Radical Relations

Radical Relations

Lesbian Mothers, Gay Fathers,

and Their Children in the

United States since World War II

Daniel Winunwe Rivers

THE UNIVERSITY OF NORTH CAROLINA PRESS
Chapel Hill

This book was published with the assistance of the
Anniversary Endowment Fund of the University of North Carolina Press.

The paper in this book meets the guidelines for permanence
and durability of the Committee on Production Guidelines
for Book Longevity of the Council on Library Resources.

The University of North Carolina Press has been
a member of the Green Press Initiative since 2003.

Library of Congress Cataloging-in-Publication Data
Rivers, Daniel Winunwe.
Radical relations : lesbian mothers, gay fathers, and their children in the
United States since World War II / Daniel Winunwe Rivers.
  pages cm
Includes bibliographical references and index.
ISBN 978-1-4696-0718-4 (cloth : alk. paper)
1. Gay parents—United States—History. 2. Children of gay parents—
United States—History. 3. Families—United States—History. 4. Gay rights—
United States—History. I. Title.
HQ75.28.U6R58 2013
306.874086'64—dc23   2013001366

Parts of this book have been reprinted with permission in revised form from "In
the Best Interests of the Child: Lesbian and Gay Parenting Custody Cases, 1967–
1985," Journal of Social History 43, no. 4 (Summer 2010): 917–43.

17 16 15 14 13   5 4 3 2 1

In memory of my best friend, Shem Tsipur,
and the lesbian households we grew up in

Contents

Illustrations

Acknowledgments

Throughout the creation of this book I have consistently felt the presence of others. Grateful as I was to have the honor of telling a story that has not been previously told—the history of lesbian mothers, gay fathers, and their children in the United States in the post–World War II era—I also felt the weight and responsibility of the project. During the research and writing years, I felt the presence not only of my dear friend Shem, with whom I grew up in a lesbian feminist community in the 1970s and who died in 1995, but of generations of families who have been illegible within an American cultural understanding of the family as always heterosexual. These people kept me company and lent inspiration when the work grew difficult. I am humbled by their example, and I hope I have honored their memory and their lives in what follows.

In more material ways, I am indebted to many individuals and institutions for their invaluable support, assistance, and advice in the researching and writing of *Radical Relations*. I have benefited greatly from the insightful advice of colleagues and mentors who have read and commented on drafts over the years, including Richard White, Al Camarillo, Paul Robertson, George Frederickson, Ellen Lewin, Ian Lekus, Judith Weisenfeld, Carol Rigolot, Gill Frank, Margot Canaday, Tiffany Wayne, Leisa Meyer, Ellen Herman, Elizabeth Pleck, Elisabeth Armstrong, Susan Van Dyne, Marilyn Schuster, and Daniel Horowitz. I am especially and deeply indebted to Estelle Freedman for her consistent guidance, mentorship, and support throughout my work on this book. Her ethics, scholarly rigor, and commitment to critical historical work are a touchstone to which I consistently return and a constant source of inspiration for me.

I could not have done this work without the generous, tireless, and talented archivists who have helped me through critical conversations about the history presented here and through their dedication to the preservation of LGBT history. I am especially grateful to Maxine Wolfe, Deborah Edel, Saskia Scheffer, Desiree Yael, Willie Walker, Marjorie Bryer, Terence Kissack, Daniel Bao, Brenda Marston, Yolanda Retter, Jenny Sayward, Terri Boggis, Beth Teper, and Arden Eversmeyer. I was also helped over the years by the invaluable assistance from interns at the San Francisco GLBT Historical Society, the Lesbian Herstory Archives, the ONE Institute and Archives, and the Human Sexuality Collection at Cornell University.

Chuck Grench at the University of North Carolina Press has been supportive of this book from an early stage and has been a dedicated and insightful editor throughout the publication process. I am grateful to him and Thadious Davis and Mary Kelley, the editors of the Gender and American Culture series, for their enthusiasm for this book. I also thank Paula Wald at the press and Liz Gray for her close reading and talented copyediting of the manuscript. In addition, I would like to express my gratitude to my indexer, Tiffany Wayne, for her excellent work.

I have been fortunate to have had assistance from several dedicated research assistants over the course of writing *Radical Relations* and am grateful for the committed work of Stacey Cotter, Catherine Dawson, Alison-Bird Pilatsky, Lena Eckert-Erdheim, Katherine Ryan, Laura Emiko Soltis, and Guirdex Massè. The research involved in the book was made possible through grants from the Social Science Research Council, the Clayman Institute for Gender Research, the Smith College Program for the Study of Women and Gender, and the James Weldon Johnson Institute for the Study of Race and Difference. Each of these fellowships provided collaborative working environments as well as financial assistance, and I am very grateful for both.

Perhaps the greatest debts of gratitude I bear are those I owe to each one of my participants, all of whom sat with me and revisited past tragedies and joys, giving me the immeasurable gift of their stories. They took me into their homes; shared photos, time, and memories; and went through the complex emotional and intellectual process of communicating their life experiences to me. This book would not have been possible without them.

I have also been supported by friends and family too numerous to mention by name. I am grateful to Vicki Gotcher, Aurora Valentine, Caren Franci, Sharon Gotcher, Richard Schweid, Linda Delgado, and Roger Delgado, and all the members of my community who listened and offered encouragement as I discovered new things and wrestled with how to convey them. I have also been honored by the support of many groups and individuals who invited me to give talks and bolstered me with their enthusiasm for the project. I would especially like to acknowledge my friends at the Atlanta chapter of SAGE who supported me in the last year of final revisions.

Finally, I want to express my gratitude to Jessica Delgado, my partner and best friend, for her unwavering support. She has read countless drafts, provided critical feedback, and consistently believed in the importance of this work.

Radical Relations

Introduction

In 1971, Carole Morton moved into a house in suburban, middle-class Union, New Jersey, with her lover, Inez, and their three sons. The two women were members and founders of the state chapter of the Daughters of Bilitis (DOB), the first lesbian civil rights organization in the United States. Although the national organization had been founded in San Francisco in 1955, Carole and Inez had only just recently helped to found the New Jersey chapter in the spring of 1971.[1] The New Jersey chapter reflected a different demographic than the New York Daughters of Bilitis, which had been founded in 1958. This newer chapter was made up predominantly of suburban lesbian mothers who had left heterosexual marriages. Morton had divorced her husband, whom she suspected had gone to gay bars himself during their marriage, shortly after attending her first DOB dance in New York in 1970. She was an early advocate for lesbian mothers; she spoke in interviews with the press about issues facing lesbians with children and organized consciousness-raising groups for lesbian mothers in New Jersey DOB. By 1972, the couple, with eight other women, was attending a therapy group for lesbian mothers run by Bernice Goodman in New York City.[2]

Things were difficult for their household in their suburban New Jersey neighborhood. Carole and Inez were visible as a lesbian couple with children; they held discussion groups for other lesbian mothers in DOB at their house and had parties where lesbians in the group socialized while their children played together in the yard. Carole and Inez also employed a Jamaican housekeeper who lived with the family and whose boyfriend played with the boys and slept over, which Carole recalled brought disapproval from others in the all-white neighborhood. Eventually, the three boys told their mothers they were harassed and beat up by other children on the block for living in a lesbian household. "No one said anything to the adults," Carole recalled; "they said things to the kids and then they took it out on our kids." This went on until one morning the family went out onto the front lawn and found a noose and a sign hung on the tree in their front yard; the sign read, "Welcome to Lezzie Land."[3]

This story, a window into historical experiences still largely invisible in American scholarship, highlights some themes that are at the heart of this book. The animosity that Carole Morton's family experienced as a lesbian household in their suburban neighborhood was grounded in the longstanding assumption in American society that parenting and same-sex orientation are, or should be, mutually exclusive.[4] In reality, however, lesbians and gay men have raised children for generations. Before the rise of lesbian and gay liberation movements these parents stayed hidden out of fear of legal and social persecution. When large numbers of Americans began living openly as lesbians and gay men beginning in the late 1960s, gay fathers and lesbian mothers nationwide faced the loss of their children in custody courts, judged unfit parents explicitly because of their sexuality. As a result of decades of activism and visibility, by the last decades of the twentieth century the demand for full domestic and parental civil rights for all lesbian, gay, bisexual, and transgender (LGBT) individuals had become a central focus of the mainstream LGBT freedom struggle.[5] By tracing the historical contours of lesbian and gay families with children in the United States, *Radical Relations* troubles the assumed heterosexuality of the American family and explores the history that this assumption has obscured for decades.

The title of this book uses the word radical in the sense of "root" or fundamental, not to define the history of lesbian mothers, gay fathers, and their children as having a single, essential political character. Indeed, at different times and in different places, lesbian and gay childrearing has been both assimilationist and avant-garde; in addition, while political organizing does play an important role in this history, much of the story also takes place outside of an explicitly political framework. However, regardless of its specific political characteristics, I want to argue that a history of lesbian mothers, gay fathers, and their children brings into focus and challenges a foundational, widely held, and erroneous belief in American culture that the family is by definition heterosexual. In this way, these families are "radical relations" both in the sense that their stories highlight core cultural beliefs about the family and in the sense that they themselves challenge these beliefs, both politically and otherwise.[6]

The history of lesbian mothers, gay fathers, and their children since the Second World War offers us a framework for understanding critical historical connections between sexuality and the family. *Radical Relations* charts the legal and social enforcement of what Adrienne Rich calls "compulsory heterosexuality" as it has been founded on a model of the family as exclusively heterosexual and has mandated the explicit separation of sexual minorities from children and all childrearing relationships.[7] Deviations from this model have been historically policed for generations, and experiences such as those of Carole, Inez, and their children bring the cultural investments behind this policing into clarity and focus. In the period from the Second World War to the present, the enforcement of the heterosexuality of the family has occurred on suburban lawns, in the holding cells of municipal jailhouses, and in family courts. Throughout this era, lesbian mothers, gay fathers, and their children existed in cultures in which their family ties were illegible and seen as virulently dangerous when they were discovered.

The idea that gay men and lesbians are pathological to children is visible not only in the historical struggles that lesbian and gay parents and their children faced, but in other manifestations of social prejudice against LGBT individuals and communities as well. During the "sex crime panics" of the 1950s, such as those in Boise, Idaho, and Sioux City, Iowa, large numbers of gay men were incarcerated based on a perception that they were dangerous to children. From the 1950s through the 1970s, lesbian and gay schoolteachers lost their jobs if their same-sex orientation was discovered, often fired explicitly to "protect" children in the classroom. In 1978, a California state legislator, John Briggs, attempted to codify this practice into law in the form of Proposition 6, known as the "Briggs Initiative." This initiative, which failed to pass, stated that any teacher found to be "advocating, imposing, encouraging or promoting" homosexuality should be fired. Anita Bryant's successful 1977 antigay campaign in Dade County, Florida, a backlash against the passage of a measure banning discrimination against gay men and lesbians, was significantly titled the "Save Our Children Campaign." Rhetoric declaring sexual minorities to be an urgent threat to children and families was at the heart of these and other similar campaigns.[8]

Demands that children must be separated from lesbians and gay men and the idea that the family is by definition a heterosexual institution have both been central underpinnings of antigay prejudice and homophobia. The loss of child custody that lesbian mothers and gay fathers faced for decades, legal and social opposition to lesbian and gay adoption and foster parenting, and the representation of lesbians and gay men in media and popular culture as detrimental to children were all fueled by a belief that children, and the family, must be kept away from same-sex relationships. The enforced separation of sexual minorities from children and the construction of the family as a heterosexual institution have been historically motivated in part by the fear that children, if exposed to lesbian and gay role models, might come to live similar lives as adults, and by the conviction that this possibility represented the destruction of the normative heterosexual nuclear family and the society built upon it.[9]

Radical Relations examines the changes over time in the experiences of gay fathers, lesbian mothers, and their children as they lived in tension with these cultural beliefs that negated their existence and condemned their experiences. Carole Morton, her partner Inez, and their children were at the boundary between an era when lesbians and gay men who raised children did so secretly and one in which lesbian and gay parents became visible for the first time in the courts and popular media. Before the late 1960s, gay fathers and lesbian mothers did their best to avoid discovery and often lived on the margins of American culture. They were aware that if their identities as lesbian or gay parents were discovered, they would face persecution and probably lose the right to parent their children. But in the liberation era, increasing numbers of lesbians and gay men with children "came out" publicly about their same-sex orientation. As they did so, they proved how prescient the fears of the earlier generation had been; in 1967, a wave of custody cases involving lesbians and gay men began, sending fear through gay and lesbian communities nationwide. Not until the mid-1980s would family courts begin to substantively challenge the assumption that same-sex sexual orientation rendered someone an unfit parent, a change brought about in large part by the legal activism of lesbian and gay parents themselves.

The story of Carole and Inez's family and their struggles in suburban New Jersey at the beginning of the liberation era also highlights the many ways that lesbian mothers and gay fathers have struggled against the social condemnation of their families. *Radical Relations* is not only a history of the family as a repressive cultural symbol; instead, it seeks to place lesbian and gay parenting within a broader historiography of the American family that approaches it as both a regulatory institution and a site of resistance. Even as social and legal definitions of the family as heterosexual obscured their very existence, lesbian mothers, gay fathers, and their children defied these proscriptions in a myriad of ways over generations of lived experience. Carole Morton's life is a clear example; even as she and her family struggled to withstand the violence and harassment they experienced in Union, New Jersey, Morton worked to organize lesbian mothers in DOB, and in 1976, she went on to found Dykes and Tykes, an important lesbian mother activist organization in New York City.

Activists such as Carole Morton were instrumental in contesting the assumption that lesbian and gay parents were unfit. In doing so, they brought to light the quiet struggles of a generation of lesbian mothers and gay fathers that had come before them. In the 1970s, driven by the emergence of gay liberation and lesbian feminist movements and the struggles of lesbian and gay parents in custody courts, lesbian mothers and gay fathers groups formed across the nation. The lesbian mothers custody movement grew out of the political commitments of lesbian feminism and framed the rights of lesbian mothers within a larger struggle for women's reproductive freedom, which included organizing against the forced sterilization of women of color and poor women, ensuring legalized and low-cost abortion, and advocating for the welfare of women and children, as well as the right of women to remain child-free. Networks of gay fathers formed across the country during these years as well, primarily to share information and offer support for gay fathers who had lost or struggled to maintain contact with their children after leaving heterosexual marriages, or in many cases, who chose to stay married in order to protect their ability to parent. From the gay father movement came a powerful politics of gay family respectability and nationwide organizational networks of gay fathers groups. Together, these movements made up a reproductive-rights revolution that was a critical but unrecognized part of the so-called sexual revolution, which I would argue, should also be thought of as a family revolution.

A history of political organizing on the part of lesbian mothers and gay fathers also provides historical context for the current focus on family/domestic rights in the modern LGBT freedom struggle. The struggle for domestic and parental rights that is a centerpiece of the contemporary LGBT civil rights movement is in fact part of a much larger history of the family and sexuality that belies the assumption that "the family" is by definition heterosexual. By the end of the twentieth century, parental and domestic rights had emerged at the center of the modern LGBT freedom struggle; *Radical Relations* argues that this was a direct result of the social activism of lesbian mothers and gay fathers, the politicization of the custody cases, and the experiences and contributions of generations of lesbian mothers, gay fathers, and their children.

As the social debate over this struggle has increased, it is not accidental that "kids of" have become important poster children and organizers in the mainstream LGBT freedom struggle of today. The children of lesbians and gay men are valuable icons for precisely the same reasons that in decades both past and present lesbian mothers and gay fathers have been under threat of losing their children in the family courts. They call into question the belief that family is always heterosexual. These children are also often consummate bridge workers.[10] The late 1980s saw the beginnings of organizing on the part of the children of lesbian and gay parents and the important role this played in the development of a consolidated focus on LGBT domestic and family rights by mainstream LGBT rights organizations in the 1990s. By the beginning of the twenty-first century, a new generation of "kids of" had followed an earlier wave of gay fathers onto television talk shows. What is being fought over in this ongoing legal and cultural debate, and what had been at issue for decades, are competing definitions of the family and sexuality that have coalesced around children and childrearing relations.

Recent scholarship in LGBT history has begun to engage important aspects of familial ties. In her book, *Not in This Family*, Heather Murray explores the cultural and emotional history of the relationships between gay men and lesbians and their heterosexual families of origin.[11] Murray argues that the way these relationships are expressed and experienced by both heterosexual parents and their gay and lesbian children illustrate important historical connections between the family and sexuality. Emotionally and culturally significant milestones in these relationships, Murray notes, such as the moments when lesbians and gay men come out to their heterosexual parents, mark contested spaces around definitions of sexuality and the family and serve as counterpoints to a conservative political agenda based on "family values" that emerged in the late 1970s. The history of lesbian and gay parents in *Radical Relations* provides a different, but complementary, perspective on many of these same cultural struggles and, together with Murray's work, articulates a history of the family and sexuality that sees the two as fundamentally linked symbols and lived historical experience; both the stories of lesbians and gay men in their heterosexual families of origin offered by Murray and the history of lesbian mothers, gay fathers, and their children illustrate the cultural construction of the family as heterosexual in the United States, as well as its contestation.

In the writing of *Radical Relations*, I have also benefited from recent work on state investments in sexual identities. In her book, *The Straight State*, historian Margot Canaday uses the history of antihomosexual regulations in three American bureaucracies—the military, the Bureau of Immigration, and federal welfare agencies—to argue that the state increasingly defined itself through the policing of same-sex sexuality during the postwar era.[12] Canaday shows how the persecution of same-sex sexuality both worked from and constituted new notions of sexuality and citizenship and argues that through these three institutions of bureaucracy, an American conception of heterosexuality as normal and homosexuality as deviant came to fundamentally define the nation. I would add that a history of lesbian and gay parents since the Second World War reveals the ways in which the policing of the family, understood as a presumably heterosexual institution, also came to define what was American and what was dangerous to the coherency of American society.

The work of Murray and Canaday, along with Nancy Cott's scholarship on the history of marriage and Elizabeth Pleck's book on the history of cohabitation and anti-adultery laws, point to the power of historical American

cultural and legal investments in defining the family as a heterosexual institution, codified through marriage.[13] The history of lesbian mothers, gay fathers, and their children throws these investments into stark relief by showing that for decades individuals have lived in contradiction of them, aware
of their precarious position and struggling to transform the ways that family
and sexuality were conceived of in American society. These histories show
us that definitions of the family and sexual identity have been intimately intertwined in the United States and give us a framework for understanding
modern struggles for same-sex marriage and parenting rights.[14]

Radical Relations also works from histories that explore ways in which the
family has functioned as a regulatory structure to police nonwhite, working-
class communities. Scholars of Native American history argue that settlers
imposed Anglo-American ideals of the patriarchal family on Native populations.[15] Historians of women's lives in the early twentieth century argue that
immigrant women and the Progressive Era reformers who sought to uplift
them constructed competing definitions of the family, while scholars of
African American history have shown that the family operated as a mobiliz-
ing symbol for both freed-slave populations and white supremacists during
Reconstruction.[16] Important scholarship by Rickie Solinger and Dorothy
Roberts has brought intersections between race and reproduction into focus
and shown how attacks against women of color and their communities often
made heavy use of a rhetoric that accused these communities of harboring
pathological families that were damaging to children and to the stability of
society itself.[17] In her book, At the Dark End of the Street: Black Women, Rape, and
Resistance—a New History of the Civil Rights Movement from Rosa Parks to the Rise of
Black Power, Danielle McGuire shows how rape and sexual assault were systematically used by white supremacists to terrorize African American populations and that women in the modern black freedom struggle fought this brutality. McGuire argues that the violent control of black women through rape,
the racist focus on miscegenation, and the courageous fight against them, are
part of a struggle over autonomy of not only sexuality but the family as well.[18]

Radical Relations is grounded in this work on the family and sexuality and
argues that the regulation and threats of regulation that have historically destabilized lesbian and gay childrearing arrangements are part of this broader
symbolic function of the family that has limited social access and supported
social divisions built on race, class, gender, and sexual identity. Where other
scholars have shown the ways that reproduction was raced and gendered,
Radical Relations argues that it was, at the same time, culturally defined as
heterosexual and that this was a crucial part of the ways that notions of the

normative family contributed to the policing of race, class, gender, and sexual boundaries.

I also seek, in this book, to underscore the elasticity of the family and its power as a force of social change, as well as to broaden our understanding of how notions of family have been used to police people's lives. Understanding the ways in which legal, religious, and cultural institutions have historically defined the family as heterosexual and how these definitions have been challenged shows us the interdependency of the family and sexuality in the history of the United States. The right to raise children, to be a "family," is one way that normative sexual ethics have been enforced and culturally reproduced. The state has taken children away from lesbian mothers and gay fathers out of a vested interest in children being raised in heterosexual homes. In the face of this heterosexist investment, lesbian mothers and gay fathers have nonetheless raised their children in openly lesbian and gay families since the 1970s, and in hiding since the Second World War; in so doing they have embodied values that lay outside of the heterosexual ideal. Consequently, the struggle for LGBT domestic and parental rights has held and continues to hold the potential to fundamentally transform the way the family is defined in American culture.

Radical Relations enacts a historical genealogy of the family and sexuality through a social history of gay fathers, lesbian mothers, and their children over the course of six decades. It opens with two chapters on the pre–gay liberation era. The first of these, "Families in Hiding: Lesbian and Gay Parents and Their Children, 1945–1969," chronicles the social pressures and legal harassment of lesbian mothers and gay fathers in the immediate post–World War II era. Given the postwar emphasis on heterosexual familial domesticity, many men and women who had already realized their same-sex orientation felt pressured into heterosexual marriage. Lesbian mothers and gay fathers in this period lived under the threat of custody loss if their same-sex sexuality was discovered, a historical antecedent of the lesbian mother and gay father custody cases of the 1970s and 1980s. Chapter 2, "The Seeds of Change: Forging Lesbian and Gay Families, 1950–1969," shows that despite these social and legal pressures, lesbians and gay men in this era did manage to parent children outside of heterosexual married life and that this era gave rise to the first signs of lesbian and gay parental organizing. This chapter includes stories of lesbian mothers raising children in 1950s working-class butch/femme communities, the first discussions of adoption as a civil right in the homophile movement, and the children of gay men and lesbians acting as bridge workers between their families and heterosexual society.

Chapter 3, "In the Best Interests of the Child: Lesbian and Gay Parenting Custody Cases, 1967–1985," focuses on the lesbian and gay custody struggles that erupted after 1967. In the gay and lesbian liberation era increasing numbers of lesbian mothers and gay fathers left previous heterosexual relationships and had to fight for custody of their children, marking them as the first generation of lesbian and gay parents to fight openly for their parental rights through the legal system. The arguments of judges and social workers in these cases vividly illustrate the legal implications of the American heterosexual family ideal explored in the first two chapters. In addition, this chapter chronicles the slow, state-by-state changes in judicial reception of lesbian and gay parenting and the role of sympathetic attorneys and psychologists in this shift.

Chapter 4, "Lesbian Mother Activist Organizations, 1971–1980," traces the nationwide grassroots network of lesbian mothers groups that emerged in the 1970s. The history of these groups, which were part of the lesbian feminist movement, demonstrates how lesbian and gay activism contributed to a reproductive-rights revolution that explicitly connected lesbian custody battles, the forced sterilization of women of color, and the economic deprivation of poor mothers. Although many of these groups disbanded by the early 1980s, their political commitments, along with networks established by gay fathers organizations, pushed the modern lesbian, gay, bisexual, and transgender freedom struggle toward its current focus on LGBT domestic and parental rights.

Chapter 5, "Gay Fathers Groups, 1975–1992," traces the development of gay fathers groups nationwide in the 1970s and 1980s. Beginning from an analysis of radical fatherhood as conceptualized in early gay liberation, it argues that gay fathers groups became less politically radical with the influx of professional, middle-class men into gay male communities in the late 1970s and 1980s. Gay fathers of this era, who primarily retained only visitation rights with their children, faced different issues than lesbian mothers and often maintained closer ties with their ex-spouses. By the late 1980s, these groups were also devastated by the AIDS/HIV epidemic. At the same time, gay fathers groups developed a politics of gay family respectability and civil rights, as well as national networks, that were formative to the adoption of family as a central concern of the mainstream LGBT freedom struggle.

Chapter 6, "The Culture of Lesbian Feminist Households with Children in the 1970s," looks at the first generation of openly lesbian families and the lesbian feminist communities in which they lived. These families were part of an alternative culture that celebrated same-sex relationships and feminist ideals of childrearing, and paved the way for the lesbian and gay baby boom of the 1980s and 1990s. This chapter analyzes tensions between lesbian mothers and lesbian separatists, some of whom were mothers themselves, over the presence of boy children in lesbian feminist communities and looks at the experiences of children raised in lesbian feminist communes and group childrearing arrangements, lesbian mothers of color and their children, and the formation of underground insemination networks linking lesbians with willing gay male donors.

The final chapter, "She Does Not Draw Distinctions Based on Blood or Law: The Lesbian/Gay-by Boom, 1980–2003," explores the changes in lesbian and gay parenting in the last two decades of the twentieth century. It looks at the expansion of lesbian and gay parental relationships, insemination, adoption, and surrogacy and carries the story of the legal struggles for lesbian and gay parental rights to the end of the twentieth century through the history of donor paternity cases, lesbian co-mother custody cases, and the development of second-parent adoption by lesbian and gay legal activists. This chapter also continues the history of lesbian and gay parental activism that runs throughout the book, exploring the founding of organizations by the children of lesbian and gay parents.

Radical Relations argues that by forging new kinds of childrearing relations and explicitly challenging legal obstacles to their family formations, lesbian mothers, gay fathers, and their children reshaped the historical relationship between sexuality and the family, drew connections with contemporary social and political struggles, and paved the way for the current focus on domestic and parental rights in the LGBT freedom struggle. Their histories show us important ways that definitions of family and sexuality in the United States have been mutually constitutive, enforcing a separation between childrearing and same-sex relationships and upholding a myth of same-sex childlessness. For decades, lesbian mothers, gay fathers, and their children have lived at the boundaries and margins of these categories, standing in contradiction to an understanding of the family as always heterosexual, living in fear of enforced separation, and changing the way that the family is seen in American culture.

CHAPTER ONE

Families in Hiding

Lesbian and Gay Parents and Their Children, 1945–1969

The years that followed the Second World War were a time of both intense repression and dynamic change for lesbians and gay men in the United States. Lesbian and gay communities in major port cities such as San Francisco, Los Angeles, and New York grew rapidly as men and women who had come out to themselves while serving in the armed forces stayed in these metropolises instead of returning to their hometowns. Other men and women discovered their love for people of the same sex working in the industrial cities of the Northeast as part of the war effort and helped to infuse these cities with a diverse working-class lesbian and gay culture. The first large-scale lesbian and gay civil rights organizations, the Mattachine Society and the Daughters of Bilitis, part of what was known as the homophile movement, originated in the 1950s. However, the postwar period was also a time of intensified persecution. Politicians nationwide used antigay campaigns to further their careers, and new laws policing gay men and lesbians went into effect. Sex-crime panics spread throughout the South and the Midwest, as gay men were blamed for changes in postwar society, and social ambivalences toward new sexual awareness led to increased fear and policing of lesbians and gay men.[1]

The media images and political voices of the 1950s emphasized a heterosexual, middle-class nuclear family model of domesticity in which women were homemakers and men were breadwinners. This strongly heterosexual culture elided lesbians and gay men and rendered lesbian mothers and gay fathers invisible. In fact, mainstream society viewed same-sex sexuality and desire as antithetical to parenting, which it understood to be exclusively an outgrowth of heterosexual intimacy. Many heterosexual people in this period strongly believed that lesbians and gay men were psychologically disturbed and prone to molesting children. Thus, most lesbian and gay parents remained completely underground during these years, in contrast to the period that followed the emergence of the lesbian and gay liberation movements. Though stifling, this invisibility served a protective function as well, for lesbian and gay parents understood that they would be perceived as deviants if exposed and that their children would be taken from them. These were difficult and dangerous years for lesbian and gay parents and their children.

It was primarily lesbians who raised children in same-sex households during the decades of the 1950s and 1960s, although gay men were sometimes a crucial part of these lesbian-headed families. Not until the development of gay and lesbian liberation movements in the late 1960s, when large numbers of gay men and lesbians came out publicly, did gay male–headed households with children form in significant numbers. A lesbian could have a child as the result of a casual encounter with a man without having to continue any sort of relationship with him, something a gay man could not do. It was also more viable for lesbians leaving heterosexual relationships to keep custody of their children, as long as they did not reveal their sexual orientation. However, as women raising children without men, they were often in economically precarious positions. For gay men, maintaining any contact at all with their children was difficult because custody courts often favored mothers, and because two men living together raised greater suspicions than did two women.[2] For most gay men and many lesbian mothers in the 1950s, parenthood was an experience either of some measure of isolation from their children or of living double lives that included both heterosexual marriage and same-sex relationships.

Understanding the history of lesbian and gay parents in the 1950s and 1960s requires that we be wary of imposing any post-Stonewall assumptions and investments in the notion of "the closet." Although "coming out" existed as lesbian and gay vernacular in this earlier era, it meant telling another lesbian or gay man about your sexuality, not declaring yourself to heterosexual society.[3] The boundaries between hetero- and homosexualities were often quite porous before the rise of lesbian and gay liberation movements in the late 1960s. Women and men with children went in and out of heterosexual marriages to seek cover from punishment; they lived double lives for years in these marriages, and their complex experiences were all marked by intense persecution and the knowledge that at any time their sexuality could be revealed and contact with their children taken away.

Postwar Pressures to Marry and Have Children

The most common way for a lesbian or gay man to become a parent in this era was to have children within a heterosexual marriage. Marriage and domesticity were core values of postwar American society, and men and women who knew that their primary attraction was to people of the same sex were under intense pressure from their families and society at large to marry and have children. Though these pressures differed for women and men, they were ubiquitous. The set of social mores that mandated heterosexuality were particularly strong in the American postwar period; the uncertainty of the Cold War led to a resurgent fear of anything outside of traditional cultural values. Public opinion held that psychologically mature citizens should take on appropriately heterosexual gender roles and teach their children that deviation from this model was dangerous and threatening to society as a whole.[4]

The recollections of gay men who married and became fathers in the postwar years illustrate the pressures on young men to marry and have children. Many gay men who married during this period remember feeling a sense of powerlessness in the face of these social mandates. Ron, a gay man who grew up in rural Maine before the war and got married in the 1950s, remembered hearing his mother referring to some men in town as gay in a derogatory manner, which made him feel that he should struggle against his own attraction to other boys. Ron experienced intense pressure to be heterosexual after coming back from the Second World War: "There was a lot of patriotism and nationalism . . . and so if you were a good man you went to college, you got a good job and in the meantime you get married and had kids." Even though Ron had known from a young age that he was much more attracted to men than to women and had fallen in love with another man in the service, it was inconceivable to him that he would not do what was expected of him. "That's what I thought everybody should do," he recalled, "and as far as I could see, everybody was doing that."[5]

William Harrison joined the navy in 1940, at the age of nineteen. At that time, he had no awareness of being a gay man. Instead, Harrison remembered, "all I thought about was getting married and having children and the normal routine of life." It was in the navy on a Pacific island that Harrison had his first sexual experience with another man "who made a successful pass at me while I was supposedly sleeping." Harrison gave this experience "little credence" at the time since he still firmly intended to return from the war and get married. He met his future wife while on leave with a fellow sailor.[6]

Many men felt shame about their same-sex attraction and hoped that marrying and having children would enable them to conform to social expectations. Richard Mason had sexual relationships with other young men in ninth grade that were very special to him but which he felt were just part of a phase he would grow beyond. However, in May 1943, Mason was inducted into the army, and while studying medicine at Hamilton College in Clinton, New

York, he fell in love with his roommate. He went to visit his roommate's family shortly before the man was shipped out to reinforce the Allied troops at the Battle of the Bulge. The heartbreak Mason endured over this loss made him depressed and physically ill. Soon after, Mason met his future wife, Virginia. He said to himself at this time, "Mason, you can cure yourself of this horrible affliction that you have by getting married, and it will all pass away." He converted to Catholicism and married Virginia in 1945 with the conviction that "God would cure" him of his love for men.[7]

Hank Vilas had a similar experience. Born in 1925 and drafted into the army in 1943, he had his first sexual experiences with other men while in the armed services. Vilas was still very ambivalent about his attraction to other men and was overwhelmed by these encounters. He rationalized his sexuality with men as an "adolescent phase" that was an unspoken part of wartime service. In 1950, Vilas went to California to attend graduate school at Stanford University. He began going to gay bars and having sex with men he met there, but he still defined himself as a "straight person going through an adolescent phase." Soon after coming to California, Vilas got married. In the heterosexual family-oriented 1950s, he "assumed that of course I had to get married and have 3 or 4 children. It was so pervasive. . . . It was so accepted that almost everybody I knew bought into this." Vilas had decided he would repress his attraction to men and be satisfied with the love he felt for his wife, which was "basically a kind of platonic love as opposed to the passionate communicative" connection he had felt with men. He convinced himself that he "was doing it for all the appropriate reasons. [He] was in love, [he] wanted a family, this seemed like the right thing to do." In retrospect, he later said, it was "homosexual panic" that caused him to marry and start a family. Terrified about his love for men, Vilas turned to the postwar, nuclear family ideal as an escape.[8]

Judgment and ridicule from parents drove some gay men to marriage. Carl Elliott was born in 1939 and grew up in an upper-class family in Washington, D.C., and New York. He began to have sexual relationships with other boys in boarding schools as a teenager. When he told his father that he was afraid he was a homosexual, his father derisively told Elliott that he had always been "a sissy." Distressed by his father's reaction, Elliott got married two days later at the age of eighteen.[9]

Gay men who married in the postwar era often did so because the cultural atmosphere of the 1950s and 1960s mandated that a successful career man have a wife and children. Only in the role of nuclear-family breadwinner could a man avoid the taint of psychological handicap. One man from Portland, Oregon, bemoaned the "150 sessions with a psychiatrist" he had in 1950 that convinced him to renounce his love for men and get married. By 1965, he had separated from his wife, with whom he had fathered a daughter.[10] In 1963, ABilly S. Jones-Hennin had a conversation with his father in which he admitted to him his love for men. His father told him that he should hide these feelings and any relationships with men, get married, and have children. Years later, after his father's death, he would learn from his mother that his father had made the same choice. "My father was my role model. He was Black, well educated, professional, rugged and tough, a husband and father, and a lover of men," he said. Jones-Hennin took his father's advice, feeling it would be the only way to become a father.[11] One gay man who married in 1962 and fathered a son with his wife, his first and only female sexual partner, said that he made his decision because of "social pressure."[12]

Jack Warner remembered the sadness he felt when a man he fell in love with in 1954 ended their relationship to marry and have children. Warner's lover, Charles, was an active member of an African American church and wanted to become a minister. Initially, Charles could not bring himself to tell Warner about the conflict between his dreams of becoming a minister and their love for each other. Warner said that "it was only later that I understood what his real problem was. . . . He had a degree in divinity and he wanted to be a minister in his church, and it was believed in the church that preachers ought to be married. Charles therefore felt strong pressure to get married and make babies." The day that Charles left to create the life he envisioned for himself, they were sitting at the table in a restaurant, and Charles admonished Jack not to cry because it would cause people to wonder what was going on. Later, after marrying and having children, Charles came back to San Francisco and told Jack that he had regretted leaving his earlier life with him.[13]

Clay Wilson was among the first African American men to graduate from the U.S. Air Force Officer Candidate School in Maxwell, Alabama, in 1952, shortly after Harry Truman desegregated the armed forces. Wilson grew up in a poor, all-black town in eastern Pennsylvania, was the first student from his high school to attend an integrated college, and since childhood had been determined to excel and challenge racist and classist obstacles to his success. He had also been aware of and acting on his attraction to other men since his teen years and in 1949, as a student at Penn State, discovered a vibrant circle of gay men through members of his fraternity. Wilson began to learn about gay male culture while spending the summer with these men. They introduced him to camp humor and the dangers of the police, whom they referred to as "Lily Law." That same year, he wrote a letter to N., a woman he had been seeing, telling her about his love for other men and his joy at finding a community of other men he could be himself with. In the letter, Wilson expressed his determination to continue this journey of self-discovery with other gay men, his growing fondness for N., and his commitment to their relationship.

Wilson had always felt the social pressure to get married, but at Air Force Officer Candidate School in 1950 and 1951, he increasingly saw marriage as critical to his career. As one of the first black officers in the newly integrated air force, he faced scrutiny and racism; he knew he had to be careful in the intensification of McCarthy-era homophobia in the early 1950s and saw that a successful officer needed to be part of a nuclear, heterosexual family unit. Writing to N., he proposed marriage, she accepted, and the two were married in March 1952. Wilson recalled feeling an intellectual and personal camaraderie with N., who he had done civil rights work with in 1948, and a sense that they would forge a partnership that would help him navigate the pressure of being a black officer in the air force in the 1950s.[14]

Just as expectations about Cold War masculinity structured the pressures gay men felt to be fathers and husbands in this era, social investments in femininity and gendered constraints shaped the experiences of women with children who "came out" to themselves in the 1950s. Del Martin remembered the pressure to get married and become a mother she felt growing up in San Francisco in the 1930s: "That was the thing you were supposed to do—to get married and have kids."[15] Shaba Barnes also experienced this social pressure growing up in an African American Jewish family in Brooklyn, New York. Barnes had always been attracted to women, but she felt she had to stifle these desires and marry. Twice she married men from Harlem's Nation of Islam Temple 7 after she got involved with the temple along with her best friend, Betty Sanders, who would later marry the temple's minister, Malcolm X.[16]

For young women in particular there were few options other than heterosexual marriage that would allow them to survive financially away from their family. In the 1940s and 1950s, many young women felt that marriage was the only way they were going to be able to leave their parent's home. Del Martin remembered that in addition to social pressure to marry and have children, she wanted to leave home and saw marriage as her chance to do that.[17] Bernie, who was born in 1926 in a small town in Wyoming, knew she was attracted to other girls when she was fifteen or sixteen years old, but in 1944 she married a man she met in the bowling alley where she worked in order to get away from her parents.[18] Vera Martin, who had relocated from Louisiana in 1939 when she was sixteen to live with her mother in Los Angeles, got married in 1942 to get out of her mother's house.[19] After the war, economic options for women grew more limited because companies pressured women to leave their positions so that men returning from the war could take them. Only certain jobs, such as nursing, teaching, or social work, were regularly open to women, and when they could find work, women were often paid less than male employees.[20]

Win Cottrell got married in 1942 because she "didn't know what else to do." Cottrell knew she was a lesbian and had shared an apartment in San Francisco with a friend of hers who was also a lesbian. There she had spent time with a small group of women with whom she would go to Mona's 440 Club, a lesbian bar in San Francisco in the 1940s. When her future husband proposed to her, she was confused and unsure of what to do. She consulted a few psychiatrists and decided to marry her suitor, who was pressuring her to say yes. In the first year of their marriage, Cottrell became pregnant with her first child, Dana. By the early 1950s, Cottrell had two daughters. Later, she recalled that it was her two daughters that kept her married, even though she knew that she loved women: "I didn't feel confident enough, and I didn't have, you know, skills that I could go out and get a good job and support them and support myself. . . . I was afraid of the responsibility of two little girls."[21] Women who were unhappy in heterosexual marriages often felt powerless to leave when faced with the lack of employment opportunities for women in postwar America.[22]

Poverty and racism often compounded these constraints. Born in 1933, Gini Morton grew up in a poor black family in Detroit, Michigan. She watched her mother and father struggle against the racism that kept them underemployed in menial, debilitating jobs. "We were poor. We were dirt poor," Morton recalled later. "My father did not have a job. . . . Nobody would hire him because he was old and black. . . . The jobs were given to the white boys returning from the war." When Morton was thirteen she became lovers with a girl from another neighborhood whom she met while visiting her grandmother. The two girls had a love affair that lasted about six months, but one night her mother heard them making love, and after Morton walked her girlfriend to the bus stop, her mother forbade her to see her lover again.

When Morton was fifteen and in high school, still sad about the end of that relationship, a group of boys began taunting her and calling her "queer." When she asked a friend of hers what that meant, he told her she was "always hiding in bedrooms and under the steps with girls and you girls are doing it." After looking up the word "queer" in the dictionary and seeing that it meant "strange," Morton decided, "I'll stop being strange, and I'll start being with boys." Later that year, at the age of sixteen, she had sex with a boy for the first time and became pregnant. Morton, who had always been an avid reader and promising student, left high school and married because "that was all that was left for you, really, back then if you were straight. . . . Even if you weren't straight you got married to shut people up." Social prejudice and economic necessity pushed women toward heterosexual marriage, disallowing any other alternative.[23]

Living Double Lives

The pressures of heterosexual domesticity were gendered and affected men and women differently in the 1950s postwar era, but both lesbians and gay men experienced them; in response, many men and women who knew they were primarily attracted to others of the same sex stayed married and led double lives. Much of the social turbulence of the following decades had its roots in underlying tensions in the immediate postwar era that belied the general cultural atmosphere of consensus, and cultural links between the family and sexuality were a part of this; these double lives foreshadow the custody cases that would be fought by lesbians and gay men in the 1970s, as men and women who had entered into double lives in the 1960s left their marriages in the liberation era, openly declared themselves to be lesbians and gay men, and found themselves forced to fight for custody or visitation of their children.

In the atmosphere of conformity that characterized the years of the McCarthy era, it was more secure for some gay men to be married with children and engage in gay relationships clandestinely than to live as bachelors. Interviewed in 1978, James, a retired diplomat, said that being married with a child gave him cover as a gay man working in the government in the early 1950s. He felt sure that if he had not been a family man, he would have fallen victim to McCarthy-era antigay purges. He also described his decision to get married as one motivated by the knowledge that only married men were successful in his field. He remembered his superior telling him that to get ahead, he needed to entertain, and for that he needed a wife.[24]

Often, anonymous sex with other men in popular "cruising areas" such as public restrooms or parks allowed married gay fathers to pursue sexual encounters with other men while still trying to protect their family life and career. Sociologist Laud Humphreys, in his 1970 book *Tearoom Trade*, studied the lives of men who had sex with other men in public restrooms in the St. Louis metropolitan area. Humphreys, who grew up in Oklahoma, was the son of a conservative father who, he later learned, had sex with men throughout his marriage to Humphreys' mother. For his research, Humphreys interviewed fifty participants he had separately seen engaging in sex with other men in public restrooms. He did not tell the majority of the men about his research and interviewed them under the auspices of a demographic study unrelated to homosexuality. Of the fifty men that Humphreys interviewed, twenty-seven were heterosexually married, three were divorced, and one was in a marital separation. Speaking about the married, working-class men with families he talked with, Humphreys said, "any personal ongoing affair" would have threatened to "jeopardize the most important thing these men possess, their standing as father of their children." One of Humphreys' participants, Tom, who was married with two children and living in "ranch-style suburbia," said, "being married has made me more stable."[25]

Sometimes lesbian and gay double lives spanned decades and formed a silent backdrop to the American suburban family. Barbara Kalish, who grew up in Los Angeles, met her husband, Chuck, in 1945 after he returned from serving in the navy. Barbara said that by the time she was sixteen her parents "were ready for me to get married. Man, were they ready." All of her friends got married and pregnant in a few years time. In 1949, Barbara and Chuck moved into a house in a Norwalk, California, housing tract, built and paid for by the G.I. Bill. Their first child, a daughter, was born in 1950, and their second daughter followed in 1952. Barbara got involved in local politics, working on political campaigns, fund-raising for the dynamic growth taking place in Norwalk and surrounding areas in the early 1950s. She also joined the PTA and became active in local school activities.

Elected president of the PTA in 1958, Barbara traveled to San Francisco for a training conference for PTA presidents. She remembered meeting Pearl, "the most gorgeous woman in the world . . . another PTA president. I fell madly in love." For both women, the mutual attraction was completely unexpected, for neither of them had previously known any lesbians. When the two women returned from their trip, Barbara found the courage to tell Pearl that she was in love with her, initiating a twelve-year relationship. Pearl lived two blocks away from Barbara and her family, with her own husband and two children.

Pearl and Barbara spent the 1960s running a grassroots political lobbying business they founded while raising children in their respective marriages. They would talk about leaving their marriages and moving in together after the children went away to college. She recalled they had a great life together, traveling all over California in a little convertible that Barbara bought, lobbying for various political causes and working on small, local elections. Neither of them knew any other lesbians: "Anyway, Pearl and I are the only lesbians in the world. I don't even know that I knew the word lesbian. I didn't know anyone else."

In 1968, when her daughters were sixteen and eighteen, Barbara decided that it was time for her and Pearl to leave their husbands and get a place together. However, Pearl was afraid that she would be unable to get medical insurance if she left her husband. As Barbara remembered, Pearl's husband, Lee, was a "sweet guy," and Pearl was unsure about leaving the life of wife and mother. So Barbara went to her husband, Chuck, from whom she had been growing more and more distant over the years and told him, "I'm going." She helped Pearl close up the business, moved out of her house, and moved into a room in the back of the Star Room, a lesbian bar in Los Angeles on the corner of Main and El Segundo. It was there, in a tough neighborhood, living in the back of a lesbian bar, that Barbara had her "life turned around."[26]

Married men and women who were leading isolated double lives sometimes found comfort in the periodicals and organizations of the homophile movement, which was emerging as the nation's first gay and lesbian advocacy movement during these years. A married father from Pennsylvania, writing into the *Mattachine Review* in 1958, told of leading "the double life that is all too common" and described himself as "plagued with fears of detection because of business, friends etc." He wrote, "As a result I find the Review like a friend; company to me in this problem with society as a whole."[27] A man from California identifying himself as "a married man with children" wrote into the *Review* in 1956, wishing to thank the editors because "the information in your magazine has helped me to solve many things for myself and others."[28] A woman from California wrote to the editors of *The Ladder* "to say DOB makes life a little brighter for one surrounded by heteros. After two marriages and two children, I'm finally waking up to the facts—unfortunately, too late. . . . DOB and its book service make life a little easier and I don't feel so lonely."[29]

However, possessing or subscribing to homophile periodicals also carried risks for men and women living double lives. A man from Corvalis, Oregon, stopped into the Mattachine Society's offices in San Francisco in April 1962—an experience that he said had given him "a tremendous lift." In a letter a month later, he expressed his wish that he could subscribe to the *Mattachine Review* but said that, "with a wife and children," he did not feel he "could take the risk."[30] A woman wrote the editors of *The Ladder* to request that her subscription be cancelled. She had recently been married "after seven years in 'gay life'" and wanted to avoid the "unpleasantness and unnecessary explanation" that "would occur if a copy fell into the hands of my husband." The woman ended her letter on a bittersweet note, emphasizing the strength of the pressures to get married: "I wish you all good luck in your work, and I'll probably wish I could have really been one of you. I just wasn't strong enough to face it all."[31] Another woman, a married mother from Chicago, wrote in a 1968 letter of being "so very afraid of being discovered in my correspondence with D.O.B." She requested that her copies of *The Ladder* be sent to her sister's address, because if her husband discovered them, she believed he would "draw and quarter me or perhaps be less sadistic and merely shoot me."[32]

Hidden, double-life relationships could cause both men and women engaged in them a great deal of guilt and psychological anguish. A man who called a San Francisco Mattachine hotline in 1966 told Don Lucas that he was married with two children and was in a relationship with another man who was also married with children. The two men co-owned property and had worked together, and the man who was calling found the relationship "quite fulfilling." However, he was concerned because his lover, who had been brought up Roman Catholic, felt very guilty about their relationship and believed he was breaking his marriage vows. The man who had called in was doubtful that the second man would talk to anyone about his feelings.[33] A married woman with four children from Oregon wrote in 1960: "I have been married 13 years. . . . They have been miserable years of fear and guilt because of my inadequacy as a wife and mother." She explained that she remained in her situation out of "love and duty."[34]

Leading a double life as a married gay man was often fraught with danger and anxiety over possible arrest. During the 1950s and 1960s, nationwide, married gay fathers leading double lives were subject to discovery and persecution during routine vice squad arrests for having sex with other men. A Southern California man, arrested on a "lewd and lascivious acts" charge, was married with one child. By 1965, he was in San Francisco and trying to go back to school and find work.[35] In 1958, a major in the U.S. Air Force was arrested on a "morals" charge in Texas. The man reportedly had a wife and daughter in England, where he had been stationed.[36]

As part of the public persecution of men caught in vice raids on gay bars and private parties in the 1950s, local newspapers often published the names of men arrested on lewd vagrancy charges. For married gay men living double lives, this practice threatened to destroy both their families and their careers. A juvenile probation officer, arrested in 1960 on charges of public indecency in the bathroom of a Woolworth's store in San Francisco, was married and had four children. At the time of his arrest, the police notified the man's employer, who subsequently fired him. His wife, also a probation officer, lost her job as well. The court eventually found the man guilty, fined him $155, and put him on a year of probation.[37] In a 1960 "crackdown" in Waukesha, Wisconsin, police arrested ten men in two local parks for "sexual perversion." One man, married with a child and a dean at a local college, lost his job after the arrest. Another married man, a local dentist and father of four children, had his name published in newspapers after having "struck up a lengthy conversation in Cutler Park on sex and homosexual matters" with another man.[38] One married gay man, arrested in a raid on a party in Memphis in 1962, committed suicide after the *Memphis Commercial Appeal* published his name in conjunction with a story on the raid.[39]

A man with five children, writing in 1959, testified to the intense fear and loneliness that he carried with him. He had known he was gay since he was young but had married on the advice of psychologists. Because he worked for years in a "sensitive government agency," he dared not visit any gay bars or hangouts. Thoughts of his family kept him from meeting other men for sex in public spaces in Washington, D.C., where "the members of the vice squad are very active and have picked up quite a number of homosexual men on the charge that they were soliciting." He felt he had to be extremely careful "not to become involved with the authorities" for the sake of his wife and children, and was consequently in a "very lonely" situation.[40] A married man in San Francisco in 1962 was too scared by the possibility of arrest and the reactions of "friends and above all relatives, including grown and married children" to go into gay bars.[41]

When married gay fathers were caught in sexual relationships with other men, it often resulted in social ostracization for them and their families. Richard Tooker described this happening to a man with whom he was having a brief affair in the 1950s in the San Francisco Peninsula, a suburban, middle-class area. Tooker would have dinner with the man and his wife and then afterwards have sex with him in the garage. Eventually policemen caught this man having sex with his wife's brother. Tooker said that the neighborhood knew about what had happened, even though it was never discussed, and that "socially" the relationship between the family and their neighbors had changed.[42]

Married gay fathers had to cover up their double lives when arrests threatened to bring the walls between their two worlds down. Hank, a married gay father, was caught up in a raid on a Seattle bathhouse called the Royal Baths. It was a heterosexual bathhouse upstairs and a gay bathhouse in the basement. The police burst through the doors and forced all of the men out of the baths. Hank remembered pleading with one of the officers, "Don't take me, I'm married with two kids." When the summons to appear came to his home, he lied to his wife, telling her that he had witnessed an accident on the way home from work and was being summoned to testify. Employed at a major corporation, Hank feared he would lose his job for years after quietly pleading guilty in court, sure that someone at his company would find out about his arrest record.[43]

Gay fathers were also frequently caught up in the "sex-crime panics" that characterized the postwar period. In her work on the history of sex-crime panics, Estelle Freedman identifies two main periods of sex-crime panic in the United States: the first from 1937 to 1940 and the second from 1949 to 1955. Sometimes these waves of persecution and incarceration of gay men followed the sexual assault and murder of a child, for which gay men became scapegoats as "sexual deviants." Other times, increased visibility of gay men drove social campaigns to police gay male communities.[44] The reason given for such campaigns was generally that the men arrested were a pathological danger to children.

In Boise, Idaho, in 1955, local police and politicians initiated a widespread attack on gay men when several teenage boys reported having sex with men for money in the downtown area. Joe Moore, a fifty-four-year-old married father who was vice president of the Idaho First National Bank was jailed in the Boise panic. Police arrested Moore on a felony charge of "committing an infamous crime against nature." Despite the fact that Moore's son testified to his father's character in court, the court sentenced him to seven years in the state penitentiary.[45]

Married gay fathers also faced incarceration and torture in mental health facilities. A 1955 article in *Mattachine Review* described how men incarcerated as "sexual psychopaths" at California's Atascadero State Hospital expressed anxiety over "their role as husbands and fathers." There is evidence that men arrested in California under a 1941 sexual psychopath law and sent to Atascadero in the 1950s and 1960s faced electroshock treatments, lobotomization, and castration.[46] Rick Stokes suffered similar treatment in Oklahoma City. Sometime after the birth of his children, Stokes's wife told her parents about his childhood same-sex love, and in 1958 they incarcerated Stokes in a mental institution in an effort to "excise this homosexual element from my character." When he first saw Stokes, the doctor said, "Well, we could castrate you, but let's try some treatments and see what we could do there." In the end, Stokes was given a series of ten to fifty electroshock treatments meant to "cure" his desire for other men, a devastating experience that left him in "utter terror."[47] Policemen detained one married gay man who was the father of three children solely because he stopped into a local gay bar in Sioux City, Iowa, in the middle of a sex-crime panic in that city that same year. Police interrogated him about his sexual history with other men, arrested him, and incarcerated him in a mental institution for three months. He lost his business and was forced to talk with his wife about his sexual attraction to other men. Years later he recalled that "my life was shattered. . . . It was gone. I was devastated and scared to death. I didn't know what was going to happen."[48]

In one of the more famous cases of police harassment of a closeted gay father, authorities arrested Walter Jenkins, a top aide for President Lyndon B. Johnson, for having sex with another man in a YMCA bathroom. Jenkins was married and the father of six children. The Washington, D.C., police apparently spied on him using a peephole in the bathroom wall. Despite Jenkins's attempts to block the story, the *Washington Post* ran it, and Jenkins immediately resigned from his post at the White House. A subsequent FBI investigation revealed that Jenkins had been arrested in the same washroom in 1959 on a charge of "disorderly conduct (pervert)." After a quarter of a century as Johnson's right-hand man, Jenkins's career was destroyed.[49]

In 1959, Massachusetts radically strengthened its obscenity laws under the direction of the governor, Foster Furcolo, who was about to run for the U.S. Senate. In 1960, as a result of the new laws, seven men from Northampton, Massachusetts, were charged with various charges, including committing "sodomy and unnatural acts" and possessing pictures of naked and semi-naked men, as well as having copies of the homophile movement periodical, *ONE Magazine*. Three of the men were married fathers.[50] In 1966, law officials broke up an extortion ring targeting gay men when the extortionists tried to blackmail a "member of Congress from an Eastern State." The authorities chose to withhold the victims' names because "many were married and have families."[51] This was of course not always done in cases involving less powerful individuals.

Gay men and lesbians of the 1950s and 1960s who chose to marry and have children did so for many reasons. Like all men and women of this era, they lived in a society that exerted strong pressures to marry and have children. In fact, many people believed that heterosexual marriage and childrearing was a sign that an individual was a psychologically mature adult, and anything else bore the taint of deviance, or at least of emotional and sexual instability. This left many men and women with no option for financial survival or success except marriage and family. The way men and women experienced these socially mandated conditions varied with gender, race, and class, but the pressures themselves were something that nearly all men and women of the era felt. In addition, many gay men and lesbians deeply and truly wanted to become parents and could see no other way to do so but to enter into a heterosexual relationship. Many then remained married after having children out of fear that they would lose their parental rights if their same-sex attraction was discovered.

The Fear of Losing Custody and Visitation Rights

Lesbian mothers and gay fathers in the era before gay and lesbian liberation faced the possibility of losing custody of their children to the state, an ex-spouse, or other family members. Denial of parental rights to anyone who openly loved someone of the same sex was part of the legal and social policing of same-sex relationships and the enforcing of heterosexuality, though this danger was often extrajudicial. There were rare, isolated cases of denials of custody based on lesbian or gay identity in this period, but more often, lesbian and gay parents simply understood that if their same-sex sexuality was discovered, there would be little possibility of retaining their custodial or parental rights. The threat of parental estrangement lay over the lives of lesbian and gay parents of this era and foreshadowed the massive loss of custodial rights that lesbian and gay parents experienced as large numbers of men and women openly declared their same-sex sexuality in the 1970s.[52]

Blue Lunden, a lesbian mother from New Orleans, moved to New York and gave guardianship of her one-year-old daughter, Linda, to a heterosexual couple that she knew, convinced that she could not provide a suitable environment for a child. However, in 1959, when she learned that her abusive godmother had taken over custody of now four-year-old Linda, Lunden returned from New York to retrieve her daughter, publicly repudiating her lesbianism in order to do so, before then returning to New York to raise her daughter while continuing to live as a lesbian. Later, when Blue Lunden went to parent-teacher meetings in Manhattan in the 1960s, she felt she had to put on a dress and act like a housewife to avoid the threat of custody loss.[53] For lesbian mothers raising their children in lesbian households in this period, any interaction with representatives of the state, including the educational system, was potentially dangerous.

Lesbian mothers raising children in lesbian-headed households also had to worry about ex-husbands using their lesbianism to take custody of the children. In 1958, Vera Martin met and fell in love with Kay, a Japanese American woman who had come to the United States at the end of the Second World War after marrying an African American serviceman. Kay had two children, and Martin had a son and daughter. The families got along well and would spend time together on the weekends. R., Vera Martin's teenage daughter, babysat for the other children when Kay and Martin wanted to go

Blue (left) and Linda Lunden, New York, mid-1960s. Courtesy of Linda Lunden.

out together. Both women feared that the authorities or their ex-husbands would take custody of their children if they found out they were in a lesbian relationship. "We knew that we had to be careful," Vera Martin remembers, "and keep the knowledge that we had kids very quiet . . . very quiet." Kay worked as a prostitute to support her family, and the two women lived in fear that someone would report them to authorities, possibly even one of the other women with whom Kay worked, in order to remove competition. They also feared that their ex-husbands would simply take their children away directly if they found out they were lesbians. Martin was an African American woman and Kay was Japanese American, and as two lesbian mothers of color, they felt particularly threatened by the courts.

Lesbian mothers who had left previous heterosexual marriages during this era lived in constant fear of discovery and exposure. One night in 1959, when Vera Martin and Kay were at the If Club, a lesbian bar in Los Angeles, a heterosexually identified man who knew Martin's ex-husband walked up, said hello to her, and left. Terrified, Martin turned to Kay and said, "That's someone that knew me when my husband and I were together, and they are still in touch." Kay understood the danger immediately and said, "I think we better get out of here." Vera Martin thought the man would use the pay phone and that her ex-husband would show up at the club or later at one of their houses. She and Kay lived in terror afterwards and did not go out in public "for a long time." When the two of them eventually went to a dance together, they asked two men to accompany them as cover.[54]

As parents, lesbians and gay men had no legal protections or recognition of their co-parent relationships in the 1950s and 1960s. As it would in later decades, this jeopardized their ability to maintain communication with their partner's children. After Kay died suddenly in the winter of 1959, Vera Martin wanted very badly to take Kay's children into her home and raise them with her own, as Kay had told her children's caretaker she wanted before she died. However, Kay's ex-husband, who lived across the country and had been brutally abusive to Kay, came into town with his new wife and took the children. "Oh, I wanted those kids so bad. . . . I was crazy about them and they were crazy about me," Martin recalled, but she had no chance of competing for custody of the two children against an intact heterosexual nuclear family. In the era before gay and lesbian liberation movements there was no chance of legal recognition for lesbian households with children. Martin despaired when Kay's ex-husband held an auction to sell all of Kay's belongings. She came up with one hundred dollars to buy Kay's address book, a potentially dangerous item in the hands of her ex-husband. In 1963, Vera Martin then married a gay man and "slammed the closet door shut behind her," because she heard rumors that her own ex-husband suspected that she was a lesbian, and she was afraid he might try to use that to obtain custody of T., her son and youngest child.[55]

Although the first openly lesbian and gay organizations were founded in the postwar period, women in these groups who had children were still under tremendous pressure to stay hidden. In 1955, Del Martin and her partner Phyllis Lyon founded the Daughters of Bilitis (DOB), the nation's first lesbian civil rights organization, in San Francisco. As the founders of DOB, Del Martin and Phyllis Lyon recalled that they knew of many lesbians with children in the 1950s that were afraid that authorities and ex-husbands would use their love for women against them in custody struggles.[56]

Archived letters to DOB show that losing custody of their children was a deep fear for lesbians even before the era of the custody cases began in earnest. In 1964, for example, a woman from Jacksonville, Florida, wrote the organization and said she was in "a most dreadful plight." The woman was the mother of three children and was "at the mercy of a divorce court exposure that may well cost me the custody of my children." She had burned all of her back copies of The Ladder but was still receiving new issues and requested that they not be sent to her anymore, lest they be used "as evidence" of her lesbianism in a custody battle.[57] Helen Sanders, of the Daughters of Bilitis, noted in 1958 that many lesbians "are mothers and have given up a great deal to retain their children."[58]

Del Martin's own ex-husband attempted to use her lesbianism to prevent their 1945 divorce. While still married, Martin had written love letters to a woman living nearby. Her husband found the letters and brought them to court to denounce Martin as a lesbian in order to keep her from leaving the marriage. The judge, however, saw only evidence of female friendship in the notes and decided that they were not indicative of a love affair. After their divorce, Martin's ex-husband and his new wife, who believed themselves unable to have children, asked her if they could raise Kendra, Martin's seven-year-old daughter. Martin gave up custody of her daughter because her own unresolved feelings about her lesbianism caused her to think Kendra might be better off in a heterosexual, nuclear family. "At that point I was really struggling with who I was," Martin remembered, "and they gave me the song and dance about having a mother and a father . . . so eventually I said yes."[59] In this era, the idea that children were better off in a heterosexual family was so pervasive that many lesbian mothers felt guilt about raising children in lesbian households.[60]

Although lesbian and gay custody cases were rare in this period, custody courts did sometimes act to take children away from lesbian mothers and gay fathers. In 1959, a brief article appeared in a New Jersey newspaper that foreshadowed the tragic struggles of many gay fathers and lesbian mothers of later decades. The article reported an appellate ruling in a contested divorce between Henry Hanson and his wife, Elizabeth Hanson, based on the assertion that she "associated with female homosexuals and refused to change her ways." Evidence used by the husband's attorney included thirty-nine letters from Elizabeth Hanson to another woman. The letters between the two women discussed their lives, their children, and their love for each other. The court gave custody of the two children to the father.[61] In 1955 a man claimed in court that his wife's "strange passions" made her an "unfit mother."[62] In another 1955 case, a woman in Pottstown, Pennsylvania, filed for divorce on the grounds that her husband was gay, although she admitted that she had known this before they got married and that besides his love for men he was a good father and provider.[63] A decade and a half later, as gay fathers and lesbian mothers began coming out in large numbers, cases like these would become all too common.[64]

For gay fathers who left heterosexual marriages during this period, the chances of maintaining contact with their children were slim. It was rare in this era for men to win custody in any case, and for gay men, even maintaining visitation rights with their children was unlikely. It was somewhat easier for lesbians to conceal their love for women while they raised their children, because women living together incurred less scrutiny than male intimacy did, and because women were expected to be the primary caregivers for young children. For most gay men, the decision to leave their marriages and pursue their love for men meant being ostracized from their children.

Ex-spouses and their families often made it clear when men admitted their same-sex sexuality that they intended to keep them from their children. William Harrison realized that he was a gay man while going to college on the G.I. Bill and living in Buffalo, New York, with his wife and daughter. When Harrison was waiting for the bus to class one evening, a man propositioned him and Harrison accepted. This man was "involved in the gay culture," and through his connection with him, Harrison became more and more aware of his love for other men. Eventually, in 1947, he and his wife separated. For some time, Harrison was still seeing his daughter once a week when his ex-wife brought her over for visits. However, when he told his ex-wife that he was gay, she told her brothers, and they were "out for blood." His ex-wife told their two-year-old daughter that he had died, after which Harrison left for New York, where he enrolled in hairdresser's school and became a hair stylist. He picked hairdressing because his perception was that all hairdressers were gay men, and he wanted "something that was going to be nearer to the gay world." Harrison's perception of the life he left behind in Buffalo was that "they didn't have any use for queers."[65] For gay fathers the divide between the gay world and fatherhood was often stark and impermeable.

When a man allowed himself to embrace his love for another man, he often had to walk away from his life as a father, so clearly did the two paths seem to be mutually exclusive. Richard Mason, who had converted to Catholicism and married his wife, Virginia, in 1945, had hoped that "God would cure" him of his love for men. However, sometime later he met a man in Saranac Lake, New York, where his wife's family lived, and this man taught him about the gay world and the possibility of living life as a gay man through their conversations together. Then in December 1949, Mason met Sam Cerasaro, when he and his wife came into Cerasaro's sporting goods store to buy a "folding baby carriage" for Mason's daughter Jeannie. By the fall of 1950, the two men were in love with each other. Mason remembers his love for Cerasaro as a godsend: "Before I met Sam," he said, "I was right on the edge of suicide . . . but he showed me that there was a chance for happiness . . . that we could live together." Cerasaro took Mason to Greenwich Village and showed him that there "was a whole different thing," declaring, "We're going to go where we have lots of company." They went to the Everard Baths, took trips to Fire Island, and together explored the gay world of New York in the 1950s.

Mason knew that in choosing a relationship with Cerasaro that he was walking away from fatherhood. Shortly after his second daughter was born in October 1950, Mason went to Saranac Lake to spend Christmas with the girls and then did not see his daughters again for almost fifteen years. The gay world in which Cerasaro and Mason lived was separate from the world of fatherhood and family. For Mason, fatherhood had been part of his heterosexual life. Cerasaro and Mason reconnected with Jean, Mason's oldest daughter, in 1965, when she was attending college in New York City. By then, Cerasaro and Mason were living in Manhattan, and it was acceptable to spend time with Mason's daughter in their world. They even took her to a party thrown by gay male friends of theirs, although they never talked directly to Jean about their relationship.[66]

Gay fathers who were able to stay in touch with their children after a divorce constantly feared being cut off from them. Hank Vilas married, but in the late 1950s, when he and his wife had three children, Vilas fell in love with Bob, whom he met at work. When his wife was away for a week-long vacation, Vilas asked Bob to stay with him. Vilas recalled that "the next morning I was a gay man." His intense relationship with Bob led to the end of Vilas's marriage. He decided to live his life as a gay man and forged friendships with several other gay fathers who had been married, all of whom feared losing visitation rights with their children. The assumption at the time was that if "the homosexual issue" came up, the judge would "take a position . . . that if you see the children you will, of course, pervert them, you will damage them, you will do awful things." Vilas considered himself lucky, since the possibility of his losing his visitation rights with his son on account of his homosexuality did not "come up" until a few years after his divorce, and he "was able to maintain a much closer relationship with my children than most of the other men I knew that were in the same boat."[67]

The 1950s and 1960s was a time of intense persecution for lesbians and gay men in the United States. The growth of lesbian and gay communities immediately following the Second World War brought with it an upsurge in police harassment and bar raids, sex-crime panics, and vice squad entrapment. The vilification of same-sex relationships in this era was exacerbated by the fact that popular American culture idealized heterosexuality and held up marriage as the only viable option for psychologically mature adults. Heterosexual marriage was seen as necessary for raising a family and maintaining a career, and for women was often the only option that would enable them to leave their parents' home and survive economically. In this postwar environment, many lesbians and gay men married and had children, and some led double lives, struggling with their sexual orientation in the face of society's insistence on heterosexuality. Being a lesbian or a gay man was widely understood as antithetical to parenting; the threat of losing custody of their children kept many men and women from leaving heterosexual marriages and enforced the silence and invisibility of those who did raise children in same-sex households.

CHAPTER TWO

The Seeds of Change
Forging Lesbian and Gay Families, 1950–1969

As difficult as the preliberation era was for lesbian mothers, gay fathers, and their children, these years also held the promise of change. When large numbers of men and women embraced their same-sex orientation and then settled in cities, it energized the lesbian and gay communities in these metropolises. Neighborhoods long known for their tolerance of diverse ways of living grew in size, and others emerged for the first time. In these enclaves, lesbian mothers raised their children, who often found themselves struggling as bridge workers between their homes and a larger society that saw lesbians and gay men as antithetical to family. These years also saw the beginnings of lesbian and gay parental activism, as members of homophile organizations such as the Daughters of Bilitis, the Mattachine Society, and the Janus Society discussed the viability of raising children in same-sex households and debated the wisdom of fighting for adoptive and foster parent rights.

The stories of lesbian households with children and lesbian and gay parenting activism in this period contribute to an emerging historical portrait of "the other fifties." Many recent historians of the postwar era have questioned the widely held view of the 1950s as an era of conformity and consensus, showing instead that the years from 1945 to 1960 were turbulent ones characterized by cultural and social changes that would lead to the radical social upheavals of the 1960s. Joanne Meyerowitz's analysis of popular magazines from the years 1946 to 1958 found that writers in mainstream popular culture often celebrated women working outside the home; they "expressed ambivalence about domesticity and presented it as a problem."[1] In her book, *Young, White, and Miserable: Growing Up Female in the Fifties*, Wini Breines argues that young middle-class white women found inspiration for rebellion against restrictive gender norms in the male counterculture iconography of the Beats and in rock-and-roll youth culture. Breines shows that young women who wanted to escape the postwar culture of marital domesticity found refuge in neighborhoods such as San Francisco's North Beach and Greenwich Village in New York City.[2]

Historians have also shown that earlier social justice movements of the 1950s predated and facilitated the activism of the 1960s. In work on women in the peace movement, Dee Garrison shows that nonviolent activists such as Bayard Rustin and Dorothy Day laid the groundwork in the late 1950s for the women's and antiwar movements of the next decade. "The civil rights struggles and peace struggles of the late 1950s," argues Garrison, "built the framework for the emergence of the New Left."[3]

Part of the nascent activism of this period was the emergence of the homophile movement, with the founding of the first organized lesbian and gay civil rights groups. In 1950, the Mattachine Society formed in Los Angeles, spearheaded by a group of communist-affiliated gay men who wanted to organize for the rights of homosexuals. In 1955, the Daughters of Bilitis (DOB), the nation's first lesbian organization, formed in San Francisco. Although DOB initially formed as a social group, it quickly began working for a greater acceptance of lesbians by mainstream American society and tried to expose the discrimination that many lesbians faced at work and in public space.[4]

Social and sexual mores were changing rapidly in postwar American society. Alfred Kinsey's studies of sexuality in men and women, published in 1948 and 1953 respectively, caused widespread controversy and signaled that sexuality was a topic of public debate. The publication of sensationalist tabloid literature and pulp novels also contributed to a growing awareness of sexual diversity. In this context, legal groups such as the American Civil Liberties Union (ACLU) began calling for the decriminalization of all sex between consenting adults based on a model penal code published in 1962 by the American Law Institute.[5]

Lesbian-headed households and gay and lesbian parental activism originated within these social changes of the postwar period. Many lesbian mothers raised their children in the same bohemian neighborhoods where young women and men began rebelling against the ideals of American postwar culture; together with Beats, sex workers, political activists, poor people, and people of color, the lesbian mothers and their children who lived in these places made up part of a growing counterculture that existed on the margins of mainstream America. Children were rarely raised in gay male–headed households in this period, but gay male activists did begin discussing the subject of parental rights for gay men in the early 1960s. Most of the activism of the 1950s would explode in full force in the 1960s, but not until the advent of gay and lesbian liberation in the early 1970s would lesbian mothers and gay fathers openly advocate for their rights. However, during the 1950s and 1960s, the seeds of liberation-era lesbian and gay parental activism were already taking root at the fringes of Cold War culture.

The growing presence of lesbian mothers raising their children within marginal communities in the United States was a part of larger changes in sexuality, gender, and the family that were occurring in the United States during the 1950s and 1960s. As women moved into the workforce and lesbian and gay urban communities emerged, lesbians could raise their children discreetly, even though they did so under constant threat of having their children taken away from them. These changes would lead eventually to widespread lesbian mother and gay father activism in the 1970s and 1980s and to the demands for full domestic and parental rights of the modern LGBT freedom struggle by the end of the century.

Lesbians Raising Children in Bohemian and Butch-Femme Communities

Because of the prevailing attitude that only heterosexuals could be parents, lesbian mothers who did raise their children outside of heterosexual marriages tended to live in the relative safety of bohemian, working-class neighborhoods. Often these communities were in cities such as New Orleans, where neighborhoods known for urbane freethinking, such as the French Quarter, gave women some degree of anonymity. The growth of bohemian communities in the 1950s and 1960s allowed lesbians raising children some freedom from oppressive social norms that would have otherwise made their lives extremely difficult. Blue Lunden, a lesbian mother who grew up and gave birth to her daughter in New Orleans, attributed the strength of the lesbian communities she was a part of to that city's cosmopolitan nature. "Well—certainly in the French Quarter at the time that I was there, there were gay bars," Lunden recalled later, but she remembered this gay scene as part of a larger community "that consisted of the guys that held the doors open for the strippers, the strippers, prostitutes, various kindsa con men and loose assorted people who were a counterculture of that time. We used to come into each other's company." Jazz musicians and female and male impersonators performed for straight, white tourists who would come to the French Quarter to see the wilder side of life. Lunden remembered musical jams starting at three in the morning that everyone would go to after "the tourists and the squares" were gone.[6] In these communities, lesbian mothers and their children found refuge from the vision of the heterosexual nuclear family promulgated in postwar America.

One of the most important bohemian centers in the United States during this time, and the most famous lesbian and gay neighborhood in the country, was Greenwich Village in New York City.[7] Blynn Garnett was born there in 1933. Her mother, Rachael, her father, Larry, and the woman who would become her mother's life partner, Evelyn, lived together in a "bohemian household." By 1936, however, Blynn's father had moved out, and Rachael and Evelyn were raising Blynn. Although the family moved from the Village to a "more middle-class neighborhood" in 1936, Blynn was raised as a "red-diaper baby" who by kindergarten "knew all the Communist and Wobbly songs, could give you my position on the Spanish Civil War, and generally knew 'which side I was on.'" Blynn remembered that she was encouraged throughout her childhood to be an active learner and thinker.[8]

Across Manhattan from Greenwich Village was the East Village, known throughout the twentieth century as a radical, bohemian neighborhood. Blue Lunden lived in an East Village apartment after she took her daughter, Linda, from her abusive godmother and brought her to New York. Blue's lover, Jeanie Meurer, had been instrumental in bringing Linda to New York, helped to raise Linda as her "Aunt Jeanie," and would remain an important figure in Linda's life even after the couple broke up. The family lived together in a neighborhood along with beatniks, radicals, and other lesbians and gay men. It was also an ethnically diverse neighborhood, with large African American and Puerto Rican populations. Jeanie and Blue Lunden, who were both white, lived in the East Village apartment for four years, raising Linda and spending most of their time in the black lesbian community of the Lower East Side. Lunden and Jeanie frequented "pay parties," house parties at private apartments that charged an entrance fee and in which drinks and food were served. These and more formal lesbian dance hall events in Harlem offered black lesbians in New York an alternative to the sometimes segregated and often racist white lesbian bars. Blue recalled that there was a sense of family gatherings about the house parties: "It was like families, I mean people would bring their kids! And it was real evident to me that a lotta Black lesbians—their families knew that they were lesbians and it was just kinda taken as a matter of course."[9] In the radical, metropolitan space of the East Village there was some measure of safety for these lesbian mothers.

Many of the children of these early postwar counterculture spaces grew up in working-class butch/femme communities. Butch/femme was a specific historical lesbian culture that emerged in the United States in the first decades of the twentieth century and was particularly prevalent during and after the Second World War. Butch/femme cultures were predominantly tough,

Left to right: Linda Lunden, Jeanie Meurer, and Blue Lunden, Jones Beach, New York, 1960. Courtesy of Linda Lunden.

working-class bar cultures by the 1950s, where butches often had to defend their community from gangs of straight men who would go to butch/femme bars to start fights. They had distinct cultural values that defined them as different from middle-class lesbian communities in the 1950s; for example, butch/femme couples often refused to pass as straight in public, often risking violence and harassment by walking openly as couples, hand in hand.

Butch/femme culture revolved around the identities of butch and femme, which engaged with American concepts of masculinity and femininity but involved unique codes and understandings. Butches wore traditionally masculine clothing, such as suits or slacks and collared dress shirts, and valued stoicism, sexual prowess, and the ability to physically protect their femme companions. Femmes, on the other hand, wore traditionally feminine clothing and celebrated toughness in their butch partners. However, it is a mistake to see butch/femme as mimicry of heterosexual gender roles. Butch and femme sensibilities were distinct from heterosexual masculinity and femininity in many ways. For instance, it was a source of pride for butches to be able to give their femme partners sexual pleasure, and sexual prowess was defined through this ability—with it often being emphasized far more than their own physical pleasure. In addition, it was often femmes who worked and maintained economic control in butch/femme relationships. This was frequently understood as a part of these couples' refusal to pass in straight society; butches frequently faced employment discrimination based on their appearance, and femmes chose to support their partners as primary breadwinners, taking the kind of jobs available to women at this time.[10] In other words, butch/femme was a specific lesbian culture, affected by the same gendered dynamics as mainstream American culture, but with its own ways of engaging and navigating these dynamics. Butches did not see themselves as male or transgender, and they were not in drag; femmes did not see themselves as feminine women having relationships with men. Butches and femmes were women, largely working-class women, who loved other women and performed their gender and lesbianism in a culturally specific way.

The development of these largely working-class communities in the United States was an important consequence of the social changes brought about by the war. Women had somewhat more freedom to dress as butches in an environment where it was more acceptable for all women to wear some aspects of traditionally masculine clothing, such as pants, as women entered the wartime industrial workforce. Also, in the economic boom years of the war, butch/femme bar communities experienced an expansion. Cities, particularly large port cities and inland manufacturing centers, opened up and changed drastically after the war. Many of these cities developed working-class, butch/femme neighborhoods and bars, such as the ones Blue Lunden found in New Orleans. In these neighborhoods, some women raised their children together. The presence of large, urban metropolises gave these parents and their children some measure of safety from social prejudice and legal persecution.

As Elizabeth Kennedy and Madeline Davis have shown in their book, *Boots of Leather, Slippers of Gold*, Buffalo, New York, had a thriving, vibrant butch/femme community by the 1950s. Buffalo was a dynamic, midsized industrial city and experienced a tremendous amount of growth in the first half of the twentieth century. This growth facilitated changes that enabled the emergence

Left to right: Norma Jean Coleman and Beverly, a butch/femme couple, and Beverly's daughter, Dennie Sue, 1958. Courtesy of the Lesbian Herstory Archives.

of strong butch/femme communities. Many of the women in this community raised children. Pat, an African American woman born in Buffalo in 1940, grew up in the butch/femme social world of Buffalo, Albany, and Toronto. Her mother was a lesbian, and Pat grew up in a house that was open to young gay men and lesbians from all over the Northeast. Pat herself, after leaving home at thirteen and coming out as a lesbian, stayed in Buffalo, where in 1957, she got her own apartment and had a daughter at seventeen years old.[11]

New York City had vibrant white and black butch/femme communities that dated back to the 1920s, in which butch/femme couples raised their children. Joan Nestle, who came out as a young, white femme in New York's Greenwich Village in 1958, described seeing Puerto Rican and African American butches yelling up to their lovers in the Women's House of Detention, reassuring them that they would take care of the children.[12] The Los Angeles area also had butch/femme communities by the Second World War. Lana Lloyd grew up with her mother, a tough butch lesbian, in such a community in San Pedro, located in South Los Angeles, in the 1950s. Lana remembered hanging out with her mother and her mother's friends playing cards.[13] Vera Martin and Kay were both femmes with children, and Martin remembered that they had been ridiculed in butch/femme lesbian circles because they were a femme/femme couple.[14]

Many of the patterns common to working-class lesbian households with children of this era are visible in the life of Blue Lunden. Lunden learned early how to navigate the streets of New Orleans and roamed the city with her brother as a young girl. Her independence caused her family to label her a tomboy. By the age of twelve, she had fallen in love with another girl, and by fourteen she had several girlfriends whom she stayed with when things got too bad with her abusive godmother. By the time she was fifteen, Lunden had been in and out of the House of Good Shepherds, a local reform school for girls run by the Catholic Church, and had moved back in with her father.

Lunden was a streetwise teenager, a young butch who smoked and organized impromptu Pentecostal revivals to give the nuns a hard time. In 1952, the father of her girlfriend Carol took Lunden to her first gay bar, the Starlet Lounge, in New Orleans. The next year, she was caught in a police raid in a lesbian bar, the Golden Rod Inn, which was raided as part of a wave of increased police hostility toward lesbian and gay bars.[15] Lunden, who turned seventeen the same month as the raid, was arrested and lied about her age to keep from being sent back to reform school; however, a local newspaper printed a list of all those caught in the raid. This effectively exposed Blue Lunden as a lesbian to everyone in her life, and she decided that she would be honest with her family about her love for women. Her father's response was to throw her out of the house and disown her.

Lunden then moved in with her lover Virginia, Virginia's husband, and their children in the French Quarter, where she became more involved with the working-class, butch/femme lesbian community there. It was a dangerous and exciting time for Lunden and those around her. Police raids were common. Later, talking about the police, she recalled, "They would just come into the bar and pick some of you out." In New Orleans, women could still be charged with wearing the clothing of the opposite sex or with vagrancy. During this time, it was difficult for Lunden to make money, and she was primarily dependent on Virginia and her husband. She spent a lot of her time at the Starlet Lounge, and one night she went home with a man who offered to pay her to have sex with him. On this night, her first sexual encounter with a man, Blue Lunden became pregnant at the age of seventeen. She then married her friend Norman, a gay man, so her child would not be stigmatized as illegitimate. They marked the occasion in a local gay bar amid ironic laughter and celebration.

Blue gave birth to her daughter in October 1954, and a year later, she arranged to leave her with a couple she knew in an informal adoption. After this, she moved first to Texas, and then to New York City in 1956 on the recommendation of her brother, Tommy, who was living with his lover, a drag queen, in Greenwich Village. In New York, Blue learned that her godmother, who had physically abused her as a child, was going to take over the care of her daughter, Linda. Alarmed at the thought of her violent godmother raising her daughter, Lunden returned to New Orleans and told her godmother that she had renounced lesbianism. Lunden's godmother relinquished the child, and Lunden took Linda back to the Village, where she raised her.[16]

As Lunden's life illustrates, butch/femme communities were situated in tough, counterculture communities where lesbians, and sometimes gay men, stood against the dominant heterosexual, middle-class ethos of the postwar era. They were also spaces where lesbians had children. Blue Lunden remembered many of the butches she knew in New Orleans getting pregnant and having children. Prostitution was one way that women became pregnant in these postwar lesbian communities. For some women who loved women and decided to live outside of the socially proscribed role of marriage, sex work provided a way they could remain economically independent while raising their families. Also, as lesbians, these women faced enormous social persecution, and they could sometimes find more safety in the social circles that surrounded the informal economies of sexuality than in society at large. Many of the women Joan Nestle remembered talking to each other through the windows of the Women's

Left to right: Doris ("Big Daddy") King, Stormy Weather, and Blue Lunden, New Orleans, 1954. Blue was pregnant with her daughter when this picture was taken. Courtesy of the Lesbian Herstory Archives.

House of Detention in Greenwich Village had been incarcerated because they were sex workers.[17] Vera Martin's lover, Kay, who had emigrated from Japan after the war and who, like Vera, was raising two children, worked in a circle of lesbian prostitutes. This work enabled Kay to raise her own children, although she was terrified that her estranged ex-husband would take them from her because of her lesbianism.[18] Several women from the butch/femme community of Buffalo, New York, remembered lesbians, both butches and femmes, getting pregnant in the 1950s from having sex with men for money.[19]

Lesbian mothers raising children during this time faced threats of violence and incarceration. Police harassment of lesbians and gay men was constant in the decades following the Second World War. Women in these communities were incarcerated for sex work charges, for being caught in a lesbian bar during a police raid, or for wearing men's clothing on the street.[20] Bernie, a lesbian mother from Wyoming who relocated to Vallejo, California, was pregnant with her first child when she was pulled off the street by a police cruiser in 1945 and put in jail for the weekend for wearing male clothing.[21] Blue Lunden had been living with her daughter, Linda, in 1955 when the constant police harassment she was suffering on the streets forced her to relocate from New Orleans to Texas and then to New York City.[22] As a gay man wrote in a 1956 letter, police harassment in Key West, Florida, had created a situation where it was "hardly safe for a deviate (male or female) to be seen on the streets, not to mention bars or restaurants."[23] Even as counterculture urban communities provided a measure of anonymity and safety for lesbian mothers, these women remained vulnerable to persecution for openly defying heterosexual norms.

Battling Bias and Building Bridges: The Experiences of Children in Lesbian Households in the Pre-Liberation Era

Children growing up in lesbian households before the pre-liberation movement, like those in later generations, faced community ostracism as a result of prejudice directed toward their families. Like children of lesbian and gay parents in later decades, they had to be careful about which of their peers they brought home with them and learned to be wary of the sexual norms of mainstream society. They also acted as bridge workers between their families and the straight world, as generations of children of lesbians and gay men would after them, negotiating the cultural investments in family and sexuality that left them and their families either invisible or abject. Unlike the children of lesbians and gay men raised after Stonewall, however, they lacked any openly politicized communities or movements advocating for their rights.

Interviewed in 1998, Richard Tooker told a story that illustrates the ways that the children of lesbian mothers in this era were subject to isolation resulting from community animosity toward lesbian-headed families. Tooker first came to San Francisco in 1942 looking for wartime work in the manufacturing industries. He found a room in a boarding house in the Western Addition and began exploring local cruising spots to have sex with other men. The boarding house, it turned out, was run by a lesbian couple whom Tooker referred to as Mrs. X and Mrs. Y. The two women were partners, although Mrs. Y was married and her husband lived in the basement. To Tooker's discomfort, largely because he was in conflict about his own sexuality, the boarding house was part of a larger lesbian and gay social circle. Mrs. X had a teenage daughter who lived in the house, and Tooker remembered that once Mrs. Y helped set up a birthday party for the girl. "Everything was all set; they had this store-bought ice cream for . . . oh, probably a dozen," he recalled, but just before the party, the phone starting ringing, and "one after another," all the parents of the girls invited to the party called to say that their daughters would not be able to attend. Someone had told the parents that the two women were a lesbian couple, and years later, Tooker said that he could "still see the dismay on Mrs. Y's face."[24]

As it would be later, warning children about homophobia was an important part of conversations between lesbian mothers and their children. In 1946, when Ira Jeffries was fourteen and came out to her mother, Bonita, who was a lesbian herself, she remembered Bonita warning her that "society does not look kindly on that kind of behavior." Jeffries also recalled detesting hearing words like "bulldagger" used in a derogatory manner to refer to lesbians in her Harlem neighborhood. As was true for children in non-heterosexual households in later generations, Jeffries knew that her family was looked down on by heterosexual American culture and was warned by her mother to be careful.[25]

Lana Lloyd, who grew up with her lesbian mother and her father in San Pedro, California, in the 1950s, remembered that life was difficult at times because of the reaction of the outside world to her family. Lloyd's mother lived as a lesbian and had a live-in lover. She and Lloyd's father had a large circle of gay male and lesbian friends who would spend time at the house. Lloyd remembers in 1958, when she was five years old, one of her friends said that she could not "play with [her] anymore because [her] mom [was] a lesbian." Growing up, Lloyd knew that "it wasn't cool to bring my friends over." Like

Bonita Jeffries, standing, with her daughter, Ira, to her left and Ira's girlfriend, Snowbaby, to her right celebrating Ira's sixteenth birthday, Harlem, 1948. Courtesy of the Lesbian Herstory Archives.

other children of lesbian and gay families, Lloyd evaluated her friends' trustworthiness by watching how they reacted to her home environment. "Friends who survived a screening period were allowed to come to [the] house," where she introduced her mother's lovers as aunts. Lloyd also saw advantages to growing up the way she did and credited it with allowing her to experiment later with relationships with women, even though she ultimately came to identify as heterosexual: "Our parents have shown us that we're gifted with sexual options." Lloyd felt that her mother had taught her how to love honestly and well.[26]

Children reacted in complex ways to the knowledge of their mother's lesbianism. In 1964, Justin Henderson's sister told him that their mother was a lesbian. He was thirteen and she was twelve, and he told her that he already knew. At that point, his sister was living with his mother and her lover in an openly lesbian household, and Justin was living with their father. Until 1961, when his parents divorced, Justin had grown up in a "semi-Bohemian Southern California family." His mother had wrestled with her lesbianism throughout Justin's childhood, and he said that even though he and his sister had never spoken of it until that day, he had always been reluctant to bring friends over to his house and had been "in some ways ashamed of her sexual nature." When given the choice to live with his mother or with his father and his new wife in their middle-class house, he chose the latter but felt guilty about it.[27] Blynn Garnett, growing up in an unacknowledged lesbian household in New York City in the 1940s, remembered that she would lie about her absent father, saying that he was off at war, even after the end of hostilities: "World War Two was a godsend to me. . . . He'll never know what an immense and prolonged contribution he made to the postwar reconstruction of Japan."[28]

In these early decades, before the lesbian and gay liberation movements brought large numbers of parents out of the closet and long before the lesbian and gay baby booms of the 1980s and 1990s, growing up in a heterosexist society as the child of a lesbian household could be an isolating experience. Life in a lesbian household, even in the East Village, was lonely for Blue Lunden's daughter, Linda. When Blue came home, it was a time she could "put my clothes on and be who I was," but most of Linda's peers might have reacted badly to Blue's butch appearance. Because of the potential reactions of other children and their parents to a lesbian household, Blue and Jeanie "didn't encourage her to bring a lot of kids home." Blue remembered that Jeanie did try to organize a piñata party for Linda's birthday when she turned five, but that "it was difficult and she did not have a lot of playmates."[29] The isolation that lesbian mothers felt in a society that celebrated heterosexuality and denigrated same-sex relationships was shared by their children.

Sometimes, as would be the case with later gay and lesbian households with children, moving from a cosmopolitan area to a more suburban or rural one made things even more difficult for lesbian mothers and their children. In 1969, a lesbian couple, Lou Ellen and Delores, wrote to the New York chapter of the Daughters of Bilitis about relocating from New York to New Jersey with their two small children. Soon after finding an apartment in a housing complex the family found themselves in "hot water." After getting settled, the women sent their oldest child, Jean, out to play. She came home crying and told her mothers that a girl she was trying to play with had said that her mother had told her not to play with Jean. The two women quickly learned that they were the first open lesbians to settle in the area and that parents were telling their children to stay away from their kids, Jean and Peter. Adults ignored the family when they went outside, and people went out of their way to avoid getting on the elevator with them, particularly with Lou Ellen, who was a butch. Neighbors made it clear that Delores was not welcome with the other wives when they sat outside together to sunbathe and talk. Finally, Lou Ellen decided to take Delores back to New York for a night, so they could spend some time with other gay people, and they asked a neighborhood teenager if she would baby-sit. The girl agreed, but she later told Delores that when she returned home her parents had grilled her about whether she had been sexually propositioned, molested, or asked to return later when the women were home.

In this case, the tension continued for the adults, but gradually over time the presence of the children began to offset the prejudice and animosity toward the family. As Lou Ellen recalled, "Slowly people started giving credit where it belonged, Delores and the kids won them over whether they liked it or not." Their daughter, Jean, once walked an elderly man with a heart condition all the way to his apartment on the twelfth floor, holding his hand the whole way, which her mothers felt helped smooth the way toward acceptance of their family by the neighbors. Lou Ellen also felt that the wonderful home that Delores kept and the "spotless and respectable" nature of the two children slowly warmed the neighbors to the family. Then "the day came when Delores and I were giving a birthday party for Jean. The kids were supposed to come at 1 pm and leave at 3 pm." In the end, fourteen children came and would not leave until eight that night. The next day the "phone rang constantly, mothers calling asking what we did, the children never stopped talking about how wonderful Delores and Lou Ellen was, how they loved us." Soon, the two women were being consulted about interior decoration and meat loaf recipes and being asked to baby-sit. "We all have our troubles," Lou Ellen concluded the letter, "but isn't it just great when we just make enough headway to walk into a restaurant and not have the waitresses in a corner whispering."[30]

The story of this butch/femme New Jersey household in 1969 highlights the ways that children of lesbians and gay men have acted as emissaries between their families and the heterosexual world for decades. Before the massive expansion of gay and lesbian organizing in the 1970s, these children helped create space for their families in a cultural milieu that saw their families as an impossibility. In doing so, they made compromises, made up stories, stood defiant, and helped to pave the way for the generation that would come after them, the first generation of openly lesbian and gay parents and their children.

The Homophile Movement and Lesbian and Gay Parenting

As repressive and uncertain as these decades were for lesbian mothers, gay fathers, and their children, they also saw the beginnings of lesbian and gay parental organizing. Unlike the lesbian mothers and gay fathers groups of the liberation era, these early organizing attempts were not aimed directly at changing the legal status of lesbian and gay parents in the custody courts. Custody cases were rare and, when they did occur, almost always tragic; it was unthinkable in this period that the law recognize lesbian and gay parents. Direct action for lesbian and gay parental rights would begin only after the emergence of a militant doctrine of lesbian and gay pride in the early 1970s. However, the right to custody was addressed in lesbian and gay publications; lesbian mothers formed support groups to talk about how they could be good parents and to assure each other that their lesbianism would not harm their children, and gay men in the homophile movement began to discuss their right to become adoptive parents. These discussions mark the emergence of lesbian and gay parental activism and would lead directly to more open organizing in the 1970s, as an increased visibility of lesbian mothers and gay fathers brought on the era of the custody cases.

The right of lesbians and gay men to be parents was clearly a consideration for both male and female homophile groups, and in 1961, they began to demand that right. In January of that year, around forty representatives of DOB and the ONE Institute came together to draft a "Homosexual Bill of Rights" at the annual ONE midwinter symposium. Attendees broke up into five committees to draft sections of the document. One committee, tasked to work on "Social Rights," listed as one of these "the right to have children, if desired," while the committee on "Legal Rights" ended its list with "the right to custody of one's children, or adoption."[31]

In 1964, the Atheneum Society, a homophile organization founded in Miami, Florida, published the views of eleven homophile organizations and publications, including their own, on a variety of issues. Two of the questions the society asked each of the organizations were, "Do you believe homosexuals should be allowed the legal bonds of matrimony?" and a follow-up question, "Do you believe these 'families' should be allowed to adopt children?" Of the eleven organizations polled, the responses from only five survive.

However, the disagreement between the five organizations tells us that the issue of whether the rights to marry and adopt were worth struggling for was highly contested in male homophile communities at this time.

The Janus and Atheneum Societies both wrote unequivocally that marriage rights were not part of their struggle and that gay men should not be allowed to adopt children, while the Mattachine Society of San Francisco reported that they did support a "legal recognition of permanent homosexual relationships" and that "adoption of children by gay couples should be permitted once we know that such a living situation would not 'convert' a child over a certain age to the homosexual situation."[32] In response to the question about marriage, the group Gay Publishing wrote that they felt "some form of legal sanction would seem to be indicated," and on adoptive rights: "Yes, providing that the individual adjustment of the child would be constructively fostered by such an arrangement." On both the question of marriage and that of gay male rights as adoptive parents, the Society for Individual Rights answered that until sexuality between two men was decriminalized, the question of marriage and adoptive rights would remain moot.[33]

The Atheneum Society itself felt that any advocacy of gay parental or domestic rights would only alienate society and set the homophile cause back. In complaining about the rise of "wild and radical" ideas among homophile organizations, the society concluded that "primary among these wild ideas is the impression given that most homosexuals are in favor of the creation of a 'third sex' with legal marriage, child adoptions, and the acceptance of these 'families' into general society."[34] A reader, "Mr. I" from Miami, Florida—possibly Richard Inman, founder of the Miami-based Atheneum Society—wrote into ONE Magazine in 1965 and said, regarding "homosexuals favoring legalization of marriages and adoption of children," that he felt the homophile movement must first focus on the "immediate goals" of overturning sex laws used against homosexuals; stopping antihomosexual employment discrimination in the private sector, the federal government, and the armed forces; defending the right of homosexuals to associate with one another; and stopping antihomosexual harassment and social bigotry. After these goals were achieved others would rise to the forefront of the freedom struggle, and "perhaps then, two of these goals will be marriage and adoption of children."[35]

Other visions of gay families in this era were more fantastical but can nonetheless be seen as antecedents to both gay liberationist and lesbian feminist revisions of heterosexual nuclear childrearing arrangements that would separate heterosexual companionate intimacy from the family. In a 1961 article in ONE Magazine, James R. Steuart called for the creation of collective childrearing groups of lesbians and gay men based on "artificial insemination" that would raise children in an environment encouraging of same-sex relationships.[36] Steuart's essay predicts the emergence of a lesbian donor insemination baby boom and has interesting similarities to lesbian feminist parthenogenesis-based visions of an Amazonian mother-daughter society. His call for lesbian-and gay-headed households that would raise children in a pro-homosexual environment was singular in this era, and whether or not he was serious, seems intended to call attention to the ways that both heterosexual and homosexual communities took the heterosexual family, queer childlessness, and the raising of children as heterosexual for granted. Letters to the editor responding to Steuart's article ranged from condemnation of it as mad to the response from one lesbian from Youngstown, Ohio, who said, "I just might be willing to discuss artificial insemination a little bit more fully."[37] A 1960 article, entitled "Augmented Families," argued for the benefits of extended childrearing arrangements that would get away from "institutions such as the heterosexual family."[38] Although rare, articles such as these demonstrate that there were individuals in homophile communities already beginning to articulate radical visions of childrearing relations outside of the heterosexual family.

The first organized discussions in the United States of lesbians as mothers emerged in this period among the members of the Daughters of Bilitis. Founded in 1955 by a group of eight women in San Francisco, California, the group was the first lesbian civil rights organization in the United States. Along with gay male organizations of the same period, DOB was part of the homophile movement, the first wave of lesbian and gay civil rights organizing. Two of the original four lesbian couples who founded DOB were lesbian mothers and co-mothers, and two of these original co-founders, Del Martin and Phyllis Lyon, later recalled that there were always mothers in the organization.[39] A participatory study of lesbians begun in 1963 by Ralph Gundlach and done with the assistance of DOB members found that 20 percent of the 226 lesbian-identified women who filled out questionnaires were mothers.[40] A questionnaire sent out by DOB to its own members in 1958 found that out of 157 participants, 23 were mothers.[41] In 1956, early in the group's existence, DOB held discussion groups on lesbian motherhood that drew from six to eight lesbian mothers and their partners. Entitled "Raising Children in a 'Deviant' Relationship," these were the first known organized discussions of lesbian motherhood ever held in the United States.[42]

Martin and Lyon recalled that many of the mothers in the early years of DOB were still wrestling with self-doubt and the fear that their lesbianism would somehow damage their children or cause them to become gay or lesbian themselves. They remembered that "when DOB got started, there were so many mothers who felt . . . they didn't want their kids to grow up to be gay and they were afraid they might." The talks that DOB held in 1956 brought in child psychiatry experts to address these concerns. Phyllis Lyon remembered one woman at the meeting, a single lesbian mother, who was "really worried that they [the kids] were going to turn out gay and she thought being gay was the worst thing that could happen to anybody." They concluded that as long as children were raised in a loving environment they would be fine and that there was no evidence they would grow up to be non-heterosexual.[43]

Gay and lesbian parents' concern that their children would be negatively affected by their homosexuality would come up frequently in discussions organized in this period. Not everybody in this early period agreed with the conclusions of the first DOB meetings on raising children in same-sex households. A series of discussions in 1958 on "homosexuality—a way of life" at ONE Institute's annual two-day midwinter symposium included a group meeting titled, "Should Homosexuals Get Married." The topic of parenting came up, and there was a "general feeling" among participants that children of "a union of one or more homosexual parents would probably end up with more problems than would be their lot under normal circumstances."[44] Such fears paralleled those felt by the first wave of organized lesbian mothers and gay fathers groups in the 1970s and 1980s.

DOB chapters and the group's nationwide publication, The Ladder, offered lesbian mothers and their children comfort and community. One thirty-six-year-old woman from Southern California, divorced with two children, wrote to DOB in 1966 asking to be put in touch with DOB members in the Claremont-Pomona area. That same year, a couple from Costa Mesa, California, with six children wrote to the DOB office in San Francisco, asking for advice on their upcoming vacation, since "vacations without the children are few and far between." The two women had never been to San Francisco before and wrote that "we are looking for a place to stay (not expensive) and the fun places to go. We like to dance (together) and drink and talk." They were interested in gay life outside the bars and asked if they could come to a DOB meeting while in town. In 1961, a woman wrote DOB president Jaye Bell to tell her that she and her daughter were moving from Danville, Virginia, to Oakland, California, and were looking forward to meeting her. The woman and her daughter had just come back from a vacation to the Greek island of Lesbos (Mytilini). Bell wrote the woman back, invited her to speak about her vacation at a DOB meeting, and told her to get in touch upon arrival in the San Francisco Bay Area if she and her daughter needed help getting settled.

A woman from Los Angeles who identified herself as a twenty-five-year-old African American, separated, with a one-year-old boy, wrote DOB national headquarters in 1965 asking for information on meeting DOB members in Los Angeles. The woman expressed her desire to "find happiness and acceptance in society being what I am."[45]

In 1966, the San Francisco chapter of DOB, in conjunction with the Council on Religion and the Homosexual (CRH), held a public "family night" panel discussion at Glide Memorial Church. In what was advertised as the first public discussion of its kind, family members of "homosexuals and/or lesbians," including children of gay or lesbian parents, spoke about the issues raised by their family situations. By 1968, the San Francisco DOB chapter was collecting letters it had received from lesbian mothers in a file in anticipation of helping with research on lesbian mothers that chapter members felt was needed.[46] In 1970, members of the San Francisco chapter of DOB told a crowd of psychiatric professionals that the community needed "family counseling for those with children wherein the parent's homosexuality would not be treated as the catch-all cause of their family's problems."[47]

In April 1967, a "Gab n' Java" meeting was set up by the New York chapter of DOB to discuss "specific issues facing homosexuals rearing children." Women attending the meeting included a lesbian who had been living with her son and daughter and her lover for five years, a woman who was raising her three-year-old daughter in a lesbian household, and a woman whose teenage daughter had been "hostile" when she met her mother's lover. None of the women had told their children about their lesbianism, and all were concerned about when and if they should do so and how their children would be affected.[48] In 1968, another New York Gab n' Java was held on the subject with topics ranging from how to deal with questions that came up from the children to the feeling shared by some women present at the meeting that the absence of male role models was "probably detrimental" to the children.[49]

These meetings, held by DOB on both coasts, were the forerunners of the lesbian mother movement that emerged nationwide in the early 1970s. In fact, only a few years later, some of these later lesbian feminist groups came in part from DOB chapters. As previously mentioned, Del Martin and Phyllis Lyon, founders of the organization in 1955 and central members of the San Francisco chapter, were two of the founders of the nation's first lesbian mother advocacy group, the Lesbian Mother's Union, in 1971. Carole Morton, whose story opens the introduction to this book, set up discussion groups in 1970 and 1971 for lesbian mothers in DOB New Jersey and DOB New York and went on to found Dykes and Tykes in New York in 1976.

The DOB discussion groups for lesbian mothers, the conversations about gay male adoptive rights in the *Atheneum Review*, and the identification of parental and custodial rights at ONE's Midwinter Institute were precursors to the lesbian mothers and gay fathers groups of the 1970s and 1980s. They also reveal the first stirrings of the political focus on domestic and parental rights that LGBT civil rights groups would eventually embrace in the last decade of the twentieth century. That these early roots of lesbian and gay parental activism dealt only with the most basic questions regarding the propriety of lesbian motherhood and gay fatherhood is a sign of the deeply and widely held belief in the postwar years that the heterosexual family was the only acceptable environment for raising children. And the fact that the *Atheneum Review* thought fighting for gay male parental and marital rights was utopian and self-defeating further testifies to the intensity of the social edict that gay men and lesbians should not be allowed to parent children. In this postwar cultural and political climate, still so antagonistic to gay men and lesbians, merely advocating the right of lesbian mothers and gay fathers to exist seemed radical and subversive.

Conclusions: Hidden Families and the Seeds of Change

Lesbian mothers and gay fathers raising children in this pre-liberation period faced constant danger in a society that saw them as deviants with no right to be parents. They lived their everyday lives with the threat of exposure and its consequences. For lesbian mothers raising their children in bohemian and lesbian communities, discovery and intervention by the state meant probable loss of their children and incarceration. Gay fathers who were living separately from their children and their children's mothers also had to be extremely circumspect, lest they be barred from any contact with their kids—and many did find themselves completely ostracized from their children. Many lesbian mothers and gay fathers, facing these prospects, chose to stay in heterosexual family relationships and lead a hidden life of a different sort. They negotiated their desires with the realities of a culture of heterosexual postwar domesticity, often sacrificing their mental and physical well-being so that they could remain close to their children. In all of these varied life experiences lay the roots of the custody struggles and gay and lesbian parental activism of later decades; eventually, these men and women, invisible in the domesticity of the postwar era, would have a profound effect on the modern LGBT freedom struggle, which would put gradual but increasing focus on domestic and parental rights.

CHAPTER THREE

In the Best Interests of the Child

Lesbian and Gay Parenting Custody Cases, 1967–1985

On November 15, 1967, Ellen Nadler appeared before the Honorable Justice Joseph Babich in the Superior Court of California, Sacramento County. It was the second time in two months that she had argued for custody of her five-year-old daughter. A little over a month earlier, on October 5, Justice Babich had awarded custody of the child to Nadler's ex-husband solely on the basis of the mother's lesbianism. The judge had done so without hearing any additional evidence in the case, stating that "the homosexuality of plaintiff as a matter of law constitutes her not a fit or proper person to have the care, custody and control of . . . the minor child of the parties hereto."[1] Ellen Nadler's trial marked the beginning of decades of lesbian mother and gay father custody cases, as men and women fought for their rights to express their same-sex sexual orientation and parent their children at the same time.

This chapter examines the early history of lesbian and gay custody conflicts from 1967 to 1985 through an analysis of 122 cases in which lesbian or gay parenting was an issue, based on court transcripts, newspaper articles, oral histories, articles in professional journals, personal letters, and lesbian and gay periodicals. Institutional antigay and -lesbian prejudice, which grew out of the same cultural assumptions that confronted lesbian mothers and gay fathers in the 1950s and 1960s, constructed same-sex sexuality as antithetical to parenting, actively stripped many lesbians and gay men of their parental rights, and kept a whole generation of lesbian and gay parents in fear of being estranged from their children.

In the 1970s, as large numbers of lesbians and gay men openly declared their sexuality, they challenged the longstanding cultural assumption that lesbians and gay men could not be parents. The greater visibility of gay and lesbian communities increased the risk of exposure and therefore loss of custody for many lesbian and gay parents, and in the eighteen years between 1967 and 1985, lesbian and gay parents lost many more court battles than they won.

However, by 1985 an increasing number of state courts were overturning decisions that had denied lesbian mothers and gay fathers custody and visitation rights. Custody cases in these critical years reveal the powerful cultural connection between sexual orientation and beliefs about what constituted a proper family as well as its slow and arduous shift. Lesbians and gay men had to fight hard to change both the perception of parenting as exclusively heterosexual and the legal practices that supported it. Their uphill battle is an important part of both why and how domestic, parental, and marital rights came to be at the center of the modern lesbian, gay, bisexual, and transgender civil right movement by the end of the twentieth century.

The majority of cases from 1967 to 1985 involved men and women who had left heterosexual marriages. Gay fathers usually fought for visitation rights, while lesbians fought for either visitation or outright custody. Gay fathers were often estranged from their children for years as a result of court orders secured by ex-wives or other family members.[2] Both lesbian mothers and gay fathers lost custodial rights regularly, and even when they were allowed to spend time with their children, they often did so at the expense of their constitutional rights of association, in the form of prohibitions against being with their same-sex partner and their children at the same time or against participating in lesbian and gay activism or social events.

When lesbian mothers and gay fathers came out in the process of a divorce from heterosexual spouses, they often faced the immediate danger of losing custody of and even contact with their children. At this time, even those lesbian and gay parents who tried to hide their sexual identity came under increased scrutiny by ex-spouses, both because there was a greater awareness of same-sex relationships in society in general and because after leaving their heterosexual marriages they often relocated to gay and lesbian neighborhoods, such as San Francisco's Castro District or New York's Greenwich Village. Once visible in a lesbian or gay community, the risk was much greater that ex-spouses or family members would use their sexual orientation against them in a custody dispute.

The various components that made up judicial prejudice against lesbian mothers and gay fathers in these custody cases were familiar ones in U.S. society. They echo longstanding aspects of antigay and -lesbian bigotry in the United States, including the belief that gay men and lesbians were more likely to be pedophiles, that they were emotionally irresponsible, that their children might be gay—which the courts assumed was a negative outcome—and that these children would face social stigma and psychological damage as the result of being raised by a lesbian or gay parent. These attitudes are similar to rhetoric that permeated legal decisions and campaigns against gay and lesbian teachers, the rounding up of gay men in the sex-crime panics of the 1950s and 1960s, and the backlash against the lesbian and gay freedom struggle represented by the 1977 "Save Our Children" campaign in Dade County, Florida.[3] All of these reactions to lesbian and gay individuals and communities share fundamental fears about the proximity of children to same-sex sexual orientation, fears that had their most direct manifestation in the virulent animosity toward gay fathers and lesbian mothers in the courts.

Those custody cases involving lesbian and gay parents that are traceable represent only the tip of the iceberg. Due to child privacy concerns and a desire to have the latitude of judges unfettered by publicity, decisions largely went unpublished. Only when a decision was appealed did it become public. Appellate decisions, therefore, make up the majority of the historical record. Thus, with a few exceptions, we know little of lesbians and gay men who lost custody of their children outright and never appealed the original decision. In addition, the public record does not include the many custody cases that were settled out of court. The cases that did become known, however, often received a great deal of attention in both the mainstream and grassroots gay and lesbian community media, which meant that legal prejudice against lesbian and gay parents, as well as its gradual lessening, had a social impact far beyond the courtroom.

A slow decline in judicial bias against gay and lesbian parents occurred in the years between 1967 and 1985 for the same reason the cases emerged in the first place; as lesbian feminist and gay liberation movements energized and made lesbian and gay communities more visible, lesbian and gay parents lost custody of their children, but political activism in these communities also heightened opposition to these losses. Lesbian mothers and gay fathers groups formed across the country, including politically active groups such as Dykes and Tykes in New York City, the Lesbian Mothers Union in Oakland, California, and the Lesbian Mothers' National Defense Fund (LMNDF) in Seattle, Washington. Gay fathers groups, although less concertedly focused on political organizing than lesbian mother' organizations, also provided personal support and financial assistance for members facing attacks on their parental rights. These organizations raised funds for lesbian mothers and gay fathers involved in custody struggles and worked with progressive attorneys such as Donna Hitchens and Roberta Achtenberg of the Lesbian Rights Project, Rosalie Davies from Custody Action for Lesbian Mothers, or Marilyn Haft with the ACLU's Sexual Privacy Project, as well as political activists from organizations such as the National Gay Task Force. The political and legal work these organizations pioneered was critical to the slow shift in custody decisions. It also played a fundamental role in turning the focus of the LGBT freedom struggle toward the rights of marriage and the family.

Also crucial in the gradual movement toward greater acceptance of lesbian and gay parenting was the reevaluation of same-sex sexuality within the field of psychiatry.[4] As psychiatrists and psychologists such as Judd Marmor, Richard Green, John Money, and Wardell Pomeroy fought to change the stance of the American Psychiatric Association (APA) on same-sex sexuality, they also argued that sexual orientation was irrelevant to fit parenthood. In the early 1970s, a few of these individuals, including Pomeroy, Money, and Green, began to testify on behalf of lesbian mothers and gay fathers in custody disputes, arguing that lesbians and gay men were not unfit to be parents because of their sexuality and would not cause psychological damage to their children. Lesbian mother activist groups and legal advocacy organizations often worked to put lesbian and gay parents facing custody battles in touch with these early sympathetic psychologists and psychiatrists.

By 1985, this social, professional, and legal activism on behalf of the parental rights of lesbians and gay men began to have an impact on custody rulings in the West and the Northeast, areas where gay men and lesbians tended to migrate as part of their coming-out process. States where sizable lesbian or gay communities had formed after the Second World War, such as California, Michigan, Pennsylvania, and New York, were early and frequent battlegrounds between gay and lesbian parents, their ex-spouses, and sometimes other family members, along with political, legal, and religious advocates on either side.[5] It was also in these locations that state supreme courts began deciding in favor of lesbian mothers and gay fathers by the late 1970s and early 1980s. Resistance to change was most visible in states traditionally dominated by Christian fundamentalism, such as North Carolina, Mississippi, Virginia, Oklahoma, and Texas.[6]

The call for custodial and parental rights from 1970 to 1985 was an important part of broader legal efforts that accompanied gay and lesbian liberation movements, and negative judicial reactions to lesbian mothers and gay fathers resemble court responses to other demands for lesbian and gay civil rights in the same period. Judges often criticized lesbians and gay men fighting for employment or privacy rights for discussing their cases with the press or for taking part in gay or lesbian political activities, factors also cited in many decisions denying lesbian mothers and gay fathers custody or visitation rights.[7] Judges also used state sodomy laws as justification for antigay and -lesbian decisions in a whole range of cases, arguing that under these laws, lesbians and gay men were admitted felons and therefore could not appeal to the legal system to uphold their rights to employment, privacy, or child custody.

This chapter examines the animosity that lesbian mothers and gay fathers experienced in custody courts from 1967 to 1985 and argues that the prevalent judicial bias was that "the best interests of the child" always lay in a heterosexual household and that this bias effectively deprived lesbian and gay parents of their civil rights. This bias and the legal losses that came from it created an atmosphere of fear that affected not only those parents who lost custody but also an entire generation of lesbian mothers and gay fathers. However, lesbian and gay custody cases of this period also challenged and began to change the widely accepted notion that same-sex sexual orientation was antithetical to parenting, and a state-by-state shift in judicial opinion became visible by the mid-1980s.

The Denial of Custody

The 1967 *Nadler* rehearing exemplifies the ways in which the legal doctrine of "the best interests of the child" was frequently used as a smoke screen for judicial bias against homosexuality and a denial of parental rights to lesbians and gay men. Judge Babich's ruling in the case had been subsequently overturned by a California court of appeals, which objected to the assumption that homosexuality per se made someone an unfit parent. The appellate court demanded that Babich rehear the case. The higher court did not necessarily disagree with his final award of custody to the father or the condemnation of lesbianism in a woman who had children. It did find fault, however, because he had not exercised the "very broad discretion" at his disposal as a judge in a custody dispute. As a matter of law, Justice Babich had erred in not hearing all of the evidence in the case with "the best interests of the child" in mind; instead he had simply declared lesbianism grounds for removal of custodial privileges with no further review.

There is little doubt that Ellen Nadler's sexual orientation was still on trial in the appeals proceedings. At the end of the long trial, during which the judge and the attorney for her ex-husband were both graphically preoccupied with her sexuality, Nadler again lost custody of her daughter. This time, however, the judge was clear in stating that it was because a heterosexual environment would be in "the best interests of the child," not because lesbian motherhood was against the law.[8]

In demanding that Judge Babich base his decision on "the good of the child," the court of appeals was working from a California state statute that had its roots in Victorian-era concepts of motherhood and childhood. Based on a vision of a private domestic sphere, and buoyed by the rise of an urban middle class, these new ideas gradually led to the development of a "maternal preference" when courts decided issues of child custody. Of course, like the "cult of true womanhood" that it accompanied, this glorification of motherhood had certain built-in restrictions based on class and race; the ideal of the virtuous mother applied explicitly to white, middle-class women of European ancestry.[9] This new Victorian philosophy replaced a colonial-era deference to a father's right to his children as property. By 1936, forty-two state legislatures had rewritten their laws regarding custody to reflect this transition. For decades, state laws embodied two principles: "maternal preference," or the "tender years" principle, as it also came to be known, and the idea that judges must prioritize the "best interests of the child."[10]

By the late 1960s, custody rulings began to revise the trend toward maternal preference, as divorce rates increased rapidly and father's rights groups lobbied for changes in custody law.[11] Men going through divorce started to question a system that they claimed almost always awarded custody to the mother. Often ex-husbands sued for custody after being ordered by increasingly stringent courts to pay overdue child support. Changes occurred faster on the books than in court decisions, but gradually, over the decade of the seventies, heterosexual fathers did begin to receive substantial custody rights.[12] The maternal preference began to fade from American family courts, leaving a strengthened "best interests" doctrine in its place.

The 1967 Nadler case serves as a symbol for the decade and a half of intense struggle that lay ahead for lesbians and gay men who fought in the courts for their right to parent their children. In some ways, the case of Ellen Nadler set a precedent in California. The state already had a "best interests of the child" statute on the books, and thus, Nadler established that a lesbian or gay man could not be declared an "unfit" parent per se, simply as "a matter of law." But this impact was limited to California, and in any case, state statutes could easily be made to fit a judge's agenda. In California after the Nadler appeal in 1967, the courts merely had to conjecture that being in the care of a homosexual parent was not "in the best interests of the child," circumventing the question of whether homosexuality per se made an individual an unfit parent. The ambiguous and slippery bias against these parents that characterized the final decision in the Nadler case, couched in a concern for the welfare of the child, was the norm for most of the decade. In state after state, family court judges hid their condemnation of gay and lesbian parents behind the logic of a "nexus ruling." Judges found reasons, remarkably similar ones from state to state, to decide that there was a definitive connection, or "nexus," between a parent's same-sex sexuality and possible harm to children and that a child's best interest always lay with having a heterosexual family.

The reasons judges gave for taking custody away from lesbian and gay parents revolved around the idea that a parent's same-sex sexuality would harm their children. Judges often brought up the concern that the children of lesbian or gay parents would be socially ostracized. In one case, a New Jersey court denied Sandra Panzino custody of her two daughters in 1977 on the grounds that her children might suffer stigmatization. Even though Panzino was a Girl Scout troop leader, had been sole caretaker of the girls for seven years, was heralded as "a devoted mother" by school officials at the custody hearings, and had recently been forced to sue her ex-husband for back child support, she lost custody because of her sexual orientation. Judge Joseph Gruccio claimed that Panzino was "too dependent" on her daughters, and his decision discussed the dangers of social alienation and ridicule the girls might face as a result of her lesbianism if they remained with their mother.[13]

This idea that the children of gay men and lesbians would suffer socially because of their parents, and that this opinion justified a denial of custody to lesbian and gay parents, was widespread. One conservative judge who declared in an article in a legal journal that lesbian mothers were to be "pitied more than condemned," listed "criticism and ostracism by the community" as one of the reasons he cautioned against out lesbians having custody of their children.[14] A Texas jury denied Mary Jo Risher custody of her nine-year-old son in a 1975 trial in which her seventeen-year-old son testified that he had suffered ridicule at the hands of his peers over his mother's lesbianism.[15]

In addition to the belief that the children of lesbians and gay men would suffer from stigma, judges were often convinced that gay men and lesbians were likely to molest their children. The supervised visits required in many court decisions were structured with these fears in mind. In the *Nadler* case, Judge Joseph Babich had remarked, "The Court—we are dealing with a four-year-old on the threshold of its development—just cannot take the chance that something untoward should happen to it."[16] In a speech given at Georgia State University in Atlanta soon after she lost custody of her son, Mary Jo Risher identified the myth that all gay people were "child molesters" as one of the cultural biases that she felt had influenced the jury in her case. Mary Jo Risher's ex-husband's attorney repeatedly asked her in court if she and her partner, Ann Foreman, performed any sexual acts in front of the children.[17] Orange County social workers accused Cynthia Forcier, a Native American lesbian mother, of molesting her five-year-old daughter in

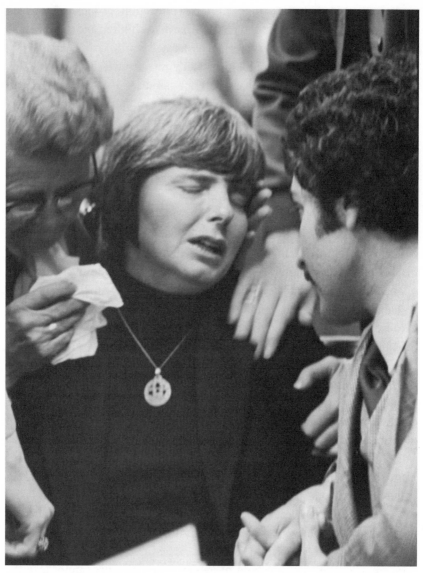

Mary Jo Risher leaving the courtroom after losing custody of her son, Dallas, Texas, 1975. AP Images.

a California custody case in which her lesbianism was also an issue. A doctor assumed that bruises in the girl's pelvic area were indications of sexual molestation and not the result of being kicked by another child, as Forcier's daughter claimed. The doctor and a social worker wrote to Orange County authorities declaring Forcier an unfit mother and linking the possible molestation with lesbianism. When an Orange County Superior Court judge ruled that Cynthia's lesbianism would not be admissible against her in court, all charges were dropped.[18]

Gay fathers also faced these accusations. Robert Johnson married a woman in the early 1970s after living as a gay man in San Francisco during the decades after the Second World War; he came out to his wife in 1983, and, in a custody battle focused on the "sickness" of his homosexuality, she accused him of molesting their son.[19] Similarly, a petition filed in 1982 on the part of a gay man's ex-wife in Dekalb County, Illinois, alleged that the man was "recruiting the children into homosexuality" and that he was likely to molest them. A county examination of the man's relationship with his children found no evidence of any abuse.[20] Cases across the nation at this time echo the concerns reflected in these examples that gay men and lesbians were a threat to their children or that being raised with lesbians and gay men harmed children in some way, socially, emotionally, psychologically, or sexually.

During the first decade and a half of lesbian mother custody cases, many of the most publicized cases involved white lesbian mothers who had left marriages to middle-class husbands. These women attracted public attention because their race and the class positions they had inhabited before coming out made them legible as mothers to mainstream society at the same time as their lesbianism made them the targets of animosity. This left the struggles of lesbian mothers of color invisible. For these women, white supremacy compounded the prejudice they faced in custody courts. In a 1979 letter to the LMNDF in Seattle, attorneys for the Lesbian Rights Project reported that they had represented lesbian mothers in four cases in 1978, and that three of these cases had involved black lesbian mothers who "confronted the multiple discrimination or our legal system—black, poor, lesbians, and mothers."[21] A woman writing from North Carolina in 1984 who identified as "a dyke of colour" and an "out dyke" asked the LMNDF for support in a custody case she was fighting. She described her fear that she would lose custody of her child in the conservative climate of her region because of her inability to afford a good lawyer.[22]

The intense vulnerability of being a lesbian mother of color was so great that in some cases it drove women to go underground with their children to keep custody of them. Earnestine Blue, an African American lesbian mother who fled California for Utah in 1974 rather than lose custody of her children to their father, described the way that racism and antilesbian bias worked together in the courtroom: "I think that homophobia plays into it, I think the racism plays into it. I think that the judge did not care because both of us were African-Americans. I think that they felt like I was way worse because I was a lesbian." Blue recalled that her lack of financial resources made her especially vulnerable: "I'm a black lesbian female, and my husband . . . he had a lot more money than I did, and I couldn't afford an attorney."[23]

Sometimes attorneys seeking to strip lesbian mothers of visitation rights or custody would use the race of their partners or their partners' children as a way to portray them as unfit mothers. In one Arizona custody case, attorneys suggested that the interracial relationship of a white lesbian mother fighting for custody might harm her children.[24] In a Virginia case, the "looseness" of a lesbian mother's household was argued based only on her lesbianism, the fact that she allowed her son to say the word "shit," and that her lover's son was black.[25]

Decisions in many cases nationwide cited the legal proscriptions against sodomy and the judges' agreement with these laws as justification for denying gay men and lesbians their right to parent their children. The use of sodomy laws to police same-sex sexual orientation throughout the twentieth century included decades of raids on gay and lesbian bars and meeting places under state statutes variously worded as "sodomy," "sexual psychopath," or "crimes against nature" laws.[26] Although states slowly repealed these laws, beginning with Illinois in 1961, some states retained them until very recently. In 1986, the U.S. Supreme Court ruled in *Bowers v. Hardwick* to uphold the sodomy laws, a ruling that held until 2003, when *Lawrence v. Texas* overturned *Hardwick*.[27] Before the *Lawrence* decision, lesbians and gay men were subject to custody discrimination in states where sodomy or "crimes against nature" laws remained in effect.[28]

In the 1975 California case *Chaffin v. Frye*, the judge explicitly referred to the laws against sodomy in denying Lynda Chaffin the right to be a mother, even though there was vigorous lobbying against these laws in the state legislature at the time. The judge argued that even though society was growing permissive, so much so that "in certain respects enforcement of the criminal law against the private commission of homosexual acts may be inappropriate," this change did not mean that lesbians or gay men could be allowed to keep their children.[29] Admitting that in some situations sodomy laws could be antiquated, this judge nonetheless cited their historical existence to bolster his opposition to lesbian parenting. In a 1985 ruling, the Virginia Supreme Court used the Virginia statute against sodomy as partial justification for limiting a gay man's visitation rights with his daughter, forbidding him from seeing her in the presence of his lover or any other gay men.[30] Assistant district attorney Ernest F. Winters referred to California's sodomy law when he demanded that Ellen Nadler relinquish the names of her female sexual partners since 1966; he told the court that these women "may be felons, and I believe there is a case in point in which continued association with felons has been ground to deny custody to a parent."[31] Over the objections of both Ellen Nadler and her attorney, the court forced her to reveal the women's names. Judges continued to cite the sodomy laws to deny lesbian mothers and gay fathers custody of their children until the *Lawrence* decision declared them unconstitutional.

Judges stripped many lesbian and gay parents of their constitutional right of free association out of a fear that even casual displays of affection between same-sex couples would be detrimental to children.[32] In case after case, gay and lesbian parents were ordered to sign affidavits agreeing never to have their partners and children in their homes at the same time, to undergo regular psychiatric examinations testifying to their repudiation of their sexual orientation, and to halt all pro–gay rights activist work in order to maintain parental rights.[33]

As gay men and lesbians fought for custody or visitation rights, the threat that they could be separated from their partners loomed large. "That was our main concern in Jeanne's case," remembered attorney Jill Lippett, who represented Jeanne Jullion in a San Francisco Bay Area lesbian mother custody case that made national headlines, "that she and her partner would not be able to live together."[34] In a 1972 California case, M v. M, the court forced Cam Mitchell to agree that she would not live with her lover, Darlene Reynolds, or even allow her children to come into Reynolds's presence, in order to keep custody of her three children. The judge replied after delivering his decision in the case that he had put these limitations on Mitchell to show he "wasn't soft on homosexuals," even though a juvenile probation officer recommended in her favor in the original custody proceedings.[35] Mitchell received assistance from the Lesbian Mothers Union chapters in San Francisco and Oakland and eventually successfully appealed the restrictions on her right of association. Ellen Nadler was also forced to agree to supervised visits in order to see her daughter after losing custody. Del Martin, one of the founders of the Lesbian Mothers Union, wrote in her personal notes about a 1973 case in which a lesbian mother was allowed to retain custody of her children only "as long as she lived alone with them."[36]

Outside of California, a range of custody decisions across the country repeated these restrictions. In a 1973 decision in *Spence v. Durham*, the Supreme Court of North Carolina overturned an appellate decision denying Susan Spence custody of her two daughters. The supreme court only granted custody to Spence based on evidence that she had refrained from lesbianism since 1968, at which time evidence had pointed to "the existence of a situation in their home . . . which was beyond the pale of the most permissive society." Without expanding on this ominous euphemism, the court awarded Spence custody with the caveat that "at least every six months" a social service agency would visit the family and file a report.[37] In two separate cases, *Schuster v. Schuster* (1974) and *Isaacson v. Isaacson* (1974), the court told Sandy Schuster and Madeleine Isaacson, two Seattle women, both open lesbians, that living together as they had been doing was not in the "best interests" of their six children and ordered them to keep their family apart.[38] One anonymous account from 1976 tells of a Boston woman identified only as "Carole" losing custody of her children and retaining visitation rights only by promising she would not sleep with her lover while the children were in the house.[39] In a New York case, *In re Jane B.*, the mother's visitation rights were restricted to daytime hours and to places where no other "homosexuals" were present. In this case, the court explicitly stated that the woman's constitutional rights had been superseded by the "best interests of the child."[40] In another New York case that began in 1971, a judge told an admitted lesbian mother that she could only visit her daughter when her lover was not present.[41]

All over the country, gay fathers also risked losing their rights of association. In a 1973 case involving an Oregon man who was "alleged" to be a homosexual, the court awarded custody to the father only with a stipulation against "any other man . . . living in the family home." The mother of the two boys involved in this case had "substantially no contact" with them for ten years during which she had not expressed a desire for custody. When she tried to claim custody in 1973, the court denied her only after ordering that the father and the boys remain under "supervision by the Clackamas County Juvenile Department." This father categorically denied having ever engaged in any homosexual behavior, although he did admit on cross-examination that he "might have possible homosexual traits and tendencies."[42] In Philadelphia, a man named Bob supported his partner Tony's efforts to reestablish contact with his children even though they both assumed that if the courts did let Tony see his children again, he would never be able to do so in his partner's presence.[43]

Family court judges often chastised lesbian and gay parents for their involvement in gay liberation political activism. Many judges saw these activities

Jeanne Jullion speaking at a rally organized on her behalf, San Francisco, 1977. Photograph by Cathy Cade. Courtesy of the Bancroft Library, University of California, Berkeley.

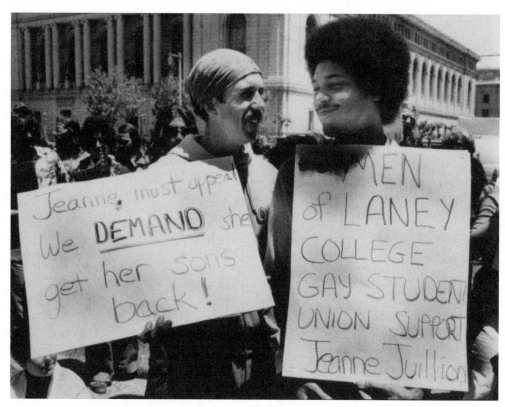

Men at a rally for Jeanne Jullion, San Francisco, 1977. Photograph by Cathy Cade. Courtesy of the Bancroft Library, University of California, Berkeley.

as sufficient cause for removal of custody. One man who was public about his gayness and active in gay liberation in the early 1970s was barred from visiting his children by a New Jersey superior court in 1974, although experts testified to his devotion as a father. The court did allow the man three weeks with his children during the summer, but forbade him from engaging "in any homosexual activities."[44] Jeanne Jullion, who lost custody of her eldest son in a long court battle, felt continuously punished by the judicial system for her work as an activist. Jullion remembered that not only did the first judge she faced ask her for the names of all the women who worked on her defense committee, but a second judge also made sure to open later proceedings with an admonishment to her for involving activist groups. "They never got over it," Jullion said, speaking of the courtroom reaction by the judge and opposing counsel to her activist work.[45] Court cases throughout these years reflected similar kinds of restrictions and criticisms aimed at keeping lesbian and gay parents from associating with other lesbian and gay individuals, including their lovers and partners, from engaging in political activism, or from participating openly in the lesbian and gay community.

Because of the difficulty in winning a lesbian or gay custody case in the 1970s, many attorneys recommended strongly that their clients settle and not bring their cases to trial. Once in court facing allegations of homosexuality, the chances of a lesbian mother or gay father retaining custodial or parental rights was slim. However, with a well-prepared feminist attorney, lesbian mothers could sometimes settle before the case went to trial. The Lesbian Mother Litigation Manual, developed by Donna Hitchens for the Lesbian Rights Project, cited judicial bias as one of the factors that "encourage an attempt at out of court resolution."[46] Faced with an increasing number of informed feminist and activist lawyers throughout the 1970s, attorneys for heterosexual ex-husbands often chose this option, frequently trading custody to lesbian mothers for an erasure of further paternal financial obligations. Rosalie Davies, who founded Custody Action for Lesbian Mothers with Mikki Weinstein in 1974, remembers that most cases she fought were settled out of court; she recalled many attorneys for the other side, expecting an easy win, settled quickly when faced with prepared lesbian feminist counsel.[47] Another lesbian feminist attorney who fought lesbian custody cases in the Midwest said in 1976 that she had represented women in over forty cases, and they had all been settled out of court.[48] Katherine English, a legal worker with the Community Law Project in Portland, Oregon, estimated in 1979 that she knew of eighty to one hundred custody cases in the Portland area where the same-sex orientation of gay and lesbian parents was an issue that had been settled out of court.[49] Rhonda Rivera, a professor of law at Ohio State University, stated in 1981 that between 1978 and 1980, only eleven custody cases involving lesbian and gay parents had been reported and that "more probably were negotiated out of court or settled unreported in trial courts."[50]

The Importance of Expert Testimony

As courtrooms became battlegrounds, the lack of studies on children raised in gay or lesbian households played a decisive role in custody denials. Judges tended to follow the advice of expert witnesses hired by heterosexual ex-spouses, who often relied on outdated American psychological models heavily influenced by Freudian psychoanalysts or developmental psychologists such as Jean Piaget and Erik Erickson. These models considered any sexual activity outside of heterosexuality to be psychosexually immature, deviant, and/or pathological.[51] In this period, despite the emergence of gay liberation movements, clinical psychologists such as Irving Bieber and Charles Socarides were still claiming that homosexuality was a mental disease that could be "cured." The influence and longevity of these perspectives is evident in the testimony of expert witnesses hostile to lesbian and gay custody.

In *Smith v. Smith* (1977) for example, Dr. William Doidge, testifying for a heterosexual father fighting for custody, described his clinical experience with homosexuality as consisting of Air Force studies conducted from 1956 to 1958 on "whether homosexuality was allied with other psychopathology." In the case of *In re Risher* (1976), Dr. Robert Gordon, a psychologist for Mary Jo Risher's ex-husband, declared it "ridiculously poor behavior" for Risher, a known lesbian, to have allowed her son to attend classes at a local YWCA and to wear a "unisex" T-shirt. He believed "it would be much better for the mother to encourage . . . masculine identifications." The doctor described Risher's oldest son as exhibiting "homosexual panic" and stressed the damage that Risher's lesbianism could have on her seemingly well-adjusted younger child, Richard, when he reached puberty.[52]

However, the range of professional opinions on homosexuality also began to diversify at this time. Psychologists who saw homosexuality as pathological represented only one part of a professional community that was divided over the question of sexual minorities and their rights. Since the publication of the reports on male and female sexuality in the United States authored by Alfred Kinsey and Wardell Pomeroy in 1948 and 1953, there had been an increasing tendency, particularly in the disciplines of sociology and anthropology, to see homosexuality as a cross-cultural phenomenon in human societies. Dissident views gradually developed in American psychiatric circles over the issue of homosexuality, affected by these disciplinary differences, as well as by the increasing agitation of gay activists.

By the early 1970s, a group sympathetic to the struggles of lesbians and gay men had formed within the American Psychiatric Association (APA), an organization long dominated by clinical psychoanalysts who saw homosexuality as pathological. APA members Dr. Judd Marmor, Dr. Evelyn Hooker, and Dr. Richard Green argued against the pathological diagnosis of homosexuality advocated by psychiatrists such as Socarides and Bieber, voicing doubts about whether all gay men and lesbians were, by definition, psychically disturbed. Many of those arguing against Socarides and Bieber were influenced by Kinsey's work. Green, Hooker, and Marmor were part of the group within the APA that ultimately defied Socarides and Bieber and spearheaded the 1973 vote to remove homosexuality from its list of mental illnesses.[53]

As lesbian mother and gay father custody battles increased in number and visibility, these changes in the psychiatric profession affected their outcomes. Just as psychiatrists sympathetic to the Freudian ideas of Bieber or Socarides testified that lesbians and gay men were "unfit" to be parents and would damage their children, other psychiatrists and sociologists began arguing on behalf of the custodial rights of gay or lesbian parents in court, declaring that there was no evidence that lesbian or gay sexuality made someone an unfit parent.

Dr. Richard Green said later that for him, the struggle to remove homosexuality from the APA's list of mental disorders was directly linked to the assertion that having lesbian or gay parents was not necessarily contrary to the "best interests of the child." For Green, the efforts to change antigay prejudice in both psychiatric and legal spheres "coalesced" in the first half of the 1970s.[54]

A year after he had participated in the APA debate, Green testified in an Ohio case, *Hall v. Hall* (1974), on behalf of a lesbian mother. *Hall v. Hall* was an early victory for a lesbian parent.[55] As was common in lesbian and gay custody cases, the judge asked explicit questions regarding lesbianism during Green's testimony in the Ohio custody trial. The judge wanted to know, in determining if the woman was a fit mother, how Dr. Green thought "the sex act between lesbians was accomplished" and whether he considered oral copulation "normal." Green answered that although same-sex sexual orientation was statistically atypical, he believed that sexual orientation in itself had no bearing on "psychological health." The mother's attorney asked Dr. Green if he thought lesbians were capable of molesting their children. In response, he replied that child sexual abuse was statistically a heterosexual problem.[56]

Green also testified the next year in another Ohio case, *Townend v. Townend*.[57] Although he offered testimony similar to the earlier case, stressing how children of "homosexual parents" were not themselves likely to be gay, the lesbian mother in this case lost custody of her children. The judge declared that if the woman had "indicated that until her children were reared she would abandon the practice of lesbianism," he might have awarded her custody, but that the court could not afford to "experiment" with giving a known lesbian custody. In a similar case, Dr. Bernice Goodman testified on behalf of a New York lesbian mother who was nonetheless denied all visitation rights.[58] The inconsistent outcome of expert testimony sympathetic to the rights of lesbian and gay parents during the early 1970s depended greatly on the strength of a judge's personal bias. In her book, *Courting Change: Queer Parents, Judges, and the Transformation of American Family Law*, Kimberly Richman argues that while the "legal indeterminacy" of family law has permitted biased custody decisions, it also offers LGBT family law activists a space to argue for new legal constructions of family.[59] In the 1970s, expert testimony negotiated the space that Richman identifies and began rearticulating a vision of the proper family separate from the assumption of heterosexuality.

In the 1970s, activists campaigned to revise attitudes toward gay and lesbian parenting and sought professional support in doing so. In 1973, gay father Bruce Voeller, then president of the Gay Activist Alliance of New York and a founder of the National Gay Task Force (NGTF), sent requests to several specialists on homosexuality asking them for a statement on gay and lesbian custodial rights. Those who replied included Dr. Evelyn Hooker, Dr. Judd Marmor, Dr. Benjamin Spock, Dr. John Money, and Dr. Wardell Pomeroy, all of whom stated unequivocally that lesbians and gay men could be fit parents. The 1979 revised version of the Gay and Lesbian Parents Support Packet, which Voeller compiled from the letters of support for lesbian and gay custody rights, included comments from Dr. Richard Green and Audrey Steinhorn, a sympathetic New York area psychotherapist who advertised herself as having extensive experience caring for the needs of gay parents.[60]

Professional studies sympathetic to lesbian mothers and gay fathers supported these efforts. In 1973, Dr. Bernice Goodman compared a group of heterosexual and lesbian mothers over a two-year period. Goodman, a practicing psychotherapist in New York City, based her findings on her clients. "As of July 1, 1975," she explained, her practice was "composed of 45 different lesbians seen at least once a week." Of the forty-five women, twelve were lesbian mothers and another seven were the partners of lesbian mothers. Goodman's study reported no negative impact on the children of lesbian mothers and suggested that in fact these children may have benefited from their childhood spent in lesbian households. Goodman, who was active on behalf of lesbian mothers, also presented a paper on the social victimization of lesbian mothers at a 1976 feminist event, the New York Tribunal on Crimes against Women held at Columbia University.[61] The same year, a scholarly study published by Martha Kirkpatrick, Ronald Roy, and Catherine Smith, based on interviews and tests conducted with twenty children of lesbian mothers in the greater Los Angeles area, found that none of the children's psychological issues concerning their parent's divorce "related to the mother's sexual choice." The study focused specifically on discrediting "red herrings often wielded as effective weapons during court custody challenges," including the idea that children living with gay parents would become gay themselves or would exhibit a reversal of gender roles and identity.[62]

Richard Green also contributed to the scholarly assault on antigay attitudes. Green had followed thirty-seven children, sixteen raised by "transsexual" parents (both male-to-female and female-to-male) and twenty-one children raised by "homosexual" parents. In a 1978 article on the study published in the *American Journal of Psychiatry*, Green specifically mentioned that the "children of the homosexual parents had mothers who were involved in child custody litigation with their ex-husbands." He reported that all the children in his study demonstrated heterosexual sexual identities and suffered little social stigma as a result of their parents' sexual orientation.[63] Unlike Bernice Goodman, who suggested possible advantages for children growing up in a lesbian household, Richard Green stressed only the similarities between children raised by heterosexual and homosexual parents. Through the 1980s, the standard argument by psychologists sympathetic to lesbian and gay parents was that lesbians and gay men raised children who did not differ in any significant way from those raised in single-parent heterosexual households. Green went on to cite his own work while testifying on behalf of several lesbian mothers.

By the early 1980s, then, psychiatrists sympathetic to lesbian and gay parenting rights who testified in court had several new empirical studies to cite that claimed lesbian mothers and gay fathers could be just as good as heterosexual parents. New scholarship continued to expand their body of usable evidence. In 1981, Martha Kirkpatrick, Catherine Smith, and Ron Roy published further results from their ongoing study involving twenty children raised by lesbian mothers, now structured along a comparative model with interviews of twenty children of heterosexual mothers. The study confirmed earlier findings that children of lesbian and heterosexual mothers experienced difficulties with divorce and the separation of their parents, but that there was no difference in increased stress sustained by the children of lesbian mothers.[64] Although most of the studies conducted in this period compared lesbian mothers with heterosexual mothers, in 1981 Frederick Bozett, a therapist who had worked with gay fathers as part of his own practice, published a sympathetic article on gay fathers.[65]

Studies such as these were among the factors that led to slow changes in legal attitudes toward lesbian and gay parents during the late 1970s and 1980s. In 1979, Byron Nester, a child psychiatrist from Berkeley, California, polled all members of a regional San Francisco Bay organization of child psychiatrists affiliated with the American Academy of Child Psychiatry. Nester's poll gives a historical picture of a profession in turbulent transition in a region that had already seen the rise of a highly visible gay and lesbian rights movement, a few highly publicized lesbian custody cases, and the development of a widespread network of grassroots activism on behalf of lesbian mothers and gay fathers. Only 15 percent of the child psychiatrists polled felt they would have to recommend a heterosexual parent over a homosexual parent in the matter of child custody. The fact that 60 percent of the psychiatrists polled responded to another question by saying they felt they had insufficient experience with the same issues betrayed ambivalence among the respondents.[66]

The Impact of the Custody Cases

The threat of losing one's children in a custody battle affected a whole generation of lesbian mothers and gay fathers who may never have seen the inside of a family court. For many parents not directly involved in a legal case, the possibility of losing custody of their children, or the right to see them, was an ever-present threat. Overwhelmingly, legal activists agreed throughout the 1970s that women and men who kept their cases out of court were more likely to retain parental rights.[67] Media stories about custody loss publicized the precarious position in which gay fathers and lesbian mothers found themselves, increasing fear and trepidation. Marty Karls's recollection of his 1977 divorce reflects this widespread anxiety. After their separation, Karls's wife moved from San Francisco to New York, where they had both grown up. Karls remembered being terrified that he would lose his son and feeling powerless to stop his ex-wife from leaving the Bay Area: "There was no possibility of suing for rights . . . of keeping her in California . . . because I could be identified as a gay man."[68]

One woman said in an interview that "child custody threats are a constant harassment," while another woman described how she lived "in constant fear of loss of job and children and possible physical harm" if her lesbianism was discovered.[69] When the members of a lesbian mother support group in Cincinnati, Ohio, were asked to send representatives to speak to a course on feminist theory at the University of Cincinnati in 1979, they wrote an anonymous statement to be read by a teaching assistant because they were too concerned with custody loss to appear in person. The group wrote: "We knew if we told you publicly who we were we would face the very real threat of losing our families and the jobs that support our families. . . . All of us at one time or another has had to deal directly with the probability of losing custody of our children in court."[70] Denise, divorced in 1980, worried that the father of her five-year-old twins would keep them each time they went to visit him. At times she suspected he was prying to confirm his suspicions about her sexual orientation.[71] An ex-wife of a man who had come out as gay in the 1980s confirmed the salience of such fears by stating that "when he said he wanted to see the kids, I just laughed and told him I would go to court and tell everyone about him. That shut him up for good."[72]

Often lesbian mothers waived child support, and both lesbian mothers and gay fathers refrained from living with their lovers or allowed themselves to be coerced into informal arrangements to appease ex-spouses and avoid a custody battle. Alex described how he and his wife had reached an informal agreement that gave him custody but left Alex unable to petition for legal divorce. As he explained: "I stopped the legal divorce because I was afraid she might change her mind about my having the children and that if she pointed out to the court that I'm gay there wouldn't be much chance of me keeping the kids."[73] Becky Logan, who raised her daughter in upstate New York, later regretted having been honest with her ex-husband about her lesbianism when they decided to separate in 1973 because "I knew that he could go to court and get the kids because I was a lesbian." Logan remembers never asking her ex-husband for child support, even when she lacked money to buy her children basic necessities, out of fear that she could lose custody of her children as a lesbian mother.[74]

Lesbian mothers and gay fathers who had won custody or visitation rights were also kept in fear by the fact that decisions in many states could always be reassessed based on a showing by one of the parties of a "material change in circumstances." Any new information that an appeals court deemed significant could endanger an original ruling, and same-sex orientation was often ruled to be a legitimate reason to reopen a case. If an ex-spouse claimed to have discovered a lesbian mother or gay father's sexuality or had remarried and could present the new option of a heterosexual nuclear household, judges could decide to hear their arguments for a change in custody. This threat of a renewed custody battle based on sexual orientation kept many lesbian mothers and gay fathers who had preserved some measure of custody or visitation in fear and unable to take part in lesbian or gay community activities.[75]

Lesbian mothers and gay fathers who lived in isolated, often conservative, rural areas, far from lesbian and gay activist networks, were particularly afraid. One woman from North Carolina wrote to a national lesbian periodical in 1976, asking that her name be taken off the mailing list. She had just taken her children and left her husband, who was "looking for any shred of evidence" that would show she was an "unfit mother," and she was concerned that the periodical "would certainly convince these backwoods judges of my 'immorality.'" The woman also asked that her partner, who was in a similar situation, be taken off the mailing list.[76] Kathy Florez, a lesbian mother involved in lesbian feminist activism who took part in speaking bureaus at Montana State University as a lesbian mother, said in 1979 that although lesbian mothers were organizing politically nationwide, she could not ask lesbian mothers in Montana to take that risk and she herself worried about losing custody of her children in a state where her "chances of winning were slim to none." Lacking the resources that men and women had in metropolitan areas, lesbians and gay men in rural areas would face custody struggles for decades after the first wide-scale shifts in judicial discrimination.[77]

Many gay men and lesbians also lived with the fear that their biological families would try to take their children away in court if they learned about their sexual orientation. One woman from New York, speaking on the radio in the late 1970s, said about her nine-year-old daughter, "My relatives would probably steal her if they knew I was a lesbian. . . . They're that backwards."[78]

Legal Changes

By the late 1970s and early 1980s, lesbian mothers and gay fathers began to win some important custody victories across the country at the appellate and state supreme court levels. These victories were brought about by the combined effort of sympathetic expert witnesses such as Dr. Richard Green, John Money, and Wardell Pomeroy and the work of community activists and attorneys fighting for the rights of lesbian mothers and gay fathers. By the end of the 1970s, attorneys who supported gay and lesbian rights, aided by groups such as the ACLU's Sexual Privacy Project and the Lesbian Rights Project in San Francisco, began to consolidate their arguments against homophobia and to win cases on appeal.[79]

Throughout this period, lesbian and gay activists both longed for and dreaded the possibility that the U.S. Supreme Court might hear a case on lesbian or gay parenting rights. On the one hand, a favorable ruling on either an expanded constitutional right to privacy protecting same-sex sexuality in general or on lesbian or gay parenting rights specifically would have been welcomed. On the other hand, as the Supreme Court became increasingly conservative in the mid-1980s, many gay and lesbian activists were relieved that it had not taken up a gay or lesbian parenting case. This was especially true as attitudes in some state courts began to shift toward recognizing lesbian and gay parenting rights. Nonetheless, legal activists continued to argue in court that constitutional rights were involved in gay and lesbian custody cases, including the right to privacy and the due process and equal protection guarantees of the 14th Amendment.

Custody cases in the 1980s had mixed outcomes, but in some states there were signs of legal change and increasing judicial comfort with the issue of lesbian and gay parenting rights. In a few states, state supreme courts ruled in favor of lesbian mothers or gay fathers. The Michigan high court, for example, ruled in 1979 in favor of Margareth Miller, who had been fighting through state courts for two and a half years for custody of her daughter, Jillian. Four lower courts had all ruled against Miller. In overturning the earlier denials, the Michigan State Supreme Court stated that sexuality should not be a consideration in custody decisions.[80] The same year, Rosemary Dempsey was awarded custody of her two children as an out lesbian by a New Jersey Superior Court judge who ruled that there was "no evidence" that her lesbianism or her living with her partner, Margaret Wales, and her three children was harmful to Dempsey's son and daughter.[81]

In many early victories that followed, state supreme courts, which were loath to interfere in family court matters, reminded the lower courts that they were obliged by the "best interests" statute to give a measured assessment to all factors in a case, and that in denying custody to a lesbian mother or gay father, they must show a specific connection, or "nexus," between the parent's sexual orientation and possible harm to the child. In *Schuster v. Schuster* (1978) and *Isaacson v. Isaacson* (1978), the Washington State Supreme Court allowed lesbian mothers Madeleine Isaacson and Sandy Schuster to continue living together, despite the earlier ruling mandating that they maintain separate residences. The court ruled that no specific "nexus" had been shown to suggest that the lesbianism of the two mothers posed any danger to their children.[82] In 1986, the New York State Supreme Court awarded a gay man custody of his twelve-year-old son, finding no proven detrimental effect of gay or lesbian households on the children growing up in them. The court said that in this case the father's sexual orientation was not contrary to the "best interests of the child."[83] Similar decisions were made during this period in Vermont, Massachusetts, and Alaska.[84] These state supreme court rulings were merely statements that lesbians and gay men could not automatically be deprived of custody based on their same-sex orientation rather than assertions that the rights of lesbian and gay parents warranted specific legal protection. Nonetheless, these decisions in favor of lesbian mothers and gay fathers, even ones based on a "best interests" statute, provided a legal history that attorneys arguing for lesbian and gay parental rights could cite.

Left to right: Margaret Wales, Rosemary Dempsey, and their children, Trenton, New Jersey, 1979. © 2013 JEB (Joan E. Biren).

Although these state supreme court cases did offer a judicial precedent in favor of lesbian and gay parental rights, this did not mean that discriminatory custody denials were impossible in these same states. Lesbian mothers and gay fathers continued to lose custody of their children, as waves of backlash against lesbian and gay civil rights washed over the state courts. In 1985, the Virginia Supreme Court overturned an earlier ruling and denied a gay man both custody of his ten-year-old daughter and any visitation in the presence of another gay man. The ruling echoed earlier decisions by arguing that exposure to "his immoral and illicit" relationship with his male partner rendered this father "an unfit and improper custodian as a matter of law." The man had fought for custody of his daughter for six years in a suit with his ex-wife, who had claimed that proximity to a gay relationship would be harmful to their daughter.[85] In *M.J.P. v. J.G.P.*, the Oklahoma Supreme Court upheld a lower court's ruling transferring custody away from a lesbian mother based on stigma the boy might suffer as a result of his mother living in a same-sex relationship. Lower court rulings were equally mixed. In 1991, the Illinois

Second District Court of Appeals upheld a family court ruling that had denied a woman the custody of her daughter because the mother "was living with another woman."[86]

As attorneys and legal groups such as the ACLU argued for the rights of lesbian mothers and gay fathers they drew analogies between the rights of lesbian and gay parents and interracial families, drawing on the legal victories of the black freedom struggle. When arguing against custody denials to lesbian and gay parents on the grounds of a perceived danger of stigma facing the child, they often cited the U.S. Supreme Court decision in *Palmore v. Sidoti*. In this 1984 case, the Court struck down a District Court of Appeals ruling that upheld a Florida court's decision to take custody away from a woman who remarried into an interracial relationship. In taking away the woman's parental rights, the lower courts had argued that the child would be subject to stigmatization for having a biracial family. Attorneys representing lesbian and gay parents argued that the same logic that the high court employed in *Palmore v. Sidoti* went against the "stigma" argument that had been used in lesbian and gay custody struggles.[87] However, in the absence of a U.S. Supreme Court decision on lesbian and gay custody rights, supportive attorneys could only argue the comparison in amici briefs and hope that family courts would find the argument compelling.

During the 1980s, the U.S. Supreme Court failed to address the issues of lesbian and gay parents, but there is evidence that the justices of the high court were aware of the impending legal issues surrounding lesbian and gay parenting rights. In her confirmation hearings in 1981 Sandra Day O'Connor sidestepped a question regarding her stance on lesbian and gay rights by conservative Alabama Republican Senator Jeremiah Denton by saying that "cases concerning the rights of people who are homosexuals in connection with being deprived of a position as an employee or having custody of children" were "very confused" at a lower court level and that she foresaw that the high court would "indeed be asked to rule" on these "unsettling" issues in the future. O'Connor's mention of lesbian and gay parenting rights marked the first time a Supreme Court nominee or justice had publicly acknowledged the legal issues related to lesbian and gay parents and custody.[88] In that same year, the Supreme Court declined to hear the case of a lesbian mother when the Kentucky Court of Appeals transferred custody of her five-year-old daughter to the father, arguing that the mother's lesbianism represented a potential danger to the child.[89]

Although the high court would not specifically address the rights of gay and lesbian parents during these years, it did undermine their chances of gaining custody through its 1986 ruling in *Bowers v. Hardwick*. In its majority 5-4 opinion upholding Georgia's antisodomy law, the court ruled that gay men and lesbians enjoyed no specific rights of privacy or intimacy such as those held by heterosexual partners. Although the case dealt explicitly only with the rights of individual gay men and lesbians to engage in sexual activity free from state control, its implications were very important for lesbian and gay parents. In *Bowers*, enumerating the rights of privacy previously accorded by the court to American citizens, Justice Byron White included the rights of "procreation" and "family relationships." He went on to state however, that "no connection between family, marriage, or procreation on the one hand and homosexual activity on the other has been demonstrated, either by the Court of Appeals or by respondent." In placing lesbians and gay men outside the legal definition of family and denying them any right to domestic privacy, Justice White and the rest of the majority left lesbian and gay parents at the mercy of the biases of family court judges.[90]

In the 1950s and 1960s, the threat of custody loss and estrangement from their children kept lesbian mothers and gay fathers hidden and in fear. When large numbers of lesbian mothers and gay fathers came out in the liberation era, they challenged society's unspoken assumption that same-sex sexual orientation and parenting were mutually exclusive and that lesbian mothers and gay fathers represented pathological threats to their children's well-being. Custody case proceedings and the atmosphere of fear they generated among lesbians and gay men from the late 1960s to the mid-1980s are evidence of a strong state investment in keeping the family heterosexual.[91] This investment was strengthened by various social conceptions of the "homosexual": that a gay man or lesbian was more likely to sexually molest their children, that the children of lesbians and gay men would face debilitating social stigma, and that gay men and lesbians would "pass on" their sexual orientation to their children. The visible struggles of lesbian and gay parents to retain custody or visitation rights pushed these assumptions and conceptions into the open as they were expressed by judges, lawyers, and the media reporting on these cases.

Lesbians and gay men who confronted these assumptions in court were part of a larger resistance movement that challenged heterosexist, racist, and misogynistic attitudes about the proper structure of the American family. Local grassroots organizations sprung up in lesbian and gay communities across the nation to advise and support men and women fearful of losing custody of their children.[92] These organizations also made connections with activists and attorneys opposing the forced sterilization of women of color and poor women, fighting for the right of all women to access to affordable, legal abortions and birth control, and advocating for the rights of families on welfare. The open denial of lesbian and gay parental rights in the 1970s and the strength of the social and legal prohibitions against the proximity of children to non-normative sexuality fueled organizing for the legal and social recognition of non-heterosexual families. The difficulty of these efforts galvanized large parts of the gay and lesbian community, and a new activist focus coalesced around these struggles. This political work, the national networks it engendered, and the success it began to have paved the way for an even greater emphasis on lesbian and gay adoption, parenting rights, and marriage. After 1985, through the expansion of many of these networks and the growth of legal, social, and political institutions born of these concerns, the modern LGBT freedom struggle increasingly made a priority of family and domestic rights, until these lay at the center of the movement by the end of the twentieth century.

Though this shift involved a great many social and cultural factors, the period of the earliest custody battles was a crucial part of it.[93] Prior to the gay liberation era, the deep cultural understanding of the family as inherently heterosexual was so widely assumed and accepted as to be almost unassailable. In this period, lesbians and gay men could only be parents by raising their children in secret or by living double lives. As women and men came out in large numbers, both as lesbians or gay men and as parents, the idea of the family as naturally and always heterosexual was exposed as just that, an idea or a social construction. As such, it had to be asserted, which judges, courts, psychiatrists, and religious figures did, along with the heterosexual spouses and relatives of the lesbians and gay men fighting for custody. The ideological and social battle that ensued was extremely difficult, and the front that was located in the courtroom during those early decades was filled with losses. It was these losses and the difficult but persistent struggle against them that focused the attention and resources of LGBT communities toward domestic and family civil rights, a tendency that only gained momentum after 1985 as the legal and social tide began to turn in the direction of greater acceptance for non-heterosexual families. After nearly twenty years of legal struggle, lesbians, gay men, and their advocates had successfully begun to chip away at the previously hegemonic notion that only heterosexual people were fit to be parents. By 1985, courts and judges began to register this ideological shift in their legal decisions.

CHAPTER FOUR

Lesbian Mother Activist Organizations, 1971–1980

In the early 1970s a network of lesbian mother activist organizations emerged across the country. These groups formed as a result of the new visibility of lesbian mothers and the social and legal condemnation they faced in the era of gay and lesbian liberation. They shared a commitment to fighting for the custody rights of lesbian mothers, and many of them organized lesbian community events and offered psychological support to lesbian mothers as well. These lesbian mothers groups were local organizations that grew out of lesbian feminist communities and were connected to a wave of grassroots, feminist reproductive rights organizing in the 1970s. They challenged the long unspoken assumption in U.S. culture that same-sex sexuality was antithetical to parenting and the family, articulated a radical vision that included a demand for the reproductive rights of all women, and argued that the denial of custody rights for lesbians was linked to the lack of support for single mothers on welfare and the forced sterilization of women of color. Although many of these groups were dissolved by the late 1980s, their political activism played a crucial role in shifting the political priorities of the later lesbian and gay civil rights movement toward lesbian and gay parental, domestic, and marital rights.

Lesbian mother advocacy groups were founded amid the politics of lesbian feminism, which emerged as a political movement in the late 1960s and early 1970s. Activists came to lesbian feminism from the women's movement, gay liberation, the civil rights movement, and the antiwar Left. As women in these other radical social movements came out as lesbians, they often experienced homophobia and sexism from fellow activists. Disillusioned and informed by the sexist and antilesbian attitudes of their would-be political allies, lesbian feminists developed a powerful critique of social and legal structures that punished women for loving other women. Lesbian feminism was part of a larger set of challenges to sexual and social norms that accompanied changes in ideas about gender, sexuality, and the family in the United States. Lesbian and gay liberation movements of the late 1960s came about along with developments such as the introduction of the birth control pill and the struggle for legalized abortion, the challenges of the women's movement to gender discrimination and sexual exploitation of women, and the rise in heterosexual relationships that lay outside of traditional companionate marriage.[1]

Early lesbian feminist political organizations such as the Furies in Washington, D.C., the Lesbian Tide Collective in Los Angeles, the Radicalesbians in New York City, and the Lavender Woman Collective in Chicago developed a political ideology that saw patriarchy and its oppression of women as a fundamental source of societal injustice and violence and called for all women to work for female empowerment. In the first issue of the Furies' newspaper, Charlotte Bunch wrote that "to be a Lesbian is to love oneself, woman, in a culture that denigrates and despises women. The Lesbian rejects male sexual/political domination; she defies his world, his social organization, his ideology, and his definition of her as inferior."[2] For Bunch, and for many other lesbian feminists, lesbian feminism held the potential to undermine racism, capitalism, and misogyny through its focus on the power of women working together and loving one another. Lesbian feminism advocated egalitarian relationships, questioned traditional nuclear family structures, and encouraged collective process.

During the 1970s, lesbian feminist communities based on these shared political values sprang up across the country. Many of these developed in urban areas, but there were also dozens of rural lesbian feminist communes nationwide, often connected to collectives and communal households in nearby cities. Working from the ideals of women's empowerment and the importance of woman-centered community, lesbian feminists founded women-owned auto-repair shops, construction crews, bookstores, record labels, and coffee houses. Chapter six examines more closely the day-to-day experiences of lesbian-headed families with children within the cultural context of these lesbian feminist communities.

Lesbian mother advocacy groups were usually organized within these lesbian feminist communities, were guided by feminist political commitments, and developed multifaceted criticisms of racial and class discrimination; at the same time, they themselves critiqued and transformed the politics of lesbian feminism. Many lesbian mother activists reported feeling alienated by a broadly anti–nuclear family and youth-oriented New Left lesbian feminism in the early 1970s as the movement developed as a political and cultural ideology. Over the decade of the 1970s, lesbian mother activism complicated lesbian separatism, redefined the lesbian feminist critique of the nuclear family, and argued for the necessity of political ties between heterosexual women of color, poor women, and lesbian activists.

The stories of lesbian and gay parental activism during this period are part of the history of a broader trend of political organizing that focused on reproduction and the family. This history includes the overturning of antimiscegenation laws, the growth of the women's health movement, and the struggles to end sterilization abuse aimed at poor communities and communities of color, to legalize and guarantee access to abortion, and to end the stigmatization of women and men who choose to remain child-free.[3] The history of this reproductive rights revolution comes into focus when we conceive of the family as a historical construct, shaped by categories of sex, race, class, and gender, and not as a static, "natural" social formation. These movements shaped the evolving concept of the family in the late 1960s by challenging ideas about sexuality and gender. In questioning normative sexual and gender categories and working against discrimination, they proposed new ways of thinking about the American family and criticized the traditional heterosexual, white, middle-class, patriarchal, nuclear family model. What was coined as the "sexual revolution"—a popular, media-friendly term—was in fact a family revolution as well, of which lesbian mother organizing was an important part.

The history of lesbian mothers groups illustrates the importance of local grassroots organizing and the impact of earlier radical social movements such as the African American civil rights movement and the movement to end the war in Vietnam on this local organizing in both the reproductive rights movement and lesbian feminist activism of the 1970s. Estelle Freedman, Ruth Rosen, Vicki Crawford, Sara Evans, Paula Giddings, Charles Payne, Danielle McGuire, and other historians have emphasized the impact of local feminisms, often inspired by the work of female African American civil rights leaders, on many of the most influential political and social projects of the women's movement.[4] Many of the women involved in lesbian mother activism had gained political experience from earlier work in the black freedom struggle and the antiwar movement. Their feminist political analysis of the family as lesbian mother activists came directly from these earlier experiences and informed their organizing.

Lesbian activists overlapped with local and regional feminist networks, which included underground abortion referral networks and abortion reform activists in the pre-*Roe* era, women's bookstores, women's music festivals, and rape and battered-women crisis hotlines. Lesbians often brought together different activist communities. They brought organizing experience to mainstream women's communities, working with heterosexual feminists in

Philadelphia, for example, to help newly divorced mothers with legal advice and childcare.[5] These coalitions are evident in the histories of lesbian mother activist networks that worked with the women's health movement to secure reproductive rights for all women and to establish ideas and institutions, such as feminist health clinics, that would in turn be instrumental in lesbians creating their own families through insemination beginning in the late 1970s and early 1980s.[6]

Lesbian mother activist groups are also part of the history of the LGBT freedom struggle as it moved from its radical roots in the early 1970s to a much more mainstream political movement by the end of the twentieth century. By working both within and outside of their communities to increase awareness of lesbian and gay parenting issues, these activists played a crucial role in shaping this political organizing, which would come to count parental rights as one of its central concerns by the mid-1980s. The political work of lesbian mother activists within lesbian feminist communities transformed the politics of these communities, sharpening their critiques of the patriarchal family and contributing greatly to a growing awareness of the social and legal struggles of gay fathers and lesbian mothers in later decades.

The Struggle for Custody Rights

All lesbian mother activist groups in the 1970s focused on lesbian mother custody battles in the family courts, whether they provided direct support or worked politically to draw attention to the difficulties these women faced. The fact that lesbian mothers groups organized all across the country during the 1970s attests to the widespread dangers of custody loss faced by lesbian mothers. Lesbian custody activism encompassed both large urban centers, where sizable gay and lesbian communities often existed, and more rural areas where lesbian mothers fighting for custody had limited community resources; often, single-case defense funds would organize around a particular custody case and would be connected to the larger, nationwide network of lesbian mother activist groups. Lesbian mothers groups helped raise money for expensive custody cases, put women in touch with sympathetic attorneys and expert witnesses, worked with family agencies to make them more responsive to the needs of lesbian mothers, and, when nothing else could be done, helped lesbian mothers go underground to avoid losing their children when they were in immediate physical danger.

The emphasis that lesbian mothers groups put on raising money for custody cases distinguishes them from gay fathers groups of the era and highlights the financial struggles faced by many women who left heterosexual marriages. In the 1950s and 1960s, sexist hiring practices and the differences between male and female wages had kept many married lesbians from leaving their husbands; in the 1970s, lesbian mothers who did leave heterosexual relationships faced not only the threat of custody struggles but poverty as well. In 1977, the group Lesbian Women from the Wages for Housework Campaign, San Francisco, declared: "Those of us who are lesbian have had to fight to get and keep every job. . . . We are also always fighting to keep custody of our children."[7] Lesbian mothers faced attacks in custody courts based fundamentally on their sexuality, and as women who had stepped away from relationships with men they often faced economic deprivation and employment discrimination. Lesbian mother activist groups understood this, incorporated it into their political analyses, and worked to offer lesbian mothers financial assistance in custody struggles.

The first lesbian mother activist group in the country, the Lesbian Mothers Union (LMU), was founded in the San Francisco Bay Area in 1971.[8] From its inception, the LMU focused its attention on custody. "As most of us know," the first edition of the group's newsletter stated, "a custody case involving a sister is happening. A meeting was set up several months ago with her and the LMU pledged its support."[9] An important part of this support was raising money to help women pay the fees associated with their custody cases. The LMU maintained a legal defense fund and in 1973 and 1974 held benefit auctions and raffles at Scott's Pit, a well-known lesbian and gay bar in San Francisco. The police threatened to shut the auction down after receiving complaints but were dissuaded by the Council on Religion and the Homosexual, who acted on the event's behalf.[10] The auctions were sponsored by lesbian and gay organizations such as the Metropolitan Community Church of San Francisco, and guest auctioneers included San Francisco gay luminaries such as female impersonators Jose Serria and J. J. Van Dyke.[11] These Lesbian Mothers Union benefits were part of larger lesbian and gay communities in the San Francisco Bay Area that formed in the 1970s and helped raise awareness over the issue of lesbian mother custody cases, and lesbian and gay parenting in general.

The Lesbian Mothers' National Defense Fund (LMNDF), founded in Seattle, Washington, in 1974 by Geraldine Cole and Lois Thetford, was one of the most influential and longest lasting of all the lesbian mother organizations founded in the 1970s. Like the Lesbian Mothers Union, the LMNDF tried to help defray the high legal costs incurred by women fighting for custody, who were often financially disadvantaged. In a 1979 article on lesbian mother organizing,

—AUCTION—

'Y MOTHER'S DAY!HAPPY MOTHER'S DAY!HAPPY MOTHER"S DAY! HAPPY MOTHER'S DAY! HAPPY MOT

SUNDAY
MAY 13
7:00 P.M.

LESBIAN
MOTHERS UNION
Benefit for legal expenses!

ITEMS TO BE DONATED FOR THE AUCTION
MAY BE DROPPED BY SCOTT'S AT ANYTIME!

GUEST
AUCTIONEERS!
Jose, J.J. Van Dyke, Bob Ross, Lady Kate

SCOTT'S PIT
10 SANCHEZ
SF

Flyer for a Lesbian Mothers Union benefit auction, San Francisco, Mother's Day, 1973. Courtesy of the Gay, Lesbian, Bisexual, Transgender Historical Society.

three members of the LMNDF wrote that "the bulk of our money goes to pay lawyers and expert witnesses."[12] After its first fundraiser, a performance by a Seattle group called Puppet Power, the LMNDF sent Lorraine Townend and Vicky Dickenson, two local women fighting a lesbian mother custody case, a check for one hundred dollars. In another instance, the LMNDF gave $400 to a lesbian involved in a custody battle in Indiana who had a "$90 a week job and an ex-husband who has not paid child support in a year."[13] In January 1976, the LMNDF began publishing detailed financial accounts in their newsletter. The published financial reports from January 1976 to May 1978 indicate that during this period the group sent out $5,490 in legal fees and $1,145 in fees to expert witnesses for lesbian mother custody struggles.[14]

To raise money the LMNDF held a variety of fundraising events. Like the Lesbian Mothers Union in the San Francisco Bay Area, the LMNDF existed in a vibrant lesbian and gay community and took advantage of this setting when organizing benefits. They announced events in their newsletter, *Mom's Apple*

Pie, which came out every two months and was an important and highly visible publication in the Seattle lesbian and gay community of the 1970s. The group also worked with a variety of Seattle lesbian and gay men's groups when organizing fundraising activities.

In June 1976, the Lesbian Entertainment Group held an event called the First Annual Women's Festival at Shelly's Leg, a well-known Seattle lesbian and gay bar. The entertainment included a lesbian mother skit, based on the legal transcripts of a lesbian mother case where the mother had lost custody of her children, along with dancing, music, a kissing booth, and a Women's Skills Auction. Among the donated items auctioned off were five hours of childcare, a double motorcycle date for a "sunny day or warm evening," donated by "2 hot dykes on 2 hot bykes!!!" and "18 woman hours of carpentry," donated by the Gertrude carpentry collective. The benefit made close to $500, 100 of which went to the Seattle Lesbian Resource Center and almost 400 to the LMNDF.[15] The defense fund also held dances and cosponsored annual lesbian talent shows with the Seattle Metropolitan Community Church.[16]

In addition to these local events, the LMNDF helped sponsor concerts and worked with musicians and promoters who were part of the women's music circuit, a network of feminist and woman-centered musicians that had emerged as part of lesbian feminist culture by the mid-1970s.[17] In October 1977, the LMNDF sponsored a concert at the Moore Egyptian Theatre featuring Holly Near and Mary Watkins, two well-known feminist musicians. Many local Seattle groups volunteered their time and labor to help with the concert, including the Feminist Karate Union, which provided event security; Leftist Lezzies, a local activist group that volunteered to usher; the Men's Resource Center, which provided childcare; and Odessa Sound, a woman's sound-engineering group. After paying all costs, the LMNDF made a profit of over $1,700.[18] In the spring of 1978, the LMNDF co-sponsored a concert of third world women's music and poetry with Olivia Records, featuring performances by poet Pat Parker and musicians Linda Tillery, Meg Christian, and Teresa Trull.[19]

Dykes and Tykes, a New York lesbian mother activist organization founded in 1976, formed an East Coast Lesbian Mother Defense Fund in June of that year to raise money for lesbians involved in custody struggles. Dykes and Tykes had originally been focused on providing social services and community support for New York City lesbian mothers who already had custody of their children; however, in its first six months, members of the organization realized the need for ongoing, organized legal assistance for lesbian mothers fighting for custody. The group's hotline was receiving twenty-five to thirty-five calls a week from women throughout the East Coast in heterosexual marriages who were afraid to be open about their lesbianism for fear of losing their children, women threatened with loss of custody by their ex-husbands, and women engaged in active custody struggles in the courts.[20]

The defense fund was overseen by the Dykes and Tykes Custody Defense Committee. The fund immediately began raising money for an appeal of a decision in a Syracuse case, which had ended with the judge denying the mother custody and stating that "a woman has the right to be a lesbian, but a lesbian does not have the right to be a mother." Dykes and Tykes immediately made a commitment to raise $1,000, and by August 1976 the committee of ten members organized a fundraiser for the Syracuse appeal and developed plans to expand beyond fundraising to legal education and outreach.[21]

In 1978, Dykes and Tykes opened the Dykes and Tykes Legal Custody Center in New York City. A member of Dykes and Tykes who was also a member of the National Lawyers Guild (NLG) suggested that the NLG, which had been fighting for progressive legal causes since the 1950s, help Dykes and Tykes to open a legal-services center for lesbian mothers fighting for custody of their children. Using a grant from the NLG, Dykes and Tykes set up a training program in the summer of 1977. For six weeks, lawyers from the guild held workshops to train twenty women from Dykes and Tykes in paralegal and peer counseling. The Dykes and Tykes Legal Custody Center opened in December 1978, offering "an exploration of the legal/emotional issues involved in fighting a court battle," including advice on how to choose a lawyer, the importance of expert testimony, and courtroom strategies. The center also gave women advice about applying for welfare and food stamps or getting protection in situations of possible domestic violence and referrals for legal services, daycare centers, community services, and lesbian mother rap groups. Childcare was provided for all women who visited the center.[22]

Dykes and Tykes and the National Lawyers Guild put together the rough draft of a pamphlet for gay parents during the summer of 1977. The next year, the antisexism committee of the San Francisco chapter of the National Lawyers Guild published it as the first edition of "A Gay Parents' Legal Guide to Child Custody." The pamphlet covered a wide range of questions relating to the custody issues both gay and lesbian parents faced, including how to choose a lawyer, custody court procedures and terms, the decision to be open to the court about one's sexuality and the consequences of this decision, and how to get help from the local gay and lesbian community in a custody battle. The pamphlet publicized the struggles faced by lesbian and gay parents as a political issue.[23]

Like the LMNDF and the Lesbian Mothers Union, Dykes and Tykes held various kinds of fundraisers for the East Coast Lesbian Mothers Defense Fund and the custody center, including a disco dance, local theatrical and musical performances, and concerts by nationally known women's musicians such as Ginni Clemens and Casse Culver. The group also held benefit screenings of films and parties. As in Seattle and the San Francisco Bay Area, these benefits involved the lesbian feminist community of the Greater New York area in lesbian mother activism.[24]

Sometimes, smaller lesbian mothers groups formed around a single lesbian mother custody case. In 1976, in Ann Arbor, Michigan, a group of women, "lesbian and non-lesbian, mothers and non-mothers," began meeting out of concern over a custody case in which a woman and her partner, "Marie and Sarah," were fighting for custody of two children with Marie's ex-husband. He had taken the children in 1975 after a weekend visit. Sarah had been heterosexually married for twenty years and also had children, who lived with Marie and Sarah. In court, Marie faced biased attitudes about her lesbianism, about which she was open, and was repeatedly told that she could get custody of the children more easily if she agreed not to live with them and Sarah. In response, the two women argued in court that their relationship was a loving, stable one that should not be judged by the fact that they were two women.

As commonly occurred in 1970s lesbian mother custody cases, their relationship was subject to the prurient interests of psychologists and the judge; Marie said she always felt as if the court-appointed psychologists wanted to ask them about their sexual practices but could not bring themselves to do it, and at one point, Marie's attorney told the two women that Sarah would only be allowed in the courtroom on "very special days," to reduce sexual fantasies that the judge was having.[25]

Calling themselves the Ann Arbor Lesbian Mothers' Defense Fund, the group committed themselves to helping Marie and Sarah with their legal bills. From the fall of 1976 to the end of 1977 the organization contributed money to the two women and acted to raise funds for their case in the Ann Arbor lesbian community. The group organized a benefit showing of the Iris Films movie on lesbian mothers, "In the Best Interests of the Children," and appealed to the Ann Arbor lesbian community for donations through local publications such as the Leaping Lesbian, an Ann Arbor lesbian newsletter. The group was in communication with the Lesbian Mothers' National Defense Fund in Seattle and was aware of Dykes and Tykes in New York City.[26]

A group called the Lesbian Defense Fund emerged in Essex County,

Members of the Lesbian Defense Fund, Essex County, Vermont, announcing their custody victory onstage at the Michigan Womyn's Music Festival, 1977. © 2013 JEB (Joan E. Biren).

Vermont, after Carol, a member of the lesbian-feminist collective Redbird, faced a custody struggle in which both her lesbianism and the fact that she was raising her daughter in the Redbird collective were used against her. "Because of my lesbianism and political activity," Carol wrote in April 1977, "all aspects of my life are coming under scrutiny."[27] After the group won its case, it decided to continue working on behalf of other lesbian mothers struggling for custody of their children. It did so throughout 1978 and 1979, corresponding with lesbians fighting for custody and other lesbian mothers groups nationwide.

Although both the Ann Arbor group and the Lesbian Defense Fund of Essex County, Vermont, envisioned their purpose as going beyond the case that had inspired each group's founding, small defense funds also grew up around particular cases with the sole purpose of supporting those cases. Like larger groups, single-case defense funds usually formed in high-density areas with politically active lesbian and gay populations, since it was usually in these

Jeanne Jullion and her sons at home, Berkeley, California, 1977. Photograph by Cathy Cade. Courtesy of the Bancroft Library, University of California, Berkeley.

areas that lesbians fighting for custody could find other women for support. In the spring of 1977, Jeanne Jullion began hearings for custody of her two sons, ages four and eleven. The previous year, Jullion had come to the San Francisco Bay Area during a separation from her husband, had come out as a lesbian, and had fallen in love. The lesbian community was a new one for Jullion, an Italian American from a traditional East Coast family. Jullion described herself as being naive about all politics, particularly those concerning the rights of sexual minorities, until her ex-husband, with the help of her own parents and siblings, challenged her custody of her two sons.

In the preliminary hearing Jullion's ex-husband's attorney interrogated her about the sleeping arrangements at the house she and her partner shared, asking whether or not the children were ever present in the bedroom, whether or not she and her partner ever expressed affection, and whether her relationship with her partner or her relationship with her children was hypothetically "more important" to her. Her ex-husband's attorney also accusingly showed her pictures of the "Wonder Woman" poster that hung in front of her house, apparently taken by a private detective in her ex-husband's employ, and asked her to confirm that it was indeed her place of residence. Most crushingly, she was shown an affidavit signed by her own parents, recommending that custody of both her sons be given to her ex-husband on account of her lesbianism. A probation report following the preliminary hearing described Jullion's home in glowing terms, but inexplicably recommended against custody. Still Jullion's lawyer failed to act.[28]

At this point, Jullion realized that without sympathetic and proactive help, she would lose custody of her two children with little protest from any of the men deciding her fate in the courtroom. Jullion and her partner began researching legal precedents for lesbian custody issues, fired Jullion's attorney, and resolved to raise the money they would need for a court battle. In the spring of 1977, with the help of a sympathetic lesbian feminist attorney, Jill Lippett, Jeanne Jullion formed the Jeanne Jullion Defense Committee at a gathering in her living room. The committee included around twenty-five women from the San Francisco Bay Area lesbian community.[29] Jullion's case eventually became a nationwide symbol for the plight of lesbian mothers in the custody courts. She spoke out across the country on behalf of her right to raise her sons, but in the end—after a year of organizing—the court gave custody of her eldest son to her ex-husband, expressing concern about leaving an adolescent male in the care of a lesbian.

Since lesbian custody cases could happen anywhere, defense funds were sometimes set up in areas that were more conservative than San Francisco or

Jeanne Jullion rally, San Francisco, 1977. Photograph by Cathy Cade. Courtesy of the Bancroft Library, University of California, Berkeley.

Seattle, although they still generally occurred in large metropolitan lesbian communities where lesbian mothers could get support from other women. This was the case with the Friends of Mary Jo Risher, which provided support for Risher when she lost custody of her son, Richard, in a Texas jury trial in 1975. The group helped raise funds for Risher's legal appeals and increased public awareness about the case. Friends of Mary Jo Risher scheduled radio and television appearances for Risher to speak on her own behalf, published articles about the case in nationwide periodicals, and organized women's music concerts as fundraisers for the appeals process, such as one given by Meg Christian in May 1977 in Dallas. Affiliated groups emerged across the country to raise funds for Risher's case.[30]

In addition to financial assistance and publicity organizing, lesbian mother activist groups also put lesbian mothers in touch with sympathetic attorneys and mental health professionals who were willing to testify as expert witnesses in lesbian mother custody cases. As discussed in the previous chapter, the increasing willingness of psychologists, psychiatrists, and social workers to testify on behalf of lesbian mothers and gay fathers was an

Flyer for a Mary Jo Risher benefit sponsored by the Huntington, New York, Mary Jo Risher Appeal Fund, April 19, 1976. Courtesy of the Lesbian Herstory Archives.

important part of changes in judicial attitudes toward lesbian and gay parenting in the 1970s and 1980s. These changes were facilitated by networks of lesbian mother activists that sought out and maintained lists of possible expert witnesses. It was also often difficult for lesbian mothers to find attorneys who would take their custody cases or who had any familiarity with lesbian issues; in many cases, lesbian mother activist organizations helped lesbians fighting for custody find attorneys in their area who could deal competently with their cases.

As part of its commitment to helping lesbian mothers, the Lesbian Mothers Union in the San Francisco Bay Area put women who were fighting custody battles in touch with attorneys who could represent them well. Cam Mitchell, for instance, who fought for custody of her children from 1973 to 1978, turned to the LMU out of frustration with her original lawyer's homophobia. Mitchell had originally won custody of her children, despite the fact that a psychiatrist who testified as an expert witness called Mitchell a "neurotic paranoid, suffering from lesbianism." However, the judge stipulated that Mitchell could not be in the presence of her lover and her children at the same time.

After realizing that her lawyer could not handle a lesbian custody case, Mitchell contacted the LMU through a web of community references that illustrates the interconnectedness of lesbian activism during this period. "I got really frantic. I just started calling phone numbers in San Jose. The Sexual Freedom League put me in contact with Gay Liberation, put me in contact with Radicalesbians, put me in contact with the Lesbian Mothers Union and Del Martin. Del Martin gave me the phone number of my present attorney, Joan Bradford." On appeal, Mitchell eventually overturned the court's limitations on the custody of her children. Mitchell credited Bradford's legal advice and her awareness of the issues facing lesbian mothers with winning the case.[31]

The LMNDF in Seattle also tried to put women who sought their help in touch with expert witnesses and attorneys who had experience with lesbian mother custody cases. Geraldine Cole and Lois Thetford always stressed that one of the most important things for a lesbian fighting for custody was a competent, understanding lawyer who was familiar with the issues surrounding lesbian custody.[32] The group kept a set of index cards with the names of sympathetic lawyers and expert witnesses. The cards included the person's name and occupation, who recommended them, the cases they had worked on in the past, and their location. With an eye to always wanting to provide resources to women in rural areas and the southern states, where lesbian communities were less vocal than in the metropolitan Northeast and West, the group filed these cards alphabetically by state. They also kept cards for attorneys and expert witnesses who had done a poor job, to let women know who to avoid. One contact list gave addresses for attorneys with experience in lesbian mother custody cases in nineteen states and Canada.[33]

The LMNDF Seattle in particular acted as a clearinghouse for information and kept lesbian mother activists in touch with similar groups nationwide. When they realized they only had one attorney referral for Michigan in 1977, they asked the Ann Arbor Lesbian Mothers' Defense Fund for references and learned of two other attorneys in Ann Arbor who had taken on lesbian mother custody cases, one of whom had a legal brief she was willing to share. This grassroots network of groups distributed legal materials, maximized resources, and facilitated change in the custody courts over the decade of the 1970s.[34]

Custody Action for Lesbian Mothers (CALM), founded in Philadelphia in 1974, offered lesbian mothers legal advice and support and provided women living in Pennsylvania with legal representation and psychologists to act as expert witnesses. Unlike other lesbian mother activist groups, CALM also provided direct assistance for gay fathers, taking cases on a case-by-case basis. CALM offered legal and financial aid to lesbian mothers in the Pennsylvania region for decades. Rosalie Davies founded the group after she lost custody of her own children in a Philadelphia custody battle in which her ex-husband used her lesbianism to argue that she was unfit as a mother. After this, Davies began working with attorneys on behalf of other lesbian mothers and decided that she would return to law school and learn how to defend them in the courtroom.

CALM had a twelve-woman board of supervisors that made all decisions. Over the course of the 1970s, the group served as a referral service for lesbian mothers concerned about custody issues nationwide as well as a local legal advocacy group, providing free legal counseling and representation for women fighting for custody in Pennsylvania. The organization offered its services free of charge due to an initial anonymous private endowment, pro bono services by legal staff, and peculiarities in Pennsylvania state law that eliminated much of the expensive legal work commonly involved in custody disputes in other states. When CALM began these efforts there was very little precedent, and Davies remembered feeling as if they were "starting from scratch."

Davies began working early on with Mary Cochran, a Philadelphia psychologist who had extensive experience counseling lesbian families. Davies put Cochran on the stand to testify that lesbians could be fit mothers. Although Davies was in contact with professionals such as Richard Green, who were testifying on behalf of lesbian mothers in other states, the expense of communicating and working with experts who had to travel long distances made the presence of a local authority very important for many of her lesbian mother clients, who were often quite poor.[35]

As these activists worked to support lesbian mothers in their custody cases, they connected with each other and created a nationwide network that linked sympathetic attorneys and mental health professionals willing to act as expert witnesses on behalf of lesbian mothers and gay fathers. By 1978, members of the Lesbian Mothers Union, the Lesbian Mothers' National Defense Fund, Dykes and Tykes, and Custody Action for Lesbian Mothers were all in touch with each other and sharing information on previous cases and referrals for attorneys and expert witnesses in various parts of the country. In a 1974 letter to Karen Burr of the Lesbian Mothers' National Defense Fund, Del Martin expressed enthusiasm for the group's founding, asked Burr for copies of case transcripts from two Seattle lesbian mother cases, and offered case information from the files of the Lesbian Mothers Union.[36] When Carole Morton, one of the founders of Dykes and Tykes, went to California to go to law school in 1976, she met with Pat Norman, a longtime Bay Area activist and one of the women who had founded the Lesbian Mothers Union. That spring, she also met two women who were a part of the Jeanne Jullion Defense Committee.[37]

The Reproductive Politics of Lesbian Mother Activism

The activists who worked in these groups brought with them extensive previous experience in other social justice movements. Women in these groups had been involved in homophile movements of the 1950s and 1960s, civil rights groups fighting for African American voting rights in the South, radical feminist activism, welfare advocacy organizations in large urban areas, and northern antipoverty programs. They had fought for the right to legal abortions, to stop sterilization abuse, for the rights of sex workers, and for affordable, feminist health care for all women. Working from a complex intersectional analysis of the ways that normative categories of sexuality, race, and gender oppressed women, lesbian mother activists developed a broad, coalition-based politics that linked critiques of heterosexism, racism, classism, and patriarchy. As they challenged the longstanding presumption in U.S. culture of the family as heterosexual, they played an important role in the feminist redefinitions of motherhood in the 1970s and helped lead the way to the current focus on domestic and family rights within the modern LGBT civil rights movement.

The founding of the Lesbian Mothers Union in the San Francisco Bay Area was the combined work of activists from the homophile, African American civil rights, women's rights, lesbian feminist, and anti–Vietnam War movements. Del Martin and Phyllis Lyon were longtime homophile activists, having founded the Daughters of Bilitis in 1955, the first national lesbian organization in the United States. Their experiences both as lesbian mothers and with other mothers in DOB in the 1950s and 1960s, as well as their work as feminist organizers in the late 1960s, had led them to see the cultural discrimination and custody struggles facing lesbian mothers as important issues in the lesbian civil rights movement.[38]

Ruth Mahaney, who was active in the LMU in the mid-1970s, was involved in the antiwar movement in Bloomington, Indiana, in 1967. With other women in the activist community there, Mahaney helped start the first women's support group in Bloomington, eventually helping to set up between thirty and forty women's support groups in the city. Mahaney lived in a communal house that served as a women's shelter, founded a cooperative childcare center, and helped organize a pre-*Roe* abortion network called the Midwest Abortion Counseling Service that helped women in the Midwest and Northeast to get abortions. The group also helped women contact the underground abortion providers, JANE, in Chicago.[39] The same commitments to women's reproductive autonomy that led Mahaney to this political work also led her to work for the rights of lesbian mothers.

Judie Ghidinelli, a co-founder of the LMU, had worked to establish an urban, cooperative preschool in a black neighborhood in Hartford, Connecticut, and went on to work on the Poor People's Campaign in Washington, D.C., building houses and cooking meals for poor families. These experiences changed Ghidinelli forever. "One of the women," she recalled, "told me that she fed her kids newspaper and water for dinner and it just changed my whole life. I couldn't pretend. . . . It just wasn't right."[40] These early experiences gave Ghidinelli insight into the ways that racism and class oppression operated to marginalize poor mothers of color that would inform her work in the Lesbian Mothers Union years later.

Cathy Cade, who was actively involved with the East Bay chapter of the LMU, worked in the civil rights movement in Albany, Georgia, in 1963. She became involved with the movement as an exchange student at Spelman, the historically black women's college in Atlanta. While at Spelman, Cade had participated in sit-in demonstrations alongside historian Howard Zinn at the Georgia State Senate. Cade spent the summer of 1963 in Albany, Georgia, and in Atlanta, working with the Student Non-Violent Coordinating Committee (SNCC) to desegregate public facilities, stop police brutality against black communities, and enforce voting rights. As a volunteer, Cade saw the repression of African Americans in the South firsthand and wrote in her letters to her family of the rape and murder of civil rights activists. The next summer, in 1964, Cade worked in Gulfport, Mississippi, as part of the movement for voter registration.[41]

For Cade, these experiences in the civil rights movement taught her about the impact that class and race had on people's lives.[42] She wrote to her parents in 1963 that she was beginning to "realize that this fight isn't something you pick up after you've done your homework, but something affecting the whole way of life of thousands of people."[43] Working with African American women in Mississippi and seeing their strength and labor in black communities and families gave Cade an early sense of women's political and social power. In

1968, Cade helped found a women's group in New Orleans with several other women who had been active in SNCC, including Dottie Zellner and Jeanette King. These women, who were instrumental in the first few meetings of the women's group, had become mothers, and the contradictions between their political lives in SNCC and their social positions as mothers were a part of the early discussions of the group. These discussions were an important part of Cade's politicization concerning motherhood and women's rights.[44]

The founders of the LMNDF in Seattle were also already activists when they began to get involved in lesbian mother advocacy. Lois Thetford was working as an antiwar organizer and pregnant with her daughter, Robin, when she met Marilyn Koop and Nancy Driver, two lesbian mothers who were fighting for custody of their children. Thetford had been working at an off-base coffee house in Tacoma, working to encourage military personnel to leave the service as conscientious objectors, helping the families of those who did, and performing civil disobedience on the bases against the Vietnam War.[45]

Carole Morton, who founded the New York group Dykes and Tykes in 1976, came from a political background that included work in the homophile movement, radical feminism, welfare advocacy, and lesbian feminism. After coming out in 1970, Morton helped found the New Jersey chapter of the Daughters of Bilitis and began organizing activities for the many lesbian mothers in the group. By November 1971, Morton was running consciousness-raising groups on "Being a Lesbian Mother" for members of New Jersey DOB.[46] In two 1971 speeches that same year, at a Gay Pride rally in Central Park and at the Gay Academic Union firehouse, Morton stressed the ways that women are punished through restrictions on their right to parent. At the same time, she began working with Lesbian Feminist Liberation and founded the Downtown Welfare Activist Center in a United Methodist Church on West 4th Street in New York City in the early 1970s.[47]

From this diverse political experience, lesbian mother activists developed a theory of the rights of lesbian mothers that argued for an intersectional analysis of the struggles of lesbian mothers. Dykes and Tykes in New York City consistently returned to connections between race and class in their analyses of state oppression of all mothers outside of a white, heterosexual, nuclear model. The group's organizational literature often focused on connections between state assaults on poor communities and communities of color and on discrimination against lesbian mothers.[48] Dykes and Tykes developed a detailed political stance that opposed the Supreme Court's decision in the anti–affirmative action case *Bakke v. UC Davis*, welfare cuts, and forced sterilization of women of color. They advocated for free abortion on demand for all women

Carole Morton with a sign that reads "Mothers of the World Come Out," Christopher Street Liberation Day march, New York, 1971. Courtesy of the Diana Davies Photographs, Manuscripts and Archives Division, The New York Public Library, Astor, Lenox and Tilden Foundations.

and for changes in the prejudiced attitudes in the custody courts against poor women, women of color, and gay men and lesbians. They called for an end to discrimination based on income, race, or sexual preference in adoption and foster placement and for the removal of antigay family court judges.[49]

Out of these commitments, Dykes and Tykes forged concrete coalitions with other New York organizations, including the Sisterhood of Black Single Mothers, the Coalition for Abortion Rights and Against Sterilization Abuse (CARASA), and the Committee to End Sterilization Abuse (CESA).[50] These political connections defined the outlines of the reproductive rights revolution of the 1970s, a political movement that demanded, in the words of Dykes and Tykes, "the right to have a family if we choose, for the custody of our children, and for the rights and resources to sustain them."[51]

On May 15, 1978, Dykes and Tykes held a Mother's Day demonstration on the steps of the Manhattan Family Court, in cooperation with the Lesbian Mothers' National Defense Fund in Seattle. The protest demanded an end

Flyer for a Dykes
and Tykes Mother's
Day demonstration,
New York, May 15,
1978. Courtesy of
the Lesbian Herstory
Archives.

to racist, sexist, and homophobic denials of custody. Women picketed and performed "guerilla theatre." Local endorsements for the event came from organizations ranging from university women's centers to revolutionary socialists and gay and lesbian activist organizations.[52] Dykes and Tykes argued that such a broad antiracist, reproductive rights political coalition was an important way to organize against what they perceived in the late 1970s as a rising conservative backlash.

Dykes and Tykes and the LMNDF held coordinated rallies on opposite coasts for Mother's Day 1978, while a group in solidarity with them met on the Boston Common. In New York, Audre Lord read her poetry, and activists spoke on abortion rights and custody issues faced by Native American women. At the Boston rally, Lee Swislow spoke, linking the fight for lesbian mother custody rights to the struggle against the forced sterilizations of poor women and women of color. She also linked the cause of lesbian mothers to the right to have legalized abortions and to social and legal attacks on poor women and prostitutes. Swislow compared the custody struggles of lesbian mothers with the custody battles faced in the 1950s and 1960s by white women who married black men. "Custody battles," Swislow declared, "are an old method of keeping women in line."[53]

Members of the LMNDF articulated a broad, coalition politics based on an antiracist, anticlassist defense of all women's reproductive rights. In an essay on organizing written for the journal *Quest* in 1978, Geraldine Cole, Lois Thetford, and Joan Pittell wrote that "mothers also lose their children because they are feminists, poorer than their children's father, handicapped, involved in interracial relationships, or politically active." They wrote that they were fighting for women's reproductive choice and linked their activism on the part of lesbian mothers to movements against forced sterilization, for legal access to abortion, and against violence to women. They also linked their work explicitly to the custody struggles of gay fathers, although they explained that they chose to focus on lesbian mother custody since they believed that gay men often had more financial resources than lesbian mothers.[54]

One LMNDF member said, "I believe that the oppression lesbian mothers face comes from the same source as the oppression of other women who face the possibility of sterilization, losing their children, being denied birth control education, etc."[55] Acting on its antiracist politics, LMNDF actively supported Yvonne Wanrow, a Native American woman accused of shooting a man who had been abusing her children when he came onto her property, refused to leave, and moved threateningly toward her. At a rally sponsored by LMNDF in support of her defense, Wanrow, who was not a lesbian herself, connected the struggle of lesbian mothers to those of Native peoples and the right of all oppressed peoples to self-defense. These politics led LMNDF to support all single mothers facing poverty and the hardships of raising children in a patriarchal society. Joan Pittell, an active member of LMNDF, remembered that the lesbian mothers in the group were very aware of the plight of all single mothers.[56] As a *Mom's Apple Pie* article argued: "A single woman with children in this society is hard pressed to exercise her right to work. . . . The need for 24-hour childcare and child abuse prevention centers is obvious to us."[57]

These political connections were a part of lesbian feminist communities, and groups such as the LMNDF were a central part of their development. One woman from the Working People's Health Clinic in Chicago wrote in to the group in 1977 asking for a subscription to their newsletter, *Mom's Apple Pie*, after reading about them in another widely circulated lesbian feminist periodical, *Lesbian Connection*. The women in the clinic had been working on a project around violence against women in Chicago and wanted to include "fighting the state's child-snatching from oppressed women—lesbian mothers, Native

American mothers, etc." The letter ended with an offer to distribute *Mom's Apple Pie* in Chicago.[58]

Sometimes women involved in single-case defense funds developed similar political perspectives as a result of their own custody battles. For the year that it was in operation from the spring of 1977 until the winter of 1978, the Jeanne Jullion Defense Committee was the hub of an enormous amount of political activity. Jullion's day planner for 1977, on which she wrote down an amazing array of contact numbers, points to the monumental act of coalition building performed by Jullion, her partner, Jill Lippett, and the rest of the defense committee. There are contact numbers or reminders to contact Elaine Brown and Erika Huggins of the Black Panthers as well as the editor of the Black Panther Party newspaper, Donna Hitchens of the Lesbian Rights Project (LRP), Bay Area Women Against Rape, Harvey Milk, the East Bay chapter of the National Organization for Women, and Gay Solidarity with Chilean Resistance, to name just a fraction of the organizations and individuals listed across the pages of Jullion's organizer. This list shows that lesbian feminist organizing around parenting rights worked through a broad coalition of activists, both radical and reformist, in the San Francisco Bay Area.[59]

The evidence of broad coalitions between various resistance movements is accompanied by an almost-daily record in the book of Jullion's own politicization during the year of her custody battle. "Affirmative action," one note scrawled in Jullion's tight script reads, "We're all losing our rights. . . . We are a threat, especially women . . . take away our kids as punishment . . . no federal funding for abortion but more than happy to finance sterilization."[60] Jeanne Jullion describes herself, as do others on the committee who knew her at the time, as someone who had until the court battle lived a life sheltered from politics and social change; however, the threat of losing custody of her children, coupled with new political and social perspectives, helped Jeanne Jullion to see connections between her own experiences and those of women fighting for other reproductive freedoms.[61]

This articulation of reproductive freedom as a political commitment linking the movement for abortion rights, welfare advocacy, and the rights of lesbian and gay parents and committed to fighting forced sterilization and domestic abuse illustrates the ideological foundations of the reproductive rights revolution of the 1970s. It often incorporated an intersectional perspective on race, class, and gender, saw state and social control of the family and sexuality as linked, and was intertwined with the women's self-health movement.[62] Many of the changes that have historically been attributed to a "sexual revolution" were at the same time part of new changes in the family, and this reproductive rights movement was critical in fighting for a new vision of sexual freedom and the American family. At the same time, these criticisms were very radical and would survive only in muted ways as lesbian and gay parental and domestic rights emerged by the late 1990s as a central focus of the mainstream LGBT freedom struggle.

Going Underground

Several lesbian mother activist groups took part in an underground network in the 1970s that enabled lesbian mothers fighting for custody to go into hiding with their children. Organizers remember this as strictly a last-resort option that was done only when the mothers were in court against ex-spouses with local political connections or a great deal of money or ex-spouses who were violent. The network operated on both coasts, involved safe houses, and helped women to develop new identities.

In Philadelphia, lesbian mother activists who worked with CALM organized what Rosalie Davies remembered as an "underground railroad" for lesbian mothers who needed to flee the threat of a loss of custody and sometimes physical violence. According to Davies, this practice began in Philadelphia with action taken in a North Carolina case involving a father who was known to beat the children but was nonetheless likely to win custody over their lesbian mother. This network of lesbian activists occasionally provided false identification for women needing to escape quickly, helped them to establish new identities, and provided them with financial support.

Although this network operated out of Philadelphia, it offered services to women nationwide, and even internationally, throughout the 1970s. Helping lesbian mothers in this way was seen as an option of "last resort." It involved a rigorous screening process to establish that the woman was a viable candidate for relocation since the process was emotionally and physically arduous. Davies estimated that she knew of "15 to 20" lesbian mothers whom Philadelphia activists helped to go underground during the decade of the 1970s.[63]

The LMNDF in Seattle sometimes helped lesbian mothers go underground, particularly if they were in physical danger from ex-husbands. Lois Thetford remembered that "women who were in real physical danger and had to escape . . . came to us and we helped them find child care and new identity stuff." Many of these women faced cases in which their ex-husbands' social and legal power as policemen or attorneys meant that there was no chance of the women gaining custody.[64] Kris Melroe, who allowed her house to be used as a safe house by LMNDF, remembers being contacted on the phone and told that a woman and her children needed to stay with her. Melroe had women on the run stay at her house "three or four" times and recalled that they were scared and on the move.[65]

Dykes and Tykes in New York City also thought of helping women to go underground as a possible last resort in lesbian mother custody struggles. Training in prelegal counseling for the staff at the Dykes and Tykes Legal Custody Center included instructions on talking to women about how to "pick up your kid and run" if nothing else was going to prevent your loss of custody.[66] Carole Morton, one of the group's founders, remembered that "we used to help women with false school papers, we used to send them to the other coast, and we used to help them dye their children's hair or their own hair. There was definitely a lesbian mother's underground railroad." Morton recalled that the group helped a "handful" of women leave the state while she was involved with it and that after they left New York the women were aided by lesbian feminist community networks in getting across the country.[67]

Lesbian Mothers Groups as Support Networks

In addition to fighting for the rights of lesbian mothers involved in custody disputes, many lesbian mothers groups also provided a crucial social network for lesbian mothers in lesbian feminist communities. Although they found invaluable support in lesbian communities, many women who were active in groups such as the LMNDF or the LMU also felt that lesbian feminist communities were unsympathetic and hostile to lesbian mothers. Lesbian feminism had as one of its foundations a critique of the oppression of women by the traditional, patriarchal nuclear family. Sometimes motherhood, even lesbian motherhood, was seen in this critique as self-enslavement. Lesbian mothers and the organizations that worked to support them often felt that members of lesbian feminist communities without children questioned their political commitment and even their lesbianism, since it was assumed they had slept with a man to have their children in the first place. Motherhood, claimed Rosalie Davies, the founder of CALM, represented "in the lesbian community, the heterosexual part of a woman," and as a result "there tends to be an attitude—now it's not a stated attitude but it's there. . . . If you left your husband, you came out as a lesbian, that was really fine, why don't you leave your children and all of the oppression behind."[68] In the youth-oriented, counterculture atmosphere of lesbian feminist communities, motherhood could become a suspiciously heterosexual activity.[69] This attitude changed drastically by the early 1980s, when lesbians began having children in large numbers through donor insemination and adoption, but it did so largely as a result of the efforts of lesbian mother activist groups in the 1970s.

The first lesbian mother activist group in the United States, the Lesbian Mothers Union, itself arose out of feelings of frustration at the lack of support for lesbian mothers in lesbian feminist communities. The LMU grew out of an impromptu workshop organized by a group of lesbian mothers at a Los Angeles lesbian feminist conference in June 1971. Between thirty and forty women met in the workshop while attending the conference of more than 200 people. As the lesbian mothers at the conference talked, they found that in addition to being angry at the lack of childcare at the conference, they had many other issues in common. Many women at the conference lived in constant fear of their ex-husbands taking custody of their children based on their lesbianism and felt resentment toward a society that saw them as unfit mothers.[70]

Many of the lesbian mothers had come from the San Francisco Bay Area, including Pat Norman, Del Martin, Phyllis Lyon, and Judie Ghidinelli. As part of a panel earlier that day, Del Martin had underscored the lack of support many lesbian mothers felt from the lesbian community. The reception the group received when they addressed the general conference after discussing their ideas was indicative of the lack of sympathy in the larger lesbian community that Martin had warned of in her talk earlier that day. Women in the original group remembered a general dismissive response to lesbian motherhood at the conference, the first lesbian feminist activist conference in the nation. Judie Ghidinelli recalled that it was as if people were saying, "Why are you bothering us, this isn't important. . . . You chose to have children, you take care of them," in reaction to the group's complaints.[71] Pat Norman remembered that there was a sentiment that "if you did have children, then that's your problem, and it's not ours, so like get out of our face" and that the founding of the LMU began very important discussions about lesbian mothers and the importance of fighting for lesbian mother rights as a feminist struggle.[72]

One member of the LMNDF in Seattle complained at a meeting, "I see theories that say a first-class lesbian should be a woman without children, certainly without male children; as opposed to saying dykes are hookers, dykes are third world women, dykes are mothers. These are the realities." A member of Dykes and Tykes remembered that shortly before the group began, a conference was held by the Gay Academic Union in Manhattan in 1976. At the conference both gay men and lesbians had expressed the feeling that if a woman was "really a lesbian" she would not have had a child in the first place. Members of Dykes and Tykes described feeling isolated as lesbian mothers in both straight and lesbian communities. They called motherhood "the last closet" in the lesbian community. Stevye Knowles, an active member of Dykes and Tykes, said in a 1978 radio interview that within lesbian communities on the East Coast in the early 1970s "it was somehow a negation of your lesbian-ism that you had this child."[73]

Women organizing single-case defense funds around their own custody cases could also feel alienated from the lesbian feminist communities of the early 1970s. While trying to distribute flyers at a lesbian concert in 1977, Jeanne Jullion received primarily negative comments from the majority of the women in response to her requests for help in a custody case involving two male children.[74]

This initial reception to Jeanne Jullion's case, like the organizational evolu-tion of the Lesbian Mothers Union, illustrates the cultural impact of lesbian separatism in the early 1970s. A complex movement, lesbian separatism grew out of frustrations with antilesbian attitudes in heterosexual feminist move-ments and a desire to construct political networks where lesbian activist work could more directly benefit lesbian communities. Having the space for self-affirmation was an important part of lesbian separatism, as it had been for black separatist movements in the late 1960s. Nonetheless, by the late 1970s, radical lesbian politics often embraced the cause of lesbian mother rights, en-couraged by women like Jeanne Jullion to see the struggle for parental rights as central to the cause of lesbian civil rights.

Lesbian mother activists felt that the elision of lesbian mothers was part of a politically rigid dogmatism in the lesbian feminist community that erased important differences in women's experiences of their lesbianism. A combi-nation of this sense of isolation within lesbian feminist communities and the homophobia of mainstream society left lesbian mothers in the early 1970s in need of social support networks, and many lesbian mothers groups served this purpose as well as helping women in danger of losing custody of their children.

Although the Lesbian Mothers' Union put a considerable focus on help-ing lesbian mothers to fight custody battles, the group also organized social events for its members and provided childcare at lesbian feminist functions in the San Francisco Bay Area.[75] These services were critical in that they created a way for lesbian mothers to reach out to each other and begin to end the iso-lation felt by lesbian mothers of earlier decades. In 1972, the gay motorcycle clubs of San Francisco organized a Christmas party for the LMU as an "op-portunity for lesbian mothers to meet socially." In 1973 and 1975, the LMU held a "toys for tots" program, and in 1977 the group held a day in the park

Lesbian Mothers Union picnic, Berkeley, California, 1973. Photograph by Cathy Cade. Courtesy of the Bancroft Library, University of California, Berkeley.

for lesbian mothers and their children, along with occasional potluck dinners for LMU members.[76] The group also held discussion groups on various topics at their monthly meetings. Topics included how to help children of lesbian mothers deal with the outside world, raising male children, co-parenting, and feeling isolated from the larger lesbian feminist community.[77] Together these events helped to create an important network of social and educational support and resources that fortified the activist work of this organization.

Dykes and Tykes in New York City regularly held discussion groups on topics such as "Mothers of Adolescent Daughters," "Lesbian Mothers and Sons," "Being a Mother Within the Lesbian Community," "Coming Out to Your Children," "Building Support Networks," and "Co-Parenting."[78] The group also held informational talks given by professionals, such as a 1977 talk on "lesbians as foster and adoptive parents and children," which included a presentation by foster care workers.[79] Dykes and Tykes organized regular events for lesbian mothers, such as women's coffeehouses, music-making gatherings, and dances, as well as visits to children's museums, ice-skating parties, and picnics for lesbian mothers and their children.[80] Long-term goals of Dykes and Tykes included the establishment of an alternative school, cooperative childcare, and a country space for children.[81]

Lesbian support groups could be particularly important in more rural or politically conservative areas. Kathy Florez, a lesbian mother living in Bozeman, Montana, called on lesbian mothers in the area to "get in touch with each other for support, exchange of childrearing books, and to rid the feeling of isolation." Florez also published her phone number in a local lesbian feminist periodical for anyone interested in forming a lesbian mothers support group.[82]

Even when lesbian mothers groups were primarily focused on raising money for custody cases, they offered a community for lesbian mothers and their children. The LMNDF Seattle organized activities for lesbian mothers and their children in the Seattle area as fundraisers. The group held talent shows, concerts, and film screenings where childcare was provided and mothers and their children could participate in the Seattle lesbian feminist community. Even organizational work meetings offered lesbian mothers and their children a place where they could feel at home. Carolyn Selene, who attended LMNDF functions and meetings in the mid-1970s as a grade-schooler with her mother, remembered that "those times were special because, those were times I got to be with other kids with no other pretense . . . and I got to be myself with my family."[83]

The Roots of the Modern LGBT Freedom Struggle

The activism of lesbian mothers groups focused attention and resources on lesbian mother custody issues and, by doing so, pushed the modern LGBT freedom struggle toward a focus on parental and domestic rights. Throughout the 1970s, lesbian mother activist groups facilitated a growing interest in lesbian and gay family law. By attending and speaking at conferences on women and the law, maintaining correspondence with attorneys and law students, writing journal articles, and even submitting amicus briefs, lesbian mother activists pushed the legal interest in lesbian and gay family rights forward. In 1974, Del Martin and Pat Norman, both members of the Lesbian Mothers Union, spoke on issues facing lesbian mothers at the University of California at Davis Law School. The following year, an invitation was extended to the Lesbian Mothers Union to send members and materials to a law conference held at Hastings School of Law in San Francisco.[84] In 1978, Lois Thetford, Pam Keeley, and Geraldine Cole of the Lesbian Mothers' National Defense Fund gave presentations at a conference on women and the law in Atlanta,

Georgia. The conference was an incredible gathering and brought together lesbian mother activists from across the country, including Del Martin, Jeanne Jullion, Nancy Polikoff, Donna Hitchens, Mary Morgan, Renee Hanover, Nan Hunter, and Barbara Price.[85]

Lesbian mothers groups also helped to generate enthusiasm about lesbian and gay parental rights in prominent LGBT movement organizations, such as the Lesbian Rights Project and the Lambda Legal Defense Fund. In 1977, Donna Hitchens wrote to the LMNDF Seattle to request membership in LMNDF and to let them know that she was starting a project on lesbian legal rights sponsored by Equal Rights Advocates, a San Francisco women's legal advocacy group. A month later, the LMNDF had responded enthusiastically to Hitchens's letter and sent her several of their court transcripts and articles on lesbian mother custody cases.[86] Throughout the late 1970s, Hitchens and the Lesbian Rights Project were in touch with lesbian mothers groups and activists, including the LMNDF and the Lesbian Mothers Union. In 1982, working from an earlier project initiated by Barbara Price with help from Del Martin, Phyllis Lyon, and Rosalie Davies, Hitchens compiled the Lesbian Mother Litigation Manual for the Lesbian Rights Project, which became a critical tool for lawyers fighting lesbian mother custody cases.[87]

The Lesbian Rights Project would eventually change its name to the National Center for Lesbian Rights (NCLR) and would become one of the most important legal organizations in the LGBT civil rights movement, with an annual budget in 2008 of $3.7 million. Over the next thirty years, NCLR would work on a multitude of issues affecting LGBT individuals, including employment discrimination, immigration rights, youth advocacy, and transgender rights, but its roots in the radical lesbian mother activist organizations of the 1970s ensured that it always kept LGBT family and domestic rights as a central focus.[88]

The Lambda Legal Defense and Education Fund, founded in 1973, also moved toward an increased focus on lesbian and gay parental and domestic rights in the late 1970s, in dialogue with lesbian mother activists. In the first three years after its founding, Lambda had gotten involved in a case involving the firing of a gay teacher, discrimination faced by a gay student organization, a police brutality case, four cases challenging state sodomy laws, a case of police entrapment under "deviant sex" laws, a case involving a gay man in the military, two immigration cases, and two cases involving lesbian mother custody. However, in September 1976, Margot Karle, representing Lambda's board of directors, wrote to the Lesbian Mothers' National Defense Fund in Seattle and told the LMNDF that "at a meeting of the Board of Directors held on September 13, 1976, the Board resolved to take a more active part in lesbian mothers' litigation." Karle had previously written to LMNDF in 1975 as an attorney in private practice and had requested an article from the group entitled "Lesbian Mother Custody Cases." Knowledge of the LMNDF and their work on lesbian mother custody cases was part of Lambda initially committing to a stronger focus on lesbian parental rights.[89]

The Impact of Lesbian Mother Activism

The diverse commitments of the women involved in lesbian mother activist groups led to a broad, coalition-based politics that argued for the reproductive freedom of all women. This political vision was based on an analysis of class, race, and gendered oppression that saw regulation of the family as one way the state controlled the lives of women. This political understanding of the family owed much of its articulation to the critique of the nuclear, heterosexual, male-dominated family central to early lesbian feminist movements; however, this political perspective supported women with children who did not fit into the traditional model and believed that fighting for their parental rights was central to the struggles for women's rights and lesbian rights. These political arguments would have a powerful impact on the LGBT freedom struggle and would help bring parental rights to the center stage. Along with the struggle for legal abortion, the women's self-health movement, welfare reform for poor families, the struggle to end sterilization abuse in communities of color, and the fight for the custody rights of gay fathers, unmarried heterosexual couples, and single women, lesbian mother activism helped contribute to a large-scale reproductive rights revolution in the United States.

CHAPTER FIVE

Gay Fathers Groups, 1975–1992

Like lesbian mothers a few years earlier, gay fathers formed their own organizations by the mid-1970s. In some ways, these groups had much in common with those organized by lesbian mothers: they publicized and fought custody court rulings, they provided spaces to discuss their shared concerns about being gay parents, and they planned activities designed for gay fathers and their children. Both gay fathers and lesbian mothers of this era resisted the longstanding cultural and legal assumptions in American society that parenting and same-sex sexuality were mutually exclusive and came together with others facing similar struggles. Both gay fathers groups and lesbian mothers groups contributed in important ways to the increased visibility of lesbian and gay parents in LGBT communities by the 1980s and the emergence of a focus on gay, lesbian, and transgender parental rights and same-sex marriage in the LGBT freedom struggle by the end of the twentieth century. At the same time, in spite of these similarities, gay fathers groups of the 1970s and 1980s were very different from lesbian mothers groups of the same era. Although gay fathers groups had their roots in a radical politics of gay fatherhood that developed in liberation-era communities, by the late 1970s they were more assimilationist in their outlook than either this earlier radical politics or lesbian mothers groups and, as such, were pivotal in the development of a new politics of gay family respectability that became increasingly influential in the 1990s.

Early expressions of gay fatherhood in gay liberationist communities in San Francisco, Detroit, and New York were based on a feminist reconceptualization of masculinity that saw the raising of children by gay men, and sometimes feminist heterosexual men, as a part of a revolutionary transformation of patriarchal systems of domination. Like lesbian mothers in lesbian feminist communities, radical gay fathers actively sought to raise their children outside of traditional heteronormative sex roles. They developed political critiques of the nuclear family, organized experimental feminist childcare projects, and called for increased support for childrearing in gay male communities as part of a larger political project.

However, by the late 1970s, the demographics and political character of many gay male neighborhoods in the United States was changing. As more men came out and migrated to these spaces, they brought with them centrist views that shifted gay politics from a revolutionary, liberationist perspective to one focused on local municipal politics and a national, assimilationist civil rights model. Gay fathers groups were especially affected by this shift, since the men who joined these organizations in gay communities of the late 1970s and 1980s tended to be older, professionally established, and more politically conservative.

By the late 1970s, most gay fathers groups were largely white, middle-class, and politically centrist. These groups did not articulate the sort of broad, anti-capitalist, antiracist, feminist platform grassroots lesbian mothers groups did. Members of these groups did, however, see their identities and struggles as gay fathers as part of a larger freedom struggle and articulated arguments for gay parental and domestic civil rights. In addition, their economic strength and mainstream political expertise provided the gay father movement with resources that would allow it to emerge as a central force in the mainstream struggle for LGBT parental and domestic rights by the early 1990s. Gay fathers groups were more likely than lesbian mother activist groups to use high-visibility mainstream forums, such as television talk shows, for asserting their rights as fathers, where they invariably found themselves working against deeply held assumptions that gay masculinity and fatherhood were incompatible.

Gay fathers groups were also different from those organized by lesbian mothers in that members were more likely to remain in heterosexual marriages, and when they did leave these marriages behind, they were less likely to have custody or even visitation rights with their children. Gay fathers groups illustrate that many men in gay communities of the 1970s and 1980s existed in two worlds, with their life divided as fathers and as gay men. Since it was rare for divorced gay men to retain custody of their children at this time, even if they managed to keep their sexuality hidden from their ex-spouses, gay fathers were forced to negotiate these two realities. Active members understood that this continuation of the double lives of the 1950s and 1960s was a reality for many men, and outreach was a fundamental goal of most gay fathers groups. Gay fathers who left marriages lived in fear that their ex-spouses might terminate their right to see their children at any time, and they faced an uphill battle to be accepted as viable fathers. Thus, providing strategies for managing these complex relationships with children and ex-spouses, as well as support for current and ex-wives of gay fathers, was an important part of gay father organizing nationwide.

An earlier generation of married gay fathers had experienced only two options: either live double lives as married gay men or leave their children altogether, but by the late 1970s and 1980s many gay fathers had organized to protect their rights as parents and support each other in this effort. Gay fathers groups formed nationwide in the very cities that spawned gay liberation: San Francisco, Los Angeles, New York, Philadelphia, Chicago, San Diego, Boston, and Cleveland.[1] They met at gay and lesbian community centers or in people's homes and provided legal and emotional support both for fathers who had come out publicly as gay men and those who had not. Outreach was an important part of the work of all of these groups, since members felt great solidarity with others who suffered in isolation. Some of the groups took public stands in local custody cases, while others provided more private spaces where men could discuss their lives in relative safety.

The history of gay father organizing reflects the contours of gay history from the gay liberation movement through the 1990s. In the 1970s and early 1980s, gay fathers groups formed in gay male neighborhoods that were largely gender segregated; in fact, although gay and lesbian parents struggled against similar legal persecution, they had little contact with each other. Although these communities, such as San Francisco's Castro District, had their roots in the counterculture politics of gay liberation, they became increasingly focused on commercial ventures and municipal politics as large numbers of men migrated there. The growing diversity of gay communities that fueled this shift can be seen in the changing membership of gay fathers groups. Increasingly, members of these groups were middle-class, professional, white men who were uncomfortable with the radical street politics of the early 1970s. In these youth-oriented "gay meccas," gay fathers often felt similar isolation to that expressed by lesbian mothers of the same period. Then by the mid 1980s, most gay fathers groups of this era were hit hard by the tragedy of AIDS, suffering huge losses. And in the 1990s, gay father activists were instrumental in the founding of groups for the children of lesbian mothers and gay fathers, and their organizing efforts led directly to the focus in the modern LGBT freedom struggle on parental rights and same-sex marriage.

Early Years: Radical Gay Fatherhood Comes Out

The first public political articulations of what it meant to be a gay father emerged amid the changes wrought by the advent of the gay liberation movement. By the late 1960s, influenced by other social movements of the era—including the civil rights, antiwar, and women's movements—young gay men and lesbians were organizing for their own rights in cities such as San Francisco and Los Angeles. These new activists often took a more militant stance than earlier homophile groups, such as the Mattachine Society or the Daughters of Bilitis. As early as 1967, protests against police harassment at bars such as the Black Cat Bar in the Silverlake district of Los Angeles signaled a growing urgency on the part of lesbians and gay men to resist discrimination. However, it was the Stonewall riots in New York's Greenwich Village in June 1969 that served as the symbolic center around which this new gay liberation movement took shape.[2]

In the first year after the Stonewall riots two important gay liberation organizations, the Gay Liberation Front (GLF) and the Gay Activists Alliance (GAA), formed in New York City. Chapters of the GLF spread across the country by the early 1970s in Boston, Denver, Philadelphia, Chicago, Atlanta, Tucson, Tallahassee, San Francisco, Los Angeles, Detroit, and Ann Arbor. In Los Angeles, members of GLF helped Morris Kight found what became the Gay Community Services Center and held the first gay pride march in the city in 1970 to commemorate the anniversary of the Stonewall riots. Gay liberationists created a movement aimed at ending the silent suffering of gay men and lesbians and centered around the political importance of coming out, fighting the perception that same-sex sexuality was a sickness and proclaiming pride in loving honestly and openly.[3]

Amid this radical, counterculture spirit was a vision of gay fatherhood that understood gay fathers as a vanguard in the struggle to transform sexist and homophobic gender roles and challenge male supremacy and the patriarchal nuclear family. Activists in New York, Detroit, and San Francisco argued that gay men helping to raise children offered a new revolutionary sense of fatherhood in which men could be nurturers and help develop nonsexist childrearing practices. These men also criticized what they saw as a commodification of sexuality in gay male communities and the alienation felt by gay fathers in these spaces.

This vision of gay fatherhood was present in the earliest days of gay liberation. It took shape as a central tenet of the politics of *effeminism*, a radical feminist movement in gay liberation that grew out of the original Gay Liberation Front in New York in the months after the Stonewall riots. The effeminist movement had its roots in an anti–male supremacist discussion group of gay and heterosexual men that met in the winter of 1969. Two members of the group, Kenneth Pitchford and Steven Dansky, were also members of

Children at the Christopher Street West Gay Rights march, Los Angeles, 1972.
Photograph by Cathy Cade. Courtesy of the Bancroft Library, University of
California, Berkeley.

Gay Liberation Front New York. Although the men's group was short-lived, it allowed Dansky and Pitchford to develop the principles of a politics of a gay male feminism that formed the foundation for a second group, the Flaming Faggots, a "consciousness-raising group of revolutionary homosexuals" that they and other gay liberationists from GLF founded in the spring of 1970.[4]

Throughout their involvement in both groups, Pitchford and Dansky conceived of radical childrearing and gay fatherhood as central to their vision. Pitchford had a son, Blake, born to him and feminist writer and activist Robin Morgan in 1969, and collective childcare by the men in each group was seen as a political act from 1969 on. Members of the Flaming Faggots took turns caring for Blake as part of their commitment to a feminist gay male political perspective that called for the rooting out of sexism in gay and heterosexual men and the eradication of sex roles propagated by the nuclear family.[5]

In 1970, Dansky wrote a piece called "Hey Man," originally published in the New Left periodical Rat and then republished as a pamphlet by Gay Liberation Front New York, in which he called for gay male activists to examine their own sexism and to integrate a commitment to women's liberation into their political analyses and organizing practices. As part of this political vision, Dansky called for the creation of Revolutionary Male Homosexual living collectives, or RMHs, to serve as building blocks for a new social vision. RMH collectives, consisting of no fewer than three and no more than twelve men, would model a way of life built around a "communistic sexuality of sharing, cooperation, selflessness, and total community." Collective members would be committed to confronting both heterosexual and homosexual male supremacy and to challenging and demanding an end to traditional cruising spaces, such as tea rooms, bars, and bathhouses, which Dansky saw as exploitative. Part of Dansky's vision was the adoption and rearing by RMH collectives of male homeless children. These children would be raised outside of the "male supremacist ideation of manhood." As originally published, the article was accompanied by a single graphic of counterculture men surrounded by children, babes in their arms.[6]

In 1973, Steven Dansky, Kenneth Pitchford, and John Knoebel wrote the "Effeminist Manifesto," a document that outlined the basic principles of the effeminist movement. The final point in the thirteen that made up the manifesto declared that "our first and most important step" was to "take upon ourselves at least our own share of the day-to-day life sustaining drudgery that is usually consigned to women alone." Through taking responsibility for the labor of childrearing and housework, the effeminists believed they could "release women to do other work of their own choosing" and "begin to redefine gender for the next generation." Childrearing by feminist gay men was seen by the effeminists as the most important element of a movement that would transform masculinity, patriarchal society, and the narrow gender and sex roles proscribed by the heterosexual nuclear family.[7]

Similar reconfigurations of gayness, fatherhood, and masculinity appeared in other gay liberationist communities as well. Don Mager became involved with radical gay activism in Detroit in the summer of 1972. Mager was the father of two small children and was in the process of separating from his spouse. The couple had lived in communal households in Syracuse, New York, and Detroit, and shared commitments to nonnuclear, egalitarian, feminist childrearing ideals. After Mager began identifying as a gay man, he joined the Detroit chapter of Gay Liberation Front and became part of an activist community that included the *Gay Liberator*, a newspaper published by a collective of the same name that had emerged from Detroit GLF and the Gay Community Center.[8]

In the spring of 1973, Mager wrote an article for *Gay Liberator* entitled, "Faggot Fathers." In the article he articulated gay fatherhood as a specific experience characterized by isolation from both mainstream heterosexual culture as well as gay liberationist communities that failed to understand the particular issues faced by gay fathers. Working from his politics as a feminist, anticapitalist father he suggested that gay fathers held the potential to destabilize repressive gender and sex roles that supported the nuclear family and that their choice to be openly gay and foster loving relationships could contribute to a "breakdown of the patriarchal family structure" and offer "new alternative models of fatherhood" centered on nurturing, caretaking roles for men. Mager argued that gay communities should embrace the radical potential of gay fathers and lesbian mothers raising children and support them through the development of communal, nonnuclear childrearing arrangements.[9]

In the mid-1970s, Mager worked to put these political ideas into practice. He organized a workshop on gay parents for the 1973 Detroit gay pride festival. The workshop was scheduled alongside ones on other liberation-era topics such as "Women's Liberation and Gay Liberation" and "Gay Liberation and Socialism."[10] Mager remembered that he conceived of the workshop "just to see who would show up," but that to his amazement thirty people came to the discussion. Out of the workshop a gay parents social group formed. For the first year of its existence, the group would hold a monthly social event, whether it was a potluck, bowling party, or skating party, that would allow all of the parents and children to get together. According to Mager, the group remained purely a social group, never a support or discussion group, because of time constraints faced by the group's members. The group met for four or five years, although Mager himself did not remain active in it for that entire time. While he was involved with the gay parents group, Mager met a man with whom he became fast friends and set up a communal living situation with in a household consisting of Mager, his partner, his friend, and their children.[11]

Mager's commitments to feminist childrearing were part of his work in a childcare collective in Detroit called Children and Adults Living and Loving and Learning Together (CALLL Together). He began working with the collective in 1974 after doing informal shared childcare in his neighborhood. CALLL Together was an independent, nonprofit cooperative dedicated to a feminist perspective in childcare that had been founded at Wayne State University after a group of student mothers occupied the president's office and changed diapers on his desk to protest the lack of campus housing for students with children. CALLL Together had an explicit policy of nondiscrimination toward gay and lesbian parents, and Mager recalled later that in the mid-1970s, when he was involved with the organization, a third of the children at any given time would have had either a bisexual or gay father or a lesbian mother.[12]

It was out of ideas and political commitments such as these that the gay father movement initially emerged. The first gay fathers group in the United States came together at the San Francisco gay pride parade in 1975, the largest such event in the country up to that date, with an estimated attendance of 82,000. The theme that year was "join us, the more visible we are, the stronger we become," a statement that testified to the groundswell of gay and lesbian activism at the time.[13] Several months before the parade, Jack Latham had published an article entitled "A Faggot Father Speaks Out" in *Gay Sunshine*, a widely read gay liberation newspaper. Latham's article struck a nerve: the number of letters in response exceeded that of any other single article published in the newspaper.[14] Latham invited all of the responding gay fathers who lived in the San Francisco Bay Area to march together at the 1975 pride parade. As the men walked in the procession, other gay fathers came out of the crowd to join them. Allen Klein later remembered, "I saw a couple of men walking and one of them was Jack, with his sign that said 'Gay Father.' . . . I ran up to them and said, 'You're a gay father, I'm a gay father too!'"[15] It was from this group that San Francisco Bay Area Gay Fathers (SFBAGF) was born.[16]

In his article, Latham chronicled his struggles as a gay father after he fell in love with another man in 1968, came out and left his marriage, and got involved in gay liberation activism as a member of a Tucson group called Gay Liberation Arizona Desert. He described feeling alienated from both heterosexual society and other gay liberationists, who could rarely relate to his

GAY LIBERATOR

25c 30¢ outside Michigan   June 1973   no. 27   Detroit

Don Mager and his two children on the cover of the *Gay Liberator* (Detroit), 1973.
Courtesy of the Gay, Lesbian, Bisexual, Transgender Historical Society.

experiences as a father. Similar to the experiences of lesbian mother activists in lesbian feminist communities, gay fathers in early gay liberation circles often felt alienated and misunderstood by other gay men. In Arizona, Latham began working with lesbian feminists and expressed his commitments to antisexist work and communal childcare through involvement in an effeminist men's group and by helping to found a feminist childcare collective, Artemis Child Experience. He felt his own gay fatherhood contained an "element of pioneering in our departure from the heterosexual nuclear family," and sought to raise his children in an atmosphere free from aggression and emotional repression.[17]

At first, San Francisco Bay Area Gay Fathers was comprised primarily of young, radical men from the ranks of the countercultural gay liberation movement. Describing the men who met him before the parade that day, Latham later wrote: "Most were end-of-the-era hippies, so 'in the moment' no one brought a camera. Several unselfconsciously enjoyed hallucinogens. Then and for several parades to come, some wore camp and other ethnic drag."[18] Bill Jones, a founding member of SFBAGF who had spontaneously joined the group as they marched that June day in 1975, remembered that "these guys all had long hair and every one of them was smoking pot."[19] San Francisco Bay Area Gay Fathers also reflected its counterculture roots in its informal organizational style. The initial monthly potluck meetings held either at Jack Latham's or Allen Klein's house were vegetarian and included both children and adults mingling in the laid-back atmosphere of the era. According to Latham, most of the men active in the early group "lived on subsistence or welfare incomes." They were part of the larger Bay Area counterculture and had preschool age children. During the first year of its existence, SFBAGF maintained a membership of around forty gay fathers, with five to ten men forming a core group.[20]

The radical roots of organizing by gay fathers demonstrated in the beginnings of San Francisco Bay Area Gay Fathers, Don Mager's experiences in Detroit, and the principles and social vision of the effeminist movement are an unexplored part of the larger history of gay liberation. They show that like lesbian motherhood, gay fatherhood in the early 1970s was conceived of as a potentially radical experience that could undermine sexism and homophobia and contribute to a revolutionary new social order. This history complicates the critique of the family and sex/gender roles in early gay liberation political materials, showing that it was a complex challenge to the normative concept of the family—one that we have seen was in conflict since the Second World War. It illustrates the ways that the family—intertwined with sexuality—has been one of the central sites of struggle and change since the late 1960s. And like the lesbian mothers groups, this genealogy of gay father organizing helps clarify the emergence of the struggle in the late twentieth century over LGBT domestic and parental rights.

A Model Minority: Increased Visibility, Outreach, and a Politics of Respectability

From this early presence in gay liberation communities, the character of gay fathers groups shifted as more and more men with children came out of traditional marriages and sought the company of other gay fathers for help in the face of the threat of custody and visitation loss, emotional support, and social interaction. By the late 1970s, urban gay communities in general had moved away from the radical politics of the decade's early years and had turned to community organizing and municipal politics. In this context, gay fathers groups played an increasingly prominent role and positioned themselves as assimilationist and contradicting the Moral Majority portrayals of gay and lesbian culture as antifamily.

The informal organizational style that had characterized San Francisco Bay Area Gay Fathers from its inception in 1975 predominated in the group's first two or three years. The members rarely took minutes, and announcements of monthly meetings spread simply by word of mouth. However, increases in membership during the second year of the group necessitated the publication of a flyer to announce the gatherings, and members began to record minutes. In 1979, when monthly attendance grew to about one hundred men, members realized they needed a more formalized organization. The group created its first steering committee in order to address expanding needs: members proposed the publication of a newsletter and created the formal position of "Chairdaddy." They still held their monthly get-togethers at member's houses, but they began discussing a permanent, community-based location for meetings.[21]

Bill Jones remembered this increase in membership as a product of a larger mobilization of the gay and lesbian communities wrought by Anita Bryant's antigay "Save Our Children" campaign in Dade County, Florida, in 1977.[22] The campaign was the most visible part of a conservative backlash to the passage of lesbian and gay civil rights legislation in several localities nationwide. By 1977, over thirty-five states and municipalities had enacted laws guaranteeing fair treatment for lesbians and gay men in areas such as employment and housing. When a similar law passed in Dade County, Florida, an antigay political campaign attempted to repeal the bill and replace it with legislation banning same-sex marriage and preventing lesbians and gay men from adopting children. In the wake of the Dade County campaign, St. Paul, Minnesota; Wichita, Kansas; and Portland, Oregon repealed gay and lesbian civil rights legislation.[23]

Anita Bryant's activism galvanized gay and lesbian communities nationwide. The singer became a symbol for antigay intolerance that helped to fuel a new determination to fight for gay and lesbian rights. In San Francisco that year, the attendance at the annual pride parade more than doubled from the previous year to 250,000. This was an increase brought about by the repeal of the Dade County civil rights ordinance three weeks earlier and the brutal hate-crime killing of a gay man, Robert Hillsborough, in San Francisco a few days before the march. The next year, California state representative John Briggs spearheaded a campaign for a statewide proposition, known as the Briggs Initiative, to bar gay men and lesbians from teaching in public schools. Due in large part to the coordinated work of San Francisco Bay Area gay and lesbian activists, the initiative was defeated.[24] During these turbulent years, San Francisco Bay Area Gay Fathers continued growing; as more men publicly came out, many among them were previously married fathers.

As gay fathers became more visible, membership blossomed; the right-wing attacks on gay men as threats to children inspired many gay fathers to organize and publicly acknowledge their roles as fathers. But increasingly, these men were among the middle-class professionals coming out and migrating to the metropoles. Gay fathers held a special significance in combating the New Right, since much of the antigay rhetoric centered on the danger that gay men and lesbians supposedly posed to children and on a reassertion of "family values." The presence of a visible gay father movement helped to refute the assertion that same-sex sexuality was pathological to children. At the same time, a politics of respectability and parental civil rights replaced earlier radical, gay liberationist views of gay fatherhood.

In San Francisco, San Francisco Bay Area Gay Fathers became a familiar fixture at the annual pride marches. From its inception, SFBAGF had attracted particular attention when it marched in the annual parades. Jack Latham described the way the "newspapers singled us out" and crowds "exploded" in cheers at the initial 1975 group. Latham reasoned that this was because gay fathers marching was "novel and startling." Throughout the late 1970s, SFBAGF marched in the annual parades, with an increasing number of fathers. In 1979, SFBAGF members who marched in the parade began wearing "gay fathers" T-shirts and carrying banners emblazoned with the same logo. This increased the group's visibility and membership.[25] From 1982 to 1984, SFBAGF won "most inspirational float" in the parade.[26]

San Francisco Bay Area Gay Fathers' parade presence was seen by some members as an important countermeasure to the visibility of highly sexualized aspects of the annual celebration that they saw as making the gay community vulnerable to attacks by the Right. In 1985, the president of SFBAGF, Bill Jones, remembered that seeing Jack Latham and other gay fathers marching in 1975 mitigated his discomfort at the "sleaziness of the overdone drag queens and the pickup trucks loaded down with obscene signs, bare rear ends, and toilet bowls." For Jones, looking back from the mid-1980s, gay fathers in San Francisco were an important representation of the diversity and respectability of the gay community in the city. "We do make a powerful political statement," he declared, "with our numbers, our clean-cut look, and most of all, with the wonderful faces of our kids who look happy and well cared for."[27] This perspective coincided with the fact that many men in the gay father movement by the 1980s were white middle or upper-middle class professionals who eschewed the more radical gay politics of the previous decade. One journalist in 1981 characterized a gathering of about one hundred members of the Gay Fathers Forum of New York as distinctly different from the youth-oriented, counterculture gay community he was familiar with: "There is more pinstripe than denim at this gathering, and there seems to be an unusually high incidence of advanced degrees. . . . These men do not remind me of the gay men I know, not today anyway; they remind me of a professional society of some sort."[28] It also highlighted the idea that gay fathers could be good fathers, and constructed a vision of "family values" that could serve as a political counterpoint to the increasingly antigay politics of the Reagan era. Later political campaigns for gay and lesbian parental rights and same-sex marriage would inherit this politics of gay familial and domestic respectability.

Gay Fathers of Los Angeles (GFLA) started in 1979 as a discussion group attended by a relatively small group of three to four men who met weekly at the Gay Community Services Center on North Highland Boulevard in Hollywood.[29] The group was more conservative than the San Francisco organization, lacking roots in the counterculture of the early 1970s. However, as in the case of San Francisco Bay Area Gay Fathers, the first two or three years of the organization were a period of growth, though not as dynamic as that of its Northern California counterpart. By 1980 the group had grown from five to fifteen regular members, and by 1983 it had over fifty members from the greater Los Angeles area.[30] The Los Angeles group, like San Francisco Bay Area Gay Fathers, included a small number of adoptive gay fathers as well as

Members of the San Francisco Bay Area Gay Fathers, San Francisco Freedom Day parade, 1980. Courtesy of Bill Jones.

"co-dads" but consisted primarily of noncustodial fathers who were in the process of leaving previous heterosexual marriages. Members who were active at the time remember the expansion as a result of both the increasing number of married men coming out and the greater visibility of GFLA.

As in San Francisco, gay fathers marching in Los Angeles's annual pride celebration brought in newcomers; one member of GFLA remembered that immediately following one march, the group had its largest meeting he ever attended, with over a hundred men at the gathering.[31] In 1984, a group of forty-five people, made up of gay fathers and their children, marched in the gay pride parade in West Hollywood alongside their float—a Volkswagen Rabbit decorated as a Red Flyer wagon. This was the largest contingent of gay fathers and their children in the West Hollywood parade up to that point.[32] Like members of San Francisco Bay Area Gay Fathers, men in the Los Angeles group expressed a belief that they and their children gave the parade a sense of respectability that stood against antigay prejudice. In a letter to the organizing committee of the Christopher Street West parade in Santa Monica, Gino Sikorski complained about the charging of admission for children at the 1983 festival and said, "We feel that our children supply an air of wholesomeness to the onlooking homophobic individual who thinks of us as drug abusing, disco dancing, diseased individuals."[33]

Gay fathers in New York also marched in the annual pride parade in the 1980s, and increased visibility and membership as a result. Members of the Gay Fathers Forum, which grew out of discussion groups in the late 1970s and was formally organized in 1980, marched in the front of the 1985 parade, many in gay fathers T-shirts made by the group. The group also staffed a booth at the fair at the end of the march.[34] In addition to the annual parades, the Gay Fathers Forum staffed booths at smaller, local gay and lesbian community events as well as larger functions. The group had a booth and passed out literature about their organization at the local Chelsea Street Fair in 1983 and had a table at the citywide Self-Help Fair, held at Battery Park in 1984. A request for members to staff the table at the Self-Help Fair noted that the group's presence at the fair the previous year had been "an important part of our outreach program" and helped "other gay fathers know that they're not alone."[35]

The presence of gay fathers in annual parades played a central role in the emergence and consolidation of the gay father movement in the 1970s and 1980s. It was Jack Latham's presence in the annual San Francisco parade that had catalyzed the founding of SFBAGF, the nation's first gay fathers group. Four years later Alan Ross was inspired to found Gay Fathers of Greater Philadelphia when he saw a man carrying a "Gay Daddies" sign in the 1979 New York parade and thought, "Wow! That's where my heart wants to be."[36]

Gay fathers groups in less urban areas also took part in annual parades. In 1985, Gay Fathers of Sacramento marched in and staffed a booth at the annual Gay Freedom Fair in Sacramento, California, with the theme, "The Next Generation."[37] At times participation in smaller events in more suburban contexts, which were often not supported by a sizable gay or lesbian community, could be dangerous. When Don Harrelson, a member of Gay Fathers of Los

Gay fathers in the New York Pride march, 1979. © 2013 JEB (Joan E. Biren).

Angeles, and his son Jon marched in the Long Beach pride parade a group of
religious protestors followed the gay fathers "jeering and throwing things."
Describing the event in a 1984 interview, Harrelson remarked that although "it
was a hard lesson that left me shaken and hurting," the incident showed that
"we must work even harder to promote a positive image of our gay families"
and inspired him to make "even more effort in making gay parenting an accepted part of our society."[38]

Groups from areas adjacent to large metropolitan areas also took part
in parades by traveling to those in nearby cities. In 1985, South Bay Gay
Fathers announced in their newsletter that they would be marching in the
San Francisco pride parade. In order to preserve their visibility as a distinct
organization, they asked the parade organizers to place them at least one
entry away from the San Francisco gay fathers group.[39] Alan Ross, one of the
founders of Gay Fathers of Greater Philadelphia, wrote in 1980 of marching
up Fifth Avenue with a crowd of "hundreds of thousands" in New York's annual pride parade along with the "other Fathers organizations from various
cities."[40]

The involvement of gay fathers groups in annual pride parades was part of a larger commitment to outreach shared by many gay father organizations of the period. Gay fathers, cognizant of the situations that married gay men had historically faced and the silence that could be brought on by fear of custody loss, made it a high priority to reach other gay fathers who remained without support. By September 1984 Gay Fathers of Los Angeles had established a twenty-four-hour recorded message "giving callers an opportunity to request information about the various Los Angeles gay parenting organizations.[41] Appearing on the nationally syndicated television program, the *Phil Donahue Show*, New York Gay Fathers Forum founder Stu Gross emphasized the importance of reaching gay fathers in the viewing audience. "I want to say to all the gay fathers out there," he said, "you are not alone, there are a lot of other gay fathers out there, and do what you need to do."[42] John Mills, who served as editor of the San Francisco Bay Area Gay Fathers newsletter in 1984, considered communication one of the "primary goals of Gay Fathers" and saw the newsletter as a fundamental part of this goal of outreach to other gay fathers.[43] One member of the group wrote in 1985 that "each fathers group has the obligation to help other gay fathers come to better understand and like themselves as individuals of worth as well as their role as father, spouse (ex-spouse), lover and citizen of the world."[44] As part of its outreach work, the Gay Fathers Forum of New York maintained a regular ad in the New York weekly the *Village Voice*.[45] The monthly "Newcomers" discussion group, often led by founder Stu Gross, attempted to reach gay fathers who were in the closet, those who were open but still married, and those who had only recently left marriages.

Men who found these groups in the 1970s and 1980s testified to the importance they had played in their own period of coming out as gay fathers. One father, Michael, wrote the Gay Fathers Forum of New York and expressed gratitude for this aspect of the organization: "As someone who's been out of the closet for only a few months, I have found the Forum to be immensely helpful."[46] Allen Klein remembered that San Francisco Bay Area Gay Fathers let him know "that there were other gay men out there with kids and that gay men could be fathers," and he recalled "feeling good that I was helping other men who were struggling through all of this, somehow get through it and find a place where they could feel comfortable talking about their child and their wife and whatever issues they were having."[47] A man who got involved in an early New York gay fathers group in the late 1970s remembered that before he joined the group, he "straddled uneasily between the gay and nongay worlds, and felt uncomfortable in both."[48]

Gay & A Father?

There is a group for you!
Focusing on our unique
EXPERIENCES
with wives and ex-wives
and our children in
building new lives for
ourselves.

MEETING WEDNESDAYS, 7:30P.M.
THE GAY COMMUNITY SERVICES CENTER
1213 N. HIGHLAND AVE.
HOLLYWOOD CA. 90038
(213) 464-7400

"Gay & A Father?" flyer, Hollywood, California, early 1980s. Courtesy of the ONE National Gay & Lesbian Archives at U.S.C.

Unlike lesbian mothers, who could hope to get custody of their children if they kept their sexuality a secret, and in many cases saw their previous marriages as being exploitative and sexist from a lesbian feminist perspective, gay fathers often remained in closer contact with their ex-spouses. Some gay fathers even stayed married after they came out about their sexual orientation. Because of this, gay fathers groups held discussion groups about issues that would arise in these relationships. A GFLA flyer declared: "Gay & a Father? There is a group for you! Focusing on our unique relationship experiences with wives and ex-wives and our children in building new lives for ourselves." Discussion topics dealing with these relationships, such as one entitled "Wives, Then and Now," were an important part of GFLA.[49] Recognizing that many gay fathers chose to stay with their wives, the Gay Fathers Forum, like other gay fathers groups, also focused on providing a place where husbands and wives could negotiate their new relationships. The rap groups it held at its monthly meetings included a "Married Men's Group" and a group on "Wives and Gay Fathers."[50]

Amity Buxton ran a support group for wives and ex-wives in SGBAGF. In 1985, she wrote that wives and former wives of gay fathers had a "special need for support" and that it was important that the gay fathers group recognized the pain and self-doubt that wives experienced when their husbands came out. The support group organized discussions and worked to foster a sense of community among these women.[51]

Concerns about outreach and recognition that many gay fathers remained married also meant that gay fathers groups sometimes had strong ties to other local men's groups. This was the case with San Francisco Bay Area Gay Fathers and the married gay men's group at the Pacific Center, a counseling and adult education center located across the San Francisco Bay in Berkeley. Many of the members of SFBAGF had first discovered the Pacific Center's married men's group when they were initially coming out. Marty Karls, who was later active in SFBAGF, attended the group at the Pacific Center in 1977, the second year of its existence.[52] Fred Sonenberg, who facilitated the married men's groups at the Pacific Center for four years, attended his first San Francisco Bay Area Gay Fathers meeting with an old friend of his from the Pacific Center group who introduced him to the fathers group. For Sonenberg, the Pacific Center offered a supportive community in which to deal with the emotional issues and fears that accompanied coming out as a gay father. He remembered the feelings of anxiety that he suffered the first time he went to a meeting of the men's group: "I went to this thing, walked around the block ten times, because I knew once I entered, once I crossed the portal, I was beginning a journey and that journey meant losing my wife, losing my child, losing my life."[53] These Pacific Center meetings were connected to San Francisco Bay Area Gay Fathers by personal ties that formed a survival network for gay fathers in various stages of coming out in the Bay Area during these years.

Pacific Center meetings served as a touchstone for gay married men who were coming out during this period. Other gay parents groups had ties to networks of men who were coming out and staying married; Parents Who Are Gay, a Washington, D.C., group, shared members with another group, Gay Married Men's Association.[54] These married men's groups are in some ways comparable to lesbian and gay community centers. They were places where gay married fathers frequently made their first declarations to anyone that they were gay, often a very emotionally difficult thing to do. These initial encounters were complex for married men just coming to terms with their same-sex sexuality and what it would mean to declare it openly and leave their marriages. They often experienced a sense of alienation and fear when they made their first forays into gay neighborhoods. John McClung, a conservative Mennonite minister who joined Gay Fathers of Los Angeles in 1984, went to his first meeting of GFLA at the Gay Community Center and waited for twenty minutes before going in, too afraid of meeting gay men and lesbians in the center to get out of his car.[55]

As concepts of gay fatherhood shifted from an early radical, gay liberationist perspective on gay fatherhood to a more assimilationist, moderate model of organizing due to the changing demographic makeup of gay fathers in gay male communities of the 1970s, gay fathers groups emerged nationwide. These organizations stressed the importance of demanding parental rights for gay men and echoed earlier, more radical formulations in articulating gay fatherhood as a model of nurturing fatherhood; however, they lacked the radical feminist politics and revolutionary outlook that had driven early work on gay fatherhood. Instead, these groups were focused on addressing the needs and struggles of professional, married gay fathers who were in the process of coming into consciousness and expression of their gay identity. In so doing, they developed a politics of gay familial and domestic civil rights that, like lesbian mother activist groups, responded to the bias faced by gay fathers in American family courts.

Custody Struggles

Like lesbian mothers groups of the 1970s, one of the main concerns for members of gay fathers groups was the discrimination they faced in custody courts. Allen Klein, who took over leadership of the San Francisco Bay Area Gay Fathers after Jack Latham stepped down, said that getting "child custody rights" was an issue raised by most SFBAGF members in the early years of the group.[56] In a speech given in San Francisco during a gay rights rally outside the 1984 Democratic Party Convention, Mark Stephens of SFBAGF proclaimed: "Throughout this country, gay fathers are being denied custody. They are having their own children taken away from them, often forbidden even from visiting with them."[57] Marty Karls, the group's 1979 chairdaddy, described the major discussion topics at SFBAGF meetings as "coming out to family and friends, legal issues, and social connecting."[58] The by-laws of the organization listed "legal problems, custody, visitation, separation, divorce" as central challenges faced by group members, a focus that persisted throughout the history of the group.[59] In 1984, when Gay Fathers of Los Angeles first replaced its informal, nonspecific, rap-group format with smaller discussion groups focused around specific topics, one of the subjects was "fathers in divorce proceedings."[60]

Gay fathers groups provided members with material and emotional support if they were going through custody struggles. By November 1984, San

Francisco Bay Area Gay Fathers had raised a thousand dollars in order to establish the Gay Fathers Crisis Fund. This legal fund, also known as the Emergency Defense Fund, had the express purpose of providing "legal aid to our fathers struggling with custody battles and visitation rights." The fund was seen as a logical extension of the group's commitment to helping gay fathers battling for custodial rights. Through it, SFBAGF administered interest-free loans to members in good standing who could demonstrate "economic hardship due to legal fees and related costs."[61]

Like lesbian mothers groups such as the Lesbian Mothers' National Defense Fund, San Francisco Bay Area Gay Fathers gathered and distributed information designed to help gay fathers fighting for parental rights. By 1982 the group had established a lending library on gay fatherhood that contained over 200 books and articles. The library included a list of "sympathetic lawyers in the [San Francisco] area," another list of possible "expert witnesses," three articles on choosing a lawyer as a gay parent, and a "20 page long bibliography on legal cases that involve gays and custody and other issues."[62]

Gay fathers groups were often the first place a man turned to after realizing that the price for being honest about his sexuality might be his right to be a parent. Andrew Hallum, a single gay man who started attending Gay Fathers of Los Angeles meetings in the early 1980s because he had heard that it was the best place to pick up "straight-seeming" gay men, was shocked by the tragic tenor of many of the meetings: "then there's somebody who's there for the first time and who starts out and pretty soon is sobbing, telling about the wife and these tendencies and got a child and doesn't know what to do . . . and they never come back again."[63] Many men, however, did come back and relied on the support of the group as they weathered difficult custody battles.

John McClung discovered GFLA after his ex-wife threatened him with the loss of all parental rights in the process of their divorce. McClung had learned of GFLA through an ad in the Los Angeles gay community magazine *Frontiers* during his search for an attorney sympathetic to gay fathers. He remembers his first foray into a gay community, when he stumbled onto the GFLA announcement advertising regular Wednesday night support groups "for men who have lost their children." In the first ten minutes of that meeting, McClung met a man who later became one of his best friends. This man referred him to an openly lesbian Los Angeles attorney, Rebecca Tapia, who had experience in gay father and lesbian mother custody cases. Tapia warned him that the case would be difficult and that homosexuality would be brought up as an issue. One year later, after he came out as a gay man and began fighting what would be a six-year custody battle for his two children, McClung began attending GFLA meetings regularly.[64]

Other members of GFLA also fought for custody of their children. Robert Johnson, the man who greeted John McClung that first night and introduced him to Tapia, had himself been in a long custody struggle with his ex-wife. Johnson's wife accused him of child molestation and had fought to keep him away from his son because of Johnson's homosexuality. Born in Marin County in 1938, Johnson had lived as an openly gay man in San Francisco in the 1950s. In 1975, he married a woman who accepted his gayness and agreed to have children with him. After he and his wife had a son in 1980, his wife experienced a Pentecostal conversion, and the couple began attending an evangelical church in Pasadena. In 1982, when their son was two years old, Johnson's wife left him, telling him that she had realized that his being gay made him an unfit father and a sinner and that she believed he had been sexually molesting their son. Seeking information about his situation, Johnson discovered Gay Fathers of Los Angeles and began attending meetings regularly. Another member of the group referred him to Rebecca Tapia.[65]

The Gay Fathers Forum of New York shared the concerns of many of the other gay fathers groups nationwide, with custody issues being a primary focus. In 1982 the Forum launched a protest campaign when Richard Gottlieb, an active member of the organization and the father of a five-year-old daughter, was denied custody and forbidden from visitations with her while in the company of "any other homosexuals" or from taking her where "known homosexuals are present." The decision was based solely on Gottlieb's identity as a gay man, seen by the judge as abnormal behavior. Two years later, the case was in appeal, and both the National Organization for Women and the Lambda Legal and Education Fund had thrown their support behind Gottlieb.[66] The October 1984 Forum meeting was dedicated to the topic of "The Rights of Gay Fathers: Adoption, Legal, and Emotional," and one of the discussion groups that month was one on legal rights, including "custody and divorce." In June 1985 the Forum held discussion groups about custody issues and estrangement from one's children, and in March 1986 the monthly meeting focused on the themes of divorce, separation, and custody, with one of the workshops entitled "Custody & the Gay Father."[67] When the New York State Assembly considered a bill prohibiting consideration of sexual orientation in awarding child custody, the Forum educated its members about the bill and encouraged them to write to state legislators demanding that they support the proposed law.[68] As in the case of San Francisco Bay Area Gay Fathers, the Gay Fathers Forum conducted a regular "Urgent Concerns" discussion at its monthly meetings.[69] Losing one's children was mentioned often in Forum newsletters as a fear many gay fathers faced.

Gay Fathers of Greater Philadelphia took the remarkable step of sending literature on gay fathers to every judge in the municipal family court, hoping that "their consciousness will be raised." In 1981, the group's general chairman, David Jenkins, wrote: "The most important service has been, and will continue to be, the opportunity to meet with others who have had or are experiencing problems with separation, divorce, custody, or visitation." Jenkins noted that the group had "a wealth of experience" regarding these issues and wanted to use it to help other gay fathers undergoing custody struggles.[70]

As prevalent as custody problems were in gay fathers groups, long, protracted challenges were the exception rather than the norm. Most men in these groups did not challenge their custody losses; instead, they attempted to work with their ex-spouses over time, hoping to gradually expand their visitation rights. Andrew Hallum recalled that most of the members of GFLA seemed more concerned with smoothing things over with their ex-wives and enjoying what visitation rights they did have rather than fighting in the courts.[71] Many had been barred from seeing their children and were estranged from them. Reflecting these realities, one of the topics the group discussed in May 1984 was the difficulty of communicating with their children over the telephone. By the mid-1980s, Stu Gross, the founder of the Gay Fathers Forum of New York, had himself been estranged from his two children for years.[72]

AIDS and Gay Fathers Organizations

One thing that set gay fathers groups apart from all other reproductive rights organizations of this period, even lesbian mothers groups, was the way their members were decimated by the onset of the AIDS crisis in the early 1980s. For anyone living outside of gay and lesbian communities during this period it is hard to understand the degree to which death and loss, and the extensive mourning that accompanied it, consumed gay communities by the mid-1980s. In 1981, the Centers for Disease Control in Atlanta had reported outbreaks of a rare pneumonia, *Pneumocystis carinii*, and a rare form of skin cancer, Kaposi's sarcoma, in gay men in San Francisco, New York, and Los Angeles.[73] These reports signaled the emergence of a new disease, soon labeled Acquired Immune Deficiency Syndrome (AIDS). Gay fathers groups emerged early in San Francisco, Los Angeles, and New York because these cities had the largest gay male populations in the United States, and for the same reason, these were also the cities hit first and hardest by the AIDS epidemic. By January 1988, San Francisco reported 4,371 cases of AIDS; of these, 3,692 (84.7 percent) were gay and bisexual men. Los Angeles reported 11,097 AIDS cases by 1990, 88 percent of whom were gay or bisexual men. In New York City, 21,242 people had been diagnosed with AIDS by April 1990, and 55 percent were gay or bisexual men.[74] As AIDS hit gay communities nationwide, the three largest urban gay centers were particularly devastated.

In Southern California, the AIDS virus ultimately devastated the first generation of gay fathers group members. John McClung, who lived through these years as a member of GFLA and who was a frequent visitor at Long Beach Gay Fathers, recalled that out of approximately sixty members in each group, only five to ten survived the worst years of the AIDS epidemic. McClung believes that AIDS effectively ended gay father organizing in Southern California. Among the first men in the group to die of an AIDS-related illness was Gino Sikorski, who had single-handedly kept GFLA going before the influx of new members in the early 1980s.[75] Memorials for GFLA members who had died began to appear in the group's newsletter.

San Francisco Bay Area Gay Fathers was also hit hard by the AIDS epidemic. In 1985, SFBAGF's active chairdaddy, Bill Jones, reported on the year's activities: "Under the able direction of our Program Director, Steve Graham, we go deeper and deeper into the AIDS crisis and have faced (and hugged) men with AIDS, and will confront our own mortality in November when an attorney, Dave Wharton, will lead a session on Wills, Health Insurance, and Tying Things Up in General."[76] By 1986, topics suggested by members of SFBAGF for discussion included "Death of my Lover," "Desire for Unsafe Sex," and "Saying Goodbye."[77] Clearly, the priorities and needs of San Francisco's gay fathers were changing as AIDS consumed their community. Bill Jones remembers this period as an awful time when the healthy members of SFBAGF became "caretakers" of the members who were dying. By the late 1980s, Jones was conducting burials at sea free of charge for SFBAGF members who had died of AIDS, and after twenty-eight such memorials for gay fathers from the group, Jones sold his boat, having "lost all the joy in it."[78]

As in San Francisco and Los Angeles, the newsletters of the Gay Fathers Forum also reflect the advance of AIDS into the gay community of the New York area. One newsletter article from 1984, when AIDS was still a scientific mystery in many ways, discussed the possibility that the amyl nitrate "poppers" used by many gay men to accentuate sex might be contributing to the spread of the new disease.[79] By the next year there was a great deal more known about the virus, and "Dealing with AIDS" had become a regular workshop at the monthly meetings.[80] By 1987, memorials and descriptions of funerals began to fill the newsletters of the organization.

The AIDS crisis shook the lives of a great many children of gay fathers, as they grappled with the deaths in their communities and the fearful responses of family members. In 1985, Marty Karls, the facilitator of the discussion group for teens of gay fathers, reported that AIDS had become one of the topics brought up by the teenagers in the group, and an "AIDS and Action" group was added to the other weekly discussion groups.[81] Earlier fears that same-sex sexuality was communicable or would be passed on to children found new expression in the fear of the HIV virus and those who carried it. Karls remembered crying with his own son when he came out to him as HIV positive in the late 1980s. It was six months before he could enter his ex-wife's house. Barred from the premises by her second husband's fears of AIDS, he would wait outside for his son when he came to pick him up for visitation.[82] In a 1986 newsletter, the Gay Fathers Forum of New York announced a discussion group on how gay fathers' relationships with their children were being affected by AIDS. It asked, "Do you find yourself restrained, either physically or emotionally with your kids because of your awareness of AIDS?"[83]

Between 70 to 90 percent of the members of gay fathers groups in San Francisco and Los Angeles died of AIDS during the 1980s, and as a result, former members recalled, the groups stalled.[84] By 1992, they expressed a shortage of members to host the group's weekly potlucks—in bold letters the newsletter asked questions of the void that had replaced the active membership: "Where Are You All? Why Aren't You Coming To Meetings? Don't You Miss Us As Much As We Miss You?"[85] In a community where large numbers of men were dying or occupied with the struggle to stay alive, there was less energy for going to meetings. The politics of the group was transformed as well, as members who were still active called for more funding for AIDS research and education.

The Gay and Lesbian Parents Coalition International: Nationwide Organizing and the Long-term Impact of the Gay Father Movement

As AIDS hit gay fathers groups in the coastal metropolises, they were sustained by a nationwide umbrella organization, the Gay Fathers Coalition International. The organization was founded on October 14, 1979, at the first National March on Washington for Lesbian and Gay Rights.[86] That day, Alan Ross, Al Luongo, and Dave Berube met and discussed the possibility of an "international network" of gay fathers groups. The three men represented gay fathers groups in Philadelphia, New York, and Washington, D.C., respectively. In May 1980, members decided to limit membership to men. By its third organizational meeting in November 1980, the Gay Fathers Coalition included representatives from New York, Washington, D.C., Philadelphia, San Francisco, Los Angeles, Westchester, Brooklyn, Rochester, Cleveland, Baltimore, and Toronto.[87]

By the time of this third meeting, the Gay Fathers Coalition also began making contact with other gay and lesbian rights organizations, including the National Gay Task Force (NGTF), the National Coalition of Black Gays (NCBG), and the Lambda Legal Defense and Education Fund.[88] These groups were at the center of mainstream LGBT civil rights organizing in the 1980s. Two of the three, NCBG and NGTF, had been involved in the 1979 National March on Washington for Lesbian and Gay Rights, which listed "end discrimination in lesbian mother and gay father custody cases" as one of the points in its five-point program. Both of these organizations had themselves been founded by gay fathers, ABilly S. Jones-Hennin and Bruce Voeller, and had a political perspective based on a civil rights model similar to 1980s gay fathers groups. Jones, the founder of NCBG, helped organize groups for gay and lesbian parents in Washington, D.C., in the mid-1970s and believed that gay and lesbian parental rights were an important part of the larger LGBT freedom struggle, while Voeller had put together an early set of materials in support of gay fathers and lesbian mothers in custody struggles.[89]

By 1981, an annual Gay Fathers Coalition meeting had been established and would occur throughout the 1980s and 1990s. The articles of incorporation of the Gay Fathers Coalition, filed in Washington, D.C., in 1982, defined the purposes of the organization as the counseling and support of gay fathers and their families, challenging and changing "prevailing social attitudes," and the attainment for "homosexual persons the same basic human rights, liberties and opportunities that are afforded to heterosexual persons."[90]

The 1979 founding of the Gay Fathers Coalition, renamed the Gay and Lesbian Parents Coalition International (GLPCI) in 1986, helped foster a sense of coalition and cooperation between gay father organizations across the country. The Gay Fathers Coalition held annual conferences in cities such as Denver in 1983, New York in 1984, and Los Angeles in 1985, bringing together representatives from organizations all over the country, including the groups from San Francisco, Los Angeles, and New York detailed in this chapter. Throughout the 1980s, the Gay Fathers Coalition/ GLPCI served as an umbrella organization for other gay fathers groups in the

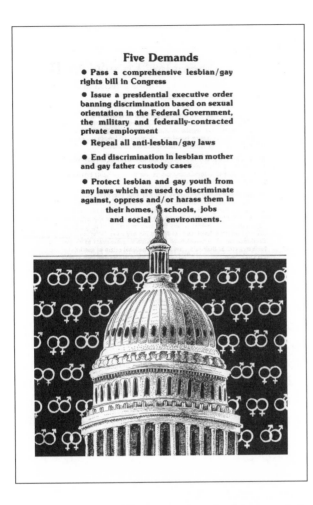

Five Demands

● Pass a comprehensive lesbian/gay rights bill in Congress

● Issue a presidential executive order banning discrimination based on sexual orientation in the Federal Government, the military and federally-contracted private employment

● Repeal all anti-lesbian/gay laws

● End discrimination in lesbian mother and gay father custody cases

● Protect lesbian and gay youth from any laws which are used to discriminate against, oppress and/or harass them in their homes, schools, jobs and social environments.

The five demands in the program for the 1979 National March on Washington for Lesbian and Gay Rights. Courtesy of the Gay, Lesbian, Bisexual, Transgender Historical Society.

United States, providing support and advice to existing groups and helping new ones to get started. Gay Fathers of Greater Boston formed in 1982 with ties to the larger organization. In 1983, a news release announced that a gay fathers group affiliated with the Gay Fathers Coalition was being formed in Long Beach after two fathers returned inspired from the annual conference in Denver.[91]

By the early 1990s, the Gay and Lesbian Parents Coalition International was increasingly central to gay and lesbian parental advocacy, particularly around issues affecting married gay men. The group served as a bridge between the earlier generation of gay father activists and newer groups that began forming around lesbian and gay families of the 1980s and 1990s, which included chosen families with a very different set of issues. Although the group changed its name in 1986 to reflect a desire to include lesbian mothers and elected the first woman to its board in the same year, the organization remained primarily aimed at gay fathers until the 1990s.

Gay fathers groups of the 1970s and 1980s accomplished a great deal: they made early inroads in discrediting homophobic social attitudes that saw gay masculinity as incompatible with fatherhood; they formed grassroots alliances between gay fathers that stretched across the country; and they struggled against losing their children in the custody courts. Unlike the members of lesbian mother activist groups of the previous decade, they also often negotiated new relationships with their former heterosexual spouses. These ongoing ties, as well as fundamental differences between the ability of gay men and lesbians to wrestle parental control from these former spouses and political differences between lesbian and gay communities of the period, made gay fathers groups less separatist and less politically radical than their lesbian counterparts. Nonetheless, both questioned the same underlying prejudices of heterosexual American society. By the late 1980s, the fathers groups had been severely damaged by the AIDS epidemic. However, as the first wave of organized gay father activism receded, a new one would emerge as part of the "gay-by boom" of the 1990s to build upon the foundations established by this generation lost to the AIDS crisis. It was the gay fathers groups of the 1970s and 1980s that would be directly responsible for the focus on gay and lesbian parental rights in the mainstream LGBT civil rights struggle of the 1990s and the first decade of the twenty-first century.

CHAPTER SIX

The Culture of Lesbian Feminist Households with Children in the 1970s

Though lesbian mothers faced legal and social persecution in the 1970s, they also created the first openly lesbian households with children from within newly formed lesbian feminist communities. The visibility of this generation of lesbian mothers was part of the political reaction against the social animosity that caused lesbians and gay men to hide in the 1950s and 1960s. While the custody cases politicized lesbian and gay parenting, lesbian feminist communities provided an alternative culture that contested the enforced silence of previous decades and paved the way for the lesbian parenting boom of the 1980s and 1990s.

These families were a part of a nationwide lesbian feminist movement in the 1970s that developed many of its own ideologies and cultural values separate from mainstream, heterosexual American society. Lesbian households with children both influenced and were shaped by the fundamental values of lesbian feminist culture, including lesbian separatism, the critique of patriarchy, and the envisioning of a lesbian nation. Children of lesbian feminist families of this era were raised with critiques of heterosexism, sexism, and misogyny and imbued with egalitarian and communal values that challenged the classic American nuclear family ideal.

In the late 1960s and 1970s, the rapid development of a radical lesbian feminist movement profoundly affected lesbian communities nationwide. As women active in the New Left came out as lesbians in the late 1960s and 1970s, they engaged with older lesbian networks, bringing with them politics and ideas from the women's movement, the antiwar movement, and the civil rights movement. Out of the synergy generated between older and younger lesbian communities, an intergenerational lesbian feminist movement emerged. Lesbian feminists challenged not only homophobia and the closet but also a global patriarchy that they viewed as the root of other political and social inequalities produced by capitalism and white supremacy.

Lesbian feminism developed alongside and interdependently with a movement that I call lesbian nationalism. I use the term nationalism to describe a specific set of principles that included a political and social criticism of mainstream American society from the vantage of a disenfranchised minority, the decision to separate from that society rather than struggle for equality through assimilation, the creation of community-based businesses and services, the development of separate spiritual and artistic cultural practices, and the belief that nationalist communities should lead to the formation of a revolutionary new state that would exist separately from the United States.

The most well-known example of these movements in the 1960s and 1970s is black nationalism. Like other nationalist movements of the same period, lesbian nationalism encouraged separatist approaches to spirituality, commercial development, and political activity, as well as the formation of new kinds of social relations. Where black nationalism envisioned separate communities based on a shared cultural experience of being African American in a white-supremacist state, lesbian nationalism sought common ground based on a shared lesbian feminist identity and antipatriarchal political commitments.

In his study of San Francisco's Castro District in the 1970s and 1980s, Manuel Castells wrote that, in contrast to gay men, "lesbians do not acquire a geographical basis for their political organization and are less likely to achieve local power."[1] On the contrary, my research suggests that lesbians did claim space, both literally and culturally, and they did so assertively, exclusively, and even militantly. More than just an ideological commitment, lesbian nationalism created separate social and geographical space, developing businesses, land trusts, and schools exclusively for lesbians and conceived of the foundation for a "lesbian nation," which sought to exist outside of the patriarchal, capitalistic nation-state.

In his book on the history of Black Power, New Day in Babylon, William Van Deburg shows that the complex black nationalist movements of the 1960s and 1970s reshaped African American society in previously unrecognized ways. Cultural nationalists such as Ron Karenga, revolutionary nationalists such as the Black Panther Party, and territorial nationalists such as the Republic of New Africa all contributed to this widespread influence. Even if black nationalism did not succeed in some of its more radical goals, such as the creation of an autonomous black state, its cultural effects were powerful and far-reaching.[2] Similarly, lesbian nationalism and lesbian feminism had profound effects on both lesbian culture and American society more generally. One such effect was the development of self-defined lesbian feminist families raising children within lesbian communities.

Lesbian feminist nationalism was a widespread cultural movement by the mid-1970s. The phrase "lesbian nation," the title of a 1973 book by *Village Voice* writer Jill Johnston, captured the political spirit. Johnston wrote that "the most radical people I knew were the radicalesbians and the message I got from them was that . . . the best thing to do was to retreat and get your own shit together and to build lesbian nation from the grass roots out of your own community of women."[3] This concept of lesbian nation had a wide appeal to a generation of newly defined lesbian feminists. In 1975, a sixteen-year-old lesbian feminist captured the spirit of this utopian movement when she wrote, "I and the women I am searching for . . . will succeed in re-building 'The Lesbian Nation,' which to me is the only Revolutionary/Evolutionary transition from Pain to Paradise."[4] In July 1976, lesbians from Ohio, Kentucky, Illinois, Tennessee, and Michigan held a conference in Bloomington, Indiana, on "Building the Lesbian Nation." The conference described itself as a "catalyst for establishing long-term goals toward complete self-sufficiency."[5] This lesbian nationalist feminist vision sometimes included a celebration of lesbian motherhood and of the mother-daughter bond as a powerful way to directly challenge and undermine patriarchy. By raising strong, empowered women, and perhaps feminist men as well, lesbian mothers could contribute to the development of a radical new society envisioned as lesbian nation.

Fueled in part by a new feminist consciousness arising out of activism among university students, lesbian feminist communities often sprang up in university towns or in the large, coastal metropolises and northeastern industrial cities where vibrant, underground gay and lesbian communities had existed since the Second World War. By the early 1970s there were sizable lesbian feminist communities in cities such as New York, San Francisco, Seattle, Los Angeles, Atlanta, Baltimore, Chicago, and Philadelphia, as well as smaller cities such as Louisville, Kentucky; Ann Arbor, Michigan; Jackson, Mississippi; Portland, Oregon; Northampton, Massachusetts; Richmond, Virginia; Tampa, Florida; St. Louis; and Cincinnati. These lesbian feminist communities created a network of activists living in distinct residential neighborhoods serviced by community-run women's bookstores, coffeehouses, car repair services, food cooperatives, childcare, restaurants, and alternative schools. These institutions were tied to local feminist projects, such as rape crisis hotlines and battered women's shelters. Urban lesbian feminist communities were also linked to a nationwide network of women's land communes, often through affiliated communal households in urban centers.[6] Lesbian rural communes existed in New Mexico, New York, Arizona, Arkansas, Missouri, Oregon, Vermont, California, Florida, Tennessee, Mississippi, Wisconsin, and Minnesota.[7]

Marchers in the San Francisco Freedom Day parade, 1978. Photograph by Cathy
Cade. Courtesy of the Bancroft Library, University of California, Berkeley.

These urban and rural lesbian feminist communities of the 1970s were the
first to see the emergence of openly lesbian families. These families were, of
course, still vulnerable to the pressures that had beset lesbian and gay parents and their children of an earlier era, but these pressures occurred within
the context of an explicitly identified lesbian community, organized around
a radical politics of resistance and empowerment. Unlike lesbian mothers
of the 1950s and 1960s, who existed in a society in which few questioned the
belief that same-sex desire was pathological and antithetical to parenthood,
lesbian feminist mothers of the 1970s were supported by a liberation-era
ethic of pride and insistence on civil rights for sexual-minority communities. The presence of these families changed the communities profoundly,

as motherhood became a central controversy in lesbian feminist culture. As lesbian feminists both celebrated and argued against motherhood and the presence of children in their communities, they reshaped lesbian feminist politics and thought. The radical experiments in childrearing in these lesbian feminist cultures also represent an important part of family history in the United States, for they illustrate post-1960s revolutions in the family and sexuality, including the separation of reproduction and heterosexual relations, as women chose to become parents with minimal or no male involvement. Lesbian mother–headed households in these communities challenged fundamental American legal and social definitions of the family as heterosexual and patriarchal.

Lesbian Feminist Family Values

Lesbian feminist families defied dominant cultural traditions. Within them, children grew up in women-centered, avowedly feminist environments that actively questioned patriarchal and heterosexual values. As part of resistance communities, lesbian feminist mothers sought to protect their children from heteronormative, sexist values in mainstream American society. In so doing, these mothers consciously destabilized heterosexual, nuclear family values at the same time as they promoted a new vision of society.

One of the fundamental motivating principles in lesbian feminist communities was the need to create a refuge away from sexism, misogyny, and the patriarchal structures of modern capitalism that sustained systems of women's oppression. For mothers this meant raising their children in a nonsexist environment. As a group of lesbian mothers explained in a self-help book published in Philadelphia, "lesbian mothers have to keep in mind that we are building something . . . an alternative to the present family structure and the present male-female role models. It's nothing less than an alternative to sexism."[8] Deborah Goleman Wolf, in her ethnography of the lesbian feminist community in the San Francisco Bay Area in the mid-1970s, wrote that "it is apparent that lesbian-feminist mothers believe themselves to be in a transitional stage, in which they try to live their lives and raise their children in terms of non-hierarchical principles."[9] One lesbian feminist, interviewed in 1975, said that "not having a patriarchal set-up inflicted on the children 24 hours a day" was one of the most rewarding things about being a lesbian mother.[10] A year later, a St. Louis woman wrote, "We are raising our female children to be stronger; we are raising our male children to be more human. We are awakening society at every point with our assertion and independence."[11]

Lesbian feminist mothers believed it was necessary to raise their daughters as warriors capable of facing society's objectification of women, so they sought to make them aware of homophobia and sexism as well as models of resistance. A Seattle woman said her daughter had "seen too many strong women to ever be dominated."[12] Lesbian feminist writer Joan Larkin wrote of her daughter Kate, "there can be *advantages* to being a lesbian mother. One is that Kate's aware—as most children are not—that there's a very wide range of possibilities for human sexual expression, and there's nothing wrong with any of them."[13] One lesbian mother described her daughter as "a little 'women's libber'" who "reads my copy of Ms. every month before I can get my hands on it."[14] Daughters in lesbian feminist households were raised to be proud feminists. Adrian Hood remembered that growing up in lesbian feminist communities with her mother, musician Alix Dobkin, was formative to her values as a feminist.[15]

Additionally, for revolutionary lesbian nationalists, raising daughters meant helping them to be strong woman-citizens of the world that lesbian nationalists hoped to create. Mothers who worked toward a matriarchal society saw this future as one in which their daughters could live as proud, strong women. As one lesbian mother wrote from Berkeley, California, "as a lesbian/feminist mother I have dreams of the lesbian community coming together to create an atmosphere where my daughter (who has been brought up believing there's nothing 'deviant' about Lesbianism) and other daughters can live in a free, matriarchal society."[16] Susie, a woman in Boston, who was raising her daughter in a household with her partner, Lynne, and their two daughters, Melanie and Jamey, saw the girls as the real hope of a matriarchal revolution because, unlike previous generations limited by patriarchy, they would be more able to embrace their strength as women.[17]

Although daughters of lesbians growing up within communities of women did learn that they could be strong and independent feminists, they also found the values of their families to be at odds with mainstream society, and some rebelled against the cultural politics in which they were raised. Celeste Cole, whose mother Geraldine Cole was one of the founders of the Seattle-based Lesbian Mothers' National Defense Fund, recalled that as a girl she longed for a "normal" family. As a teenager, Cole chafed against some of the cultural values of the lesbian feminist community in which she had been raised. In junior high school she would stop on the way to school and secretly apply eye shadow. She also, like many girls raised in heterosexual families, pretended to be less physically and mentally capable than she was to avoid threatening boys her age. However, Cole recalled that she believed from a young age that

Lynne (left) and Susie and their daughters, Melanie (left) and Jamey, Boston, 1978. © 2013 JEB (Joan E. Biren).

women were strong and capable of anything. Daughters of lesbian feminist families were deeply influenced by the fundamental values of lesbian feminism, but they sometimes compartmentalized these lessons in order to navigate the space between their families and the gender norms of the larger culture in which they existed.[18]

During this period, lesbian mothers with sons believed that it was part of their responsibility as revolutionary radical lesbians to raise their male children to stand against patriarchy and treat women in a nonsexist manner. Judy Barlow wrote of raising her son Eli: "My goal is to impress my child with the need for revolutionary change and release him knowing that he has a responsibility to be ethical and accountable in his continuing struggle."[19] A lesbian feminist from Seattle expressed her belief that "one of the hopes of this revolution is to raise male children with strong women."[20] Lesbian feminists believed that daily, intimate exposure to strong women could counter sexist social and cultural conditioning their sons received outside the family. For this reason, the Children and Youth Committee of Sisterspace, a lesbian community center, actively supported raising boys to be nonsexist and to respect the need for women's space.[21] Cathy Cade consciously decided to raise her son, Carl, as a feminist in Oakland, California, in 1978.[22] Karen Burr of the Lesbian Mothers' National Defense Fund wrote in 1974 that "no one is better qualified [than lesbian mothers] . . . to rear male children and to teach these children that women are strong and capable and are not subservient to men."[23] Similarly, a lesbian mothers support group in Boston that formed in 1973 discussed "raising male children to be nonchauvinist."[24] A member of Dykes and Tykes told a New York City public radio audience in 1978 that since "some of our daughters are not going to be lesbians when they grow up. . . . It's up to those of us who are lesbian mothers to raise our sons so that they'll be better for lesbian mothers' daughters."[25]

Trying to raise their male children outside social norms of masculinity could be disheartening for lesbian mothers. Jeanne Jullion helped found a support group for lesbian mothers with male children in the San Francisco Bay Area in the late 1970s and recalled the challenges of raising boys in a nonviolent atmosphere. Even though the women forbade their sons from playing with toy guns, the children simply improvised and forged their own imaginary weapons. "We would be all sitting in the living room," she recalled, and their sons "would come thundering down the stairs armed with Tinkertoy guns."[26] Other lesbian mothers found it difficult to raise boys as feminists while they were also living with the influence of their fathers and the male values of mainstream society. A lesbian mother from Detroit reported in 1978: "I had five sons. The one I was able to raise without much interference from his father is a splendid man; the other four got pretty mixed-up from the tantrum and chauvinism of their father."[27] As these stories suggest, lesbian feminists often found themselves in an enclave society surrounded by values contrary to their own.

Children raised in lesbian feminist households also grew up in an environment that challenged the heterosexism of society; they were raised outside of what author Adrienne Rich called "compulsory heterosexuality," the unquestioned assumption that heterosexuality is natural and superior to same-sex sexual orientation. Their mothers celebrated love between women as beautiful and criticized mainstream heterosexual culture for its prejudice against lesbians. One woman, Laura, interviewed in 1973, explained that she was glad that she had been raising her daughter in a lesbian household because she did not want "her to get too fucked up by [a] heterosexual atmosphere."[28] At Sappha Survival School, a rural lesbian community in the Cascade Mountains of Washington where children were reared, one mother proudly proclaimed in

1975 that "Freedom and Dykepride [ran] strong."[29] The same Seattle woman who had expressed her belief in the importance of raising sons around strong women also acknowledged that "our household is strongly dyke."[30] Or, as a woman from New York put it, "The children know that the people they interact with [at home] are perfectly all right. . . . They just can't believe what society is trying to tell them about lesbians not being okay."[31]

Children in lesbian feminist households learned first-hand about their mothers' efforts to achieve civil rights. Irene Yarrow, a lesbian mother from New York City, took her daughter to the hearings on a gay and lesbian rights bill. Watching an older lesbian testifying for the bill, the girl asked, "she looks just like grandma, is she for us or against us?" The children of lesbian mothers, in Yarrow's words, saw "us suffering from all the different kinds of lesbian oppression" and were strengthened by the experience.[32] Children from families such as these would later form their own political organizations, and some would eventually move to the forefront of the lesbian, gay, bisexual, and transgender freedom struggle.[33]

Lesbian feminists often subscribed to an ethic of egalitarian childrearing. The same commitments to self-empowerment that led to the establishment of lesbian feminist auto repair and self-defense courses led many mothers in lesbian feminist communities to want to raise their children to think and make decisions for themselves. Their own critiques of normative gender roles led many lesbian feminists to encourage their children to develop as independent individuals. In Ithaca, New York, Becky Logan often saw her daughter offend other adults who expected children to be unquestioningly obedient, but Logan felt that "so many decisions were made for them [the children] that they had no control over; I thought they deserved to have control over the small, basic things in their lives." She would rarely make her children eat something they did not want to and allowed them to choose their own clothing. When her son was nine, Logan remained quiet when he wore a pink dress to school even though she was afraid that he would be ridiculed.[34] Other children of lesbian mothers remember being raised with similar commitments. Kate Alfaro described her upbringing in upstate New York as one shaped by ideals of egalitarian childrearing.[35]

Lesbian feminist communes proved to be exciting and unorthodox places for many children to grow up. Cynthia McCabe lived with her mother in Colchester House, a commune located in Burlington, Vermont. She remembers long nights of consensus meetings over a myriad of political issues. Among them was monogamy. Philosophically opposed to the focus on the romantic bond in the heterosexual nuclear family ideal, lesbian feminists often attempted to set up communal limitations on adult nuclear pairing. "There was the whole ideology thing—figuring out, this is the world as we're going to live it, and they are not all agreeing—there was a huge fight about monogamy, all the time—I learned more about monogamy as a small child."[36]

As part of these same commitments, these families often raised their children communally in both rural and urban settings with all the adults responsible to some degree for meeting the needs of the children. These collective childcare arrangements were influenced by lesbian feminist beliefs about community responsibility, a nationalist impulse to create autonomous lesbian institutions, and a perceived need for family structures outside the traditional, middle-class, nuclear, heterosexual model. In Los Angeles in 1973, three lesbian feminists discussing the advantages of living in collectives professed that they were better than traditional family structures because "the kids grow up thinking and believing in a lot of people" and that the collectives provided "an alternate to the nuclear family."[37] Alix, a woman interviewed in 1973, described a communal household that she envisioned creating in Woodstock, New York: "I would like to have a big house in the country and then other smaller houses where people could be alone. And there'd be provisions for children and older women, women of all ages."[38]

Influenced by the women's movement of the 1960s, many lesbian feminists saw traditional maternal roles as oppressive because they so often meant women giving up their creative lives and sacrificing themselves for their children. One possible solution was the development of more communal forms of childrearing in which the labor and responsibilities could be shared. Cynthia McCabe's childhood included living in several lesbian land collectives: "I would be running through the living room and there would be this twenty-six-year-old woman, and I would ask her to read me something, and she'd say okay." McCabe felt that all the women around her were people she could turn to for care, to ask for something to eat, or to engage with in conversation.[39] The sense of communal responsibility often tied into desires to have children raised in a community of women. Interviewed by Joan Biren in 1979, lesbian mother Denyeta said she hoped her daughter, Darquita, would "listen, learn and experience from her womyn-folks because they have stories to share with her."[40]

One lesbian mother from Seattle described a communal system of childcare set up between lesbian mothers in that city in 1976. A two-and-a-half-year-old girl named Robin was the biological child of a lesbian and a gay man whose childcare providers included both her father's and her mother's close friends. These individuals all lived in separate households and were members

Denyeta and her daughter, Darquita, Alexandria, Virginia, 1979.
© 2013 JEB (Joan E. Biren).

of what they called the Robin's Parents' Association (RPA). The RPA held meetings "about every three months" to decide who would pick her up from day care and with whom she would spend nights and weekends. Another child, Celeste, who was three and a half years old, was being raised by a lesbian childcare collective of five women with additional help from Red Hen, a Seattle lesbian collective household. A group of five lesbians were raising a seven-year-old child named Myrah and identified themselves as a collective called "Myrah's Mothers."[41]

Lesbian mothers who were part of lesbian feminist communities were often at odds with the world outside. Because of their commitment to new ways of raising children, and because they were concerned about the stigma their children faced in schools, they often felt animosity toward the public school system. Barb and Murf described their fears about public school, because their three children "personally hold very different values than the other students. There's a lot of conflict there. I don't want them to believe society's values or internalize them."[42]

These dissatisfactions with mainstream education prompted many lesbian feminists to place their children in the alternative schools that had sprung up in the early 1970s within the heterosexual counterculture. Rachel, a lesbian mother interviewed in 1976 for the first issue of the periodical *Lesbian Connection*, enrolled her children in a Free School, an alternative school system outside the lesbian feminist community, which she described as "somewhat favorable to alternative lifestyles."[43] Children of lesbian mothers sometimes felt safer in these environments. Jon Givner, who grew up on a lesbian feminist commune in the mountains outside Santa Fe, attended a small alternative school with the other children of lesbians from the commune and found it to be free of overt homophobia and sexism.[44] At other times, the alternative commitments of nonmainstream schools did not extend to a critique of homophobia. Alix Dobkin's daughter, Adrian Hood, reported that even though the Quaker boarding school she attended for high school in the 1980s was leftist in its orientation, she did not feel safe being open about her mother's lesbianism.[45]

The desire to raise children in an atmosphere true to the values of lesbian feminist culture caused many lesbian mothers to create their own educational systems dedicated to a nonsexist and nonhomophobic education. Like black nationalism, lesbian cultural nationalism included the development of separate educational programs for children that came from families outside of normative American social values. In 1970 in Oakland, California, a group of lesbian mothers from Oakland Women's Liberation (OWL), one of the first lesbian feminist groups in the San Francisco Bay Area, formed a cooperative preschool in a member's basement. Eight of the families involved were headed by lesbian mothers who shared information and resources related to childrearing and custody concerns.[46] One of the goals of the New York lesbian mothers advocacy group Dykes and Tykes was to create a school for children of lesbian mothers.[47] A woman in rural Maine with two daughters sought other mothers and girls to open a home school in September 1977, with the eventual goal of forming a "community of women in this general area—rotating class time in each other's homes."[48]

These educational experiments were often explicitly geared toward raising children outside of traditional heterosexual and patriarchal roles and included a commitment to educating both female and male children. Womanstar, a lesbian mother from Berkeley, California, wanted to found a school with her partner in their home that was based on feminist, child-centered principles. They had looked for other options for their two children, a boy and a girl, but the only feminist school in the area was exclusively for girls, and they felt all the other alternatives were " 'straight' and 'capitalist' by default, by omission." Womanstar felt that these other schools had not respected the autonomy of their children, "forcing them to accept authority blindly and obediently."[49] Womanstar and her partner believed the only option was for them to create a school of their own in which to educate both their daughter and son in a feminist, nonheterosexist environment that respected their autonomy as human beings.

Other educational systems that lesbian feminists built emerged as part of collective-living experiments, both urban and rural. In 1975, seven white, middle-class lesbians and eight children founded A Women's Place on land in Athol, New York. One of the visions for the land was "an alternative feminist education institution, complete with library and structured alternative learning situations." From the beginning there was "talk of a summer camp for girls."[50] The members of Redbird, a lesbian feminist collective in Vermont, envisioned it as a place for lesbian feminists and their children from its inception in Burlington, where members lived in a building known as the Archibald Street House. The collective organized programs for neighborhood children and built a playground in their front yard. Years later, when it was a rural collective on land outside Burlington, Redbird drew up plans for an alternative, fully accredited school for the children of lesbians and for battered children. The school was to be named Oreithyia School, after a Greek goddess of northern winds, but Redbird faced intense community harassment from the town of Burlington over the establishment of the school. Although the commune went to court and won the right to establish Oreithyia, the group disbanded over ideological issues before it could be opened.[51]

Many lesbian feminist mothers of color shared this desire to raise their children away from a society tainted by sexism and patriarchy, but they felt that their families' struggles against white supremacy were unappreciated by white lesbian feminists focusing exclusively on patriarchy as the source of women's oppression. These critiques were part of a larger articulation of the specificity of the experiences of lesbians of color in the late 1970s and early 1980s. The topics of race and ethnicity were powerful engines of change and growth in lesbian feminist communities at this time. Lesbian feminist communities discussed the presence of racism in their communities as a part of their commitment to interdependency and group consciousness-raising; such discussions led to both conflict and change, two common elements of lesbian communal living arrangements. Lesbian feminists of color talked about their experience of racism within lesbian communities and asked white lesbian feminists to interrogate the assumption that patriarchy and sexism were at the root of all other forms of social oppression.[52] Although lesbian feminists of color acknowledged the need to fight against sexism and the assumptions of a male-dominated society, they also argued for the need to see white supremacy as an equally powerful system of domination that demanded its own analysis.

Mothers of color who lived in lesbian feminist collectives felt strongly about providing a new kind of education for their children, but they wanted to raise their children not only in a nonsexist environment but also one in which indigenous and nonwhite traditions could be celebrated. A woman from Arco Iris, communal land for women and children of color founded in Arkansas in 1977, described her goals for the education of children of color and children from biracial families: "We teach our children here what schools could never teach them and what schools would never teach them. . . . We teach them all of the things that have to do with living besides arithmetic, although we do teach them these things." One of the focuses at Arco Iris was training young women of color to be strong and proud warriors. "I feel that because our womyn children are being brought up in this environment," she wrote, "they could handle any young warrior that may grow up here easily, with one hand tied behind their back."[53]

Lesbian feminist mothers of color living on the land during the high days of lesbian nationalism often felt alienated from white lesbian feminists and some of them established their own communal experiments. The experiences of Juana María Paz, a Puerto Rican lesbian mother then working as a welfare-rights advocate for poor women in Los Angeles, illustrate the racial tensions. In 1977, Paz read an ad in *Sister* about women's land called Nourishing Space. When she moved there Paz felt alienated by the white women, who told her of some land reserved for women of color and suggested that she might be more interested in living there than on their land. "The rest of the womyn couldn't live there because they were white. They let me know that they felt real bad about that, excluded and hurt and oppressed by the unsisterly behavior." Paz subsequently helped to found La Luz, a communal space in Southern Oregon, intended as land for women of color, but soon after its inception, La Luz began to disintegrate in a tangle of personality conflicts and power struggles. Paz felt betrayed but strengthened as she realized that she would have to continue on at La Luz with her daughter, despite breakdowns in communication between herself and the other women. In her words, "Allright, I hear it. It is my dream and I will live here and create it. Mary Ann is my daughter and I will feed her when she is hungry, not wait for lovers and warriors to save me." Eventually, she and her daughter fled La Luz amid an argument with a group of Jewish lesbian feminists, who arrived with the belief that as Jewish women they should be considered women of color. Paz eventually left Oregon and settled with her daughter at Arco Iris in Arkansas. The lessons she learned about the importance of women not fighting each other when they could be working together stayed with her: "I hope that the womyn who read this and then settle on land will avoid some of the mistakes . . . [such as] competing with each other, especially the womyn of color and the Jewish womyn, who by rights should be powerful allies and not adversaries."[54]

Lesbian feminist households with children reflected the values of lesbian feminist culture, but they also had to deal with the realities and pressures of an outside world hostile to these values—a world from which they could never completely remove themselves, in spite of nationalist and separatist aspirations. These families also reflected differences and unresolved tensions within lesbian feminist communities around issues of race, questions about monogamy and nuclear relationships, and how to best organize childrearing labor. In raising children to be strong feminists, lesbian mothers consciously attempted to remove them from mainstream heteronormative, patriarchal values. While the children of lesbian feminists took these lessons to heart, they also had to negotiate the distance between the values of the larger society and those of their radical families.

The Experiences of Children in Lesbian Feminist Households: A Generation of Bridge Workers

As the children of lesbian mothers and gay fathers had in previous eras, the children of lesbian feminist families often acted as mediators between their families and a larger society that saw their homes as deviant. Unlike in previous eras, however, the children of lesbian feminist families in the 1970s negotiated the distance between radically open lesbian families and a dominant heterosexual society. Whereas in earlier decades, children of lesbian mothers had moved between their families and mainstream heterosexual society tacitly, the children of lesbian households in the 1970s were much more visible because their families demanded the right to openly exist. These children were bicultural in that they belonged to a vocal oppositional minority culture but also had to operate within the dominant culture that questioned the viability of their families. These children grew up in lesbian households that were more assertive than those of earlier decades, but compared to children of the later lesbian and gay baby boom, they still found their home and family lives to be very separate from mainstream society.

Children who attended public schools in rural, often conservative areas were often on the frontlines of cultural change, negotiating the unmitigated homophobia they encountered at school or elsewhere and the radical lesbian feminist principles they learned at home. Many of them had been uprooted from a more anonymous urban environment into a rural one where all eyes were on their families. For some children, these conflicts proved stressful. Adrian Hood and her mother, Alix Dobkin, moved from New York City to Schoharie, New York, when Adrian was almost five. Alix and her partner, Liza, were out lesbians, and Adrian remembers that older children called her "lezzie" while other children teased her on the school bus, saying that her mother and Liza "looked like boys." Eventually Adrian returned to Manhattan to live with her father.[55]

Similarly, an eleven-year-old child growing up in the rural area around the Northern California town of Willits in 1977 later described the tenuous acceptance and fear that characterized the school experience of many children living on lesbian land: "When I first moved to the land I was very scared. The next day Sage enrolled me in school. That year was fine. . . . The next year wasn't as good as the first." Her explanation of what happened that second year reflects the lack of safety these children often felt in their relationships with their peers: "I had made friends with Chris, who was in the 6th grade. . . . I told her about Sage and the other women I live with and that they were lesbians. She promised that she would not tell a soul. And she didn't until one day we got into a fight. Then she told her friend and it got around school." She went on to describe her mother's efforts to mitigate the stigma the child was suffering at school: "It was very bad until Sage told my teacher, who is a man, that she wanted me to have a woman at school to talk to. Now I see Mrs. Norman, the school nurse. She is a big help to me. Now it is not so bad. Maybe they will get bored and stop."[56]

What was true for women and children transplanted from urban areas to rural communes was also true for individual lesbian feminist families living in more rural, conservative areas. A self-identified radical feminist lesbian mother, speaking anonymously in 1983, described her daughter's decisions to be open or not about their home life in the public schools of a "small Southern town" in the 1970s as "extremely tricky."[57] Children of lesbian households also had to mediate between hostile, and often homophobic, local authorities and their families. Kate Alfaro, who lived with her mother in Searsburg, in rural upstate New York, remembers the police coming to her house after she wrecked her car in 1986. Alfaro told her mother and her mother's lover to stay in bed because she was terrified of the reaction of the small-town police to her mother's lesbianism. Alfaro, who felt isolated in the rural community, remembers finding solace in relationships with teenagers from heterosexual counterculture families who did not care that her mother was a lesbian and who also felt like misfits in the rural, conservative setting.[58]

Although children of urban lesbian households often enjoyed larger support networks that might include other children growing up in lesbian families, they nonetheless faced similar struggles as did those growing up in rural areas. Melanie, a six-year-old growing up in the lesbian feminist community in Boston, described how her friend in public school had reacted negatively to her openness about lesbianism: "She said 'who do you think you're going to have a crush with when you grow up,' I said, 'some woman,' and she said, 'you're gonna be gay, you're gonna be gay, and she starts teasing me." Melanie thought the girls made too much out of what was "no big deal."[59] Bonnie, who lived with her mother in Baltimore, was upset by local children teasing her by calling her mother a "lezzie." "Lesbian is O.K.," she told her mother, "but I don't like Lezzie."[60] Like Melanie, she felt that there was nothing wrong with her mother being a lesbian, but the other children's condemnation still hurt her. After her mother reassured her that she felt no pain as a result of this social prejudice, Bonnie learned to say "so what" when other children in her neighborhood commented on her mother's lesbianism.

Children of lesbian households often used the decision to open up to peers about their families as a litmus test for who they could really trust. Celeste Cole recalled that by the time she was in fourth grade, "it was a very conscious choice to tell someone" about her mother's lesbianism, which she thought of as a "big secret." She remembered that she would use it to see if she could truly trust those who were her best friends. Kay, who grew up in a lesbian feminist household in Ithaca, New York, maintained a "don't ask, don't tell" policy except with other friends who also had lesbian mothers. Some children, such as Carolyn Selene, learned that they should lie when questioned by their peers about their mothers because they had already lost friends to whom they had told the truth.[61]

In addition to prejudice about their mothers being lesbians, children in lesbian-headed households of the 1970s often had to confront classism from others. Many lesbian feminist mothers lived with their children on a subsistence income, in part because they were often single mothers responsible for all parenting tasks, limiting the available time for securing income for food and housing. In addition, some lesbian mothers came from traditional heterosexual marriages in which their ex-husbands had frowned on them working outside the home. With little experience in the workforce they had to train themselves in employable skills. One lesbian mother from San Jose, California, who had left her abusive ex-husband described working to support her two daughters and "barely making ends meet."[62]

In addition to the economic and labor-intensive burdens of motherhood, many lesbian feminists who had come from the middle class were "downwardly mobile" as a result of actively repudiating achievement in the capitalist workplace in favor of dedicating themselves to political activism. Though the demands of single parenthood made it difficult for some lesbian mothers to find time for political work, they remained a part of lesbian communities that were strongly anticapitalist and discouraged career-oriented work.

Some lesbian mothers utilized the welfare system to survive. They studied welfare regulations and helped others to do the same in order to negotiate the federal food stamp and Aid to Families with Dependent Children programs.[63] When asked about the impact of her lesbianism on her children, one woman linked her child's consciousness of being part of the lesbian community to a working-class resistance consciousness: "Being on welfare," she stated, "lets us both know how 'society' (male institutions) feels about us anyway—so—no big deal."[64] However, for the children of lesbian feminist mothers, this class-consciousness was sometimes gained through pain, living in a society that looked down upon them both for their lesbian feminist culture and for their poverty. Kate Alfaro remembers that in middle school, she was ashamed of her family being on welfare and of her participation in free breakfast and lunch programs. Her mother, Mary White, remembered that as a high school student Alfaro hated having to use food stamps in grocery stores where her middle-class classmates worked.[65]

Like other families within politically radical and counterculture communities during these years, such as the antiwar movement and the black nationalist movement, lesbian feminist families were resistance families. In other words, they consciously stood in defiance of the American state and passed on to their children principles of both resistance to dominant culture and reserve in the face of it. Maxine Wolfe remembers raising her daughters in Brooklyn and telling them to exercise caution about talking to straight people about lesbianism; she impressed on the two girls that letting the larger world in on what were mundane realities in their home could have dire consequences.[66] Because of social and legal disapproval of lesbianism and the publicity surrounding custody cases, lesbian feminist mothers were often afraid of having their children taken away from them. For example, a woman in a lesbian mothers group explained, "its difficult being out to them because then you have to instill in them the cautiousness, that fear. Now they have to think about how their friends are going to react before they let them know."[67] Kay remembered as a child knowing that she could not talk about her mother being a lesbian because they were on welfare and the police could take her away from her mother if anyone found out. A cartoon published in 1980 in the newsletter of the Atlanta Lesbian Feminist Alliance expressed the tension inherent in this dynamic of resistance and reserve for children of lesbian feminist families. It featured a worried-looking young boy looking up at his mother and asking, "but Mom, if there's nothing wrong with your being a lesbian, why can't I tell my friends?"[68]

These fears were not without reason. Children who were raised in radical lesbian feminist communities might also be subject, along with their mothers, to hate-crime violence. Nicole Joos wrote at age ten about Izbushka, a house built on lesbian land in upstate New York near Schenectady as a refuge after "two boys, with the help of their mother's boyfriend, vandalized the lean-to" that had been the main dwelling on their land for seven years.[69] Lesbian feminist mothers, as part of counterculture communities, could also be subject to increased scrutiny from juvenile authorities. In 1977, for example, a group of lesbians and two children who lived in a rural women's collective picked up two female hitchhikers. The children "were playing dress-up," and the little boy unselfconsciously donned a woman's dress. The women, who were "obviously lesbians and not the children's biological mothers," also mentioned marijuana. The hitchhikers reported the women to the juvenile authorities, who removed the children and placed them in foster homes. Although these children were eventually released back to the women when the biological mother returned from traveling out of state, the episode illustrates the dangers that mothers raising their children in lesbian feminist communities had to negotiate.[70]

Lesbian Separatism

Many lesbian feminists grew tired of battling straight and gay male attitudes and of devoting substantially more time and labor into the maintenance of feminist networks and institutions than did their straight female allies, whom, they argued, invariably put a significant amount of their focus on their relationships with men. Separatists asserted that lesbian feminists should minimize the energy that they gave to men and straight women, and they sought to create spaces where lesbians would not have to interact extensively with nonlesbians, including women-only communes, bookstores, cafes, and music concerts.[71]

Many of the principles women expressed in the development of lesbian separatism echoed the complaints of black civil rights workers in organizations such as the Student Non-Violent Coordinating Committee (SNCC), who argued for the importance of separatist black organizing. Lesbian separatists argued that meaningful political work was undermined by having to constantly address the needs of nonlesbians, such as gay men and heterosexual women, and that only separate political work would allow lesbians their full organizing potential.[72] Margaret Sloan-Hunter, founder of the National Black Feminist Organization, compared the empowering aspects of black separatism with the need for lesbian solidarity. Cathy Cade, a white activist in SNCC in the early 1960s, gained a new understanding of the need for a black separatist movement through her own experience with lesbian separatism. Jill Lippett, who had been active in New Left poverty programs in South Chicago, also developed a new understanding of black separatism when she became a lesbian separatist.[73] Many lesbian feminists saw separatism much in the same way that black separatists did: as a way of regrouping and gathering internal energy within a disenfranchised community without the drain of translating for those outside of the community and responding to their needs and concerns.

The presence of lesbian mothers with boy children, however, complicated lesbian separatism. Driven by the needs of these mothers, lesbian feminist communities tried to negotiate what a commitment to women-centered, nonpatriarchal space required and how the needs of lesbian mothers of sons could be met while still preserving those commitments. Lesbian separatism, a complex, multifaceted ideology, included a range of attitudes toward boy children.[74] Many lesbian separatists believed that the creation of lesbian-only spaces necessitated the exclusion of boy children of any age, in addition to adult men and straight women. The most radical of separatists felt that the effort lesbian mothers put into raising male children was misplaced, for these boys would inevitably grow up to be incorporated into the patriarchy as oppressors of women. A Seattle group, the Lesbian Separatist Group, wrote in 1973, "it is a waste of time and energy for at least white lesbians to raise male children." A year later, the group modified their position to include lesbians of color in this assessment, having decided that although communities of color were often under threat of genocide from white supremacy, it was racist to exclude lesbian mothers of color from their analysis.[75] One woman from St. Louis, a mother of three sons, wrote that she had read articles by separatists encouraging women with male children to give the boys to their fathers to raise, since there was no place for them in a separatist community.[76] The Gorgons of Seattle wrote in 1977 that many lesbians had been humiliated, beaten down, and raped by their brothers in their own families, and that "lesbians who keep sons around in the lesbian community are keeping brothers around."[77] For some lesbian separatists boy children were little men, capable of the same violence and patriarchal arrogance as grown ones.

In contrast, other lesbian separatists did not advocate any particular position on the raising of male children, but they did want to designate some women-only spaces that could be free of all men, including male children. Alix Dobkin, a popular lesbian feminist musician, who in 1971 recorded the first lesbian music album, *Lavender Jane Loves Women*, asked mothers who came to her women-only concerts to leave their sons at home. Dobkin remembered later, "I felt that women-only meant females only, of any age, and I still do, actually." However, she also saw the establishment and maintenance of women-only space as very different from the behavior of separatists who were outspokenly antagonistic toward boy children in lesbian spaces. "I was never mean to little boys," Dobkin recalled. "Some separatists were very mean to them, and I hated that." Dobkin felt that the sons of lesbians might actually learn an antipatriarchal respect for women's space by accepting the fact that there were some places that were not for them.[78]

As divisive as the issue of separatism could be within lesbian feminist communities, the premium placed on consensus and an appreciation for the needs of various groups of women often led to compromise on the issue of male children in lesbian feminist spaces. For example, childcare for boy children was organized at lesbian feminist events, which facilitated the preservation of women-only space. A 1978 political rally in Seattle advertised that both "girl-care" and "girl & boy-care" would be available, attempting to preserve the option of female-only space for the young daughters of the lesbian mothers present at the rally.[79] A meeting on "Separatism and Child Care—Our Sons in Our Community," held in Los Angeles in 1977, reflected the connection between separatist concerns about boy children and the broader issue of childcare in lesbian feminist communities.[80]

At a concert given by Alix Dobkin at the Seattle Women's Coffee Coven in April 1977, the event organizers offered childcare to mediate Dobkin's request for a women-only space and the desire of lesbian mothers with children to attend her women-only concerts. The policy of having childcare for both female and male children and making the concert an adult-only space generated protests from lesbian feminist groups on both sides of the issue. The Gorgons, a Seattle separatist group, protested the WCC's decision to bar female children from the event, saying that it was ageist and denied the girls the chance to be a part of a women-only space. At least two girls who had been barred from the concert also protested, and they were eventually admitted with the blessings of everyone present. One lesbian mother of a male child, who noted that she supported Dobkin's right to limit her concerts to a female audience, later celebrated the WCC's attempt to understand the difficulties faced by lesbian mothers of sons.[81] When the Lesbian Feminist Center in Chicago closed in 1978, they cited the controversy over their policy of banning male children from the center and its bookstore as one of the contentious issues for which the Chicago lesbian feminist community had attacked the center.[82]

Some groups developed policies that set an age limit for boys' admissibility to lesbian communal space. The Atlanta Lesbian Feminist Alliance (ALFA) had an informal policy from 1974 until 1982 that only male children under twelve years of age be allowed in the ALFA house. In 1982, the teenage son of an ALFA member came into the house, which disturbed some members present, and as a result of the ensuing discussion, the group formally confirmed the earlier policy, with the exception that emergency situations would be left to the discretion of the mother of the male child. The point of the rule and the membership discussion of the issue was to "provide a woman-only space while at the same time not preventing women with male children from coming to the house." One of the ALFA women who had originally protested the male presence explained that she had lived with a lesbian mother with a son for a year and a half and had endured the "ideas, the manners, the abusive and selfish attitudes toward women he brought home from school."[83] The mother of a teenage daughter herself, this woman complained that she already had to deal with the presence of her daughter's boyfriend in her own home and would prefer no men or boys of any age in the ALFA house, but she felt bound by the majority decision allowing boys under twelve years of age.

Many lesbian mothers saw these "no boy children" policies as politically regressive. One lesbian mother of an eight-year-old son and a five-year-old daughter wrote, "If you reject me because I happened to have a male child (and by totally rejecting him, you are rejecting me), then you are as oppressive to me as is the society who oppresses and denies me support because I am a single woman with children."[84] A member of Dykes and Tykes commented that disapproval toward lesbian mothers from the larger lesbian community "comes down especially heavy when you're the mother of a son. Because there is a tremendous feeling among a large segment of our community . . . that boys have no place in our community."[85] In this woman's opinion, these attitudes were tantamount to fascism. A woman from St. Louis, who signed her letter to a lesbian publication "mother of a male child," wrote angrily, "is there a place where one can trade male children in for acceptable female ones? You are talking about human beings, not Irish setters versus Collies."[86] When Judie Ghidinelli brought her infant son, Guthrie, to a Diana Press meeting in the early 1970s and was told that he was not welcome there, she responded by telling the women present that "they had problems if they were worried about a penis the size of a cashew."[87] These issues also came up for lesbian feminist mothers as their sons grew older. Bluebird, a lesbian mother of a son in Atlanta who was a member of ALFA, wrote that she understood "the usefulness of separatism as a strengthening process," but that it made her "angry when I feel as if my sons are rejected simply just because they are male." She and others also believed that lesbian mothers of male children had "an opportunity to raise sons to be caring individuals and should be honored by the community for trying."[88] Lesbian mothers with sons felt that community resentment toward their children was unjust and called for a reevaluation of community commitment to lesbian mothers with sons based on the goal of supporting all lesbians equally.

A major controversy over male children emerged at women's music festivals, which were an important component of national lesbian feminist networks. Part of the larger development of the women's music industry, the groups that played annually at these festivals recorded their music on women-run labels such as Olivia Records and played a nationwide circuit of women's bookstores and coffeehouses. The largest and longest- running of these festivals, the Michigan Womyn's Music Festival, has been held annually in August since 1976, and reactions to the festival's policies about boy children provide a measure of evolving lesbian politics over the decades.

The first Michigan Womyn's Music Festival, organized by a group of five women called the We Want the Music Collective, took place in August 1976 on land near Mt. Pleasant, Michigan, where 2,000 women camped for several days of concerts.[89] For the next five years the festival took place near Hesperia, Michigan. The organizers then bought land nearby to provide a permanent home for this event, which was still attended by approximately 4,000 women and children annually in the early 2000s.[90]

As space dedicated to women's strength and spirit, the Michigan festival has always celebrated the power of the mother-daughter bond and affirmed the lesbian feminist/nationalist commitment to raising strong daughters

Childcare space for girls, Michigan Womyn's Music Festival, 1983. © 2013 JEB (Joan E. Biren).

within a vision of a matriarchal women's community. By 1979, the festival billed itself proudly as "a gathering of mothers & daughters" for "womyn of all ages." Childcare was always provided, although by some accounts it was minimal in the early years, and daughters of lesbian mothers were invited to be part of the celebration of women at the festival.[91] Adrian Hood "grew up at Michigan," attending from age ten to twenty-five, and she felt that the experience of being a part of a vibrant community of strong women at the festival was central to her identity. "I was around and being taught by these incredible women. . . . The community has been a huge blessing to me." Although Hood remembered a "handful" of other daughters of lesbians at Michigan, she recalled that in the early years there were never many children.[92]

Because the Michigan festival defined itself as a woman-only space, the presence of male children provoked controversy. Every year the organizers at the festival provided some childcare for both girls and boys, but the policy concerning male children changed over time. At the first festival, the policy was informal, leaving to the discretion of lesbian mothers whether to bring

Boys' camp, Michigan Womyn's Music Festival, 1983. © 2013 JEB (Joan E. Biren).

male children. The second festival left it up to each campsite to allow or disallow the presence of male children over the age of six. These policies aimed to let women attending the festival control their own environment while balancing the needs of mothers of sons with attendees wanting a women-only space. However, some women complained about the possibility of conflict when boy children wandered into spaces where they were not welcome.

By the third festival in 1978, a more defined policy required mothers with sons over the age of six to leave them at a childcare site adjacent to the festival. The fifth festival had relocated the site for male children to a National Forest campsite thirteen miles away. Supportive male volunteers from the Michigan community took charge of childcare, and shuttles took mothers of sons from the campsite to the festival grounds. When the seventh festival relocated to a new location, a male childcare area "for sons under 12" moved adjacent to the festival grounds. Since 1983 the space for male children has been known as Brother Son Boys Camp.[93] Currently, festival policy asks that all mothers with sons between four and twelve years of age leave them at Brother Son for the duration of the festival.

The Michigan festival policies on the presence of boy children proved to be very controversial in lesbian feminist communities. As one group of lesbian feminists from New Orleans wrote in 1978, "We feel it is important for all of our children to be exposed to womyn's culture as much as possible." They strongly opposed the festival organizers' decision to exclude male children over age six and argued that lesbian feminist political goals demanded more attention to the inclusion of the sons of lesbian mothers: "If they do not experience acceptance in our cultural events and have the opportunity to learn with us the joys of a matriarchal experience, then we, in effect, are pushing them toward a reactionary position, causing them to seek their acceptance in the patriarchy."[94] A woman from Bloomington, Indiana, complained that the policies would leave lesbian mothers with sons feeling excluded from the event.[95] Susan Wolfe wrote in the early 1980s that, "forced to choose between my summer time with Jeffrey and attending the Michigan Women's Music Festival, I preserved my sisters' space by staying home." To Wolfe, a Jewish lesbian mother, it was unthinkable that she would put her son in an encampment for boys. "I refused to place my son in a camp because of his undesirability to lesbian separatists," she wrote, claiming that "the festivals organizers' ignorance of the Jewish experience with institutionalized camps was disappointingly apparent."[96] Other lesbian feminists supported the actions of the festival organizers, agreeing with them that the importance of women-only space, a rare possibility in everyday life, justified the policy concerning male children.

Separatism and the desire for women-only space created tensions within rural lesbian communes as well. Lesbian feminist communes varied in their ways of dealing with the presence of sons of lesbian mothers. At Arf, the New Mexico anarchist lesbian feminist commune with a strong commitment to local process, members did not define themselves as separatists and allowed boy children on the land at all times. Other women's communities worked through the question of boys on a more personal level, even resolving it on a case-by-case basis. Adobe, caretaker of Adobeland in Arizona, said, "there have been some boy kids here. I had trouble with some of these kids. Others I loved. They're kids. . . . I can't say I don't like male children. It depends a lot on the conditioning you've had."[97] Maria, of Arco Iris, explained in 1985 that "if a male child grew here and learned our ways and decides that he wants to stay here with us, at that time it would be taken before the women's counsel and decided upon." Arco Iris welcomed all women and children of color and conceived of itself as a "survival space."[98]

Other women's land groups had more restrictive policies on male children. Dragonwomon Outpost in southern Missouri, a lesbian feminist commune, switched from a "boy children–allowed" policy to a "no biological men on the land" policy as the result of a transfer of power from one group of lesbian feminists to another.[99] Hannah, a woman from Golden, women's land in southern Oregon, said in a 1982 interview that as a separatist at Golden in 1980 and 1981, she had been comfortable with one boy on the land, but when a woman moved in next door with a son, the two boys were too much male presence for her.[100] Women on Land, who lived on eighty acres in northwest Arkansas, said simply, "we will live only with dykes. We wish to relate to female children only—male children would be too sexist an influence on a developing women's environment."[101] A group of women hoping to form a land trust in 1977 advertised themselves as "lesbians in the eastern part of the country wanting to be living in lesbian-only space where no men, boy children, or straight women could ever come or visit."[102]

Despite these policies, a sanction ran deep in lesbian feminist communities against rejecting a mother with a child of either gender. Joyce Cheney said of Redbird in Burlington, Vermont, that they were challenged by some women over their "arrangement of being a lesbian separatist collective, and raising two boy children. We did have inconsistencies!"[103] Similarly, Cynthia McCabe remembers a childhood story told by her mother about a woman who showed up at Colchester House in 1974 with a male child. An intense long night of discussion ensued, in which collective members talked earnestly to the woman about giving the boy up to his father. In the end, after much debate, the woman came to the decision that she could not give the child up, because she needed him with her even if he was a male child. She then asked to stay at the commune anyway, and both she and her son ended up living there. Although separatism was a powerful and important part of lesbian feminism, so were consensus process and a disinclination to do harm to a woman who needed help. Members of a lesbian feminist collective met in Richmond, Virginia, and resolved to "make more of a commitment to provide childcare at dances and other LF events" to ensure that lesbian mothers would not feel excluded.[104]

Reclaiming Reproduction: Imagining Parthenogenesis and Creating Insemination Networks

The presence of lesbian mothers with children from previous heterosexual relationships in lesbian feminist communities belied the heterosexist cultural assumption that lesbianism and motherhood were antithetical concepts. As lesbian mothers fought custody cases, organized lesbian mothers groups, and carved out space in lesbian feminist communities for their families, they gave other lesbians a model for motherhood. By the mid-1970s, women in lesbian feminist communities were discussing ways to have children without men. This lesbian reclamation of reproduction sometimes took the form of interest in parthenogenesis, a process of asexual reproduction in some reptile and avian species that produces female offspring. By the late 1970s, however, lesbian feminists were also organizing underground donor insemination networks that would lead to a boom in lesbian parenting by the 1980s.

For some lesbian feminists, the ideal condition of motherhood was one in which daughters and mothers related to each other free of male presence. This vision, which came directly from lesbian nationalism, was one in which tribes of mothers and daughters would populate the new matriarchal lesbian nation. Many lesbian feminists believed that this future mother-daughter society had a precursor in ancient Amazonian culture. Jill Johnston, writing on lesbian motherhood, described how the Amazons had engaged in an annual reproductive ritual with a neighboring tribe of men to ensure that the next generation of Amazon women would be born: "Whatever girl children were born became Amazons and the boys were sent to the Gargarensians who because they had no means of ascertaining their paternity distributed them by lots among their huts. Modern Amazons are lesbians with or without their children."[105] For Johnston, the Amazonian precedent spoke clearly of the power of the mother-daughter bond and its ability to transform the patriarchy of the modern world.

Other lesbian feminist writers also invoked this vision of a matriarchal world of mothers and daughters. Sally Gearhart, in her lesbian feminist science fiction utopian novel *The Wanderground* (1979), created a matriarchal female society, the Hill Women, who had escaped the cities. Away from the dislocation from the land and the disconnect from spirit brought about by male violence, the Hill Women had returned to a deeper, clearer relationship with the earth and manifested psychic powers naturally available to women. One of these powers was the ability to impregnate themselves through spiritual connection with the energies of the earth in a sacred space, the Deep Cella. Shaped like a conch shell, the Deep Cella was a passage into the earth where Hill Women who had decided to engage in an "implantment" voyage descend to be impregnated in energetic dialogue with the earth.[106]

These lesbian feminist visions of mother-daughter reproduction had a corollary in an ongoing interest in parthenogenesis in lesbian feminist culture. Parthenogenesis is the process whereby a female egg is induced to double its chromosomes without the introduction of a male gamete. Parthenogenesis is closely related to gynogenesis, which also results in an egg splitting without introduction of new genetic material, but the sperm is required to irritate the egg, which initiates the process. The result of both parthenogenesis and gynogenesis is an XX chromosome each time, since the egg is reproducing only from its own haploid genetic material. Parthenogenesis occurs naturally in some species, including honey bees, lizards, and turkeys. For lesbian feminists, parthenogenesis, or partheno, as it came to be known, offered the hope of giving birth to female children without the presence of male sperm or the possibility of becoming pregnant with a boy child. Despite evidence that it did not work in human populations, parthenogenesis continued to interest lesbian feminist separatists throughout the 1970s as a means of imagining a female matriarchy.

Calls for parthenogenesis recurred in lesbian feminist writing of the 1970s. In her classic essay, "Lesbians in Revolt," Charlotte Bunch suggested that lesbian feminists could eventually use science to create a mother-daughter society without male involvement. "The Lesbian threatens the ideology of male supremacy," Bunch wrote, "by destroying the lie about female inferiority, weakness, passivity, and by denying women's 'innate' need for men (even for pro-creation if the science of cloning is developed)."[107] In 1974, Laurel Galana's "Radical Reproduction: X Without Y," advised women who wanted to sex-select for daughters that selective alternative insemination, gynogenesis, parthenogenesis, and cloning could enable them to have "daughters entirely without recourse to men or their sperm." Galana noted that parthenogenesis was the most productive of all these processes for lesbian feminists because it eliminated the need for sperm, and she argued that it was probable that parthenogenesis occurred naturally in a small percentage of the population. Her technical and very detailed scientific discussion encouraged lesbian feminists to learn about the developments in reproductive technologies in the hopes that parthenogenesis could lead to consistent mother-daughter reproductive cycles, although her article noted that male scientists were unlikely to support this research because of its implications for female-only reproduction.[108]

Interest in parthenogenesis and other ways of ensuring female offspring was widespread in lesbian feminist communities. Liza C. May Chan, a woman from New York, posted a letter in the March 1976 issue of *Lesbian Connection* citing Galana's article and expressing interest in parthenogenesis.[109] Writing a year later, in a letter addressed "Dear Amazon Sisters," she reported having received an "absolutely overwhelming response" from other lesbian feminists who had sent her encouraging words and their own collections of clippings and research findings on parthenogenesis. Chan expressed optimism that women were indeed "superior in this respect—that we can have (female) off-spring by ourselves without the unwelcome interference from men and their sperms."[110] Suzi Kehler, a lesbian feminist from Cheyenne, Wyoming, in arguing for lesbian separatism and against the necessity of men to society, cited parthenogenesis as evidence that reproduction is possible in an all-female society: "Reproduction? There is such a thing as parthenogenesis—natural and induced. One of the beauties of parthenogenesis is that inevitably the offspring is female."[111] A meeting of local lesbian feminists and feminists to talk about matriarchal possibilities in Richmond, Virginia, included discussion of "what role technology, cloning, and parthenogenesis should play in our future."[112] Parthenogenesis was part of the utopian vision of radical lesbian feminism, a vision that foresaw an Amazon nation of mothers and daughters that would operate according to feminist principles of anticapitalist egalitarianism.

The desire to create a parthenogenic birth process was also linked to lesbian feminist spiritual beliefs. At a workshop held at the fifth annual Michigan Womyn's Music Festival, many of the women who attended saw parthenogenesis as primarily a matter of psychic and spiritual energy work—part of their continuing commitments to women's space and spirituality. One woman wrote later that, "since the Festival I have been working to prepare a space where my daughter can be embodied and born. A rural [lesbian] community is our dream."[113] This woman was part of a lesbian feminist spiritual circle that had been helping her envision and make psychic contact with her intended daughter's spirit. In letters they received after the festival, the workshop coordinators were encouraged in their work by women who had been contemplating the feasibility of parthenogenesis. Some women were strengthened in their pursuit of mother-daughter reproduction by the precedent of ancient matriarchal societies. One letter, "from a well-known women's health clinic," hypothesized that the information on how to control parthenogenesis may have been lost with goddess worshipping societies. She continued, "I don't know if anyone is into hypnosis for the purpose of finding out about 'past' incarnations, but we might be able to find lost knowledge through other incarnations of ourselves."[114] One of the organizers of the workshop spoke of the importance of lesbian feminist community in her own preparations for parthenogenesis: "I go to Michigan for cleansing, sharing rejoicing, and glimpsing the vision of amazonation which still seems just beyond our reach. There I hear wondrous and magic tales to support my dreams of one day creating life through a baby daughter."[115] These lesbian feminists saw taking control of their bodies through parthenogenic reproduction as part of the claiming of lesbian feminist space.[116]

Parthenogenesis did not materialize, but the desire and efforts to take control of the process of reproduction did lead lesbian communities to a technology that would have a profound effect on LGBT family history, the history of the LGBT civil rights movement, and the history of the family in the United States. Influenced by the women's self-health movement, lesbian feminists around the country began to explore the possibility of having children through donor insemination. This interest grew out of broader feminist commitments to women's control over their bodies and reproductive capabilities, evidenced by the women's health movement and publications such as Our Bodies, Ourselves.

By the mid-1970s grassroots insemination networks formed in Boston; New York City; Burlington, Vermont; and Oakland, California. Cathy Cade, one of the women who founded the nation's first lesbian donor insemination network, had already investigated parthenogenesis and decided that the science was too remote. In the mid 1970s, Cade became part of an informal group of friends and fellow lesbian feminist activists in the San Francisco Bay Area who wanted to become pregnant and raise children. They organized and exchanged ideas, information, and resources about donor insemination, and around 1974, the first couple succeeded in getting pregnant through a donor arrangement with a brother of one of the women. The two women made this choice out of a desire to include the brother in their new family. Cade remembered that she and her friends had also heard of groups of lesbians doing the same thing in the New York and Boston areas. The Boston networks would later lead to the insemination programs at the Fenway Community Health Center, one of the first medical clinics in the United States to openly assist lesbians with insemination. In 1975, "artificial insemination" was one of the workshops, along with others on dyke separatism and home/ auto repair, held at a "lesbian-oriented" conference in Philadelphia.[117]

When Cade herself became pregnant after eight months of trying, she did so with an anonymous sperm donor who was a volunteer from a group of gay men in the San Francisco Bay Area who helped lesbians to conceive and who also provided childcare for the children of lesbian mothers out of a political commitment to childrearing.[118] Cade had opted for an anonymous donor arrangement because she understood the danger lesbian mothers faced of losing custody of their children to any man who could claim biological paternity. When her son, Carl, was born, Cade changed her mind and decided she wanted to give him the option of contacting his donor. She was unable to find him again, however.[119]

In 1979, Cathy Cade and seven or eight other women who had all conceived through donor insemination created an informal mothers group in the San

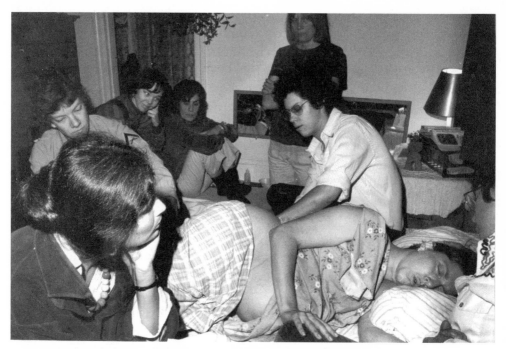

Cathy Cade in labor with friends, Oakland, California, 1978. Photograph by André. Courtesy of the Bancroft Library, University of California, Berkeley.

Francisco Bay Area. As lesbians who had openly taken control of their own process of reproduction, they were not embroiled in the issues central to the lesbian mother advocacy groups of the 1970s. They rarely spoke about the fear of custody battles or trepidation about coming out to one's children. Most of these women were already veteran lesbian feminists when they made the choice to become mothers. Nonetheless, many of their conflicts with the larger lesbian community resembled those of mothers who came out of heterosexual relationships. Both groups worked to change negative attitudes toward male children, for instance. At the first West Coast Women's Music Festival in 1980, Cade's lesbian mothers group addressed the audience and asked them for "support in raising our boys, saying we have the power to raise them with our values."[120]

By the late 1970s, the discussion of donor insemination spread within lesbian communities. In 1977, Sioux Sawyer wrote a letter to *Lesbian Tide*, a Los Angeles publication, asking about donor insemination and methods for ensuring female children. She remembered "seeing information about 3 years ago concerning diet, douches, and monthly timing," and said that she knew "several lesbians contemplating motherhood who could use this information."[121] In 1979, the Moonstorm lesbian feminist collective of St. Louis, Missouri, published an issue of their newsletter on lesbian motherhood that included instructions on how to self-inseminate. Illustrating ongoing separatist concerns they reminded readers that "while many different theories exist on procedures to determine the sex of the child, these are only theories! . . . If you simply must have a daughter, then artificial or self insemination might not be for you."[122] An article on self-insemination written by a woman in Connecticut appeared in *Lesbian Connection* in 1979 and stated that "in spite of what the medical profession wants us to think, there is nothing difficult or complicated about getting pregnant by artificial insemination."[123] The year after Cathy Cade and her friends had formed their group in 1979, a whole new support group of mothers who had become pregnant through donor insemination formed in the San Francisco Bay Area. These radical experiments in reproductive empowerment formed the roots of the lesbian and gay baby boom of the 1980s.[124]

The lesbian families that emerged in the historical context of lesbian feminist nationalism were a critical part of this larger movement. Through analysis of the categories of "mother" and "lesbian mother," lesbian feminist communities processed some of their most controversial political programs, such as separatism and the lesbian nationalist desire to found an Amazonian state and begin anew outside of patriarchy. Culturally, lesbian communities shifted toward a broader acceptance of lesbian reproduction in the years between 1970 and 1985, and lesbian feminist families of the 1970s were a crucial part of that change.

The history of lesbian feminist mothers and their children also illustrates ways in which lesbian feminist nationalism survived the 1970s. Just as those who have declared black nationalism dead ignored its far-reaching impact on American culture, so too the apparent decline of lesbian feminist nationalist ideals masks its lasting impact on women's culture. Aside from bookstores, rape crisis centers, and schools founded by lesbian feminists, the impact of lesbian feminism can be found in the resistance culture in which lesbian mothers educated their children and passed on their ideals to a new generation. Lesbian feminist families with children were themselves part of a new chapter in American family history. Like earlier "red-diaper babies" of the old Left, children from white, heterosexual counterculture families, or radical families of color during the 1960s and 1970s, lesbian feminist families were resistance families. They made contingency plans for going underground to escape the law; they developed their own schools based on radical social principles; and they developed separatist principles based on a mistrust of the American government. Lesbian feminist mothers tried to raise their daughters to be strong and to arm them with knowledge of social and cultural misogyny. They tried to raise their sons to be nonsexist men. They founded schools and raised children in communal families committed to an egalitarian concept of motherhood, always under the fear of state removal of their children. By defying the opposition between lesbian and mother, these families paved the way for the gay and lesbian parents of the 1990s and helped to keep lesbian feminist ideals alive into the next generation.

CHAPTER SEVEN

She Does Not Draw Distinctions Based on Blood or Law

The Lesbian/Gay-by Boom, 1980–2003

The 1980s and 1990s witnessed immense change for lesbian and gay parents in the United States. Over the course of these two decades, lesbian parenting through donor insemination grew beyond earlier underground networks until, by the late 1980s, lesbians were getting pregnant and having children all across the country, not just in the large cities and university towns that had sustained the lesbian feminist communities of the 1970s. More gay men also began to have and raise children, through surrogacy, adoption, and co-parenting agreements. The emergence of large numbers of lesbian- and gay-headed families that did not involve a previous heterosexual relationship flourished in part because of the parental activism of the preceding decade. Lesbian mothers and gay fathers who fought for their custodial rights and gained visibility in the 1970s served as models of lesbian and gay parenthood for others by undermining the cultural perception that gay and lesbian lives were inherently childless.

Along with challenges faced by previous generations, lesbians and gay men who had children through donor insemination, surrogacy, or adoption also experienced new forms of social discrimination. Many sperm banks would not inseminate single women or those they knew to be lesbians, and state agencies opposed gay and lesbian foster parenting and adoption. In seeking prenatal care and in their encounters with adoptive and social services, lesbians and gay men experienced new manifestations of the social acrimony against non-heterosexual parenting that affected generations of families before them. The battle for legal recognition in the custody courts also continued; gay fathers and lesbian mothers with children from previous heterosexual relationships still struggled for their right to parent in these years, particularly in the Midwest and the South. However, a new kind of custody case also emerged, as gay and lesbian couples who had children together broke up and sued each other for custody. The outcome of many of these "co-parent" and "donor" custody cases, as they became known, highlighted the continuing difficulties created by the absence of legal recognition for lesbian and gay relationships and child-drearing arrangements. In response, legal activists developed a new strategy for two-parent lesbian and gay families known as second-parent adoption to make up for the absence of legal recognition at the federal level.

The organizational character of lesbian and gay parental activism also transformed during these years. Some lesbian mothers and gay fathers groups from the 1970s faded away. Others changed their scope to include transgender and bisexual parents and to address the needs of new kinds of LGBT families. These groups still tried to provide information and support for lesbians and gay men fighting custody battles but increasingly focused on issues important to prospective and new parents, such as insemination, adoption, co-parenting agreements and the law, newborn and infant care, and new parents feeling isolated from their community. As the children raised in gay and lesbian families of the liberation era matured, they too began to organize, and groups led by children of lesbian and gay parents became an important political force in LGBT family activism.

As more and more lesbians and gay men openly made the choice to become parents and the activism of LGBT families expanded, domestic partnership, same-sex marriage, and parental civil rights came to be a central focus of the modern LGBT freedom struggle. The political fight for domestic partnership flourished in the 1980s but gradually gave way to the struggle for same-sex marriage, though not without criticism from some activists at the heart of the movement. These changes were fueled by a new appreciation for the importance of gay and lesbian domestic civil rights that was derived in part from the AIDS crisis and the pain of partners who were not allowed to be a part of medical and legal decisions for partners suffering from HIV/AIDS. This increasing focus was also founded in the activism of lesbian mothers and gay fathers groups of the 1970s and 1980s. While in the 1970s and 1980s, lesbian mothers and gay fathers often found themselves arguing for inclusion of parental politics within their communities, by the end of the twentieth century, their cause had become central to mainstream LGBT activism.

The Increase in Donor Insemination

Over the course of the 1980s, increasing numbers of lesbians chose to have children through donor insemination. In the late 1970s, the Lesbian Rights Project of San Francisco received an average of three calls a month from lesbians interested in insemination. By 1984, the group received thirty-five such calls a month.[1] By 1989, directing attorney Roberta Achtenberg told the *New York Times* that those numbers had "quadrupled" and that when she held workshops on the legal aspects of donor insemination, often as many as 500 women attended. From 1982 to 1989 the Sperm Bank of Northern California in Oakland, California, saw a doubling of the number of self-identified lesbians who sought sperm for the purposes of insemination.[2] This increase in interest was not restricted to coastal metropolises such as Los Angeles, San Francisco, or New York. Nationwide, lesbians began to hear about and pursue the possibility of donor insemination. The work that lesbian mothers and gay fathers groups had done to repudiate the idea that same-sex orientation was incompatible with parenting and the sharing of information about parenting within lesbian feminist communities was having a widespread social impact. The Lesbian Mothers' National Defense Fund in Seattle began distributing an "Alternative Insemination" informational packet in 1981 and was soon receiving requests for information about donor insemination from across the country. Women sent letters from rural areas, small towns, and big cities in the states of New York, Massachusetts, Minneapolis, Minnesota, Washington, Wisconsin, Indiana, New Mexico, Michigan, California, Virginia, Pennsylvania, and Montana.[3]

In the early 1980s, many lesbians interested in donor insemination found it difficult to get information from formal institutions, and fertility doctors and sperm banks often denied them services. Most fertility clinics and studies understood donor insemination, or "artificial insemination," as it was most commonly called, as a medical procedure appropriate only for married heterosexual couples experiencing difficulty conceiving children.[4] In 1984, Donna Hitchens wrote that "some doctors and clinics will refuse to inseminate a single woman, especially if they know that the woman is a lesbian."[5] A woman from Houston, Texas, wrote in 1987 that she and her female partner had "met with opposition from the medical community in Houston" and had been told that donor insemination was only for married women.[6] Nancy Langer, the public information director for the Lambda Legal Defense and Education Fund wrote in the mid-1980s that even when infertility clinics would work with single women, they drew "the line at lesbians."[7] The authors of a handbook on home insemination intended for lesbians and gay men addressed the difficulty in finding doctors who would "agree to inseminate you if they know you are a lesbian."[8] An article in *Lesbian Tide* described a lesbian couple being told by several clinics that insemination was only available for "married (heterosexual) women."[9] The proposal for the Fenway Alternative Insemination Program noted in April 1983 that "in Boston and the surrounding area there are very few health practitioners who are willing to inseminate lesbians, and then only as a small portion of their practices."[10]

This bias against lesbians and unmarried women came in part from the belief that they would not make fit mothers.[11] Roberta Achtenberg recalled doctors expressing "medical ethical problems" with inseminating lesbians.[12] Dr. Sherwin Kaufman, the director of the Lenox Hill Hospital Infertility Clinic in New York City, said he had ethical reservations about assisting in children being born out of wedlock. The prevailing idea was that donor insemination was to be performed only to aid the construction of heterosexual nuclear families. Some doctors also feared facing legal or political action against them if they inseminated unmarried women or lesbians. One doctor in Philadelphia refused to inseminate an out lesbian after consulting with a hospital attorney.[13] In 1979, there was at least one doctor in Seattle who would inseminate known lesbians in his office, but this doctor went unnamed in an article about donor insemination, which said that "most doctors are reluctant to publicize the operation to the general public" because "some persons and groups take violent exception to it."[14]

In response to the discrimination lesbians faced in seeking medically administered donor insemination and fueled by the anti-institutional, grassroots political perspective of lesbian feminism, networks to help lesbians find potential sperm donors and self-inseminate sprung up across the country. Sometimes early insemination networks relied on the labor of a few individuals. In Seattle, for example, Maidi Nickele began helping lesbians become parents in 1980, after she herself was helped to conceive. At a Fourth of July party, Nickele learned of a woman who worked at a local women's health clinic who had helped another lesbian inseminate. This woman found a sperm donor and inseminated Nickele in her home. Shortly before her son, Jordan, was born, Nickele began to expand on this grassroots, word-of-mouth network by asking gay men to be donors, delivering sperm to lesbians who wished to become pregnant, and holding "Make a Baby" classes on insemination and parenting at the Seattle Lesbian Resource Center. In the San Francisco Bay Area, a woman named Lily also helped lesbians inseminate using local gay male volunteers as donors. Like Nickele, she organized sperm donations and taught women to self-inseminate. Other insemination networks were organized out of small groups of lesbians interested in getting pregnant.[15]

Three feminist collectives published separate guides to self-insemination in 1979: *Lesbian Health Matters*, *Woman Controlled Conception*, and *Artificial Insemination: An Alternative Conception*.[16] These books had the stated purpose of helping lesbians and single heterosexual women gain control over their own

Mother's Day picnic, San Francisco, 1985. Photograph by Cathy Cade. Courtesy of the Bancroft Library, University of California, Berkeley.

reproductive decisions. The Lesbian Mothers' National Defense Fund recommended these guides and sent out full copies or excerpts as part of their "A. I. Packet" to women across the country. Lesbians interested in donor insemination in the San Francisco Bay Area circulated them as well.[17] These publications included information for women about charting their ovulation cycles by taking their basal temperature and monitoring cervical mucus, keeping sperm viable, and the actual process of self-insemination.

The accessibility of these grassroots networks played an important role for the increasing number of lesbians who chose to get pregnant. From 1980 to 1986, Maidi Nickele estimates that she assisted in approximately twenty inseminations that led to births and equally as many inseminations that did not result in pregnancy. Lily recalled that by 1980, she was at times inseminating as many as ten women a month. And neither Nickele nor Lily were the only women performing these services in their respective communities; Nickele said she saw many other babies born to local lesbian couples whom she had not inseminated and assumed that there must have been other women assisting lesbians as well. Similarly, by 1980, Lily knew of at least two other women in the San Francisco Bay Area organizing insemination networks. These organizers sometimes helped women far away from their locale. Nickele remembered one woman who called from Lawrence, Kansas, because she could not find a donor there; she came to Seattle for a conference, and Nickele found a sperm donor and inseminated her while she was there. She and her partner went back to Lawrence and had a baby.[18] Lily inseminated women who lived in the country and drove four or five hours to San Francisco for the procedure, and she received letters from women in the Midwest asking for help because they could not find donors where they lived.[19]

The connection fostered between gay male and lesbian feminist communities through these early insemination networks was based on shared appreciation of the importance of reproductive freedom to both groups' civil rights. A gay couple who regularly donated sperm for Lily had originally met her at a conference for gay parents when they themselves were considering becoming fathers. Although they eventually decided against having children, they liked the idea of helping lesbians do so and saw it as a way to bridge cultural divides between lesbian and gay communities. Some lesbians in the late 1970s and early 1980s used gay male sperm donors because they felt connected to the gay community politically and personally. In 1984, Roberta Achtenberg described how many lesbians in the late 1970s and early 1980s had "strong feelings that they wanted the sperm to be from a gay man."[20] Lynn Mathison had three of her gay male friends donate sperm jointly when she got pregnant with her daughter in 1978 in San Francisco.[21] Many women also felt that it would be safer to use gay men as donors because a heterosexual man would be more likely later to sue successfully for custody of the children on the grounds that lesbianism made the mother an unfit parent. When Sunny Rivera and her partner needed a donor for their first child, they asked one of Rivera's family members, who was a gay man, to act as a donor for Rivera's partner. They said they would not have been comfortable using a heterosexual relative because of the possibility of being later sued for custody.[22] For Maidi Nickele it was simply easier to ask gay men to be donors because, unlike heterosexual men, they did not find anything objectionable about lesbians becoming mothers. In fact, Nickele remembered that most gay men she asked got excited about "helping create families even if they weren't a part of that family."[23]

Although informal insemination networks were widespread and gave many lesbians the information they needed to self-inseminate, a few sperm banks and health clinics did offer insemination services to lesbians by the mid-1980s. The first two clinics to inseminate lesbians and single women in the

United States grew out of the women's health movement of the 1970s. Women at the Feminist Women's Health Center in Los Angeles were discussing and participating in inseminations by the mid-1970s, and the Vermont Women's Health Center in Burlington, Vermont, began performing inseminations in 1974.[24] Carol Downer and Lorraine Rothman founded the Los Angeles clinic in 1971 as the first women-operated clinic in the country and helped start the women's health movement. These clinics and the women's health movement in general were based on a feminist vision of women's empowerment through health education and focused on women's right to control their own health and reproductive choices. Their commitment to offering the power to decide to become pregnant to all women, particularly lesbians who had been systematically denied the right to be parents, grew out of this political perspective.[25]

A number of other local feminist health clinics responded to the growing number of lesbians interested in donor insemination by the early 1980s, continuing the political commitments of the earlier programs in Vermont and Los Angeles, by creating insemination programs and sperm banks open to lesbians. In 1983, the Fenway Community Health Center in Boston began an Alternative Insemination Program, expressly for the purpose of providing lesbians and unmarried heterosexual women an option for insemination. In describing the need for such a program, the Fenway clinic cited the work of earlier feminist women's health centers and the existence of cultural biases against lesbian mothers.[26]

In 1982, the Oakland Feminist Women's Health Center established a sperm bank to serve the growing needs of lesbians nationwide. One year into the program, one quarter of its 230 recipients and one third of its 50 calls a day were from lesbians.[27] In 1989, almost half of the sperm bank's recipients self-identified as lesbians.[28] By 1988, the Elizabeth Blackwell Health Center for Women in Philadelphia was also willing to give sperm to single women.[29] In addition, at least one mainstream New York sperm bank, Ident, which in 1987 was the largest sperm bank in the world, apparently provided frozen sperm to clinics that openly inseminated single heterosexual women and lesbians.[30]

By the mid-1980s, these clinics became increasingly important as growing concern over HIV/AIDS made noninstitutional donor relationships more difficult. By 1987, doctors with the Centers for Disease Control in Atlanta were calling for all clinics and medical practitioners of donor insemination to screen sperm donations for HIV.[31] The clinics that catered to lesbians and took sperm donations from gay men began screening donor sperm for HIV by the late 1980s. The Elizabeth Blackwell Center was testing for HIV by 1987 or 1988.[32] The Oakland Feminist Women's Health Center in the San

Francisco Bay Area, hit early by AIDS, discontinued use of gay male sperm donors in 1984.[33] Donor forms began to ask detailed questions about behaviors considered high risk for HIV/AIDS.[34] By 1988, there had been no confirmed cases of women infected with the HIV virus through donor insemination, but there were thought to be a few cases in Australia and Canada.[35]

Over time, concern about the possibility of HIV infection as a result of informal donor networks grew within lesbian communities. One woman wrote to Lesbian Connection in 1986 that those contemplating donor insemination should "give some serious thought to the source of semen for artificial insemination and, if using an established bank, to question its techniques for assuring the noncontamination [by HIV/AIDS] of the semen."[36] Maidi Nickele remembered that she slowly became worried about HIV/AIDS and insemination in Seattle. Unlike San Francisco, Los Angeles, and New York, Seattle was not an initial epicenter of the disease, and Nickele recalled that the local media did not focus on HIV/AIDS until heterosexual people began to contract the virus in large numbers. In the first years of the virus, Nickele remembers that she was still thinking of it as a form of cancer and was not connecting it to insemination. When her partner, Jan, became pregnant with their second son, Brett, in early 1985, they were not worried about the possibility of HIV/AIDS, even though by that time the Oakland Feminist Women's Health Center was very concerned. "But shortly after that, in terms of doing insemination," Nickele began to see that using gay male donors meant she needed to be aware of the possibility of HIV/AIDS in her donors. She developed a policy in which she only accepted sperm from men who agreed to be either celibate or monogamous, get tested to verify they were HIV-negative, and inform her privately if they had sex outside of their relationship.[37] By the late 1980s, the fear of HIV/AIDS had noticeably slowed the use of gay men as donors within lesbian communities.

Lesbian donor insemination, which grew out of both the women's health movement and the lesbian mother activism of the 1970s, contributed to reshaping the American family. Lesbians and their gay male donors continued the earlier challenges to the notion that parenthood was exclusively heterosexual, and although the fear of HIV/AIDS infection diminished informal donor relationships between lesbian and gay communities, such relationships continued after tests could confirm that gay men were HIV-negative. By the 1990s a significant number of sperm banks on each coast and in universities around the country inseminated lesbians and unmarried women. Private doctors nationwide also grew more comfortable with inseminating lesbians, although prospective lesbian mothers could still encounter surprise and bigotry from medical staff. Lesbians who had persisted in their desire to get pregnant and have children in the 1970s and 1980s, in spite of the opposition, pushed along this gradual expansion of donor insemination services across the country, contributing to the separation of parenting from mandated heterosexuality.[38]

The Increase in Gay and Lesbian Adoption

At the same time as lesbians and gay men were creating new families through donor insemination relationships, they were also becoming adoptive parents more frequently than in previous decades. This was true in spite of the fact that gay men and lesbians faced great obstacles to adopting children and becoming foster parents throughout the 1970s and 1980s. During this time, the increasing visibility of gay and lesbian parenting also led to a social and legal backlash against gay and lesbian adoption and foster parenting. This trend began to change by the mid-1990s, as an increasing number of states began to support gay and lesbian adoptive and fostering rights.

Bill Jones, who would later be a longtime member of San Francisco Bay Area Gay Fathers, became the first single man to adopt in the United States in 1968 and did so as a closeted gay man.[39] In the 1970s, following Jones, a small number of gay men quietly adopted as single parents. Many adoption agencies followed an informal policy of "don't ask, don't tell" in dealing with these adoptions.[40] When Bill Jones was trying to adopt his son Aaron the adoption worker knew that he was gay but did not want him to tell her so directly for fear she would have to tell the adoption committee. Just before the adoption was final, however, word leaked that Jones was a gay man and the committee tried to reverse their decision. After months of controversy, the adoption agency, which had earlier assured Jones everything would go through, bowed to his threats of a lawsuit and finalized the adoption.[41] Don Harrelson recalls that adoption officials never asked if he was gay when he adopted his son Doug in Los Angeles County in 1976 and let him know that "they didn't want to know."[42]

Gay men who were open about their sexuality had a very difficult time adopting children at this time. In 1974, adoption agencies told two gay men in Minneapolis that their chances of adopting were "remote." After searching in vain for an agency that would assist openly gay men, the two men filed discrimination complaints against the agencies that had refused to help them.[43] Randy Chapman, a gay man in Fort Worth, Texas, lost custody of his four-year-old adopted son in 1982, even though his wife had voluntarily relinquished custody in 1980 because her new husband "objected to the boy's

Bill Jones (second from left) appears on the *Mike Douglas Show* as "a bachelor who adopted a son" with his son, Aaron, and Ozzie and Harriet Nelson, 1969. Courtesy of Bill Jones.

race." In her suit for custody transfer, Chapman's ex-wife, Ann, contended that Randy Chapman's gay identity made him an unfit parent.[44] In 1974, *The Advocate* ran a story about a boy being adopted by an openly gay man in Northern California but left the story anonymous so they would not jeopardize the placement.[45]

In spite of the bias against gay and lesbian adoption, there were tacit programs in a few cities to place at-risk gay teens with gay male couples as foster parents. In 1973, the director of the Department of Children and Family Services of Illinois admitted that the office had been quietly placing children with "homosexual tendencies" with gay foster parents. The New Jersey Department of Human Services formally announced the opening of such a program in 1979.[46] Bruce Voeller mentioned in a newspaper interview that he knew of two dozen of these cases that were "quietly negotiated" by the adoption agencies and gay couples.[47] These programs were small, however, and most were shut down after public outcries.

In general, it was not until the late 1970s that known gay men and lesbians began to adopt children. The first openly gay man or lesbian to publicly adopt a child in the United States was the Reverend John Kuiper of Catskill, New York, in 1979. Kuiper was a pastor with the Good News Metropolitan Community Church in Albany and legally adopted a thirteen-year-old boy.[48] Will Dixon Gray adopted his son in 1983, after New York state laws prohibited denial of an adoptive parent solely on the basis of sexual orientation.[49] These adoptions by single parents, notable for the fact that the man or woman adopting the child was an open lesbian or gay man, represented an enormous move toward legitimizing gay and lesbian parenthood.

In a second type of adoption, joint adoption, two men or women, neither of whom were the child's biological parent, adopted a child together. Joint adoption offered a type of two-parent family formation that attempted to sidestep the lack of legal recognition for lesbian and gay domestic partnerships. Even though these couples still could not be legally married, they could guarantee critical parenting rights, such as inheritance, medical guardianship, and power of attorney, through legal adoption. In 1986, two joint adoptions by two different lesbian couples took place in the San Francisco Bay Area, marking the first year in which a court in the United States had approved a gay or lesbian joint adoption.[50] In New York, Wayne Steinman and his partner, Sal Iacullo, finalized the adoption of their daughter, Hope, in the fall of 1988.[51] Years of social science research by a generation of experts who had testified in the custody cases of the 1970s had produced a critical mass of evidence that supported these adoptions, while the activist work in support of lesbian and gay custody struggles had begun to shift prevailing legal opinion.

These parents were part of the first wave of openly lesbian and gay adoptions through state agencies that were the culmination of debates in the 1960s homophile organizations over the appropriateness of demanding adoptive rights. After two decades, courts in certain jurisdictions were beginning to uphold these rights for gay men and lesbians. Just as homophile activists of the 1960s had predicted, this ignited a political firestorm. Although there had been institutional opposition to lesbian insemination, it was largely on the part of private doctors and sperm banks. The backlash to the increase in gay and lesbian adoption, however, came from state legislatures and federal policy makers.

The oppositional reaction to gay and lesbian adoption was severe and built on earlier antigay legislation of the 1970s. Florida had been the first state to explicitly ban lesbians and gay men from adopting children. The Florida ban was instituted in 1977 as part of the antigay Christian Right political backlash in Dade County. Led by Anita Bryant, the Save Our Children campaign was started in response to a gay civil rights bill in Dade County and made gay adoption one of its primary targets.[52] These reactions were not limited to the South. In 1985, Massachusetts governor Michael Dukakis issued regulations that declared heterosexual foster families to be "the foster placement of choice" in state policy. This measure followed an antigay media outcry supporting the removal of two foster children from the home of Donald Babets and David Jean, a gay couple. The *Boston Globe* editorialized that the state should not help "homosexuals . . . to acquire the trappings of traditional families" and supported Dukakis in his adopting rules favoring so-called normal families. The Massachusetts law did not deal directly with the issue of adoption rights, but it contributed to an atmosphere in which gay men and lesbians would be discouraged from attempting to adopt a child.[53] New Hampshire followed Massachusetts in taking a stand against gay and lesbian family rights and in 1987 became the second state after Florida to institute an outright ban on lesbian or gay adoptions.[54] However, whereas the Florida law had applied to adoptions only, New Hampshire also forbade lesbian and gay foster parenting. In 1988, President Ronald Reagan's task force on adoption released a report calling for a focused expansion of the pool of adoptive parents, but specifically recommended against gay men and lesbians, even though Roberta Achtenberg of the Lesbian Rights Project had submitted a brief to the task force arguing for the adoptive rights of lesbians and gay men. A member of the task force, arch-conservative Gary Bauer, had been quoted as saying that the majority of Americans found same-sex sexual orientation "deeply offensive."[55]

The first lesbians and gay men to adopt openly in the courts experienced homophobia similar to the reactions of family courts toward lesbian mothers and gay fathers fighting for custody of their children in the 1970s. Rebecca Smith and Anne Affleck, the first lesbian couple in the country to adopt a child jointly, initially applied to adopt in 1983 in Alameda County, California, where they received a surprised but friendly reaction. However, they later applied for a child in neighboring Santa Clara County, a much more conservative locale. The two women remembered the public defender for their daughter's birth mother talking in court about the child needing a "normal family" and questioning whether this was a "homosexual placement." Later in the hearings process, Santa Clara Department of Social Services (DSS) workers worried about whether the couple would be able to "raise a girl to be appropriately subservient and submissive." The court ruled a supportive therapist's testimony as inadmissible, and the DSS workers asked questions about what the girl would be "exposed to" in their household and "what kind of touching" would occur. As in the custody cases of the 1970s and the sex-crime panics of the 1950s, the court linked same-sex orientation to pedophilia. After this hearing, the couple decided they were "hitting discrimination" and called Roberta Achtenberg at the Lesbian Rights Project, with whose help they eventually won the right to adopt their daughter.[56]

As in custody cases between biological parents, some judges used the presence of sodomy laws to justify their decisions in adoption cases. In a 1986 California case, *Matter of Appeal in Pima County Juvenile Action B-10489*, the trial court ruled against permitting a bisexual man to adopt. The court reasoned that "it would be anomalous for the state on the one hand to declare homosexual conduct unlawful and on the other create a parent after that proscribed model, in effect approving that standard, inimical to the natural family, as head of a state-created family."[57] In the same year that the U.S. Supreme Court affirmed the constitutionality of the sodomy laws, this judge used these laws to justify the assertion that same-sex relationships were antithetical to the family, here naturalized as exclusively heterosexual.

Because of the local nature of adoption decisions, bias against lesbians and gay men as parents could come up at any time in the process, even in regions where there was a stated policy of nondiscrimination; but this bias could also change as individuals involved in the process revised their opinions. When Steven Rudser went to a DSS meeting in San Francisco in 1983 or 1984 as an openly gay man, he was told that the agency did not discriminate against single or gay individuals. However, even with a favorable DSS home study, Rudser encountered a social worker at the agency who said that as a gay man, Rudser was inappropriate for the boy he was trying to adopt. Rudser remembers the woman coming to his home and making him feel as if she did not want to touch anything for fear of contracting AIDS while she grilled him on his sexual history. The woman's discomfort with a gay adoptive father made the process extremely difficult, but eventually Rudser did succeed in adopting his son, Michael. Rudser recalled that a year and a half later, on one of her home visits, this woman told him how wonderful Michael looked and that among all of her cases, Rudser's was among the least worrisome. Apparently, seeing a gay man as a successful father had altered her original response.[58]

By 1996, California, Vermont, Rhode Island, and New York had all permitted lesbian or gay adoptions. However, like custody rulings, adoption regulations allowed a great deal of latitude for the judge, and favorable outcomes did not necessarily clarify adoptive rights for lesbians and gay men in general. Favorable rulings for lesbians or gay men in single-parent adoptions did not necessarily imply that the same court approved of joint adoption by lesbian and gay couples. In California, for example, state policy denied joint adoptions to unmarried couples. The individual family court judges who approved of lesbian and gay joint adoptions did so in direct contradiction to this policy; sympathetic judges simply ignored DSS recommendations in these cases. This pattern held in California until a 2003 Supreme Court decision expressly allowed lesbian and gay couples to adopt.[59] In a sizable number of states, courts and legislatures began to positively assert gay and lesbian adoptive rights by the mid-1990s.

New Legal Struggles: Paternity Suits, Co-Parent Custody Cases, and Second-Parent Adoptions

As lesbians and gay men demanded their parental rights in new ways in the 1980s and 1990s, they faced new types of legal struggles. Custody challenges arose between gay men who had served as donors and the lesbians they had assisted and between lesbian co-mothers who broke up and challenged each other for custodial and visitation rights. Like the gay and lesbian custody cases of earlier periods, these legal conflicts were made more difficult by the lack of state recognition for lesbian and gay families with children. They galvanized the movement to guarantee legal protection for lesbian and gay parental rights and helped to drive first domestic partnership reform and then the adoption of same-sex marriage as central goals of the LGBT freedom struggle.

Paternity Suits

When many lesbians began using donor insemination to become pregnant in the 1970s, they did so without the legitimization of legal and medical institutions. Most donor arrangements between lesbians and gay men were informal, and the participants assumed that shared political commitments and verbal agreements would be enough to keep them out of court. Custody struggles had always been between heterosexual ex-spouses and lesbian or gay parents, so most lesbians and gay men who entered into parenting or donor agreements were not initially concerned about the lack of legal safeguards for their family relationships. However, the legal regulation of donor insemination was based on its definition as a tightly controlled medical procedure designed to assist heterosexual married couples. For this reason, the law in most states only voided paternity rights when a sperm donation was made to a doctor. The law did not acknowledge or address informal arrangements in which donations were not made through a doctor or a medical facility, leaving open the possibility that donors could sue for paternity rights.[60]

Most of the early donor insemination arrangements were made without a doctor involved. In addition, many early donor insemination arrangements were between friends, which unlike the use of anonymous sperm donations, made future paternity suits possible. Although the use of a go-between, an individual who delivered sperm from donor to recipient and set up the insemination, sometimes allowed donor and recipient to remain unknown to each other, some lesbian and gay legal activists grew concerned that the courts would subpoena these individuals and force them to reveal the identities of donors and recipients. By the early 1980s, the first cases of donor paternity suits and co-parent lesbian custody cases began to appear, demonstrating that as long as lesbians and gay men were forced to enter into extrajudicial reproductive agreements, conflicts of this kind were inevitable.

The first donor paternity suit brought against a lesbian mother was a 1980 California case, *Jhordan C. v. Mary K.*, in which the donor, Jhordan C., filed for paternity after agreeing to be a sperm donor for Mary K. and Victoria T. Mary was a nurse and had performed the insemination herself with only a verbal contract stipulating that Jhordan would have no paternal relation to the child. Soon after Mary and Victoria's son, Devin, was born, Jhordan began demanding regular visitation and then brought a paternity suit. A trial court ruled that according to California statutory law on insemination, the paternity claim must be upheld because the sperm donation had not gone through a licensed physician. An appeals court upheld this ruling. In August 1983, after Mary and Victoria had broken up, Victoria attempted to win joint custody of Devin with Mary, as did Jhordan. The trial court awarded sole custody to Mary, declared Jhordan Devin's legal father, and gave both Victoria and Jhordan visitation rights.[61] Like custody cases against heterosexual ex-spouses, donor cases were often very expensive. A letter from Mary K., the defendant in the case, to the Lesbian Mothers' National Defense Fund in 1985, testifies to the hardships that these cases put people through. Asking for economic help, she said: "since the donor was granted visitation numerous court battles have ensued. My lawyer's fees are constantly over $7000 and mounting."[62]

Although courts were very reluctant to give gay fathers even visitation rights in custody cases when these men had left previous heterosexual relationships, when faced with the question of a gay male sperm donor seeking parental rights from a lesbian couple, courts could be very defensive of paternal rights.

Roberta Achtenberg recalled a judge in *Jhordan C. v. Mary K.* haranguing the attorneys from the Lesbian Rights Project for defending the rights of the lesbian couple under the original donor agreement. "At least nine times in the six hearings that preceded the final determination of this man's paternity of this child," Achtenberg remembered, "did the judge say to us, 'This child is entitled to a father,' 'What about father's rights?' . . . 'You women should be ashamed of yourselves' . . . and he basically said, 'I'll be goddamned if I'm going to let you give this child's father away.'"[63] Achtenberg noted that this focus on "father's rights" could make entering into a donor agreement with a known donor and without a doctor or a written contract very risky.

The reasoning in *Jhordan*—that the insemination statute about relinquishing paternity rights was only valid if a sperm donation was made with a doctor—appeared in many of the donor cases in the 1990s. In 1994 a donor in New York sought an "order of filiation and visitation" for a child who had been conceived through donor insemination and was being raised by her mother and her mother's partner. The court based an award of paternity to the donor on the basis of a New York statute that required that a licensed physician be involved in donor insemination for paternity rights to be waived, and on the fact that the donor and the lesbian mother had no written contract.[64] In the same year, a judge awarded paternity to a sperm donor in an Ohio case. In this case, a lesbian couple had entered into an agreement with a gay man and his partner to have a child through donor insemination, and there was a dispute over how much involvement the donor had agreed to have with the child. When the woman and her partner denied him visitation, he sued for paternal rights. The judge ruled in the man's favor based on the fact that insemination had been done without medical supervision and therefore did not void paternity rights under Ohio's statutory law and because there seemed to have been an agreement that the donor would have some relationship with the child.[65]

At the same time that donor relationships were fraught with legal dangers, which often made unknown donors preferable for lesbians having children through insemination, some activists questioned whether parents had the right to keep this information from their children. Jenifer Firestone was the director of the Fenway Alternative Insemination program from 1990 to 1996, during which time she established Fenway's LGBT Family and Parenting Services program. Firestone warned that the combination of a lack of recognition for lesbian and gay households with children; a desire to replicate two-parent nuclear, heterosexual models; and the widespread fear of donor custody cases was superseding considerations of whether it would be better for the children to have more extended support networks of lesbian and gay adults, even if that would be more complex for the adults involved. In her time at Fenway, she increasingly felt that the A.I. program, and those families who used its services, had moved away from the progressive commitments of the lesbian feminist and women's health movements.[66]

Along with an increased institutionalization and commodification of reproductive technologies, however, lesbians and gay men who have raised children since the advent of the lesbian and gay baby boom have subtly challenged the companionate, nuclear family ideal. Though not as overtly political as the intentional lesbian feminist communal families of the 1970s like Myrah's Mothers, some lesbians and gay men have chosen to raise children in groups of three or four or have included male donors in the role of extended family members, like "uncles" or godparents. These arrangements have challenged the assumption that family must always be based on sexual intimacy and nuclear relationships. Jenifer Firestone herself co-parented a child with two gay men, explicitly choosing not to parent within an intimate relationship. Although the baby boom has in many instances embraced nuclear family ideals, it has also been a quiet revolution of sorts.[67]

Co-Parent Custody Cases

Donor paternity cases highlighted the precariousness of lesbian and gay domestic relationships in the absence of clear federal recognition. As long as lesbians and gay men lay outside the law in their intimate relationships, their parental rights were legally unclear. Nowhere was this clearer than in the emergence, in the 1980s and 1990s, of what came to be known as "co-parent" custody cases. Typically, these cases arose when a lesbian couple who had children through donor insemination broke up and the biological mother contested the custody or visitation rights of the co-mother. The first co-mother custody case in the United States arose in Oakland, California, when Mary Flournoy denied visitation rights to her ex-partner, Linda Loftin. Flournoy and Loftin had been married in 1977, in a church ceremony at the Metropolitan Community Church in Dublin, California, and decided to have a child through donor insemination. Loftin's brother donated the sperm "so that Flournoy could bear a child who was given the family name Loftin." Flournoy carried the child to term, and the couple put Linda Loftin's name in the space provided for "father" on the birth certificate. In 1980, the couple broke up. Loftin paid child support willingly, but Flournoy soon denied her the right to see their daughter, Sparkle Cristel Loftin. After a custody battle that went on for more than a year, the two women reached an out-of-court settlement that allowed Loftin supervised visits with the six-year-old girl.[68]

In the decade after the Flournoy/Loftin case, co-parent custody became more frequent. After living together for fifteen years, Michele and Nancy jointly parented two children, Kate, born in 1980, and Seth, born in 1984. Nancy gave birth to both children, and the couple put Michele's name in the space for "father" on both birth certificates. The women were Quakers and were perceived as co-mothers in the Berkeley, California, Quaker community to which they belonged. They separated in 1985 but continued to co-parent the two children until 1988. Both women agreed that Michele would have primary custody of Kate, and Nancy would have primary custody of Seth. In March 1988, Nancy signed a notarized letter saying that Kate was "residing permanently with her co-parent, Michele." From 1985 to 1988, the two women lived apart but co-parented the children; both were listed on school and medical records as the children's mothers. However, in 1988 Nancy decided she was no longer happy with the custody arrangement and began to assert that, as the biological mother, her parental rights superseded those of her co-parent. In September 1988, Nancy filed a restraining order to prevent Michele from contacting the children and a declaration stating that Michele was not a legal parent of either child. In February 1989, a trial court in Alameda County declared that Michele had no right to see either of the children and that her attorney's argument that she was a "de facto" parent based on years of care and support was not persuasive. Although the appeals court recognized that Michele had served the role of a "loving mother" to the children, particularly to Kate, it ultimately affirmed the original court's decision.[69]

To mitigate the lack of state recognition for their families and to ensure the rights of both parents, many women began drawing up formal co-parent agreements. This did not always help, however. After living together for approximately five years, Georgia and Kerry decided to have a child through donor insemination. Using sperm from an unknown donor, Kerry became pregnant and gave birth to their daughter in July 1985. At this time, Kerry and Georgia signed an extensive co-parenting agreement that stated their "intention to jointly and equally parent the child, and provide support and guidance," and to submit to arbitration in the event that ill feelings between them threatened this parenting arrangement. When the two separated five years later, they maintained equal custody of their daughter, who lived three days a week with each woman and one day a week with a mutual friend. In April of 1991, however, Kerry began to ask for increased time with their daughter. In June of that same year, Kerry told Georgia that she intended to exercise "her legal prerogative to raise her daughter alone, with all decisions concerning the girl to be made solely by Kerry and visitations with Georgia limited to every other weekend." She refused to participate in binding arbitration as dictated by their written agreement. Georgia then brought a parental suit, and Kerry moved to terminate any rights Georgia had to see her daughter. A trial court in Sonoma County, California, found that Georgia was neither the biological nor the adoptive parent.[70]

Not all co-parent cases ended in a ruling against the nonbiological parent, however. In a New Mexico case decided on appeal in 1992, an appellate court ruled for the plaintiff, a lesbian co-mother, overturning the original ruling saying that the trial court had erred in declaring the co-parenting arrangement unenforceable under New Mexico state law and that "sexual orientation, standing alone, is not a permissible basis for the denial of shared custody or visitation." It appears that no further legal action was taken in this case. There were other signs that judges were sometimes uncomfortable with ruling against the rights of lesbian co-mothers. In 1990, a Baltimore judge gave partial visitation rights to "A.C.," a lesbian co-mother who had a child with her partner in 1982. The judge ruled that A.C. had "a significant relationship not amounting to a parental relationship" that was in the girl's best interests to maintain. She gave A.C. limited visitation rights, restricted to the second weekend of every month and a half-hour phone conversation every week.[71] Sometimes judges would express their displeasure at the limits of existing family law even as they ruled against the rights of a lesbian co-mother. In Los Angeles, Judge Dana Henry ruled against Terri Sabol, whose partner had conceived with sperm donated by Sabol's brother. However, in her decision, the judge acknowledged that co-parent custody cases represented a serious issue and that the state legislature would have to examine the existing law to "adequately deal with the increasing number of homosexual couples."[72] In 1996, a Missouri court awarded custody to a biological mother in a co-parent case but awarded the co-mother "significant visitation and right to participate in major life decisions of the child."[73]

Second-Parent Adoption

In reaction to the precarious legal position of gay and lesbian co-parenting arrangements, lesbian activists developed a concept they called "second-parent adoption."[74] Inspired by stepparent adoption, in which courts allowed stepparents to adopt the children of their new spouses, organizations such as the Lesbian Rights Project, the Lambda Legal Defense Fund, and the American

Civil Liberties Union began arguing in court for a similar arrangement where nonbiological lesbian parents could adopt their children and by so doing become legal parents along with the biological mother. This legal arrangement mitigated the lack of protection for nonbiological parents under state and federal law in the absence of legalized same-sex marriage. However, unlike stepparent adoption, second-parent adoptions resulted in children having two legal and unmarried parents of the same gender, something often explicitly prohibited under state statutes. Stepparent adoption and the statutes against having two legal mothers or two legal fathers, like legal policies concerning donor insemination, were designed to facilitate childrearing by married, heterosexual couples. Thus, the state's historical investment in families based in heterosexual marriage continued to endanger lesbian and gay parental rights. When second-parent adoptions were granted, however, they offered a legal option for a lesbian couple who wanted to create a family in which one of the women became pregnant from donor insemination or one person in a gay or lesbian couple had adopted a child as a single adult.

Attorneys Donna Hitchens, Nancy Davis, and Roberta Achtenberg of the Lesbian Rights Project were the first to fully develop second-parent adoptions as a legal procedure allowing both members of a lesbian or gay couple with children the security of full parental rights. Davis and Hitchens petitioned to adopt their own children in the state of California, and their case became the first published second-parent adoption in the United States.[75] They had already made the decision to start a family in 1984, after being together for seven years. At that time, Hitchens had applied to adopt their daughter, K., as a single adoptive parent. In 1987, with Achtenberg acting as their attorney, the couple petitioned to jointly adopt a second daughter, M., and the family court approved her adoption as well. After bringing M. into their family, however, they wanted to give the same security of having two legal parents to their other daughter, K., so Nancy Davis petitioned to adopt K. as a second parent. The petition, written by Achtenberg, argued that being legally related to both her parents was clearly in K.'s best interests and that "she has bonded psychologically to both and views both as her parents. She does not draw distinctions based on blood or law."[76]

The fact that the legal endorsement of a new type of adoption was being proposed here did not escape the staff at the Department of Social Services; in fact, a recommendation scrawled on a draft of the petition circulated internally read: "deny on basis—child does not need additional parent/has a parent—not up for adoption—to truly a stepparent—male/female." Whoever wrote this comment understood that it was a request for a form of adoption that had previously been reserved for heterosexual stepparents. This note notwithstanding, the court approved this adoption.[77]

Over the next decade, courts nationwide approved second-parent adoptions as lesbians and gay men utilized the new process to protect their families legally. Courts approved the first second-parent adoptions in New York in 1992, New Jersey in 1993, and Illinois in 1994.[78] By 1993, second-parent adoptions had been granted in Alaska, California, Minnesota, New York, Oregon, Vermont, Washington, Texas, Washington, D.C., Michigan, and Rhode Island, and an estimated total of 200 to 300 second-parent adoptions had taken place.[79]

Changes in Lesbian and Gay Parental Activism

During the 1980s, lesbian and gay parental activism also changed radically. Gay liberation had given way to a large-scale, mainstream LGBT civil rights movement by the mid-1980s, and by the 1990s, parental and domestic rights became one of its central focuses. Inspired by the grassroots activism of the 1970s and furthered by the explosion of lesbian and gay parenting in the 1980s and 1990s, the rights of lesbian mothers, gay fathers, and their children moved to the center of the LGBT freedom struggle. This shift complemented a greater focus on domestic and relational rights that grew out of the AIDS crisis. As hospitals denied access to the partners of individuals with HIV/AIDS and shut them out of crucial legal and medical decisions made by families of origin, lesbian and gay rights activists became more concerned with rights previously reserved for heterosexual marriage. These medical and legal exclusions combined with the decade-long struggles of lesbian mothers and gay fathers in custody courts to make LGBT domestic and parental rights a focal point for LGBT civil rights. As the larger LGBT community embraced the struggle for domestic and family civil rights, the character of family rights groups themselves changed shape. Children of lesbian mothers and gay fathers began to organize on behalf of their families and became a powerful new force in LGBT activism, and the lesbian and gay parents groups that continued from the 1970s expanded their focus to reflect the growing diversity of LGBT families.

In the 1970s, lesbian mother and gay father activism was largely a grassroots enterprise. Activists formed groups such as the Lesbian Mothers' National Defense Fund in Seattle and Dykes and Tykes in New York City with very little money, while gay fathers groups largely consisted of support networks for gay fathers, many of whom were estranged from their families.

March on Washington, 1993. Photograph by Cathy Cade. Courtesy of the Bancroft Library, University of California, Berkeley.

Lesbian mothers who came out and left heterosexual marriages were often poor and raised their families in radical, counterculture communities. Gay fathers were often limited in their ability to be activists by the ever-present fear that they would be completely cut off from their children if they were perceived as fighting for gay rights. However, by the 1990s, although many of the smaller lesbian mothers and gay fathers groups had faded away, several large-scale movement organizations responded to the rapidly increasing numbers of lesbian and gay parents and prospective parents by developing focused initiatives centered around LGBT family and domestic rights. At the same time, although these groups represented a new development in lesbian and gay parental activism, they were founded in and intertwined with earlier activism; in fact, they were often dependent on groups such as the Gay and Lesbian Parents Coalition International and the Lesbian Rights Project.

The work of the Lesbian Rights Project was an important part of this transition from grassroots to large-scale political activism. The Lesbian Rights Project had been working on lesbian and gay parenting cases since 1977 and served as legal counsel on the first donor paternity cases, co-parent custody/visitation cases, and second-parent adoptions in the 1980s. The LRP also worked in cooperation with other large legal groups such as the Lambda Legal Defense Fund and the National Gay and Lesbian Task Force (NGLTF).[80] As donor insemination and adoptive families transformed lesbian and gay parenting in the 1980s, the LRP, with its origins in the lesbian mother activism of the 1970s, served as the bridge between the activist politics of lesbian mothers groups and the larger, mainstream LGBT civil rights movement that emerged in the 1980s.

The Lambda Legal Defense Fund, the first gay and lesbian legal defense fund in the country, began to focus more on custody, domestic partnership rights, and second-parent adoption cases when Paula Ettelbrick served as legal director from 1986 to 1992.[81] Ettelbrick and Lambda worked with the Lesbian Rights Project on several co-parent custody and second-parent adoption cases in the mid-1980s.[82] Once appointed, Ettelbrick took advantage of an already growing interest in lesbian and gay childrearing at Lambda. In 1983, none of Lambda's major programs directly addressed LGBT family issues, but in 1985, the organization held a conference in New York entitled "Securing Our Relationships/Securing Our Families" that included workshops on the legal implications of donor insemination, adoption and foster parenting, and custody and visitation rights.[83] Lambda's work in the 1980s on the rights of HIV-positive people also contributed to these new foci, since many of the struggles faced by people suffering from HIV/AIDS involved the state refusing to recognize their intimate relationships. As attorneys argued for power of attorney and domestic rights for partners of men who were HIV positive, many of the legal issues overlapped with LGBT parenting issues; indeed, gay fathers who faced discrimination because of their HIV status often simultaneously were deprived of recognition of their relationship with their partners and suffered attacks on their rights as fathers. Lambda had worked on some lesbian mother and gay father custody issues in the late 1970s, but the new interest in parenting in lesbian and gay communities, along with the need to focus on the domestic rights of HIV-positive individuals and the continuing work of lesbian feminist attorneys trained in the atmosphere of the lesbian mother activist groups of the 1970s, pushed the increasingly powerful and financially solvent organization toward lesbian and gay parenting and domestic rights. Culminating this trend in 1989, Lambda founded the Lambda Family Relationships Project to "stress the growing importance of our work on lesbian and gay family issues."[84]

The National Gay and Lesbian Task Force also worked with the LRP and intensified its focus on lesbian and gay parenting issues and domestic rights. In 1989, the same year that Lambda launched its program, the NGLTF inaugurated its Lesbian and Gay Families Project under the leadership of Ivy Young. The project was a joint effort with the Lesbian Rights Project, by then known as the National Center for Lesbian Rights (NCLR).[85] Like the Lambda project, the task-force initiative combined a focus on gay and lesbian parenting rights with work on domestic partnership, employment and insurance benefits, and the right for lesbians and gay men to be involved in medical and legal decisions about their partners.[86] In the early 1990s, the Lesbian and Gay Families Project lobbied for the passage of domestic-partner benefits at the municipal and state level and fought existing laws prohibiting gay adoption in states such as Florida and New Hampshire. They also worked to oppose the nomination to the Supreme Court of Robert Bork, who had been involved in passing the New Hampshire law before his nomination.[87]

At the time of the Families Project's founding, only six cities in the United States had some form of domestic partnership legislation in place. The most brutal period of lesbian and gay custody struggles and the early years of the AIDS epidemic, during which many people with AIDS had been denied the most basic rights of family and association, were in the immediate past and served as important motivations for the project's founding. The work of the Families Project brought together veterans of both lesbian mother and gay father activism and represented the increasing focus on domestic and family rights in the larger LGBT freedom struggle.[88]

On March 1, 1990, a special commission held hearings on the feasibility of enacting domestic partner legislation for the District of Columbia. Ivy Young spoke as head of the Families Project and urged the commission to follow the lead of family diversity commissions in cities such as Los Angeles and San Francisco in calling for inclusive domestic partner benefit programs. She spoke of the lack of legal recognition for diverse, intergenerational lesbian and gay households both with and without children, discrimination faced by lesbian and gay parents, and the need for equitable hospital visitation and health care policies.

Young was joined in speaking to the commission by James Fagelson, the co-founder of the Gay and Lesbian Parents Coalition of Metropolitan Washington. Fagelson used his personal experience as a gay father in a committed relationship raising two teenage daughters to convey the cost of exclusion to members of the commission. He told them that because of marital discrimination, his partner, a full-time student, did not receive health coverage under Fagelson's insurance plan.[89]

These hearings illustrate the growing centrality of domestic and family issues to the LGBT freedom struggle and the direct impact that the history of gay and lesbian parental activism, embodied in groups such as the National Center for Lesbian Rights and the Gay and Lesbian Parents Coalition International, had on these changes. In the late 1980s, domestic partnership legislation was the primary focus of this political organizing, but it would soon be superseded by a growing movement for same-sex marriage, beginning in 1993, when a Hawaii Supreme Court decision opened the possibility of same-sex marriage reform. As this transition from a focus on domestic partnership to same-sex marital rights occurred, some activists who had been central to the struggle for gay and lesbian parental rights criticized the shift. In 1989, Paula Ettelbrick wrote that marriage as a goal would not address the diverse forms of queer intimacy and kinship that were possible under domestic partnership reform.[90]

Transformations in gay fathers groups and lesbian mothers groups reflected the changing face of lesbian and gay families with children. To be sure, older groups such as the Lesbian Mothers' National Defense Fund still helped women who had come out as lesbians after having children in heterosexual marriages. In the 1980s, however, the women writing to them asking for help were often from rural areas or regions of the country where lesbian and gay civil rights had little popular or political support. The threat of custody loss for gay fathers and lesbian mothers was slowly changing, and in certain counties of some states, lesbian mothers and gay fathers who had the money to hire an attorney familiar with custody struggles involving sexual orientation could hope to protect their custodial or visitation rights. These changes were strongly dependent on region, and women and men who were poor, who faced racial discrimination, or who were in parts of the country where there was still severe social condemnation of lesbian and gay parenting often still had little chance of winning custody or visitation.

In the 1980s, the Lesbian Mothers' National Defense Fund began distributing information on donor insemination, a sign of the changing demographics of lesbian families. By 1990, it had changed its name to the Lavender Families Resource Network, under the direction of Jenny Sayward, reflecting both a commitment to LGBT families of all types and a move away from the group's previous focus on lesbian mother custody activism. Sayward, who often did much of the group's work alone, still counseled lesbian mothers afraid of custody struggles with heterosexual ex-spouses, but recalled that they were often women calling from rural areas or poor women who lacked resources to fight a custody battle. Sayward was also increasingly contacted by women in co-mother custody battles.[91]

Gay fathers groups also changed. The Gay Fathers Coalition continued to grow throughout the 1980s, even though many of its member groups were devastated by the AIDS crisis. In 1986, the group changed its name to the Gay and Lesbian Parents Coalition International to include lesbian mothers. Don Harrelson, who served as president of the organization in 1985 and 1986, remembered that until about 1990 this change was in name only; however, by 1993, 45 percent of GLPCI's members were women.[92] This change reflects a growth in the number of lesbians having children and a shift away from the more radical, multi-issue lesbian mother activist groups of the 1970s. In 1991, GLPCI developed two new positions that reflected the changes in lesbian and gay parenting during this era: director of co-parenting issues, "to represent partners of parents," and director of alternative parenting resources, to "address adoption and donor insemination issues."[93] In 1996, GLPCI organized its first Gay and Lesbian Family Week in Provincetown, Massachusetts, a week-long gathering for gay and lesbian parents and their children.[94] The continuing growth of GLPCI attests to the expanding focus on gay and lesbian parenting in the mainstream LGBT movement, a shift that would bring growing economic and political resources to the struggle for lesbian and gay parental and domestic rights.

Local groups often articulated new issues facing lesbians and gay men who were adoptive parents or who had children through donor insemination or surrogacy. Center Kids, founded in 1988, was initially an organization of gay and lesbian adoptive parents who came together in New York City to share stories and offer each other support. These parents, who were among the first openly lesbian and gay adoptive parents, began to meet regularly at the Lesbian, Gay, Bisexual and Transgender Community Center and became officially affiliated with the center in 1989. At first, the group was primarily a parent's group and hosted talks such as "Legal Issues for Gay Families," with attorneys Paula Ettelbrick and Judith Terkel in 1989, and "Considering Parenthood: A Support Group for Lesbians Considering the Possibilities," in 1993.[95] By the late 1990s, Center Kids was a politically active organization, taking part in the growing emphasis on domestic/familial rights in the LGBT freedom struggle. In 1998, the executive director of the NGLTF spoke at the New York community center as part of a Task Force "Family Tour." The event was co-sponsored by Center Kids and covered topics such as marriage, custody, domestic partnership, adoption, and schools.[96]

In Columbus, Ohio, an organization for lesbian mothers called Momazons was formed. The group published a newsletter chronicling the experiences of lesbian mothers who wrote to them from across the nation. Although there were still stories of women who had children through heterosexual relationships before coming out, many of the letters had to do with women choosing to become mothers as lesbians. The newsletter listed sympathetic sperm banks and fertility clinics across the country with an emphasis on supporting women in nonmetropolitan regions who lacked access to large lesbian communities.[97]

During this period, the children of lesbians and gay men began to organize politically for the first time as well. For the most part, this movement grew out of networks established previously by gay fathers groups nationwide. By 1989, the annual GLPCI gathering had workshops for teenage children of lesbian mothers and gay fathers, as well as ones for younger children, and a newsletter entitled Just for Us, all organized by a man named Ed Lamano. In 1990, young adult children of gay fathers and lesbian mothers came to the workshops and asked if they could run them autonomously. Lamano agreed, a steering committee was elected, and Just for Us, an organization operated entirely by children of gay men and lesbians expressly to deal with their own particular issues was born. Just for Us took over a newsletter of the same name that Lamano had been publishing and began organizing annual conferences for the children of lesbian and gay parents, held concurrently with the GLPCI annual conference. In 1993, the group changed its name to Children of Lesbians and Gays Everywhere (COLAGE).[98] The group grew rapidly. By 1996, COLAGE had chapters in Arizona, California, Colorado, Indiana,

COLAGE founders, Ali and Carrie Dubin, with a "Just for Us" banner in the West Hollywood Pride parade, 1991. Courtesy of the Gay, Lesbian, Bisexual, Transgender Historical Society.

Massachusetts, Minnesota, New York, Oregon, Texas, Virginia, Washington, and the District of Columbia.[99]

Social and Cultural Changes

The sharp increase in women and men having children openly as lesbian and gay parents brought with it large-scale social changes in the United States. While lesbians and gay men had been parents for generations, and openly so for at least one generation, the families of the 1980s and 1990s created through donor insemination, adoption, and surrogacy were different. First, children who had spent their whole lives in lesbian and gay families and communities differed from children who had gone through the breakup of a heterosexual family. For example, the experience of a five-year-old raised from birth by two mothers was much different than that of a twelve-year-old whose mother had come out as a lesbian. Young children who had only known a gay or lesbian family were less likely to be consistently secretive about their family. It is much more difficult to teach a three-year-old child that his or her family is not something to speak openly about, and, in any case, the growth of the LGBT civil rights movement diminished the need for such discretion. Secondly, the lesbian families of the 1980s and 1990s were often more integrated into mainstream American society. Lesbian feminism was still a powerful movement, and many of these mothers identified with it, but separatism and the radical politics of lesbian nationalist communities of the 1970s had receded; as a result, in the 1980s and 1990s, many lesbian mothers with small children found themselves increasingly negotiating space with mainstream heterosexual society.

As lesbian and gay families with children became more visible in American society, they faced manifestations of the same animosity that had beset lesbian and gay parents for generations; for many in the United States, lesbian and gay parenting was still a contradiction in terms, and the increased visibility of lesbian and gay families with children made them feel afraid, threatened, and angry. Children of lesbians and gay men, as they had since the Second World War, faced the hostility of society toward their families and became bridge workers between their homes and the heterosexual world. Much of the hatred they faced was unchanged from decades past. They heard the same words on the playground, but increasingly these children spoke out in defense of their families and communities and found resources to help them manage the intolerance they encountered.

Letters sent in to the organization COLAGE illustrate vividly the isolation and struggles faced by children of lesbians and gay men of this era; unlike children who grew up in the political lesbian and gay enclave communities of the 1970s, these children frequently lived in communities where they were the only child of lesbian or gay parents. A letter from a lesbian mother in North Little Rock, Arkansas, asked for membership information for her five-year-old daughter, whom she said felt "very isolated."[100] In 1997, another lesbian mother from Boulder, Colorado, wrote in on behalf of her twelve-year-old daughter, Sara, whom she said was "especially needing support right now" and did not know "any other kids with a family like ours."[101] A fourteen-year-old daughter of lesbian mothers living in Kihei, Hawaii, wrote in to request a COLAGE pen pal and said that she wanted a friend and did not know anyone else with lesbian parents.[102] Laura Bernard, a junior in high school in Essex Junction, Vermont, wrote in 1995 that she only knew "one other girl my age with a gay father." Laura was applying for a COLAGE internship and was looking forward to the chance to be "more open and vocal about my family situation."[103] Although their parents had gone through difficult personal struggles to come out as lesbians or gay men, the children of lesbian mothers and gay fathers in the 1980s and 1990s still often felt as if they were on the front lines in the ongoing tension over the presence of gay men and lesbians in American culture.

Children of lesbians and gay men in this era experienced antigay attitudes in school and mediated between heterosexual society and their families; a decade later, schools would begin to develop institutional frameworks designed to support the children of lesbian mothers and gay fathers. Ian Mobley, an eleven-year-old boy growing up in Kailua, Hawaii, explained in a 1999 interview that he felt "embarrassed and angry and sad" when kids said "that's so gay" in school because he knew that they were speaking about people like his mother and her partner; whether he ignored the hurtful words or, as he sometimes did, told the speaker to "shut up," any defense of his family was his "responsibility 'cause no one else there will do anything."[104] Children of the lesbian and gay baby-boom years had a deep sense of both the need to combat casual homophobia and their own role and responsibilities as bridge workers.

As they had in previous eras, children of lesbians and gay men who had divorced a heterosexual ex-spouse in these years sometimes had more difficulty challenging social bias about their families. One fourteen-year-old girl from Jacksonville, Florida, with a lesbian mother who had divorced her father in 1996 wrote to COLAGE requesting a pen pal and said, "I'm 14 years old and I need advice . . . and help. . . . My mom is lesbian and I don't know how to deal with it."[105] Another girl, fifteen years old, from Centralia, Washington, wrote requesting a pen pal. Her father had left her mother in 1998, three years earlier, and had come out as a gay man. The girl wrote, "It has been very difficult. . . . I feel like everyone wants me to believe their way but I don't want to disappoint anyone." She wanted COLAGE to help her find a pen pal who "I can be honest with and . . . is going through some of the same things as me."[106]

Children of lesbian mothers and gay fathers in conservative, rural regions sometimes expressed feeling particularly isolated. One fifteen-year-old wrote to COLAGE from a town of 3,000 in Texas requesting a pen pal and said that "most people where I live would think differently of me if they knew that my mother was lesbian so I have problems explaining to people why they can't come over." A girl in sixth grade from a town in Alabama with a population of 6,000 wrote to COLAGE, saying that she was "having a lot of problems in school because of my family" and that she wanted to correspond with another person "who has had the same problems in school." A boy with two moms from a town in Pennsylvania with just over 2,000 inhabitants said that he did "get teased in school for having two moms" and that he would like to be pen pals with a boy about his age "to talk to about school and the challenges of having two moms."[107]

As more and more children grew up in lesbian and gay families, children's services emerged to meet their needs. Infused with children from the increase in lesbian and gay families, summer camps for the children of LGBT parents emerged in the 1990s. Camp It Up! had its first year in 1990 as a summer camp near Yosemite for "all kinds of families." One of its organizers, Ellie Schindelman, herself a lesbian mother, had previously led gay and lesbian parenting groups.[108] In 1992, Camp Lavender Hill, the first summer camp exclusively for "children of lesbian, gay, bisexual families," was founded in northern California.[109] In that same year Mountain Meadow Summer Camp was founded as a feminist summer camp for "LGBT and other progressive families" in the Northeast.[110] By 2000, Keshet Camp, named after the Hebrew word for rainbow, offered a "weekend-long Jewish camping experience for lesbian, gay, and bisexual families" in California.[111] Camp Ten Trees, in Washington State, had its first year as a summer camp for LGBT youth and children of LGBT families in 2001, with campers coming from Montana, Oregon, and Washington.[112] These camps gave the children of lesbian and gay parents an opportunity to spend time with each other in a space where they did not have to mediate between the heterosexual assumptions of mainstream American society and the culture and realities of their families.

In response to the growing number of children being raised in lesbian and gay households, publishers released new children's books speaking to their family situations. In 1989, Alyson Publications published *Heather Has Two Mommies*, by Lesléa Newman. The book told the story of Heather, a three-year-old girl, and her two mothers, Mama Jane and Mama Kate. In the first few pages of the book the reader learns about Heather's dog, Midnight, and how her mothers fell in love and decided to have a baby through insemination. The story then focuses on one day at daycare when the children are read a story about a father who is a veterinarian. Heather, realizing for the first time that she has no father, wonders if everyone but her has a father, and begins to cry. Molly, Heather's caregiver, explains to her that she has two mommies, which is "pretty special," and the children talk about all the different kinds of families each have, including others with no father. The book openly celebrated family diversity and spoke to everyday issues experienced by the children of lesbian mothers.

A flood of books followed *Heather Has Two Mommies*, seeking to address the needs of a new generation of children with lesbian mothers and gay fathers.

Camp It Up! summer camp, northern California, 1997. Photograph by Cathy Cade. Courtesy of the Bancroft Library, University of California, Berkeley.

In 1990, Alyson published *Daddy's Roommate*, by Michael Willhoite, a book about a boy whose father and mother split up after the man realizes he is gay. It describes the everyday activities of the boy, his father, and his father's partner, Frank, and celebrates the love and sense of togetherness shared by the family. In 1991, the press published *Gloria Goes to Gay Pride*, the story of a girl and her two mothers at a gay pride march. Gloria sees antigay protesters at the march and wonders why people hate her family. Other books for the children of lesbians and gay men such as *How Would You Feel If Your Dad Was Gay?* by Anne Heron and Kris Kovick, grappled with the issue of homophobia in schools. The book told the story of a brother and sister who hear antigay slurs in school. As a result of their fathers talking to the school principal, an assembly is called where family diversity is explained.[113]

These books caused an uproar. The idea that lesbian and gay families with children would be presented in a positive light in elementary schools was unacceptable to many heterosexual parents. The community of Goldsboro, North Carolina, was divided over the issue of having *Daddy's Roommate* in the public library. Karen Grant, who led the opposition to the book, had discovered it when her son picked it up and started looking at it. Grant called the book "anti-family" and argued that it taught young people that same-sex orientation was acceptable. Parents both defended and attacked the book at a library board meeting where one adult son of a gay father said that he would have been greatly helped by the book if it had been available when his father came out as a gay man.[114] By 1993, county library boards in New Jersey, North Carolina, Missouri, Virginia, and Georgia had reclassified either *Heather Has Two Mommies* or *Daddy's Roommate* as "adult non-fiction."[115] After reclassification, library patrons often had to ask specifically for the books by name. In Oregon, the Oregon Citizen's Alliance used *Heather Has Two Mommies* and *Daddy's Roommate* to argue for a statewide antigay measure that would have classified same-sex relationships as "abnormal, wrong, unnatural, and perverse."[116] In New York City, opponents defeated a citywide program called the Rainbow Curriculum in part because of its proposal to teach books such as *Heather Has Two Mommies, Daddy's Roommate*, and *Gloria Goes to Gay Pride* in New York elementary school classrooms. The president of a Queens school board that opposed the curriculum called the books "dangerously misleading lesbian/homosexual propaganda."[117] And in the U.S. Senate, Senators Jesse Helms and Robert Smith used *Heather Has Two Mommies* as an example of "disgusting, obscene material" in arguing for the Helms-Smith Bill, which cut off all federal funds to schools that taught "homosexuality as an acceptable way of life." The bill passed in 1994.[118] This federal legislation testifies to the growing visibility of lesbian and gay parents and the fears of conservatives that alternative families had gained a foothold in mainstream American life.

As would increasingly happen over the next fifteen years, the children of lesbians and gay men became the spokespeople for their families in these controversies over school libraries. In Rutland, Vermont, in June 1995, sixteen-year-old Erin Gluckman stood up at a town library hearing over whether to restrict access to *Daddy's Roommate*. That hearing was the first time that Gluckman had spoken openly about having a lesbian mother. "I really wanted not to hide. It kept me so uptight," she remembered. "After the hearing, the next day I went into school and all my friends were cheering for me and saying great things. It was terrific." Based on the hearing, the Rutland library decided not to restrict access to Michael Willhoite's book.[119]

The increase in lesbian and gay parents that occurred in the 1980s and 1990s had its roots in the decades of lesbian and gay families with children that had come before them. By defying fundamental cultural perceptions of the family as an exclusively heterosexual institution, gay fathers and lesbian mothers in the decades that followed the Second World War opened up the possibility of lesbians and gay men choosing to become parents and raising children in openly nonheterosexual environments. These families were met by hostility similar to that encountered by the men and women that had come out within previous heterosexual marriages, but by the 1980s and 1990s lesbian and gay parents were achieving legal recognition through second-parent adoption, although this recognition still remained precarious. Unlike the radical resistance families that emerged in lesbian feminist communities of the 1970s, this new generation of gay- and lesbian-headed households openly challenged the heterosexual assumptions of American culture by demanding inclusion; as lesbian mothers and gay fathers sat in hospital maternity wards, shopped for preschools and daycare centers for their children, and inspired the production of books and summer camps aimed at their children, they drove a shift toward family and domestic advocacy in the LGBT civil rights movement and fundamentally challenged the assumption in American society that the family was, by definition, heterosexual.

Epilogue

Lesbian Mothers, Gay Fathers, and Their Children
after Lawrence v. Texas

In 2006, a group of 200 LGBT households with children wearing rainbow leis converged on the annual White House Easter egg roll. An annual event since its inauguration in 1878 by Rutherford B. Hayes, the egg roll is traditionally open to the public and tickets are passed out on a first-come-first-serve basis. The groups of LGBT parents and their children were attending the annual event to bring attention to the Bush administration's antigay policies, specifically its policies on same-sex marriage and same-sex parenting, at the invitation of the Family Pride Coalition. The president had recently weighed in clearly on the issue of same-sex parenting. In 2005, when asked about a Florida Supreme Court case on gay adoptive rights, President George W. Bush said: "Studies have shown that the ideal is where a child is raised in a married family with a man and a woman." In addition, that same year Margaret Spellings, the secretary of education, had criticized PBS for airing a children's show with one segment on two lesbian mothers and their daughters in Vermont. Some socially conservative groups such as the Institute on Religion and Democracy condemned the Family Pride Coalition's action as the political exploitation of children. It was noted that the president and the first lady were conspicuously absent when the families, including about one hundred of the LGBT families that had managed to get tickets, were allowed onto the White House South Lawn.[1]

In 2009, President Barack Obama explicitly extended an invitation to LGBT parents to attend the annual function. The administration gave tickets for distribution to lesbian and gay parents to the Family Pride Coalition, which had by then changed its name to the Family Equality Council, as well as to the Human Rights Campaign and the National Gay and Lesbian Task Force. Members of gay and lesbian civil rights organizations heralded the move as a sign of solidarity with lesbian mothers, gay fathers, and their children. Jennifer Chrisler, head of the Family Equality Council, said that the administration wanted "gay families there, and they are an important part of the American family fabric." In an open letter on the organization's website, Chrisler credited "the efforts of LGBT parents in their communities, in their schools and in their places of worship" as being responsible for a political atmosphere in which their families would be explicitly included in an event with such national visibility.[2]

The cultural discussion over the presence of lesbian mothers, gay fathers, and their children at the annual White House egg roll is indicative of several developments in lesbian and gay family history in the first decade of the twenty-first century: it shows the continuing and growing influence of organizations with foundations in the gay father and lesbian mother movements described in previous chapters; it demonstrates the ways in which same-sex parenting came to be a central focus of both the mainstream LGBT freedom struggle, the media, and political struggles between the two major American political parties; and it illustrates how lesbian and gay parenting was increasingly bound up with the issue of same-sex marriage, though these two issues had in fact often been connected in the homophile literature of the 1950s and in LGBT organizing since the mid-1980s.

Family Pride Coalition, the group that facilitated the gathering of LGBT parents and their children at the 2006 egg roll, changed its name in 2009 to the Family Equality Council, but until 1998 the organization had been known as the Gay and Lesbian Parents Coalition International. GLPCI was the nationwide organization that had grown out of the gay father movement of the 1970s and 1980s. Over the decades GLPCI and COLAGE, a group founded by children of GLPCI parents in 1989 under the name Just For Us, had emerged as major organizations in the LGBT freedom struggle.[3] In 2008, the group was energized by a merger with Rainbow Families, a Minneapolis-based organization founded in 1997. The merger allowed the Family Equality Council to incorporate over 2,000 LGBT families with children served by the Minneapolis organization when it became the Midwest office.[4] In the years after *Lawrence v. Texas*, the 2003 Supreme Court decision that declared sodomy laws unconstitutional and overturned the Court's previous ruling in *Bowers v. Hardwick*, the organization that had emerged from the gay father movement as the Gay Parents Coalition International became increasingly visible as a national voice in the struggle for LGBT domestic and parental rights.

The Family Equality Council was joined in its activism on the part of lesbian and gay families with children by COLAGE, Parents and Friends of Lesbians and Gays—an organization that increasingly defined itself as concerned with the rights of lesbian and gay parents, not just as an organization of the parents of lesbians and gay men—as well as lesbian and gay civil rights organizations such as the National Center for Lesbian Rights, the Lambda Legal Defense Fund, Gay and Lesbian Advocates and Defenders, the National Gay and Lesbian Task Force, the Human Rights Campaign, and the ACLU's Lesbian and Gay Rights Project, the descendant of the Sexual Privacy Project, founded in 1986. The primary foci of LGBT parental activism in the first decade of the twenty-first century were same-sex marriage, inclusive family curriculum and LGBT family advocacy in schools, custody and foster/adoptive rights, and media outreach.[5] These areas of political activity resonate with the earlier periods of lesbian and gay family history discussed in previous chapters, but also mark significant developments in the period from 2003 to 2011.

The fight for lesbian and gay custody continued into the era after *Lawrence v. Texas*. However, the battles were increasingly restricted to the regions of the South and the Midwest. Virginia, in particular, remained a very dangerous place for lesbian mothers and gay fathers. In this state, same-sex sexuality remained per se justification for removal of custody or visitation rights, and lesbians and gay men who had been previously married still faced the danger of losing custodial or parental rights. In a 2007 case, R.S. *v.* A.S., a Virginia appeals court upheld restrictions on a lesbian mother's visitation rights, affirming a lower court decision that prevented overnight visits by adults to whom the mother was not married in the company of the children. Although the mother claimed in her appeal that this was a punitive decision based on her lesbianism that deprived her of equal protection rights, the appeals court noted that the original decision had stipulated that the restrictions on overnight visits were gender neutral; however, it was known to the Virginia courts at the time of both decisions that the mother had been in a relationship with another woman in Oregon throughout the period of the custody struggle. Although the Virginia courts denied that same-sex sexuality played any role in the decision, the result echoed decades of restrictive custody decisions regarding lesbian mothers and gay fathers, denying the mother her right to be with her female partner and her children at the same time.[6]

In a 2004 Idaho custody case involving a gay father, Theron McGriff, the Idaho Supreme Court distanced itself from custody rulings based on homosexuality at the same time as it affirmed lower court rulings restricting the rights of a gay father. In December 2000, Shawn McGriff had filed for a modification of custody based on her ex-husband's "intimate relationship with a person of the same sex" and allegations that he had "failed to deal with his homosexuality in a responsible and emotionally stable manner." In 2002, a magistrate judge upheld the request to modify custody, awarding legal and physical custody to Shawn McGriff and restricting visitation to times when the "father is not residing in the same house with his male partner." Although the magistrate judge cited Theron McGriff's decision to "openly co-habit with Nick Case, his partner," as a factor in affirming the change in custodial circumstance, the Idaho Supreme Court found that same-sex sexuality had not been an issue in the decision and affirmed it, thereby upholding the restrictions on Theron McGriff. In a decision that mirrored earlier rulings in the 1970s and 1980s, the court declared that homosexuality could not be the sole determinant of custody, while also upholding a decision that restricted a gay father's right to visitation with his children in the company of a same-sex partner.[7]

Other cases stemming from previous heterosexual marriages show that family courts in this period were increasingly reluctant to declare same-sex sexuality to be incompatible with parenting. In deciding a case, *M.A.T. v. G.S.T.*, that involved a divorce where the mother had informed her ex-husband that she was in a relationship with another woman, the Pennsylvania Superior Court overturned a lower court ruling awarding primary custody to the father and officially overruled a twenty-five-year-old legal presumption in the state that same-sex orientation rendered an individual unfit as a parent.[8] In 2004, the Tennessee Court of Appeals struck down a lower court ruling that restricted Joseph Hogue, a gay father, from "exposing the child to his gay lover(s) and/or his gay lifestyle."[9] A Louisiana appeals court affirmed a lower court's ruling in favor of a gay father in a case where the mother had argued that the lower court "was manifestly erroneous in disregarding the [father's] open homosexual lifestyle when considering what was in the best interest of the minor child."[10] In a 2009 case, the Georgia Supreme Court overturned a trial court's decision in *Mongerson v. Mongerson* that had prohibited a gay father from allowing his children to be in the presence of his "homosexual partners and friends."[11]

Co-parent custody cases during these years also showed an increased willingness on the part of some state courts to recognize same-sex families with children and the rights of estranged co-parents.[12] In 2005, a Pennsylvania appeals court upheld a trial ruling that found it in the "best interests" of two children for them to be in the primary custody of their lesbian co-parent, and not the biological mother.[13] A circuit judge in Oregon ruled in 2011 that a lesbian co-mother was a legal parent and could seek custody and visitation rights based on the two women having previously established a same-sex partnership.[14] Sometimes, same-sex marriages and civil unions were used as determinants of co-parent status; in a 2010 decision, the New York Court of Appeals ruled in favor of a lesbian co-mother's parental rights based on the fact that the two women had entered into a civil union in Vermont. Under Vermont law the two women were legally co-mothers.[15] A similar ruling occurred in New Jersey, based on that state's domestic partnership law.[16]

There was evidence in these years that the overturning of the sodomy laws in *Lawrence v. Texas* would contribute to decisions favoring lesbian and gay parental rights. In a 2006 decision, the Maryland Court of Special Appeals overturned restrictions on Ulf Hedberg, a gay father, that forbade him from living with his partner with whom he had been raising his son for more than five years. Susan Sommer from the Lambda Legal Defense Fund had argued in a 2005 hearing of this case that the restrictions on Hedberg violated the 2003 *Lawrence* decision.[17] The Idaho Supreme Court decision in *McGriff v. McGriff* explicitly cited *Lawrence* in its determination that sexual orientation could not be the sole factor in a determination of custody.[18] However, resistance remained to *Lawrence* and to any impact it might have on lesbian and gay custody decisions; in 2004, the Alabama Court of Civil Appeals upheld a lower court's decision to modify an earlier custody ruling due in part to the father's revelation of his ex-wife's lesbianism. In its decision, the court rejected an argument that *Lawrence* invalidated a denial of custody based solely on sexual orientation.[19]

As the ongoing growth of open parenting in LGBT communities led to the increased visibility of children of lesbian and gay parents in America's schools, the issue of creating a safe atmosphere for these children in the classroom became a central issue of LGBT parental activism and its opponents. In 2006, Tonia and David Parker filed a suit in Lexington, Massachusetts, against the local school district after their five-year-old son was given a book, *Who's in a Family*, in his kindergarten class at Estabrook Elementary that included portrayals of same-sex families with children. They were joined in the lawsuit by another couple, Joseph and Robin Wirthlin, whose son's teacher had read the books *King and King* and *Molly's Family* in his second-grade classroom. The lawsuit stipulated that the school district should have given the parent's advance warning about the books' classroom usage and the chance to prevent their children from being present. In 2008, the First U.S. Circuit Court of Appeals decided the case, *Parker v. Hurley*, in the district's favor; in October of that that same year, the U.S. Supreme Court refused to hear the case, essentially upholding the appeals court ruling.[20]

A cultural struggle over lesbian mothers, gay fathers, and their children was at the heart of *Parker v. Hurley*.[21] The book that originally prompted David Parker to protest his son's curriculum, *Who's in a Family*, was a picture book about the diversity of families; it included children being raised by their grandmother, multiracial families, single-parent families, and both a lesbian mother–headed household and a family with two gay fathers. In its original ruling in favor of the school district's right to include *Who's in a Family* in the curriculum, later upheld by the First Circuit Court of Appeals, the Massachusetts District

Court explicitly identified the interests of children of lesbian mothers and gay fathers:

> It is reasonable for public educators to teach elementary school students about individuals with different sexual orientations and about various forms of families, including those with same-sex parents, in an effort to eradicate the effects of past discrimination, to reduce the risk of future discrimination and, in the process, to reaffirm our nation's constitutional commitment to promoting mutual respect among members of our diverse society. In addition, it is reasonable for those educators to find that teaching young children to understand and respect differences in sexual orientation will contribute to an academic environment in which students who are gay, lesbian, or the children of same-sex parents will be comfortable and, therefore, better able to learn.[22]

The amicus briefs filed in the Massachusetts District Court on behalf of the school district by several LGBT freedom struggle organizations also focus on the needs of the children of lesbian mothers and gay fathers. "If a teacher were forced to silence children's discussion of their families if they have gay parents," the brief declares, "because other students' parents had not been given prior notice and the right to opt out, the teacher's conduct would clearly convey to such children the terrible message that their families were unworthy of recognition, indeed unmentionable." This incident marks one of the first, and rare, times in which a U.S. court has raised and affirmed the rights of children of lesbian and gay parents to representation in a democratic society.

The debate over *Parker v. Hurley* highlights the extent to which lesbian and gay families with children have become tied to the struggle for same-sex marriage rights. Of the three books objected to by the plaintiffs in the case, only *King and King* was about same-sex marriage, while *Molly's Family* and *Who's in a Family* were both about the experiences of diverse families, not necessarily involving marriage. Yet in their objection to these materials being introduced to their children, the parents claimed that the district was attempting to devalue their belief that "homosexuality is immoral and that marriage is necessarily only a holy union between a man and a woman."[23] In its decision in favor of the district's inclusive policy, the Massachusetts District Court drew the same connection by explicitly connecting *Hurley* with the 2003 *Goodridge v. Department of Public Health* decision that established the state constitutional right to same-sex marriage in Massachusetts. The court argued that the inclusion of the books under debate in the elementary school curriculum was "rationally related" to the Massachusetts Supreme Court's "goal of eradication," as stated in the *Goodridge* decision, of the hardship imposed on lesbians and gay men by a ban on same-sex marriage.[24]

The conservative opponents of both same-sex marriage and LGBT family and domestic rights also saw these connections and cited them in the *Hurley* case decision as a sign of dangerous national trends. In 2011 congressional hearings over a bill that would have repealed the Defense of Marriage Act (DOMA), Timothy Minnery, senior vice president for public policy for the conservative organization Focus on the Family, told Congress the story of the four *Hurley* plaintiffs and argued that it showed how "when same-sex marriage becomes the law of the land, public school officials can argue that it is now part of the general culture and civil society, and therefore can be brought up at any time in any subject or grade level—without any parental notification or consent." In the same speech, Minnery stated that one of the most compelling reasons for continuing to ban same-sex marriage was "its impact on children" and that heterosexual families were better for children than ones with same-sex parents; in fact, in testimony arguing for the preservation of DOMA, Minnery spent the majority of his allotted time speaking about the dangers of lesbian mother–and gay father–headed households for children.[25] For Minnery and the organization he represented, the issues of same-sex marriage and lesbian and gay parenting had become inextricably fused. Similarly, in the debates over California's Proposition 8 to ban same-sex marriage, television ads featuring Joseph and Robin Wirthlin argued that what happened in Massachusetts could happen in California, linking the growing visibility of same-sex families with children and same-sex marriage. During the debates over Proposition 8, the Wirthlins spoke at rallies opposing same-sex marriage, linking their struggle about the depiction of families in Massachusetts schools with the proposed law in California.[26] William Tam, the head of the Traditional Family Coalition, a conservative group that supported Proposition 8, warned that the legalization of same-sex marriage could lead to children believing that same-sex relationships were valid choices.[27]

In the years after the *Lawrence* decision, lesbian mothers, gay fathers, and their children came increasingly to feature centrally in the political struggle for same-sex marriage nationwide. As cultural investments in both queer childlessness and the assumedly heterosexual family came to a head in American society, gay and lesbian families with children became the focal point of both conservative fears about social permissiveness around same-sex relationships and the political struggle for the legal recognition of same-sex relationships. In early 2008, the staff at the Los Angeles Lesbian and Gay Center began giving lesbian mothers, gay fathers, and their children clipboards that they could decorate and display in their homes for Valentine's Day as "a reminder to discuss marriage equality with anyone who visits."[28] One picture captured a child at a rally after Proposition 8 was passed on November 15th, 2008, sleeping next to a sign that read, "Mommy and Mama, Please Make the Scary Bigots Go Away!"[29] Members of COLAGE, including eleven-year-old Samuel Berston, marched with a banner in a San Francisco protest on March 4, 2009, one day before the California Supreme Court began hearing oral arguments for and against the state ban on same-sex marriage. That night, Samuel spoke to the crowd, saying, "My moms deserve love just like everyone else." Speaking at a 2012 news conference in support of same-sex marriage in California, seventeen-year-old Spencer Perry said, "When Proposition 8 doesn't allow parents like mine to marry, it isn't just defining their love as taboo or wrong, it says that our family—that my brothers, that my mothers—shouldn't belong."[30] In 2006, Andy Newman and Gregory McGuire testified on behalf of same-sex marriage to the Massachusetts state legislature with their children.[31] The testimony of twelve-year-old Evann Orleck-Jetter to the Vermont legislature was cited by lawmakers as a central reason why they voted for a bill legalizing same-sex marriage.[32] In Iowa, the Lambda Legal Defense Fund focused on the rights of the children of lesbian mothers and gay fathers in their successful arguments that a state ban on same-sex marriage was unconstitutional. In that same state, Zach Wahls, the son of two lesbian mothers, made a speech to the state legislature that became an internet sensation.[33]

The intense visibility of lesbian mothers, gay fathers, and their children in the struggle for same-sex marriage and the focus on them by opponents of lesbian and gay marital rights in the first decade of the twenty-first century are directly tied to the sixty-year history in *Radical Relations*. Since the Second World War, American culture has linked notions of intimacy, sexuality, and the family in ways that presumed queer childlessness and heterosexual family and saw marriage as the line separating the two. In the 1950s, when men and women in the homophile communities of the era debated the viability of same-sex marriage, both as a political goal and a relationship model, the presence or absence of children in same-sex relationships was often held up as a part of the debate. In the 1970s and 1980s, when family judges expressed their belief that same-sex sexuality was incompatible with parenting, it was often a remarried heterosexual spouse that offered the model of family that was legible to the courts and that seemed a more suitable place for children. In the 1980s and 1990s, as lesbians and gay men for the first time had children in large numbers *after* coming out about their sexuality, the struggles of legal activists to develop a model of family legality that would offer some protection and permanence wrestled with the fact that only heterosexual parenting, codified through marriage, was visible in the eyes of the law.

Throughout the six decades of this history, the existence of lesbian mothers and gay fathers was repeatedly illegible in an American culture that could only see childless queerness and heterosexual family. As the struggles of lesbian and gay parental activists and the lived experience of generations of lesbian mothers, gay fathers, and their children drove this contradiction to the center of the freedom struggle, the children of same-sex households increasingly became the focal point of political change and social anxieties.

Notes

Abbreviations

The following abbreviations for archives and collections appear throughout the notes.

CKA   Center Kids Archives, Lesbian, Gay, Bisexual and Transgender Community Center, New York, NY

CNOF   COLAGE (Children of Lesbians and Gays Everywhere) National Office Files, San Francisco, CA

GLBTHS   Gay, Lesbian, Bisexual, and Transgender Historical Society, San Francisco, CA

HSC   Human Sexuality Collection, Carl A. Kroch Library, Cornell University, Ithaca, NY

LHA   Lesbian Herstory Archives, Brooklyn, NY

LMNDF Files   Lesbian Mothers' National Defense Fund Files, Jenny Sayward Personal Collection (digital copies of entire collection in author's possession)

LMP   Phyllis Lyon and Del Martin Papers, 1924–2000, Gay, Lesbian, Bisexual, and Transgender Historical Society, San Francisco, CA

OLOHP   Old Lesbian Oral Herstory Project, Sophia Smith Archives, Smith College, Northampton, MA

ONGLA   ONE National Gay and Lesbian Archives, University of Southern California, Los Angeles, CA

Introduction

1. Carole Morton, interview with author, San Francisco, CA, March 10, 2007. On the founding of New Jersey DOB in 1971, see also letter from Jan Rubin to the national DOB headquarters, March 29, 1971, box 1, folder 21, LMP.

2. Carole Morton, interview with author, San Francisco, CA, March 10, 2007.

3. Ibid.

4. This belief is still a powerful one in the United States and is connected to the notion that lesbian and gay parents are a novel cultural development that came about only with the advent of new insemination technologies and surrogate births in the 1980s and 1990s. If parenting is not solely heterosexual, goes the current manifestation of this idea, it has at least been so until very recently.

5. I use the phrase "freedom struggle" here instead of "civil rights movement" to indicate that this larger movement encompasses, but has not been limited to, the pursuit of legal civil rights. In this usage, I follow Clayborne Carson's use of the term in his work on the African American freedom struggle. Clayborne Carson, *In Struggle: SNCC and the Black Awakening of the 1960s* (Cambridge, MA: Harvard University Press, 1981). See also Clayborne Carson, "Civil Rights Reform and the Black Freedom

Struggle," in *The Civil Rights Movement in America: Essays*, ed. Charles W. Eagles (Jackson, MS: University Press of Mississippi, 1986), 19–32. By "domestic and parental rights," I mean to link foster/adoptive parental rights, custody rights, and same-sex marriage rights—including the struggles of transnational queer families for citizenship rights and the legal recognition of same-sex unions in matters of health and illness, medical care, and death. The historical experiences detailed in *Radical Relations* propelled all of these demands, along with the constitutional rights to privacy, equal protection, and due process that underlie them, to the fore of the modern LGBT freedom struggle.

6. Although this book focuses on the history of lesbian mothers, gay fathers, and their children, I believe that histories of transgender and bisexual parents are also critical components of understanding these historically normative connections between family, gender, and sexuality and the ways parents and children have challenged them. It is my hope that *Radical Relations* will suggest avenues of research and inquiry for this future work.

7. Adrienne Rich, "Compulsory Heterosexuality and Lesbian Existence," in *Blood, Bread, and Poetry: Selected Prose, 1979–1985* (New York: W. W. Norton & Co., 1986): 23–75.

8. On the Briggs Initiative, see Susan Stryker and Jim Van Buskirk, *Gay by the Bay: A History of Queer Culture in the San Francisco Bay Area* (San Francisco: Chronicle Books, 1996), 78. On Anita Bryant and the "Save Our Children Campaign," see Perry Deane Young, *God's Bullies: Power Politics and Religious Tyranny* (New York: Holt, Rinehart, and Winston, 1982), 36–40. For a detailed history of the struggles of lesbian and gay teachers, see Jackie M. Blount, *Fit to Teach: Same-Sex Desire, Gender, and School Work in the Twentieth Century* (Albany, NY: State University of New York Press, 2005). On the use of child protectionist rhetoric in several conservative campaigns in the 1970s, including Dade County, Florida, anti-busing campaigns and organizing against the Equal Rights Amendment, and the connection between this rhetoric and opposition to African American civil rights, see Gillian Frank, " 'The Civil Rights of Parents': Race and Conservative Politics in Anita Bryant's Campaign against Gay Rights in 1970s Florida," *Journal of the History of Sexuality* 22, no. 1 (January 2013).

9. In her book, *In a Queer Time and Place* (New York: New York University Press, 2005), cultural theorist Judith Halberstam argues that we can chart the discursive emergence in U.S. culture of "queer time" and "straight time," where reproduction is ideologically defined as part of a notion of heteronormative, capitalist citizenship. I believe that the cultural trajectories Halberstam identifies are bound up in this identification of the family and childrearing as exclusively heterosexual.

10. Sarah Wildman, "Children Speak for Same-Sex Marriage," *New York Times*, January 20, 2010. This article relates the testimony of ten-year-old Kasey Nicholson-McFadden before the New Jersey State Senate in December 2009, in which he describes how the senate's vote against same-sex marriage, in support of which his two mothers petitioned the state for years, relegated his family to an inferior social position.

11. Heather Murray, *Not in This Family: Gays and the Meaning of Kinship* (Philadelphia: University of Pennsylvania Press, 2010).

12. Margot Canaday, *The Straight State: Sexuality and Citizenship in Twentieth-Century America* (Princeton, NJ: Princeton University Press, 2009).

13. Nancy Cott, *Public Vows: A History of Marriage and the Nation* (Cambridge, MA: Harvard University Press, 2002); Elizabeth Pleck, *Not Just Roommates: Cohabitation after the Sexual Revolution* (Chicago: University of Chicago Press, 2012).

14. Other scholarship has illustrated ways that these investments have manifested in reaction to large-scale changes in the heterosexual, white, nuclear, middle-class family since the 1950s. On the production of nostalgia over a postwar family/marital ideal, see Stephanie Coontz, *The Way We Never Were: American Families and the Nostalgia Trap* (New York: Basic Books, 1992). On changes in the American middle-class family since the 1950s, as well as cultural struggles over the meaning of these changes, see Jessica Weiss, *To Have and to Hold: Marriage, the Baby Boom, and Social Change* (Chicago: University of Chicago Press, 2000).

15. For example, Anglo settlers often saw the fact that Native women were in charge of agriculture as proof of Native inferiority to Europeans. Joan Jensen, "Native American Women and Agriculture: A Seneca Case Study," in *Unequal Sisters: A Multicultural Reader in U.S. Women's History*, ed. Ellen DuBois and Vicki Ruiz (New York: Routledge, 1990), 51–65. For similar uses and abuses of the Native family in California, see Albert Hurtado, *Indian Survival on the California Frontier* (New Haven: Yale University Press, 1988), 172–73. Also of importance are the ways that "Indian boarding schools" sought to inculcate Anglo values in Native children. See Robert Trennert, "Educating Indian Girls at Nonreservation Boarding Schools, 1870–1920," in *Unequal Sisters*, 224–49; and K. Tsianina Lomawaima, *They Called It Prairie Light: The Story of Chilocco Indian School* (Lincoln: University of Nebraska Press, 1994).

16. Linda Gordon, *Heroes of Their Own Lives: The Politics and History of Family Violence* (New York: Viking, 1988). See also Herbert Gutman, *The Black Family in Slavery and Freedom, 1750–1925* (New York: Vintage Books, 1976); Laura Edwards, *Gendered Strife and Confusion* (Urbana: University of Illinois Press, 1997); and Brenda Stevenson, *Life in Black and White: Family and Community in the Slave South* (Oxford: Oxford University Press, 1996).

17. Rickie Solinger, *Wake Up Little Susie: Single Pregnancy and Race Before Roe v. Wade* (New York: Routledge, 1992); Dorothy Roberts, *Killing the Black Body: Race, Reproduction, and the Meaning of Liberty* (New York: Pantheon, 1997).

18. Danielle McGuire, *At the Dark End of the Street: Black Women, Rape, and Resistance—a New History of the Civil Rights Movement from Rosa Parks to the Rise of Black Power* (New York: Random House, 2010). On the systematic control of black women's bodies under slavery, see Angela Y. Davis, "The Legacy of Slavery: Standards for a New Womanhood," in *Women, Race, and Class* (New York: Random House, 1981), 3–29.

Chapter 1

1. On the importance of World War II in the development of lesbian and gay communities, see Allan Berube, *Coming Out Under Fire: The History of Gay Men and Women in World War Two* (New York: Free Press, 1990). On the emergence of homophile organizations during this period, see John D'Emilio, *Sexual Politics, Sexual Communities: The Making of a Homosexual Minority in the United States, 1940–1970* (Chicago: University of Chicago Press, 1983), and Marcia Gallo, *Different Daughters: A History of the Daughters of Bilitis and the Rise of the Lesbian Civil Rights Movement* (Emeryville, CA: Seal Press, 2007).

For a historical overview of crackdowns and sex-crime panics of the 1950s, see Estelle Freedman and John D'Emilio, *Intimate Matters: A History of Sexuality in America* (New York: Harper & Row, 1988), 293–95. For the story of the impact of a sex-crime panic on one community, see Neil Miller, *Sex-crime Panic: A Journey to the Paranoid Heart of the 1950s* (New York: Alyson Books, 2002). On the persecution of gay men and lesbians in the McCarthy era, see John D'Emilio, "The Homosexual Menace: The Politics of Sexuality in Cold War America," in *Making Trouble: Essays on Gay History, Politics, and the University* (New York: Routledge, 1992), 57–73, and David K. Johnson, *The Lavender Scare: The Cold War Persecution of Gays and Lesbians in the Federal Government* (Chicago: University of Chicago Press, 2004).

2. In a 1964 issue of *The Ladder* one woman wrote about her feelings of being hidden in a suburban home with her partner and her son. She reflected that "even though I love the girl I live with, and we both love my son, we aren't recognized as a family." Although the woman longed to be a part of visible lesbian organizing, she felt she couldn't afford to do so, out of fear that her son would face social opprobrium for her choices. She expressed feeling as if her family was in hiding, and the lingering question of how much the other families in her neighborhood suspected: "I do wonder sometimes what thoughts might flit through the minds of those married couples we may happen to meet as we maneuver the grocery-laden carriage to the check-out aisle." "I Want to Stand Up and Be Counted," *The Ladder*, January 1964, 6.

3. "Post-Stonewall" refers to the era that began with the Stonewall riots, which occurred on June 28, 1969, in Greenwich Village, New York, and mark the onset of widespread gay and lesbian liberation movements. On the midcentury use of "coming out," see Berube, *Coming Out Under Fire*, 6.

4. On postwar heterosexual, nuclear family domesticity, see Elaine Tyler May, *Homeward Bound: American Families in the Cold War Era* (New York: Basic Books, 1988), and Stephanie Coontz, *The Way We Never Were: American Families and the Nostalgia Trap* (New York: Basic Books, 1992). On the importance of heterosexual marriage in this cultural framework, see Nancy Cott, *Public Vows: A History of Marriage and the Nation* (Cambridge, MA: Harvard University Press, 2000), 190–99. For a discussion of marriage, both opposite-sex and same-sex, as a topic in the homophile periodicals of the 1950s, see Craig Loftin, *Masked Voices: Gay Men and Lesbians in Cold War America* (Albany, NY: State University of New York Press, 2012), 157–79.

5. Ron, interview with author, Santa Barbara, CA, May 7, 2003. Throughout the text, pseudonyms will be indicated by the use of first names only.

6. William Harrison, interview, undated, 98-025, Oral History Files, GLBTHS.

7. Sam Cerasaro and Richard Mason, interview with author, Rancho Mirage, CA, January 28, 2006.

8. Hank Vilas, interview, Berkeley, CA, April 11, 1983, Before Stonewall Special Collection 87-2, LHA.

9. David Leddick, *The Secret Lives of Married Men* (Los Angeles: Alyson, 2003), 6.

10. Letters, *ONE Magazine*, March 1965, 28.

11. A. Billy S. Jones [sic], "A Father's Need; A Parent's Desire," in *In The Life: A Black Gay Anthology*, ed. Joseph Beam (Boston: Alyson Publications, 1986), 143; ABilly S.

Jones-Hennin and Christopher Hennin, interview with author, Washington, D.C., June 29, 2012.

12. "A Husband Divorces After Finding Male Lover," *Vector*, September 1972, 44.

13. Jack Warner, interview with author, San Francisco, CA, October 6, 2006.

14. Clay Wilson, interview with author, San Jose, CA, October 7, 2007.

15. Del Martin and Phyllis Lyon, interview with author, San Francisco, CA, February 17, 2006.

16. Shaba Barnes, interview with Arden Eversmeyer, Apache Junction, AZ, January 2003, OLOHP; Jess Stearn, author of *The Grapevine*, a sensationalist 1964 book on lesbianism, reported meeting Belle, a "middle-aged, staid-looking" lesbian mother, at a meeting of the Daughters of Bilitis that he attended at the invitation of the group. Belle, Stearn wrote, had married to please her family and escape her love for women. "Even the lesbian," Belle had told Stearn at the meeting, "reflects the prejudices of the majority." *The Grapevine: A Report on the Secret World of the Lesbian* (Garden City, NY: Doubleday, 1964), 26.

17. Del Martin and Phyllis Lyon, interview with author, San Francisco, CA, February 17, 2006.

18. "Bernie's Story . . . A Herstory, An Oral History Taken by Katie Gilmartin," *OLOC Reporter*, March 1994, 3, Old Lesbians Organizing for Change Records, Sophia Smith Archives, Smith College, Northampton, MA.

19. Vera Martin, interview with author, Apache Junction, AZ, September 22, 2006.

20. Sara Evans, *Born for Liberty: A History of Women in America* (New York: Free Press, 1989), 229–34, 236, 252–53. One woman, writing to *The Ladder* in 1957, emphasized the possible economic dependence of married lesbians in discussing the "numbers of women who are not prepared to risk a life alien to what they have been taught all their lives to believe was their 'natural' destiny—AND—their only expectation for ECONOMIC security" (emphasis in original). This reader went on to say that "I think it is about time that equipped women began to take on some of the ethical questions which a male-dominated culture has produced," and that "homosexual persecution has at its roots not only social ignorance, but a philosophically active anti-feminist dogma." Readers Respond, *The Ladder*, August 1957, 28–30.

21. Win Cottrell, interview with JoAnn Castillo, February 3, 1980, 98-025, Oral History Files, GLBTHS.

22. In the period from 1950 to 1965, women faced a particularly difficult time securing employment that would offer economic security outside of heterosexual marriage, and this reality had a huge impact on married lesbians. These gendered pressures are reflected in the pattern of national divorce rates. Historian Jessica Weiss notes that divorce rates are higher in "periods of enhanced economic opportunity for women: during World War II and after 1965." Jessica Weiss, *To Have and to Hold: Marriage, the Baby Boom, and Social Change* (Chicago: University of Chicago Press, 2000), 179.

23. Virginia "Gini" Morton, interview with Arden Eversmeyer, St. Louis, MO, April 2003, OLOHP.

24. James, interview with Deborah Goleman Wolf, September 4, 1979, Spoken Word Audio File 108 and 109, LHA.

25. Laud Humphreys, *Tearoom Trade: Impersonal Sex in Public Places* (Chicago: Aldine Publishing Company, 1970), 106, 112–15.

26. Barbara Kalish, interview with Arden Eversmeyer, Long Beach, CA, January 2001, OLOHP.

27. Readers Write, *Mattachine Review*, November 1958, 30.

28. Ibid., June 1956, 33. A married man with three children, writing in 1962, told the magazine, "We need a lot more progress. . . . You are doing good and much needed work. I like your editorial style, the factual articles, and the refreshing fiction." Ibid., July 1962, 32.

29. Readers Respond, *The Ladder*, October 1960, 20.

30. Letters dated April 23, 1962, and May 9, 1963, box 4, file 4, Donald Stewart Lucas Papers, GLBTHS.

31. Readers Respond, *The Ladder*, May 1960, 26.

32. Box 3, folder 10, LMP.

33. Notecard dated February 4, 1966, box 6, file 5, Donald Stewart Lucas Papers, GLBTHS.

34. Readers Respond, *The Ladder*, November 1960, 22.

35. Notecard dated December 8, 1965, box 6, file 5, Donald Stewart Lucas Papers, GLBTHS.

36. Tangents, *ONE Magazine*, May 1958, 23. Although I have not found stories of married lesbians arrested in bar raids in my research, suggesting this was a rarer occurrence, lesbians in general were frequently harassed and arrested in bar raids. Further research on the historical experiences of married lesbians caught in bar raids is needed.

37. "Legal Aid and Referals [sic]," October 20, 1960, box 6, file 4, Donald Stewart Lucas Papers, 1941–98, GLBTHS.

38. See "Waukesha Police Arrest 10 in Parks," *Milwaukee Journal*, September 7, 1960; "Carroll College Dean Has Quit," *Milwaukee Journal*, September 8, 1960; "Six Accused of Perversion in Park Quiz," *Chicago Daily Tribune*, September 8, 1960.

39. Daneel Buring, *Lesbian and Gay Memphis: Building Communities Behind the Magnolia Curtain* (New York: Garland Publishing, 1997), 49.

40. Toward Understanding, *ONE Magazine*, September 1959, 26–27.

41. Readers Write, *Mattachine Review*, May 1962, 23.

42. Richard Tooker, interview with Peter Toscani, January 16, 1998, 98-046, Oral History Files, GLBTHS.

43. Hank, interview with author, San Francisco, CA, October 6, 2007.

44. Freedman notes that in the late 1940s and 1950s, the resurgent social fears surrounding sexual difference driving the second wave of sex-crime panics was part of an emphasis on the traditional, heterosexual nuclear family as essential to American society. Estelle B. Freedman, " 'Uncontrolled Desires': The Response to the Sexual Psychopath, 1920–1960," *Journal of American History* 74, no. 1 (June 1987): 83–106.

45. John Gerassi, *The Boys of Boise* (New York: Collier, 1966), 12, 60, 86.

46. "Sex Offenders Tell of Helping Themselves," *Mattachine Review*, December 1955, 12–15. On the founding of the Atascadero sexual psychopath program, see Freedman, " 'Uncontrolled Desires," 83–10. On the program and its treatment of queer inmates,

see Nan Alamilla Boyd, *Wide-Open Town: A History of Queer San Francisco to 1965* (Berkeley: University of California Press, 2003), 163.

47. Rick Stokes, interview with author, San Francisco, CA, January 15, 2007.

48. Miller, *Sex-Crime Panic*, 112–15, 160.

49. "The Senior Staff Man," *Time Magazine*, October 23, 1964. See also "Editorial," *ONE Magazine*, November 1964, 4–5.

50. Jonathan Ned Katz, "Hunting Witches in Massachusetts, 1960: How an Antiporn "Reign of Terror" Destroyed Seven Gay Lives," *The Advocate*, August 15, 1989, 44–45. See also Barry Werth, *The Scarlet Professor—Newton Arvin: A Literary Life Shattered by Scandal* (New York: Nan A. Talese, 2001).

51. Jack Roth, "Blackmail Paid By Congressman: Victim among Thousands Preyed Upon by Ring of Extortionists," *New York Times*, May 17, 1967.

52. The dangers facing married lesbian mothers were culturally salient enough to make it into lesbian pulp fiction of the era. In the classic, haunting 1952 novel, *The Price of Salt*, by Claire Morgan (Patricia Highsmith), two women, Carol and Therese, who are falling in love embark on a cross-country trip and are chased by a private detective hired by Carol's ex-husband to get proof of their love affair. The ex-husband uses the evidence and a love letter that Therese has written Carol to strip Carol of her parental rights and access to her daughter, Rindy. Carol returns to New York and fights the decision but refuses to promise she will no longer see Therese. She is left with only a few days of supervised visits with Rindy every year. At the novel's end, Therese and Carol have reunited in New York, and the novel ends with the two of them in love and moving in together. The novel uncannily predicts the custody court orders of the 1970s, demanding that lesbian mothers disavow their relationships with women in order to retain their parental rights. Claire Morgan, *The Price of Salt* (New York: Coward-McCann, 1952). *The Other Way*, a more conventional, pornographic, and lesser-known 1969 pulp novel by Robert Hadley, actually opens with a young mother, Lisbeth Fields, in court fighting for custody of her son, Tommy. Lisbeth's husband, Martin, has sued for divorce after walking in on her and another woman, Dr. Niccole Duvall, making love. Lisbeth, out of fear that Martin would reveal her relationship with Dr. Duvall in court and ruin Dr. Duvall's career helping needy children, unconditionally gives up custody of her son and flees to Cape Cod. The novel ends with Lisbeth being "saved" from lesbianism by Dirk Trainer, a virile, muscular bohemian who lives as a beachcomber and quotes poetry. As the book closes, Dirk declares that he is going to "find a preacher and make an honest woman out of her." Although very different, both novels illustrate cultural prohibitions against lesbian motherhood in the postwar era. Robert Hadley, *The Other Way* (New York: Midwood, 1969).

53. Blue Lunden, interview with Quinn, December 1989, Blue (Doris) Lunden Special Collection 83-04, box 1, folder 2, LHA.

54. Vera Martin, interview with author, Apache Junction, AZ, September 22, 2006. The specter of having your children taken away by the courts in deference to a heterosexual alternative loomed large in many ways in the lives of lesbian mothers raising their children in this era. Linda Lunden remembers that her mother discouraged and finally severed her contact with her former adoptive father out of fear that even though Blue Lunden was Linda's biological mother, she would lose in court if the

man challenged her for custody. Linda Lunden, interview with author, Key Biscayne, FL, March 17, 2012.

55. Vera Martin, interview with author, Apache Junction, AZ, September 22, 2006.

56. Del Martin and Phyllis Lyon, interview with author, San Francisco, CA, February 17, 2006.

57. Box 1, folder 14, LMP.

58. "Readers on Writers," ONE Magazine, October 1958, 25.

59. Del Martin and Phyllis Lyon, interview with author, San Francisco, CA, February 17, 2006.

60. In 1966, The Ladder ran a short story that involved a lesbian mother, Lee, surprised in the midst of her weekend plans with her lover by her ex-husband and daughter home early from a scheduled weekend visit. In frustration and self-doubt she tells her ex-husband, "You and Ann can give her a normal home, the kind you approve of, I can't." "Let Us Out of Here!" The Ladder, July 1966, 7.

61. Unidentified newspaper (AP) article, "New Jersey Legal Precedent: Divorce Granted—Wife Homosexual," 1959, Subject Files, Passing 10010 folder, LHA. I believe this case was H. v. H. and that the decision was upheld by the New Jersey Superior Court in 1960. See story in Here and There, The Ladder, November 1961, 11.

62. Tangents, ONE Magazine, August 1955, 10.

63. ONE Magazine, November 1955, 9.

64. One woman writing to the DOB did report winning a custody case as an admitted lesbian, even in this early period. In 1965, "Mrs. B" wrote: "I reached a personal crossroads in 1964. After eighteen years of marriage and four children . . . I sued for divorce and openly declared my love for a woman and our intention to make a future life together. With the custody of four minor children at stake. I gambled because I believe deeply that there is justice for the homosexual." Much of the debate here seems to have centered on whether, her lesbianism notwithstanding, "Mrs. B" fit appropriate models of postwar femininity; she reported that "the most prevalent response was, 'But she is so good, a good mother, a good housekeeper, a good person.'" "Living Propaganda," The Ladder, January 1965, 13–14.

65. William Harrison, interview, undated, 98-025, Oral History Files, GLBTHS.

66. Sam Cerasaro and Richard Mason, interview with author, Rancho Mirage, CA, January 28, 2006.

67. Hank Vilas, interview, Berkeley, CA, April 11, 1983, Before Stonewall Special Collection 87-2, LHA.

Chapter 2

1. Joanne Meyerowitz, "Beyond the Feminine Mystique: A Reassessment of Postwar Mass Culture, 1946–1958," in Not June Cleaver: Women and Gender in Postwar America, 1945–1960, ed. Joanne Meyerowitz (Philadelphia: Temple University Press, 1994), 229–62.

2. Wini Breines, Young, White, and Miserable: Growing Up Female in the Fifties (Boston: Beacon Press, 1992), 126–66.

3. Dee Garrison, "Our Skirts Gave Them Courage: The Civil Defense Protest Movement in New York City, 1955–1961," in Not June Cleaver: Women and Gender in Postwar

America, 1945–1960, ed. Joanne Meyerowitz (Philadelphia: Temple University Press, 1994), 201–26.

4. On the early homophile groups as trailblazers for later LGBT freedom struggle movements, see Martin Meeker, *Contacts Desired: Gay and Lesbian Communications and Community, 1940s–1970s* (Chicago: University of Chicago Press, 2006); John D'Emilio, *Sexual Politics, Sexual Communities: The Making of a Homosexual Minority in the United States, 1940–1970* (Chicago: University of Chicago Press, 1983); and Marcia Gallo, *Different Daughters: A History of the Daughters of Bilitis and the Rise of the Lesbian Civil Rights Movement* (Emeryville, CA: Seal Press, 2007).

5. Although the ACLU consistently refused to advocate for same-sex rights or denounce sodomy or unnatural acts laws in the 1950s, they changed this stance in the 1960s, largely due to the encouragement of gay civil rights pioneer Frank Kameny. Joyce Murdoch and Deb Price, *Courting Justice: Gay Men and Lesbians v. the Supreme Court* (New York: Basic Books, 2001), 61–62. On the model penal code and sodomy laws, see William N. Eskridge, *Dishonorable Passions: Sodomy Laws in America, 1861–2003* (New York: Viking Press, 2008), 123–27.

6. Blue Lunden, interview with Quinn, December 1989, Blue (Doris) Lunden Special Collection 83-04, box 1, folder 2, LHA.

7. Interviewed in 1999, Paul Coates remembered that he and his lover had no problem renting a place together in Greenwich Village in January 1947: "this was Greenwich Village, this was New York, and it was right after the war. And, you know, this is great." Paul Coates, interview with Martin Meeker, July 28, 1999, 99-020, Oral History Files, GLBTHS.

8. Blynn Garnett, "Memoirs of a Lesbian's Lesbian Daughter," in *Lavender Culture*, ed. Karla Jay and Allen Young (New York: New York University Press, 1978), 315–24.

9. Blue Lunden, interview with Quinn, December 1989, Blue (Doris) Lunden Special Collection 83-04, box 1, folder 2, LHA; Linda Lunden, interview with author, Key Biscayne, FL, March 17, 2012.

10. In her essay, "My Fem Quest," Joan Nestle describes a specificity of femme identity that cannot be reduced to heteronormative femininity through specific connection to the economic struggle of women: "For whatever reason, 'femininity' carries a heterosexual marker that does not signify what I mean when I speak of my femness. . . . It was always working-class clear to me that I had to earn my living in a very concrete way to make my erotic survival possible. Economics and my version of gender were inextricably tied." Joan Nestle, *A Fragile Union: New and Selected Writings* (San Francisco: Cleis Press, 1998), 129–30. On butch/femme culture, see also Elizabeth Lapovsky Kennedy and Madeline D. Davis, *Boots of Leather, Slippers of Gold: The History of a Lesbian Community* (New York: Routledge, 1993), and Lillian Faderman, *Odd Girls and Twilight Lovers: A History of Lesbian Life in Twentieth-Century America* (New York: Columbia University Press, 1991), 159–87. On butch/femme experiences in Florida, including lesbian motherhood in a working-class butch/femme community, see Merril Mushroom, "At Yalla's Place—1960," *Common Lives/Lesbian Lives: A Lesbian Quarterly* no. 11 (Spring 1984), and "Bar Dyke Sketches—1959," *Common Lives/Lesbian Lives: A Lesbian Quarterly* no. 5 (Fall 1982). For a firsthand account by Mabel Hampton of African American butch/femme communities in 1930s Harlem, see "Mabel H.," Spoken Word Audio File 58, LHA.

11. Pat B., interview, Boots of Leather/Slippers of Gold Special Collection 98-1, box 2, file 27, LHA.

12. Joan Nestle, interview, Jezebel Productions Interview Transcripts Special Collection 2004-34, box 1, folder 7, LHA. Also, Joan Nestle, correspondence with author. In an interview, Red Jordan, a lesbian who lived in Greenwich Village in the 1940s, remembered that women would come to the Women's House of Detention and wave at their lovers who were incarcerated there. Red Jordan, interview, Before Stonewall Special Collection 87-2, LHA.

13. "Kids of Gays: A Lesbian's Daughter Straightens Out the Children of Homosexual Parents," US *Magazine*, July 6, 1982, 26–27.

14. Vera Martin, interview with author, Apache Junction, AZ, September 22, 2006.

15. Blue Lunden, interview with Quinn, December 1989, Blue (Doris) Lunden Special Collection 83-04, box 1, folder 2, LHA. See also Elly Bulkin, "An Old Dyke's Tale: An Interview with Doris Lunden," *Conditions: Six*, 26–45, and Blue Lunden, interview with Jonathan Ned Katz, January 4, 1974, Spoken Word Audio Files 844, LHA. On the 1953 raid on the Golden Rod Inn and the police campaigns to which it was connected, see Richard Clark, "City of Desire: A History of Same-Sex Desire in New Orleans, 1917–1977" (Ph.D. diss., Tulane University, 2009), 118–19.

16. Blue Lunden, interview with Quinn, December 1989, Blue (Doris) Lunden Special Collection 83-04, box 1, folder 2, LHA. See also Joyce Warshow's beautiful documentary about Lunden, *Some Ground to Stand On* (Women Make Movies, 1998).

17. Interview with Joan Nestle, Jezebel Productions Interview Transcripts Special Collection 2004-34, box 1, folder 7, LHA. Also, Joan Nestle, correspondence with author.

18. Vera Martin, interview with author, Apache Junction, AZ, September 22, 2006.

19. For example, see Annie, interview, July 10, 1985, box 2, file 3, and Bobbie, interview, June 30, 1984, box 2, file 8, Boots of Leather/Slippers of Gold Special Collection 98-1, LHA.

20. In the 1957 "opening shot" of a "war against perverts" the Tampa police raided Jimmie White's tavern and arrested twelve women because they were wearing "mannish dress." Tangents, ONE *Magazine*, October–November 1957, 19. In 1958, there was a series of vice raids in New Orleans aimed "primarily against homosexuals, but also hitting night club strippers, jazz spots, and even a quiet club of nudists." Tangents, ONE *Magazine*, September 1958, 19. See also Clark, "City of Desire," 126–52. A 1960 letter spoke of a "nightmare" string of raids in New York City and described the situation in one bar where "the police came in every half hour or so, and when they weren't inside they were parked in front and kept flashing their spotlight into the bar." Letters, ONE *Magazine*, January 1960, 28.

21. "Bernie's Story . . . A Herstory, An Oral History Taken by Katie Gilmartin" *OLOC Reporter*, March 1994, 3, OLOHP.

22. Blue Lunden, interview with Quinn, December 1989, Blue (Doris) Lunden Special Collection 83-04, box 1, folder 2, LHA.

23. Letters, ONE *Magazine*, August–September 1956, 44.

24. Richard Tooker, interview with Peter Toscani, January 16, 1998, 98-046, Oral History Files, GLBTHS.

25. See recorded recollections/testimony of Ira Jeffries and Regina Shaver about growing up as African American lesbians in New York City, www.griotcircle.org., accessed September 30, 2012; copy in author's possession.

26. "Kids of Gays"; and Ann Japenga, "Network for Children of Gays," *Los Angeles Times*, January 14, 1982.

27. Justin Henderson " 'Mom's A Lesbian,' My Sister Said, 'I Know,' I Said" *L.A. Weekly*, May 6–12, 1983.

28. Garnett, "Memoirs of a Lesbian's Lesbian Daughter."

29. Blue Lunden, interview with Quinn, December 1989, Blue (Doris) Lunden Special Collection 83-04, box 1, folder 2, LHA.

30. Letter reprinted in Lesbian Herstory Archives Newsletter (Winter 1984).

31. "Homosexual Bill of Rights Sizzles and Fizzles," *The Ladder*, March 1961, 11, 18.

32. "What We Are," *Atheneum Review*, October 1964, Newsletter Collection (Legal Size), GLBTHS.

33. "What We Are," *Atheneum Review*, December 1964, 10, Newsletter Collection (Legal Size), GLBTHS.

34. "Homosexuality Needs Study," *Atheneum Review*, September 1964, 6, Newsletter Collection (Legal Size), GLBTHS.

35. Letters, *ONE Magazine*, September 1965, 30. Male homophile organizations were also aware of the struggles of married gay fathers. At the ONE Midwinter institute of 1960, organized around the theme "The Homosexual in the Community," one discussion "centered around the individual who is married and has children before he consciously recognizes that he has homosexual tendencies." Discussion participants distinguished between situations where the men do not feel safe enough to reveal their homosexuality to their wives and ones where "the problem can be worked out to the best interest of the family." Sten Russell, "ONE Institute: Homophile in the Community," *The Ladder*, March 1960, 19. In a September 1962 article in *ONE Magazine* entitled "Should a Homosexual Be Advised to Marry?," Paul Britton claimed that the "police files are full of the middle-aged one-time offender" who was arrested in a park or public bathroom. Britton bemoaned the effect that scandals had on wives and children, asking: "Who stops the scandal? Saves his job? Who repairs this hell then?" *ONE Magazine*, September 1962, 18–19.

36. James R. Steuart, "Homosexual Procreation," *ONE Magazine*, March 1961, 6–8.

37. Letters, *ONE Magazine*, May 1961, 29–30.

38. J. P. Starr, "Augmented Families," *ONE Magazine*, February 1960, 6–9.

39. Del Martin and Phyllis Lyon, interview with author, San Francisco, CA, February 17, 2006.

40. See "The Gundlach-Reiss Report on Lesbians, Section IV: Social Relations, Love, Sex, and Identity," box 8, folder 14, LMP. Gundlach began asking for participants in *The Ladder* in 1963.

41. "DOB Questionnaire Reveals Some Facts about Lesbians," *The Ladder*, September 1959, 17.

42. "Raising Children in a Deviant Relationship," *The Ladder*, October 1956, 9.

43. Del Martin and Phyllis Lyon, interview with author, San Francisco, CA, February 17, 2006. One reader from New York City wrote in to express interest in the

topic, asked to know more, and inquired whether there was a way to get in touch with others interested in DOB in the New York area. Readers Respond, *The Ladder*, April 1957, 16.

44. "ONE Symposium: Homosexuality—A Way of Life," *The Ladder*, February 1958, 21.

45. Letter from Claremont, CA, box 3, folder 3; letter from Costa Mesa, CA, box 3, folder 6; letter from Danville, VA, and reply from Jaye Bell, box 2, folder 16; letter from Los Angeles, CA, box 3, folder 2, LMP.

46. Daughters of Bilitis San Francisco Chapter Newsletter, July 1966, box 5, folder 14, LMP.

47. Daughters of Bilitis San Francisco Chapter Newsletter, July 1968, March 29, 1970, box 5, folder 14, LMP.

48. Daughters of Bilitis Newsletter–New York Chapter, April 1967, 3, and May 1967, 3, DOB New York Area Chapter folder 2, Newsletter Collection, LHA. The question of whether to come out to one's children was a concern for gay fathers in this early era as well. In April of 1965, "E.A.," a gay grandfather wrote that "the homosexual parent must dissemble. The question is how long should he afford this protection? . . . Time has a way of promoting parents into grandparenthood. Then there are grandchildren to be shielded." Letters, *ONE Magazine*, April 1965, 30.

49. Daughters of Bilitis Newsletter–New York Chapter, April 1968, 4, DOB New York Area Chapter folder 2, Newsletter Collection, LHA.

Chapter 3

1. *Nadler v. Nadler*, 255 C.A. 2d 523; 63 Cal. Reporter 352. See also court transcript of *Nadler v. Nadler*, box 124, folder 18, LMP.

2. On court-ordered estrangement of gay fathers from their children, see Robert L. Barret and Bryan E. Robinson, *Gay Fathers* (Lexington, MA: Lexington Books, 1990), 68. A pamphlet entitled "A Gay Parents' Legal Guide to Child Custody," put together by the Anti-Sexism Committee of the National Lawyers Guild in 1978 said, in reference to gay fathers: "It is especially important that as gay fathers you realistically assess the options open to you. Gay fathers face a very difficult double bind. Judges refuse to acknowledge that men are able to provide adequate home environments in the absence of women . . . you should be prepared to argue against the attitude that because you are gay your *visitation rights* would be detrimental to the child" (16; emphasis in original). Copy in Subject Files, Lesbian Mothers—General 08080 folder, LHA.

3. One judge dissenting in a Washington Supreme Court ruling granting two lesbian mothers the right to live together with their children from a previous marriage cited an earlier ruling in that state against a gay man who fought to keep his teaching job in Tacoma, Washington, writing: "I am unable to understand how the court can declare that a schoolteacher who only admitted his preference as a homosexual and did not engage in any overt act is guilty of immorality, and yet, in the instant case, we can find perfectly moral the conduct of the respondents." "2 Lesbian Mothers Win in Court," *Gaysweek*, October 25, 1978.

4. For an excellent overview of these changes and their impact on the courts from the perspective of a clinical psychologist, see Dr. Laura Benkov, *Reinventing the Family: Lesbian and Gay Parents* (New York: Crown Trade Paperbacks, 1994), 9–12, 34–81.

5. Occasionally, local religious figures involved with the Christian Right would ally themselves with ex-spouses and attempt to persuade judges that letting a gay father or a lesbian mother spend time with their children was morally wrong and tantamount to child abuse. For a striking example of this, see the involvement of Pentecostal minister Maurice Gordon in the struggle between Frank and Betty Lou Batey over custody of their son, Brian. "Brian Batey Is 14," *60 Minutes*, December 8, 1985.

6. A number of the states where lesbian and gay parenting cases continued to appear in the 1990s and the first decade of the twenty-first century were also states that retained their sodomy laws until they were overturned by the U.S. Supreme Court in *Lawrence v. Texas* in 2003. Examples include Idaho, Virginia, and Alabama.

7. Joe Acanfora, the plaintiff in *Acanfora v. Board of Education of Montgomery County*, the first case involving the firing of a teacher for sexual orientation to reach the Supreme Court, had his termination upheld by a federal judge on the basis that he had given public interviews about the case. In 1973, the Supreme Court refused to hear the case, leaving Acanfora without legal recourse. Joyce Murdoch and Deb Price, *Courting Justice: Gay Men and Lesbians v. The Supreme Court* (New York: Basic Books, 2001), 179. On legal cases involving lesbian and gay teachers, see Jackie M. Blount, *Fit to Teach: Same-Sex Desire, Gender, and School Work in the Twentieth Century* (Albany: State University of New York Press, 2005), 113–21.

8. The detailed focus on Ellen Nadler's sexual activities here was gendered; although the presence of gay male sexuality in a household is routinely cited as reason for denying gay men contact with their children in custody cases from this era, it is rare that family judges express any confusion as to what this sexuality might entail. This speaks to the general aggressive interrogation of women's sexuality in family courts in custody battles as well as the cultural illegibility of lesbian sexuality. Ellen Nadler was also forced by the judge to name the three women with whom she had been lovers on the stand as "possible felons," over objections by her attorney. This intensified scrutiny of female sexuality is linked to judicial hostility that women have faced in custody trials for any expression of sexuality that falls outside of normative definitions of heterosexual, feminine maternity. As Susan Deller Ross and Ann Barcher, the authors of the ACLU handbook, *The Rights of Women*, put it in 1983: "She [a woman who wants custody] should be discreet about any relationship with another man or a sexual relationship with a woman. The legal system still imposes a double standard, and a mother will be judged more harshly for extramarital affairs than will a father." Susan Deller Ross and Ann Barcher, *The Rights of Women: The Basic ACLU Guide to a Woman's Rights*, rev. ed. (New York: Bantam Books, 1983), 231. Although this double standard did not protect gay fathers in the period from 1967 to 1985, the sexual harassment of Ellen Nadler and other lesbian mothers is nonetheless specific and historically related to the more general policing of female sexuality through notions of the "fit" family. Gay fathers would benefit from cultural hostility toward female-headed households in a later era when judges gave gay male sperm donors paternity rights in cases involving

lesbian mothers by insemination and the absence of a heterosexual option for the court to choose over lesbian motherhood and gay fatherhood.

9. For example, while Protestant Anglo reformers of the early twentieth century were concerned with a low birthrate among white, educated, propertied women, they advocated compulsory sterilization and castration for the poor. Elaine Tyler May, *Barren in the Promised Land* (Basic Books: New York, 1995), 96–108.

10. These changes also accompanied a rise in divorce rates beginning in the first decades of the twentieth century. See Mary Ann Mason, *From Father's Property to Children's Rights* (New York: Columbia University Press, 1994), xiii, 114. See also Nancy Cott, *Public Vows: A History of Marriage and the Nation* (Cambridge, MA: Harvard, 2000), 107.

11. Mary Ann Mason, *The Custody Wars* (New York: Basic Books, 1999), 3. For contemporary news accounts of single fathers groups and a discussion of the advancement of paternal custody rights, see "And Now . . . Equal Rights for Father," *San Francisco Examiner & Chronicle*, June 3, 1977; and Caroline Drewes, "When Daddy Gets Custody of the Kids," *San Francisco Examiner & Chronicle*, June 18, 1978.

12. The transition from "maternal preference" to a gender-blind "best interests" philosophy was haphazard and varied from state to state. In a 1979 study, 48 percent of California family lawyers surveyed said that they would still caution all fathers against seeking custody. Barret and Robinson, *Gay Fathers*, 6. Legal scholar Martha Fineman argues that the move toward "gender equality" has masked a continuing patriarchal state investment in family courts in a definition of fit motherhood that forces women into economic dependence and justifies state intervention into their family life. Martha Fineman, *The Illusion of Equality: The Rhetoric and Reality of Divorce Reform* (Chicago: University of Chicago Press, 1991).

13. On *Panzino v. Panzino*, see Rosalie C. Davies, "Representing the Lesbian Mother," *Family Advocate* (Winter 1979): 1.

14. Judge Ross Campbell, "Child Custody: When One Parent Is a Homosexual," *Judge's Journal* 17, no. 2 (Spring 1978): 38–41, 51–52.

15. Guy Gifford, with Mary Jo Risher, *By Her Own Admission: A Lesbian Mother's Fight to Keep Her Son* (Garden City, NY: Doubleday, 1977), 173. Dr. Richard Green was asked, while testifying on behalf of a lesbian mother in 1974, about possible stigma faced by the children of lesbian or gay parents by the attorney for the woman's ex-husband. Richard Green, *Sexual Science and the Law* (Cambridge, MA: Harvard University Press, 1992), 37–38.

16. For a discussion of the assumption of the danger of sexual molestation in the case of lesbian mothers and gay fathers, see R. A. Basile, "Lesbian Mothers I," *Women's Law Reporter* 2, no. 2 (December 1974): 9; and Marilyn Riley, "The Avowed Lesbian Mother and Her Right to Child Custody: A Constitutional Right That Can No Longer Be Denied," *San Diego Law Review* 12, no. 4 (1975): 853.

17. Gifford and Risher, *By Her Own Admission*, 271. On the Mary Jo Risher case generally, see Mary Jo Risher Special Collection 99-35, LHA.

18. On the Cynthia Forcier case, see "Lesbian Mothers Win," undated *New Women's Times* article, and Sharon McDonald, "Lesbian Mothers: In Court," both in Subject Files, Lesbian Mothers—Custody Issues 08100 folder, LHA. See also box 124, folder 9, LMP.

19. Robert Johnson, interview with author, Pasadena, CA, June 18, 2003.

20. Karlis Streips, "Sexuality Is Crux of Visitation Dispute," *Gay Life*, December 9, 1982, 8.

21. Letter from Donna Hitchens to the Lesbian Mothers' National Defense Fund, February 5, 1979, LMNDF Files.

22. Letter to the Lesbian Mothers' National Defense Fund, September 30, 1985, LMNDF Files.

23. Earnestine Blue, interview with Shad Reinstein and Jody Lane, July 24, 2005, Seattle, WA. See also *Mom's Apple Pie: The Heart of the Lesbian Mother's Custody Movement*, directed by Shad Reinstein and Jody Lane (Seattle: Three Big Dykes Productions, 2006).

24. Brent Whiting, "Phoenix Lesbian Wins Custody of Young Daughters from Court," *Arizona Republic*, April 14, 1980, A1.

25. Jill Clark, "Lesbian Mother Fights for Son," *Gay Community News* (Boston), August 9, 1980, 1.

26. Sodomy laws have also been used historically to justify other forms of legal discrimination against sexual minorities. In 1979, Richard Longstaff, a legal immigrant to the United States from England who had opened a clothing business in Texas after a decade of living in the United States, was denied citizenship based on the criminality of his assumed sexual activity as a gay man. Longstaff appealed the 5th Circuit decision to the Supreme Court, which refused to hear the case. In 1978, Oklahoma legislators passed the Helms Bill, authored by Oklahoma state senator Mary Helms. The bill used Oklahoma's "crime against nature" antisodomy statute to bar any lesbian or gay teacher from working in Oklahoma's public schools. In 1985, the U.S. Supreme Court upheld the law as constitutional. Murdoch and Price, *Courting Justice*, 233, 252. Sodomy laws and "sexual psychopath" laws were also used sporadically throughout the postwar era to round up "sexual deviants" in regional gay purges that left hundreds of men jailed, incarcerated in mental facilities, or with their lives ruined through publicity and social vilification. On the history of sodomy statutes and their use to police lesbians and gay men throughout the twentieth century, see Mary Bernstein, "Abominable and Detestable: Understanding Homophobia and the Criminalization of Sodomy," in *The Blackwell Companion to Criminology*, ed. Colin Sumner (Oxford: Blackwell Publishing, 2004), 309–24; and "Liberalism and Social Movement Success: The Case of the United States Sodomy Statutes," in *Regulating Sex: The Politics of Intimacy and Identity*, ed. Elizabeth Bernstein and Laurie Schaffner (New York: Routledge, 2005), 3–18.

27. Published in 1975, the ACLU handbook, *The Rights of Gay People*, reported that eight out of the fifty states had repealed their sodomy laws. E. Carrington et al., eds., *The Rights of Gay People: The Basic ACLU Guide to a Gay Person's Rights* (Sunrise Books, 1975), 138. On Illinois' 1961 repealing of their sodomy law and activism against the law in the 1920s, see Henry Gerber "The Society for Human Rights," *ONE Magazine*, September 1962, 5–11.

28. At the time of the *Lawrence* decision, these laws remained in fourteen U.S. states, Puerto Rico, and the U.S. military. Of these districts, four states—Oklahoma, Texas, Kansas, and Missouri—had laws that applied only to homosexual conduct.

29. "A Display of Homophobia in Appeals Court," *The Advocate*, March 12, 1975. On *Chaffin v. Frye*, see box 124, folders 7 and 8, LMP. California's law against oral copulation between consenting adults was repealed in May of the same year, just two months after the Chaffin decision.

30. *Roe v. Roe*, 228 Va. 722 (1985).

31. See court transcript of *Nadler v. Nadler*, box 124, folder 18, LMP.

32. Attorneys who fought lesbian mothers for their parental rights in court would play upon these heterosexist fears in the courtroom. When Dr. Richard Green offered expert testimony on the part of Sallie Hall, opposing counsel interrogated him as to whether the child had "admitted" to witnessing acts of affection between her mother and her mother's partner. The attorney for the lesbian mother's ex-husband asked Dr. Green if he had asked the child if she had ever witnessed the women in graphic sex acts. Testimony of Dr. Richard Green, box 124, folder 10, LMP. The same two topics were intertwined in the interrogation of Ellen Nadler by opposing counsel as well as the judge. See court transcript of *Nadler v. Nadler*, 255 C.A. 2d 523, 63 Cal. Rptr. 352, box 124, folder 18, LMP.

33. On the issues surrounding the constitutional rights of association and privacy in the case of lesbian and gay parents, see Benna F. Armanno, "The Lesbian Mother: Her Right to Child Custody," *Golden Gate University Law Review* 4, no. 1 (Fall 1973): 15. See also Marilyn Riley, "The Avowed Lesbian Mother and Her Right to Child Custody: A Constitutional Challenge That Can No Longer Be Denied," *San Diego Law Review* 12, no. 4 (July 1975): 842.

34. Jill Lippett, interview with author, Jenner, CA, December 5, 2003.

35. *M. v. M.* (Cal. Super. Ct. Santa Clara Cty. June 8, 1972). See also interview with Cam Mitchell in *CFC: A Weekly Communication to the People*, July 10, 1973, 4–5, Subject Files, Lesbian Mothers Newspaper Articles 08210 folder, LHA.

36. Box 124, folder 5, LMP.

37. *Spence v. Durham*, 283 N.C. 671, 198 S.E. 2d 537. The silence of the court about the particular nature of Susan Spence's crime was remedied in this case in the dissenting opinion, written by Justice Lake. Justice Lake apparently took great exception to the awarding of custody to an individual he called a "sexual deviant."

38. On *Isaacson v. Isaacson* and *Schuster v. Schuster*, see "Lesbian Custody Case," *Off Our Backs* (February 1978): 3; "Lesbian Mothers Win Suit over Custody of Children," *New York Times*, September 5, 1974; and *Seattle Gay News*, October 13, 1978. See also Patricia Leitch, "Custody: Lesbian Mothers in the Courts," *Gonzaga Law Review* 16, no. 1 (1980): 166; and Donna Hitchens and Ann Thomas, eds., *Lesbian Mothers and Their Children: An Annotated Bibliography of Legal and Psychological Materials*, 2nd ed.(San Francisco: Lesbian Rights Project, 1983), 20–21, Subject Files, Lesbian Mothers—Papers, Studies 2 08240 folder, LHA.

39. "Custody Defeat," *Gay Community News* (Boston), January 17, 1976.

40. *In re Jane B.*, 380 N.Y.S. 2d 848 (Sup. Ct. 1976).

41. "Fleischer v Fleischer," *New York Law Journal*, November 10, 1975, 10. On appeal, the mother had her visitation rights completely taken away for a period of three years. For a discussion of the original decision and appeal, see *A State by State Guide to Child Custody* (San Francisco: National Center for Lesbian Rights, 1996), 59.

42. *A v. A*, Or. App. 514 P 2d 358.

43. M. Tway Smith, "Gay Daddies: They Fight Ex-Wives Hostility and a Biased Court System," *Gay News* (Philadelphia), June 27–July 10, 1980.

44. *In re J.S. & C.*, 129 N.J. Super. 486 (1974).

45. Jeanne Jullion, interview with author, Oakland, CA, May 21, 2002.

46. Donna Hitchens, J.D., *Lesbian Mother Litigation Manual* (San Francisco: Lesbian Rights Project, 1982): 38, box 124, folder 3, LMP. There is also a copy of the first edition of the manual in the LMNDF Files.

47. Rosalie Davies, interview with author, Haverford, PA, September 12, 2002.

48. Lois Thetford, "Report," *Mom's Apple Pie*, July 1976, 5.

49. "Custody Rights for Gay Parents," *The Fountain*, March 1979, National Gay and Lesbian Task Force Records, box 88, Clippings, 1974–80 folder, HSC.

50. Rosemary Armao, "More Gay Parents Turning to Courts," *Los Angeles Times*, November 26, 1981.

51. These Freudian developmental theories existed alongside biological determinist ones that saw homosexuality as related to possible endocrine imbalances or differences in brain structure; however, the majority of the courtroom arguments made by expert witnesses against lesbian or gay parenting rights were of a Freudian, developmental nature.

52. Both cases quoted in Donna Hitchens and Barbara Price, "Trial Strategy in Lesbian Mother Custody Cases: The Use of Expert Testimony," *Golden Gate University Law Review* 9, no. 2, 451–79.

53. The Board of Trustees vote to remove homosexuality from the APA diagnostic manual as a mental pathology occurred on December 15, 1973. For a detailed discussion by Dr. Judd Marmor and Barbara Gittings of their recollections of this struggle within the APA, see Eric Marcus, *Making Gay History* (New York: Harper Collins, 1992), 178–83. See also Ronald Bayer, *Homosexuality and American Psychiatry: The Politics of Diagnosis* (New York: Basic Books, 1981), 101–54.

54. Dr. Richard Green, interview with author, San Francisco, CA, April 22, 2006.

55. *Hall v. Hall*, No. 55900, Ohio C.P. Court Domestic Relations Div., Licking County, October 31, 1974.

56. Richard Green, M.D., *Sexual Science and the Law* (Cambridge, MA: Harvard University Press, 1992), 31. See also materials on *Hall v. Hall*, box 124, folder 10, LMP.

57. *Townend v. Townend*, No. 74 CV 0670, Court of Common Pleas, Portage County, Ohio, April 4, 1975.

58. Bernice Goodman, *The Lesbian: A Celebration of Difference* (Out and Out Books: New York, 1977), 44; copy in Subject Files, Lesbian Mothers: Narratives 08201 folder, LHA.

59. Kimberly Richman, *Courting Change: Queer Parents, Judges, and the Transformation of American Family Law* (New York: New York University Press, 2009).

60. Copy of 1973 NGTF Gay Parent Support Packet with letters in Subject Files, Lesbian Mothers Custody Issues 08110 folder, LHA; 1979 revised version of the support packet, Subject Files, Gay Parents II folder, ONGLA; partial version of the packet in box 126, folder 5, LMP. The NGTF was later known as the National Gay and Lesbian Task Force.

61. Bernice Goodman, "The Lesbian Mother," *American Journal of Orthopsychiatry* 43 (1973): 283–84. See also Goodman, *The Lesbian: A Celebration of Difference*, LHA.

62. See "A New Look at Lesbian Mothers," *Human Behavior* 5, no. 8 (August 1976): 60–61.

63. Richard Green, M.D. "Sexual Identity of 37 Children Raised by Homosexual or Transsexual Parents," *American Journal of Psychiatry* 135, no. 6 (June 1978): 696. In the introduction to her landmark anthropological study of lesbian mothers, Ellen Lewin discusses how she was motivated in her graduate study by a desire to provide research material that might "help dispel the stereotypes that prevailed in custody challenges" of the period. Ellen Lewin, *Lesbian Mothers: Accounts of Gender in American Culture* (Ithaca, NY: Cornell University Press, 1993), xv. See also Lewin's essay "Lesbianism and Motherhood: Implications for Child Custody." *Human Organization* 40, no. 1 (Spring 1981).

64. Martha Kirkpatrick, M.D., et al., "Lesbian Mothers and Their Children: A Comparative Survey," *American Journal of Orthopsychiatry* 51, no. 3 (July 1981): 545–51. In a 2001 interview, Dr. Martha Kirkpatrick noted that her study occurred at a time when "newspapers began reporting on women in court custody battles because of their lesbian relationships" and that there was a "chance to study how these children were developing." Vernon A. Rosario, "An Interview with Martha J. Kirkpatrick, M.D.," *Journal of Gay & Lesbian Psychotherapy* 6, no. 2 (2002): 88–89.

65. Frederick Bozett, R.N., D.N.S., "Gay Fathers: Evolution of the Gay-Father Identity," *American Journal of Orthopsychiatry* 51, no. 3 (July 1981): 552–59.

66. Bryon L. Nestor, "Attitudes of Child Psychiatrists toward Homosexual Parenting and Child Custody," *Conciliation Courts Review* 17, no. 2 (September 1979): 21–23.

67. In the lesbian feminist classic *Sappho Was a Right-on Woman* (New York: Stein & Day, 1972) authors Sidney Abbott and Barbara Love wrote that "the most acute legal problem facing many lesbians is the one facing lesbian mothers. In any child custody case lesbianism is grounds for being declared an unfit mother" (57).

68. Marty Karls, interview with author, San Francisco, CA, August 9, 2004.

69. Barbara S. Bryant, "Lesbian Mothers," (master's thesis, California State University at Sacramento, 1975), 148.

70. Anonymous, "Lesbian Mothers Presentation," *Dinah* (Cincinnati, Ohio), March 1979, 11, Newsletter Collection, LHA.

71. Rosemary Armao, "3 Million Children Have Homosexual Parents: More Gay Parents Turning to Courts," *Los Angeles Times*, November 26, 1981.

72. Barret and Robinson, *Gay Fathers*, 112.

73. The Boston Women's Health Collective, *Ourselves and Our Children: A Book by and for Parents* (New York: Random House, 1978), 173.

74. Becky Logan, interview with author, Seattle, WA, May 13, 2005.

75. Hitchens, *Lesbian Mother Litigation Manual*, 9. In 1978, several activists from the lesbian mothers group Dykes and Tykes discussed how the fear of a reopened case based on a "material change in circumstance" affected lesbian mothers on a radio show in New York. "Dykes and Tykes Legal Custody Center," *The Real Live Lesbian Show*, WBAI New York, WBAI Collection, Spoken Word Audio Files, LHA.

76. Letter, *Lesbian Connection*, November 1976, 21.

77. Kathy Florez, "Lesbian Mothers," *Amazon Spirit* (March/April 1979), 7.

78. "Lesbian Mother's Day," Everywoman's Space, WBAI New York, WBAI Collection, Spoken Word Audio Files, LHA.

79. The first time that the ACLU acted on behalf of a lesbian or a gay man in a custody battle was in 1971, when Anne Elwell represented Jerry Purpura, a gay father

who was fighting for custody of his children in New Jersey. See "Homosexual Barred from Seeing Sons," *Sunday Record* (Hackensack, NJ), April 15, 1973. The second case was that of Sallie Hall, a lesbian mother. The ACLU provided Hall with legal representation. This effort was spearheaded by Marilyn Haft and the Sexual Privacy Project of the ACLU. See "Lesbian Mother Fights Court," *Syracuse Sun*, Sunday, February 6–19, 1974. See also letters from Marilyn Haft to Del Martin concerning the Hall case, box 124, folder 10, LMP.

80. In the original ruling against Miller, Judge Frederick Ziem said that the mother's behavior was "immoral" and "a major consideration" and overlooked the eleven-year-old daughter's request to live with her mother. "Lesbian Mother Wins Custody Case," *Women and Revolution, Journal of the Women's Commission of the Spartacist League* (Spring 1979), 11, Subject Files, Lesbian Mothers Custody Issues 08100 folder, LHA.

81. E. R. Shipp, "A Lesbian Who Won a Custody Battle," *New York Times*, September 5, 1980. See also Jill Clark, "Activist Lesbian Mother Wins N.J. Custody Battle," *Gay Community News*, August 16, 1980.

82. *Seattle Gay Community News*, July 28, 1979.

83. M.A.B. v. R.B. 510 N.Y.S. 2d 960 (Sup.Ct. 1986). See also "Gay Father Wins Custody Battle," *Workers World Newspaper*, October 23, 1986.

84. *Medeiros v. Medeiros*, 8 Family L. Rptr. 2372 (Vt. Super. Ct. 1982); *Bezio v. Patenaude*, 410 N.E. 2d 1207 (Mass. S.J.C. 1980); *S.N.E. v. R.L.B.*, 699 P. 2d 875 (Alaska, 1985). In the Alaska case, the Alaska Supreme Court held that it was unconstitutional under state law to deny a lesbian mother custody based on a perceived danger of stigma to the children.

85. "Virginia Supreme Court says Gay Father 'unfit,'" *Washington Blade*, January 1, 1985.

86. M.J.P. v. J.G.P., 640 P.2d 966, 969 (Okla. 1982). See also Nancy D. Polikoff, "This Child Does Have Two Mothers: Redefining Parenthood to Meet the Needs of Children in Lesbian-Mother and Other Nontraditional Families," *Georgetown Law Journal* 78 (1990): 554. On the Illinois ruling, see "Court Rules Gay People May Be Denied Custody of Children," *New York Native*, December 9, 1991. The circuit court judge who had delivered the original ruling reportedly stated that he would have given the mother custody if it were not for the fact that she was in a lesbian relationship.

87. *Palmore v. Sidotti*, 466 U.S. 429 (1984).

88. Murdoch and Price, *Courting Justice*, 214.

89. Jill Clark, "High Court Justice Grants Stay in Custody Case," *Gay Community News*, March 21, 1981. On the denial of certiorari, see *A State by State Guide to Child Custody* (San Francisco: National Center for Lesbian Rights, 1996), 32–33.

90. For an excellent discussion of *Bowers* and its impact on gay and lesbian rights in the United States, see Morris Kaplan, *Sexual Justice: Democratic Citizenship and the Politics of Desire* (New York: Routledge, 1997), 207–38.

91. Historian Nancy Cott argues that legal and political advocacy for monogamous, heterosexual marriage has been commonplace in the twentieth century. Cott, *Public Vows*.

92. The history of lesbian mother and gay father organizing is the subject of chapters four and five.

93. Estelle Freedman has compellingly argued that the struggles of life partners of people diagnosed with HIV/AIDS in the 1980s and 1990s also helped drive the focus on domestic/parental/marital rights in the modern LGBT freedom struggle. *Feminism, Sexuality, and Politics: Essays by Estelle B. Freedman* (Chapel Hill: University of North Carolina Press, 2006), 192.

Chapter 4

1. On lesbian feminism's emergence from the women's movement, see Ruth Rosen, *The World Split Open: How the Modern Women's Movement Changed America* (New York: Viking, 2000), 164–75; and Lillian Faderman, *Odd Girls and Twilight Lovers: A History of Lesbian Life in Twentieth-Century America* (New York: Columbia University Press, 1991), 204–13. For an account of one lesbian feminist experience in the early gay liberation movement, see Karla Jay, *Tales of the Lavender Menace: A Memoir of Liberation* (New York: Basic Books, 1999). On the changes in sexuality, gender, and the family in the 1960s, see Estelle Freedman and John D'Emilio, *Intimate Matters: A History of Sexuality in America* (New York: Harper & Row, 1988), 240–325.

2. Charlotte Bunch, "Lesbians in Revolt," *The Furies: Lesbian/Feminist Monthly* 1 (January 1972): 8.

3. For information on forced sterilization of poor and immigrant women in the first decades of the twentieth century, see Linda Gordon, *Woman's Body, Woman's Right: Birth Control in America* (New York: Grossman, 1976), and Philip Reilly, *The Surgical Solution: A History of Involuntary Sterilization in the United States* (Baltimore: Johns Hopkins University Press, 1991). On forced-sterilization abuse in communities of color, see Dorothy Roberts, *Killing the Black Body* (New York: Random House, 1997), and Angela Y. Davis, *Women, Race, and Class* (New York: Vintage, 1981); and on social pressures to have children, Elaine Tyler May, *Barren in the Promised Land: Childless Americans and the Pursuit of Happiness* (New York: Basic Books, 1995).

4. Estelle Freedman, *No Turning Back: The History of Feminism and the Future of Women* (New York: Ballantine Books, 2002), 84–88; Rosen, *The World Split Open*, 96–110; Vicki Crawford, "Beyond the Human Self: Grassroots Activists in the Mississippi Civil Rights Movement," in *Women in the Civil Rights Movement: Trailblazers and Torchbearers, 1941–1965*, ed. Vicki L. Crawford, Jacqueline Anne Rouse, and Barbara Woods (Bloomington: Indiana University Press, 1990), 13–26; Sara Evans, *Personal Politics: The Roots of Women's Liberation in the Civil Rights Movement and the New Left* (New York: Vintage Books, 1980); Paula Giddings, *When and Where I Enter: The Impact of Black Women on Race and Sex in America* (New York: William Morrow, 1984), 261–324; Charles Payne, *I've Got the Light of Freedom: The Organizing Tradition and the Mississippi Freedom Struggle* (Berkeley: University of California Press, 1995), 265–83; Danielle McGuire, *At the Dark End of the Street: Black Women, Rape, and Resistance—A New History of the Civil Rights Movement from Rosa Parks to the Rise of Black Power* (New York: Random House, 2010).

5. In a 1975 interview on local Philadelphia radio, CALM cofounder Mikki Weinstein appeared with Jennifer Fleming of Women in Transition, a group that offered emotional and legal counseling to newly divorced women and women suffering

through domestic violence. *The Women's Consciousness-Raising Hour with Diane Trombley*, Spoken Word Audio Files, LHA.

6. I document the emergence of grassroots lesbian insemination networks in chapters six and seven.

7. "Lesbian Women Have Rights and so do Our Children!" Statement drafted by Lesbian Women from the Wages for Housework Campaign, San Francisco, in response to Anita Bryant's 1977 "Save Our Children" campaign and distributed at International Women's Year Conferences in San Francisco, Pennsylvania, Massachusetts, and New York. Subject Files, Lesbian Mothers—General 08080 folder, LHA.

8. The group initially formed two branches, one in San Francisco and the other in Oakland. By May of 1973, the LMU had more than a hundred members in the San Francisco Bay Area and was mailing its newsletter to more than thirty members in Chicago, New York, and Boston. Judith Anderson, "Motherhood and the Gay Woman," *San Francisco Chronicle*, October 23, 1971; "Lesbian Moms Court for Kids," in the *Berkeley Barb*, February 4, 1972; and "Motherhood and the Gay Woman" in *San Francisco Chronicle*, November 23, 1971. See membership estimate for LMU in Barbara Trecker, "Lesbian Mothers: Are Only Heterosexual Couples Able to Love and Raise a Child," *Cosmopolitan*, May 1978, 98; an LMU membership list dated "May 1973" reported fifty-eight members in the East Bay, thirty-three members in San Francisco, and eight members in the Peninsula. A separate membership list dated "2/9/72" included thirty women from regions outside the San Francisco Bay Area. LMU membership information in box 124, folder 2, LMP.

9. Lesbian Mothers Union Newsletter #1, box 124, folder 2, LMP. Pat Norman, one of the LMU's founders, recalled that "at that time, again, we could have had our children taken away because someone next door didn't like the way we looked, called up CPS, and said 'These people are lesbians.' And that was a fear. That still was underlying throughout the entire time we were mothers." Pat Norman, interview with Joan Biren for the film *No Secret Anymore: The Times of Del Martin and Phyllis Lyon*, November 1999, transcript in Joan E. Biren Papers, Sophia Smith Archives, Smith College, Northampton, MA.

10. "The SF Report," Metropolitan Community Church of San Francisco Newsletter (June 1973), box 126, folder 5, LMP.

11. Flyers and event notices, box 124, folder 2, LMP. At one event the LMU raised $2,200 dollars for legal fees. For a historical view of Scott's Pit and the community it was a part of, see Nan Alamilla Boyd, *Wide Open Town: A History of Queer San Francisco to 1965* (Berkeley: University of California Press, 2003), 149. On the 1970s San Francisco gay and lesbian bar scene in general, see Susan Stryker and Jim Van Buskirk, *Gay by the Bay: A History of Queer Culture in the San Francisco Bay Area* (San Francisco: Chronicle Books, 1996), 43, 69. Anthropologist Deborah Goleman Wolf conducted interviews in the lesbian feminist community of the San Francisco Bay Area and describes the culture of lesbian bars and lesbian mother organizing in her book, *The Lesbian Community* (Berkeley: University of California Press, 1979).

12. "Organizers' Dialogue: Lesbian Mothers Fight Back," *Quest: A Feminist Quarterly* 5, no. 1 (Summer 1979): 63.

13. "Case Updates," *Mom's Apple Pie*, January 1976, 2.

14. "Financial Report," *Mom's Apple Pie*, January 1976, 1; ibid., February 1976, 5; ibid., May 1976, 5; ibid., July 1976, 8; ibid., September 1976, 8; ibid., January 1977, 12; ibid., March 1977, 7; ibid., September 1977, 10; ibid., May 1978, 11.

15. "LEG Benefits" folder, Geraldine Cole, Personal Collection. See also "Financial Report," *Mom's Apple Pie*, September 1976, 9, and news item in *Mom's Apple Pie*, July 1976, 3.

16. On the benefit dance, see *Mom's Apple Pie*, July 1977, 2. For the talent shows, see Third Annual Lesbian Talent Show flyer, Geraldine Cole, Personal Collection.

17. On the emergence of women's music and music festivals in the 1970s, see Bonnie Morris, *Eden Built by Eves: The Culture of Women's Music Festivals* (Los Angeles: Alyson, 1999).

18. Holly Near and Mary Watkins Benefit Material, Geraldine Cole, Personal Collection. For a detailed financial breakdown on the concert, see *Mom's Apple Pie*, November 1977, 4.

19. "A Traveling Festival of Women's Music and Poetry," *Mom's Apple Pie*, March 1978, 7. Olivia Records was a lesbian feminist record label founded in 1973.

20. Carole Morton, interview with author, San Francisco, CA, March 10, 2007. In a letter to Del Martin and Phyllis Lyon dated April 19, 1976, Carole Morton discussed the recent founding of Dykes and Tykes in New York. Morton told Lyon and Martin that the organization already had a mailing list of sixty lesbian mothers and thirty nonmothers, and that the group had heard of two cases in New York where women lost custody of their children because of lesbianism. Box 125, folder 19, LMP.

21. See Dykes and Tykes Newsletter, June 1976, Dykes and Tykes (Org. and Legal Custody Ctr.) NYC folder, Organizations Files, LHA.

22. See Dykes and Tykes Newsletter, March–April 1978, Dykes and Tykes (Org. and Legal Custody Ctr.) NYC folder, Organizations Files, LHA.

23. Both the original 1977 edition as well as the revised 1980 edition of "A Gay Parents' Legal Guide to Child Custody" are in the Subject Files, Lesbian Mothers Custody Issues 08110 folder, LHA.

24. For custody center benefit flyers, see Subject Files, Lesbian Mothers Custody Center, NY 08350 folder, and Dykes and Tykes folder, Organizations Files, LHA.

25. "Interview with Marie and Sarah, February 28, 1977," LMNDF Files.

26. See "Statement of Structure, Policies, and Goals by the Ann Arbor Lesbian Mothers' Collective," "Benefit Flyer," and "Correspondence with Lesbian Mothers' National Defense Fund in Seattle," LMNDF Files.

27. "Lesbian Defense Fund," *Lesbian Connection*, April 1977, 12. On the Lesbian Defense Fund in Essex County, Vermont, see Lesbian Defense Fund Special Collection 83-10, LHA.

28. Jeanne Jullion, interview with author, Oakland, CA, May 21, 2002; Jeanne Jullion, *Long Way Home: The Odyssey of a Lesbian Mother and Her Children* (San Francisco: Cleis Press, 1985).

29. Jill Lippett, interview with author, Jenner, CA, December 5, 2003; Jeanne Jullion, interview with author, Oakland, CA, May 21, 2002.

30. Mary Jo Risher Special Collection 99-35, LHA.

31. Interview with Cam Mitchell in *CFC: A Weekly Communication to the People*, July 10, 1973, 4–5, Subject Files, Lesbian Mothers Newspaper Articles 08210 folder, LHA.

32. At a 1976 talk in New York City, Cole and Thetford said, "The primary thing is that we try to get a hold of lawyers through lists that we have put together, through ACLU contacts or legal services contacts . . . it's a lot harder to find a lawyer in some parts of the country than others . . . and we try to educate the lawyer with a lot of legal material." "The Lesbian Mothers' National Defense Fund," *The Lesbian Radio Spectacular*, WBAI New York, WBAI Collection, Spoken Word Audio Files, LHA.

33. LMNDF *Training and Operations Manual* (self-published, 1978), 25, Geraldine Cole, Personal Collection; List of Attorneys, Geraldine Cole, Personal Collection.

34. Letter signed "Kathy—take care, in sisterhood," to the LMNDF Seattle, in care of Joan Pitell, LMNDF Files.

35. Rosalie Davies, interview with author, Haverford, PA, September 12, 2002. See also CALM pamphlet, Subject Files, Custody Action for Lesbian Mothers folder, John J. Wilcox Jr. Archives, William Way LGBT Community Center, Philadelphia, PA.

36. Letter from Del Martin to Karen Burr, November 13, 1974, LMNDF Files. On connections between these groups, see also letter from Rosalie Davies to Geraldine Cole, February 3, 1976, and correspondence between Lesbian Mothers' National Defense Fund and Kathy Kozachenko about a summer legal-training program developed by Dykes and Tykes and the National Lawyers Guild, April 1, 1977, LMNDF Files.

37. Carole Morton's Day Planner, 1976, and handwritten notes, Carole Morton, Personal Collection.

38. Del Martin and Phyllis Lyon, interview with author, San Francisco, CA, February 17, 2006.

39. On JANE, see Laura Kaplan, *The Story of Jane: The Legendary Underground Abortion Service* (New York: Pantheon, 1995).

40. Judie Ghidinelli, interview with author, Oakland, CA, April 15, 2003.

41. Cathy Cade, *My Family, the Movement, and Me: How My Being in the Civil Rights Movement Affected My White Family* (self-published, 2002), 1–3.

42. Cathy Cade, interview with author, Oakland, CA, June 23, 2004.

43. Cade, *My Family*, 20.

44. Cathy Cade, interview with author, Oakland, CA, June 23, 2004.

45. Lois Thetford, interview with author, Seattle, WA, March 15, 2005.

46. Letter to Sonia Polanski from DOB New Jersey, November 6, 1971, Carole Morton, Personal Collection. While in New Jersey, sometime in 1971, Morton also tried to organize an East Coast Homosexual Parents Union for lesbian mothers in DOB New Jersey, but women were too scared of discovery to get involved. Carole Morton, interview with author, San Francisco, CA, March 10, 2007. See also letter from Carole Morton to Del Martin and Phyllis Lyon, April 19, 1976, box 125, folder 19, LMP.

47. Carole Morton, interview with author, San Francisco, CA, March 10, 2007.

48. See Dykes and Tykes Flyer, "Lesbian Mothers Need Your Support," Dykes and Tykes (Org. and Legal Custody Ctr.) NYC folder, Organizations Files, LHA.

49. "DRAFT—Demands for Mother's Day Demonstration May 14, 1978," Dykes and Tykes (Org. and Legal Custody Ctr.) NYC folder, Organizations Files, LHA.

50. See Dykes and Tykes Newsletter, March–April 1978, Dykes and Tykes (Org. and Legal Custody Ctr.) NYC-2 folder, Organizations Files, LHA. On the coalition between CARASA, CESA, and Dykes and Tykes, see "International Women's Day—'78

Flyer," Dykes and Tykes (Org. and Legal Custody Ctr.) NYC folder, Organizations Files, LHA.

51. Dykes and Tykes Flyer, "Celebrate Lesbian Motherhood with Dykes & Tykes on Mother's Day," Dykes and Tykes (Org. and Legal Custody Ctr.) NYC-2 folder, Organizations Files, LHA.

52. Ibid. See also Dykes and Tykes Newsletter, May–June 1978, box 125, folder 19, LMP.

53. "Mother's Day 1978," *Mom's Apple Pie*, August 1978, 2. See also Julie Palmer, "Hundreds Attend Lesbian Mother's Day Rally," *Gay Community News*, May 27, 1968, 1, and "Come Rally with Us on Mother's Day," flyer, Subject Files, Lesbian Mothers: Announcements 08090 folder, LHA.

54. "Organizer's Dialogue: Lesbian Mothers Fight Back," *Quest: A Feminist Quarterly* 5, no. 1 (Summer 1979): 63.

55. "Did You Know," *Mom's Apple Pie*, April 1979, 4.

56. Joan Pittell, interview with author, Seattle, WA, May 14, 2005.

57. "Thorns in Our Side: Childcare—A Privilege That Should Be a Right," *Mom's Apple Pie*, September 1975, 2.

58. Letter from Jessica Robbins to Lesbian Mothers National Defense Fund, August 20, 1977, LMNDF Files.

59. Jeanne Jullion, Day Planner, 1977, Jeanne Jullion, Personal Collection.

60. Ibid.

61. Jeanne Jullion, interview with author, Oakland, CA, May 21, 2002; Jill Lippett, interview with author, Jenner, CA, December 5, 2003.

62. For example, Joan Gibbs and Claudette Furlanga, the editors of the *Azalea* special edition on third world lesbian mothers, connected the issues of forced sterilization, poverty, lack of access to day care and health care, racism in adoption policies, the lack of access to reproductive technologies for poor women, and custody struggles. "Introduction," *Azalea: A Magazine by Third World Lesbians* (Winter 1979–80): 1.

63. Rosalie Davies, interview with author, Haverford, PA, September 12, 2002.

64. Transcripts of Lois Thetford interview with Shad Reinstein and Jody Laine for their documentary, *Mom's Apple Pie: The Heart of the Lesbian Mother's Custody Movement* (Frameline, 2006).

65. Kris Melroe, interview with author, Seattle, WA, May 15, 2005.

66. "Lesbian Custody and Gay Rights Project," *Mom's Apple Pie*, July 1977, 8.

67. Carole Morton, interview with author, San Francisco, CA, March 10, 2007.

68. "Custody Action for Lesbian Mothers I," *Learning to Fly*, produced by Radio Free Women, Philadelphia, Spoken Word Audio Files, LHA.

69. In personal notes from a conversation in 1975, Del Martin jotted down some details about the woman she had spoken with: "44, Madison, WI. lesbian mom & children divorced. no support in community; radical young people." Box 126, folder 4, LMP.

70. Judith Anderson, "Motherhood and the Gay Woman," *San Francisco Chronicle*, October 23, 1971; "Lesbian Moms Court for Kids," *Berkeley Barb*, February 4, 1972, "Motherhood and the Gay Woman," *San Francisco Chronicle*, November 23, 1971. Del Martin wrote that thirty women signed up for the group at the workshop that day. See manuscripts in box 124, folder 2, LMP. Pat Norman, another of the LMU's founders,

remembered in an interview with Joan Biren that around forty women came to the impromptu workshop for lesbian mothers. Pat Norman, interview with Joan Biren for the film *No Secret Anymore: The Times of Del Martin and Phyllis Lyon*, November 1999, transcript in Joan E. Biren Papers, Sophia Smith Archives, Smith College, Northampton, MA.

71. Judie Ghidinelli, interview with author, Oakland, CA, April 15, 2003.

72. Pat Norman, interview with Joan Biren for the film *No Secret Anymore: The Times of Del Martin and Phyllis Lyon*, November 1999, transcript in Joan E. Biren Papers, Sophia Smith Archives, Smith College, Northampton, MA.

73. *Mom's Apple Pie*, June 1975, 3; *The Real Live Lesbian Show*, January 1–7, 1978, WBAI New York, WBAI Collection, Spoken Word Audio Files, LHA. On the story of the Gay Academic Union event, see also Getting Together Column, "Dykes and Tykes," *City Star*, July 1976, 18.

74. Jeanne Jullion, interview with author, Oakland, CA, May 21, 2002.

75. Judie Ghidinelli, interview with author, Oakland, CA, April 15, 2003.

76. On the Christmas party organized by the San Francisco motorcycle clubs, see "Christmas Is Coming," LMU Newsletter, October 19, 1972. On the toys for tots programs, see LMU Newsletter, October 29, 1973, and LMU Newsletter, January 1975; "Lesbian Mothers Day in the Park," LMU Newsletter, May 14 1977; and LMU Newsletter, November 1974, box 124, folder 2, LMP.

77. "S.F. Bay Area L.M.U. Newsletter," March 25, 1974, box 124, folder 2, LMP.

78. On the rap group for mothers of adolescent children, see Dykes and Tykes Agenda for August and September 1976, Dykes and Tykes (Org. and Legal Custody Ctr.) NYC folder, Organizations Files, LHA; Lesbian Mothers and Sons group announced in Dykes and Tykes Newsletter, May–June 1978, Dykes and Tykes (Org. and Legal Custody Ctr.) NYC-2 folder, Organizations Files, LHA. On other rap groups, see "At Last the Rap Sessions You've Been Waiting For," Dykes and Tykes (Org. and Legal Custody Ctr.) NYC folder, Organizations Files, LHA.

79. Dykes and Tykes Newsletter, February–March 1977, Dykes and Tykes (Org. and Legal Custody Ctr.) NYC-2 folder, Organizations Files, LHA.

80. For events, see Dykes and Tykes Newsletter, March–April 1978, Dykes and Tykes (Org. and Legal Custody Ctr.) NYC folder, Organizations Files, LHA. On picnics, see "Calendar" (1976), Dykes and Tykes (Org. and Legal Custody Ctr.) NYC-2 folder, Organizations Files, LHA.

81. "Women Loving Women Loving Children" flyer, Dykes and Tykes (Org. and Legal Custody Ctr.) NYC folder, Organizations Files, LHA.

82. Kathy Florez, "Lesbian Mothers," *Amazon Spirit* (March/April 1979), 7; "Lesbian Mothers Group," *Amazon Spirit* (May/June 1979), 5.

83. Carolyn Selene, interview with author, Lynnwood, WA, March 13, 2005.

84. Letter from LSA Speakers Forum to Del Martin, November 4, 1974, and letter to LMU from the Bar Association of San Francisco, February 19, 1975, box 126, folder 6, LMP. Norman remembered that educating people both inside and outside the lesbian feminist community was a high priority for the LMU. "That [education and the lesbian mothers movement in general] happened by us taking responsibility for teaching people who had any say in our lives. Social workers, judges, doctors, psychologists, psychiatrists. We actually went to schools, we went to high schools, we went anywhere

there were people that we could talk to, to explain not only homosexuality and gay rights, but also lesbian mothers and lesbian mothers' rights. And children of lesbian mothers as well." Pat Norman, interview with Joan Biren for the film *No Secret Anymore: The Times of Del Martin and Phyllis Lyon*, November 1999, transcript in Joan E. Biren Papers, Sophia Smith Archives, Smith College, Northampton, MA.

85. Geraldine Cole, interview with author, Seattle, WA, March 14, 2005. On the Atlanta conference in general, see "LMNDF Travels: Atlanta—Women and the Law," *Mom's Apple Pie*, May 1978, 2. On the various panels at the conference, see "9th National Conference on Women and the Law, April 6–9, 1978, Atlanta, Georgia" program, Geraldine Cole, Personal Collection.

86. Letter from Donna Hitchens to the Lesbian Mothers' National Defense Fund, November 8, 1977, LMNDF Files.

87. "Acknowledgments," first edition of the Lesbian Mother Litigation Manual, 1982, LMNDF Files.

88. Information on 2008 budget is taken from the website of the National Center for Lesbian Rights, www.nclrights.org., accessed September 30, 2012, copy of filed tax form in author's possession. On the history of the LRP/NCLR, see Wendell Ricketts, "Quietly Making History," *The Advocate*, May 1988, 46–49.

89. On cases that Lambda was involved in from 1973 to 1976, see "Lambda News," 1976, Lambda Legal Defense and Education Fund, New York, Organizations Files, LHA. Initial letter to the LMNDF, Seattle, from Karle requesting materials while in private practice, dated November 3, 1975, and letter to LMNDF on behalf of Lambda Legal dated September 23, 1976, both in LMNDF Files.

Chapter 5

1. For information about the San Francisco Bay Area Gay Fathers, see newsletter files entitled "Gay Fathers of the San Francisco Bay Area" and "San Francisco Bay Area Gay Fathers," GLBTHS; on the Gay Fathers of Los Angeles, see Subject Files: "Gay Fathers of Los Angeles," ONGLA; on gay fathers groups in New York, Chicago, San Diego, Boston, and Cleveland, see files on these groups in the records of the International Gay Information Center at the New York Public Library, as well as subject files for the Gay Fathers Forum of New York, ONGLA. On the Gay Fathers of Greater Philadelphia, see Subject Files, Gay Fathers of Greater Philadelphia folder, John J. Wilcox Jr. Archives, William Way LGBT Community Center, Philadelphia, PA.

2. Lillian Faderman and Stuart Timmons, *Gay L.A.: A History of Sexual Outlaws, Power Politics, and Lipstick Lesbians* (New York: Perseus Books, 2006), 154–58; John D'Emilio, *Sexual Politics, Sexual Communities: The Making of A Homosexual Minority in the United States, 1940–1970* (Chicago: University of Chicago Press, 1983), 176–95. Other important pre-Stonewall signs of a shift toward a new defiance in American queer communities include the riot at Compton's Cafeteria and the founding of *Vanguard* in San Francisco in 1966, the 1965 protest at Dewey's lunch counter in Philadelphia, and the 1959 riot at Cooper's Donuts in Los Angeles. On the Compton's riot and *Vanguard*, see Susan Stryker, *Transgender History* (Berkeley, CA: Seal Press, 2008), 63–78; on the Dewey's protest, see Marc Stein, *The City of Brotherly and Sisterly Loves: Lesbian and Gay Philadelphia*,

1945–1972 (Chicago: University of Chicago Press, 2000), 245–46; on the Cooper's riot, see Lillian Faderman and Stuart Timmons, *Gay L.A.: A History of Sexual Outlaws, Power Politics, and Lipstick Lesbians* (New York: Perseus Books, 2006), 1–2, and Stryker, *Transgender History*, 59–62.

3. On gay liberation in New York, see David Eisenbach, *Gay Power: An American Revolution* (New York: Carroll & Graf, 2006), 117–81; Martin Duberman, *Stonewall* (New York: Dutton, 1993); David Carter, *Stonewall: The Riots That Sparked the Gay Revolution* (New York: St. Martin's Press, 2004); and Karla Jay, *Tales of the Lavender Menace: A Memoir of Liberation* (New York: Basic Books, 1999). For a classic, detailed account of the emergence and spread of gay liberation, see Donn Teal, *The Gay Militants* (New York: Stein and Day, 1971). On the rapid growth of GLF, see D'Emilio, *Sexual Politics, Sexual Communities*, 233–36, and Eisenbach, *Gay Power*, 140–41. On the founding of the Gay Community Services Center in Los Angeles, see Moira Rachel Kenney, *Mapping Gay L.A.: The Intersection of Place and Politics* (Philadelphia: Temple University Press, 2001), 80–84, and Faderman and Timmons, *Gay L.A.*, 191–95. John Howard discusses the history of GLF Atlanta in *Men Like That: A Southern Queer History* (Chicago: University of Chicago Press, 1999), 234. See also histories of GLF Atlanta's first years written by one of its founders, Berl Boykin, and an early member, Dave Hayward: Berl Boykin, "First Person: Pride 1971," *Southern Voice*, June 22, 2007, 52, and Dave Hayward, "First Person: Pride 1972," *Southern Voice*, June 22, 2007, 54.

4. Kenneth Pitchford, interview with author, New York, NY, September 19, 2009. On the founding of the Flaming Faggots out of GLF New York, see Kenneth Pitchford, "Where We Came From and Who We Are," box 1, folder 1, Steven F. Dansky Papers, 1968–2006, M. E. Grenander Department of Special Collections & Archives, State University of New York Albany.

5. Kenneth Pitchford, interview with author, New York, NY, September 19, 2009.

6. Steven Dansky, "Hey Man," *Rat*, May 8–21, 1970, 20. Republished as *Gay Flames Pamphlet no. 8* (Gay Liberation Front New York).

7. Steven Dansky, John Knoebel, and Kenneth Pitchford, "The Effeminist Manifesto," *Double-F: The Magazine of Effeminism* 2 (Winter/Spring 1973): 2–3. Copy in box 1, folder 3, Steven F. Dansky Papers, 1968–2006, M. E. Grenander Department of Special Collections & Archives, State University of New York Albany.

8. Don Mager, interview with author, Charlotte, NC, March 28, 2008. For a description of the Gay Liberator Collective in 1974, see "Just Us!" *Gay Liberator* 36 (March 1974): 1, GLBTHS. On the Detroit Gay Community Center in 1973, see "Community Center Open," *Gay Liberator* 28 (July 1973): 1, GLBTHS.

9. Don Mager, "Faggot Fathers," *Gay Liberator* 27 (June 1973): 8–9, GLBTHS.

10. Don Mager, interview with author, Charlotte, NC, March 28, 2008. See also "Michigan Gay Pride Week" announcement, *Gay Liberator* 27 (June 1973): 12–13, GLBTHS.

11. Don Mager, interview with author, Charlotte, NC, March 28, 2008.

12. Ibid.

13. Pat Murphy, "Hands over Heart, Step Smartly," *San Francisco Sentinel*, June 23, 2007.

14. Jack Latham, "A Faggot Father Speaks Out," *Gay Sunshine Journal* 24 (Spring 1975): 10–11, GLBTHS. Jack later used the name Nick; I use "Jack Latham" in the main

body text throughout to avoid confusion. Latham discussed the size of the response in "The Roots of Gay Fathers," in *Gay Fathers Exposed* (self-published, 1985), 9. *Gay Fathers Exposed* was written by the members of the San Francisco Bay Area Gay Fathers to help other gay fathers groups get started. I am deeply grateful to Bill Jones for the copy in my possession.

15. Allen Klein, telephone interview with author, March 23, 2005. Marty Karls, still married and a young father in 1975, remembered seeing Klein in the parade that day and joining him. For Karls, the parade—where he had sex with a man in the man's camper—represented a freedom that he had denied himself since his teen years. That day was a critical moment in his coming out both as a gay man and a gay father. Marty Karls, interview with author, San Francisco, CA, August 9, 2004.

16. For a description of the first day, see Nick Latham, "The Roots of Gay Fathers," 9.

17. Jack Latham, "A Faggot Father Speaks Out," *Gay Sunshine Journal* 24 (Spring 1975), GLBTHS.

18. Nick Latham, "The Roots of Gay Fathers."

19. Bill Jones, interview with author, Sausalito, CA, May 19, 2004.

20. Nick Latham, "The Roots of Gay Fathers."

21. Marty Karls, "Early Days," in *Gay Fathers Exposed*, 10–11.

22. Bill Jones, interview with author, Sausalito, CA, May 19, 2004. Allen Klein, who was also with SFBAGF during this time, confirmed this perception. Allen Klein, telephone interview with author, March 23, 2005.

23. John D'Emilio and Estelle Freedman, *Intimate Matters: A History of Sexuality in America* (New York: Harper & Row, 1988), 346–47. See also John Gallagher and Chris Bull, *Perfect Enemies: The Religious Right, the Gay Movement, and the Politics of the 1990s* (New York: Crown Publishers, 1996), 7.

24. On the turnout for the 1977 parade, see Murphy, "Hands over Heart," and on the impact of the Bryant campaign and the Briggs Initiative on the gay community in the San Francisco Bay Area, see Susan Stryker and Jim Van Buskirk, *Gay by the Bay: A History of Queer Culture in the San Francisco Bay Area* (San Francisco: Chronicle Books, 1996), 70–82.

25. Nick Latham, "The Roots of Gay Fathers"; Marty Karls, interview with author, San Francisco, CA, July 3, 2004. On the adoption of T-shirts and banners by the group and the effect, see typewritten notes on the history of SFBAGF, Bill Jones, Personal Collection, and Tom McGee, "1980–1981," in *Gay Fathers Exposed*, 11.

26. Bill Jones, "President's Message," SFBAGF Newsletter, June 1985, 3, San Francisco Bay Area Gay Fathers folder, GLBTHS.

27. Ibid.

28. Thomas Garrett, "The Pain and Pride of Gay Fathers," *New York Native*, November 16–29, 1981.

29. Reference to being five years old in GFLA Newsletter from May 1984, Gay Fathers of Los Angeles folder, ONGLA.

30. Alan Tarsky, interview with author, Los Angeles, CA, February 25, 2003.

31. Don Harrelson, interview with author, Seattle, WA, June 30, 2003.

32. "Fathers and Kids Show up in Full Force for Gay Pride Parade," Gay Fathers of Los Angeles Newsletter, August 1984, Subject Files, Gay Fathers of Los Angeles folder, ONGLA.

33. Letter from Gino Sikorski to the Christopher Street West Festival Committee, July 2, 1983, Subject Files, Gay Fathers of Los Angeles folder, ONGLA.

34. On the group's participation in the parade, see Gay Fathers Forum Newsletter, June 1985, Subject Files, Gay Fathers Forum of New York folder, ONGLA. There were quite a few gay fathers groups in the greater New York area by the mid-1980s. Though the Forum was the largest, there was a smaller one called Gay Fathers of New York I that had been founded in 1976. On the founding of the Forum, its relative size, and other groups, see Joe Dolce, "Gay Daddies Shatter Steeotypes," *The Advocate*, January 6, 1983, 25–27. On the earlier group, see also Brad Mulroy, "Bill Goddard Talks about Life for a Gay Father," *New York City News*, November 17, 1982. Gene Santamasso, a member of Gay Fathers of New York I, talked about the group's founding in 1976 in a taped panel on gay fathers at the 6th annual Lesbian and Gay Health Conference in 1984, Taped Conference Proceedings, Library, LHA. A 1985 Forum newsletter lists the gay fathers–related groups in the greater New York area as: "Gay Fathers of New York I," "Gay Fathers of Manhattan II," "Gay Fathers of Brooklyn," and "Gay Fathers of Long Island," in addition to "Gay Fathers of Westchester," "Gay Fathers of New Jersey," and "Gay Fathers of Greater Philadelphia." Gay Fathers Forum Newsletter, May 1985, Subject Files, Gay Fathers Forum of New York folder, ONGLA. For a detailed first-person account of the Gay Fathers Forum and Gay Fathers I and their connection to the larger gay father movement by a gay father who was active in the groups throughout the 1980s, see John C. Miller, " 'My Daddy Loves Your Daddy': A Gay Father Encounters a Social Movement," in *Queer Families, Queer Politics: Challenging Culture and the State*, ed. Mary Bernstein and Renate Reimann (New York: Columbia University Press, 2001), 221–30.

35. Gay Fathers Forum Newsletter, April 1983, and Gay Fathers Forum Newsletter, September 1984, Subject Files, Gay Fathers Forum of New York folder, ONGLA.

36. Alan R. Yoffee, " 'Maybe If You Met the Right Woman . . . ': Gay Fathers, Ex-wives, and Their Children," *Au Courant Newsmagazine* (Philadelphia, PA), March 12, 1984, 1, 7.

37. Gay Fathers of Sacramento Newsletter, May 1985, Bill Jones, Personal Collection.

38. "Long Beach Experience Proves an Enlightening Experience for GFLA Marcher," Gay Fathers of Los Angeles Newsletter, August 1984, Subject Files, Gay Fathers of Los Angeles folder, ONGLA.

39. South Bay Gay Fathers Newsletter, May 1985, Bill Jones, Personal Collection.

40. Letter/newsletter from July 1980 that begins "Dear Daddies," Subject Files, Gay Fathers of Greater Philadelphia folder, John J. Wilcox Jr. Archives, William Way LGBT Community Center, Philadelphia, PA.

41. Gay Fathers of Los Angeles news release, "Gay Fathers Stresses Management of Pressures at September Meetings," September 1984, Subject Files, Gay Fathers of Los Angeles folder, ONGLA.

42. Undated video clip, *Phil Donahue Show*, 1980s, in author's possession. Members of other gay fathers groups also appeared on local and national television shows during these years. Don Harrelson and his son Jon appeared on local television shows in the Los Angeles area such as *Alive and Well* (1985) and national shows such as the *Today Show* (May 31, 1985) and the *Phil Donahue Show* (May 31, 1985), where they appeared with Bill Jones and his son Aaron. Members of Gay Fathers of Greater Philadelphia appeared in 1983 on a local television show, *Perspectives*. Video clips of Don and Jon Harrelson's and Bill and Aaron Jones's television appearances in author's possession. On Philadelphia gay fathers' appearances, see September 1983 newsletter, Subject Files, Gay Fathers of Greater Philadelphia folder, John J. Wilcox Jr. Archives, William Way LGBT Community Center, Philadelphia, PA.

43. John S. Mills, "Notables on Newsletters," in *Gay Fathers Exposed*, 23.

44. Ron Scholz, "Information Resource Center of the SFBAGF," in *Gay Fathers Exposed*, 27.

45. "Outreach to Gay Fathers Begins," Gay Fathers Forum Newsletter, March 1986, Subject Files, Gay Fathers Forum of New York folder, ONGLA.

46. Gay Fathers Forum Newsletter, May 1985, Subject Files, Gay Fathers Forum of New York folder, ONGLA.

47. Allen Klein, telephone interview with author, March 23, 2005.

48. Joe Dolce, "Gay Daddies Shatter Stereotypes," *The Advocate*, January 6, 1983, 26.

49. Gay Fathers of Los Angeles flyer and news release, "Gay Fathers: The Women in Their Lives," both in Subject Files, Gay Fathers of Los Angeles folder, ONGLA.

50. See "Married Men's Groups," in Gay Fathers Forum Newsletter, May 1985, October 1984, and September 1984. A special session of the Married Men's Group entitled "The Wives in our Lives" was facilitated by wives and ex-wives of men in the gay fathers group, Gay Fathers Forum Newsletter, August 1984; "Wives and Gay Fathers" group, in Gay Fathers Forum Newsletter, June 1985, Subject Files, Gay Fathers Forum of New York folder, ONGLA.

51. Amity Buxton, "Former (or Current) Wives of Gay Fathers Support Group," in *Gay Fathers Exposed*, 17.

52. Marty Karls, interview with author, San Francisco, CA, July 3, 2004.

53. Fred Sonenberg, interview with author, Guerneville, CA, June 6, 2004.

54. On Parents Who Are Gay and Gay Married Men's Association, see Catherine Gunther, "Gay Dads and Gay Moms: The Kids Are Alright," *City Paper* (Baltimore, MD), July 13, 1979.

55. John McClung, interview with author, Apple Valley, CA, May 22, 2003.

56. Allen Klein, "Early Days," in *Gay Fathers Exposed*.

57. Mark Stephens, "Speech before the National March for Gay and Lesbian Rights during the Democratic National Convention in San Francisco, 1984," in *Gay Fathers Exposed*, 6–7.

58. Marty Karls, interview with author, San Francisco, CA, July 3, 2004.

59. "GFSF By-Laws," in *Gay Fathers Exposed*, 34.

60. Gay Fathers of Los Angeles Newsletter, October 1984, Subject Files, Gay Fathers of Los Angeles folder, ONGLA.

61. Joe Towner, "Crisis Fund," in *Gay Fathers Exposed*, 6.

62. Ron Scholz, "Information Resource Center of the SFBAGF," in *Gay Fathers Exposed*, 27.

63. Andrew Hallum, interview with author, Lynden, WA, June 27, 2003.

64. John McClung, interview with author, Apple Valley, CA, May 22, 2003.

65. Robert Johnson, interview with author, Pasadena, CA, May 8, 2003.

66. Brad Mulroy, "One Gay Father's Custody Fight," *New York City News*, November 17, 1982; "NOW Supports Gay Father in Custody Case," Gay Fathers Forum Newsletter, September 1984. On the outcome of Gottlieb's case, see "N.Y. Court Voids Homophobic Decree on Gay Father," Gay Fathers Forum Newsletter, June 1985, Subject Files, Gay Fathers Forum of New York folder, ONGLA.

67. Gay Fathers Forum Newsletters, October 1984, June 1985, and March 1986, Subject Files, Gay Fathers Forum of New York folder, ONGLA.

68. Gay Fathers Forum Newsletter, April 1983, Subject Files, Gay Fathers Forum of New York folder, ONGLA.

69. Examples of "Urgent Concerns" discussion groups in Gay Fathers Forum Newsletters, December 1984, May 1985, November 1985, and August 1987, Subject Files, Gay Fathers Forum of New York folder, ONGLA.

70. August 1983 and April 1981 newsletters, Subject Files, Gay Fathers of Greater Philadelphia folder, John J. Wilcox Jr. Archives, William Way LGBT Community Center, Philadelphia, PA.

71. Andrew Hallum, interview with author, Lynden, WA, June 27, 2003.

72. Gay Fathers of Los Angeles News Release, "Gay Fathers Open May with Topics on Family Relations," Subject Files, Gay Fathers of Los Angeles folder, "Fathers without Children: Living without the Kids," Gay Fathers Forum Newsletter, March 1985, Subject Files, Gay Fathers Forum of New York folder, ONGLA.

73. David Black, *The Plague Years: A Chronicle of AIDS, the Epidemic of Our Times* (New York: Simon and Schuster, 1985): 49–53. *Pneumocystis carinii* and Kaposi's sarcoma (KS) were opportunistic diseases that infected people with AIDS in these early days of the outbreak, before antiretroviral drugs that fought the disease were developed.

74. San Francisco Department of Public Health, *AIDS in San Francisco: Status Report for Fiscal Year 1987–88 and Projections of Service Needs and Costs for 1988–93*, April 22, 1988; Los Angeles County AIDS Epidemiology Program, Surveillance Unit, *AIDS Monthly Surveillance Report*, December 31, 1990; Bureau of Communicable Disease Control, New York States Department of Health, *AIDS Surveillance Monthly Update for Cases Reported Through April 1990*, April 1990.

75. John McClung, interview with author, Apple Valley, CA, May 22, 2003.

76. Bill Jones, "1985," in *Gay Fathers Exposed*, 14.

77. San Francisco Bay Area Gay Fathers Newsletter, June 1986, GLBTHS.

78. Bill Jones, interview with author, Sausalito, CA, May 19, 2004.

79. Gay Fathers Forum Newsletter, June 1984, Subject Files, Gay Fathers Forum of New York folder, ONGLA.

80. Gay Fathers Forum Newsletter, May 1985, Subject Files, Gay Fathers Forum of New York folder, ONGLA.

81. On the teen group, see Marty Karls, "The Teen Group," in *Gay Fathers Exposed*, 16, 17; on the AIDS/Action discussion group, see San Francisco Bay Area Gay Fathers Newsletter, June 1985, GLBTHS.

82. Marty Karls, interview with author, San Francisco, CA, July 3, 2004.

83. Gay Fathers Forum Newsletter, March 1986, Subject Files, Gay Fathers Forum of New York folder, ONGLA.

84. This estimate is based on interviews I conducted with members of both the San Francisco and Los Angeles groups.

85. Gay Fathers of Los Angeles Newsletter, August–September 1992, Subject Files, Gay Fathers of Los Angeles folder, ONGLA.

86. Originally founded as the Gay Fathers Coalition, the group referred to itself briefly as the Gay Fathers Coalition International to reflect the membership of Gay Fathers of Toronto before changing its name in 1986 to the Gay and Lesbian Parents Coalition International, the name it would be known by throughout the 1990s.

87. GLPCI, "History of the Coalition," *Publications for Member Chapters Pamphlet*, 1, Bill Jones, Personal Collection.

88. Ibid.

89. On Jones-Hennin's founding of gay parent and gay and bisexual married men's groups in the mid-1970s in Washington, D.C., see Catherine Gunther, "Gay Dads and Gay Moms: The Parents Are Alright," *City Paper: Baltimore's Biweekly Newspaper*, July 13, 1979. Jones-Hennin's group, Parents Who Are Gay, actually held a "rap group" and an "open house aboard a boat" as part of the 1979 march events, and it is possible that he and Voeller helped influence the awareness of gay and lesbian custody struggles. See National March on Washington for Lesbian and Gay Rights Official Souvenir Program, 23, and "Make It Happen" (pamphlet), "March on Washington (1979)," folder, "Marches on Wash.," Ephemera Collection, GLBTHS. For a copy of the 1973 Gay Parents Support Packet put together by Bruce Voeller, see Subject Files, Lesbian Mothers Custody Issues 08110 folder, LHA; 1979 revised version of support packet, Subject Files, Gay Parents II folder, ONGLA. See also a discussion of gay fatherhood as a personal and political issue in Bruce Voeller and James Walters, "Gay Fathers," *The Family Coordinator* (April 1978): 149–57. On the 1979 March on Washington, see Dudley Clendinen and Adam Nagourney, *Out for Good: The Struggle to Build a Gay Rights Movement in America* (New York: Touchstone Press, 1999), 403–5, 407–9.

90. "Gay Fathers Coalition Articles of Incorporation," box 2, GLPCI folder, COLAGE (Children of Lesbians and Gays Everywhere) Records, 1982–2000 Special Collection, GLBTHS.

91. On the 1986 renaming of the Gay Fathers Coalition International as the Gay and Lesbian Parents Coalition International, see GLPCI, "History of the Coalition," in *Publications for Member Chapters Pamphlet*, 1, Bill Jones, Personal Collection, and Phil Conway's report on the 1986 annual convention in Chicago in "President's Message," San Francisco Bay Area Gay Fathers Newsletter, July 1985, GLBTHS. For the founding of Gay Fathers of Greater Boston, see "Spotlight on Local Parent Groups," *The Family Tree* (Winter 1998–99), 2, Periodicals Collection, GLBTHS. See also Gay Fathers of Greater Boston Newsletter, April 1984, Bill Jones, Personal Collection. On the Long

Beach group, see "News Release," Subject Files, Gay Fathers of Los Angeles folder, ONGLA.

Chapter 6

1. Manuel Castells, *The City and the Grassroots: A Cross-Cultural Theory of Urban Social Movements* (Berkeley: University of California Press, 1983), 140.

2. William Van Deburg, *New Day in Babylon: The Black Power Movement and American Culture, 1965–1975* (Chicago: University of Chicago Press, 1992).

3. Jill Johnston, *Lesbian Nation* (New York: Touchstone, 1973), 22.

4. *Lesbian Connection*, August 1976, 9.

5. For articles on the conference, see *Lesbian Connection*, March 1976, 23; and ALFA *Newsletter*, May 1976, 6. The ALFA *Newsletter* was later known as *Atalanta*.

6. For a general overview of lesbian feminist communities and lesbian nationalism during the 1970s, see Lillian Faderman, *Odd Girls and Twilight Lovers: A History of Lesbian Life in Twentieth-Century America* (New York: Columbia University Press, 1991), 237–45; on 1970s lesbian feminist community in New York City, see *The Lesbian Feminist*, 1973–76; in the San Francisco Bay Area, see Deborah Goleman Wolf, *The Lesbian Community* (Berkeley: University of California Press, 1977), and Susan Stryker and Jim Van Buskirk, *Gay by the Bay: A History of Queer Culture in the San Francisco Bay Area* (San Francisco: Chronicle Books, 1996); in Seattle, see *Mom's Apple Pie: The Newsletter of the Lesbian Mothers' National Defense Fund*, 1974–80, and *Out and About: Seattle Lesbian/Feminist Newsletter*, 1976–80, Newsletter Collection, LHA; in Los Angeles, see Lillian Faderman and Stuart Timmons, *Gay L.A.: A History of Sexual Outlaws, Power Politics, and Lipstick Lesbians* (New York: Perseus Books, 2006), 181–92, and *The Lesbian Tide*, 1971–80; in Atlanta, see Saralyn Chesnut and Amanda C. Gable, "Women Ran It: Charis Books and More and Atlanta's Lesbian-Feminist Community," in John Howard, *Carryin' On in the Gay and Lesbian South* (New York: New York University Press, 1997), 241–84, and *Atalanta: Newsletter of the Atlanta Lesbian Feminist Alliance*, 1973–80; in Baltimore, see *Desperate Living: A Lesbian Newsletter*, 1973–77; in Chicago, see *Lavender Woman: Chicago's Lesbian/Feminist Newspaper*, 1971–76; in Philadelphia, see Marc Stein, *City of Brotherly and Sisterly Loves: Lesbian and Gay Philadelphia, 1945–1972* (Chicago: University of Chicago Press, 2000), 341–70; in Louisville, Kentucky, see Kathie D. Williams, "Louisville's Lesbian Feminist Union: A Study in Community Building," in *Carryin' On in the Gay and Lesbian South*, 224–40, and *Lesbian Feminist Union News*, 1975–78, Newsletter Collection, LHA; in Ann Arbor, see *The Leaping Lesbian*, 1977–80, and *Lesbian Newsletter*, 1975–76, Newsletter Collection, LHA; in Jackson, Mississippi, see *Lesbian Front*, 1975–76, Newsletter Collection, LHA; and in Portland, Oregon, see Elizabeth Barnhart, "Friends and Lovers in a Counterculture Community," in *Old Family/New Family: Interpersonal Relationships*, ed. Nona Glazer-Malbin (New York: D. Van Nostrand Company, 1975), 90–155. One 1977 letter described Portland, Oregon, as having "four mountains, thirty-six camping sites, two rivers, one hundred forty-three grassy knolls, nine safeways, two Lesbian softball teams, one resource center, one bookstore, one 'people's' café, one women's bar." "Portland, Oregon," *Lesbian Connection*, September 1977, 15. On 1970s lesbian feminist community in Northampton, Massachusetts, see Study Group, "Analysis of

a Lesbian Community," *Lesbian Connection*, July 1977, 6; in Richmond, Virginia, see *Lesbian Feminist Flyer*, 1977–80; in Tampa, Florida, see "Tampa, Florida," *Lesbian Connection*, July 1977, 19; in St. Louis, see *Moonstorm*, 1973–80; and in Cincinnati, see Susan K. Freeman, "From the Lesbian Nation to the Cincinnati Lesbian Community: Moving toward a Politics of Location," *Journal of the History of Sexuality* 9, no. 1/2 (January–April 2000): 137–74, and *Dinah*, 1976–80, Newsletter Collection, LHA. For a sociological study of a lesbian feminist community in one midwestern university town, see Susan Krieger, *The Mirror Dance: Identity in a Women's Community* (Philadelphia: Temple University Press, 1983).

7. Joyce Cheney, ed., *Lesbian Land* (Minneapolis: Word Weavers, 1985).

8. *Women in Transition: A Feminist Handbook on Separation and Divorce* (Philadelphia: Women in Transition, Inc.), 86–87, quoted in Wolf, *The Lesbian Community*, 151.

9. Wolf, *The Lesbian Community*, 152.

10. Barbara S. Bryant, "Lesbian Mothers," (master's thesis, California State University at Sacramento, 1975), 140.

11. Bev, "She Ain't Heavy, She's My Sister," *Moonstorm*, Spring 1976, 4.

12. "Growing Up with the Wiz Kids," *Seattle Gay News*, April 13, 1979, 3, Subject Files, Lesbian Mothers Newspaper Articles 08210 folder, LHA.

13. See "Joan Larkin," biographical article on Larkin with a photo of her and her daughter Kate, Subject Files, Lesbian Mothers Narratives 08201 folder, LHA.

14. Bryant, "Lesbian Mothers," 137.

15. Adrian Hood, interview with author, New York, NY, April 12, 2005.

16. *Lesbian Connection*, November 1975, 9.

17. "Lynne and Susie Interview with Joan Biren Tape 1," Spoken Word Audio Files, LHA. See also Joan Biren, *Eye to Eye: Portraits of Lesbians—Photographs by JEB* (Washington, D.C.: Glad Hag Books, 1979), 24–25.

18. Celeste Cole, interview with author, Seattle, WA, March 18, 2005.

19. *Big Mama Rag* 8, no. 5, 12.

20. *Mom's Apple Pie*, January 1976, 5.

21. *Lesbian Connection*, October 1978, 9.

22. Cathy Cade, interview with author, Oakland, CA, June 23, 2004.

23. Karen Burr, "Male Children—A Lesbian Mother Perspective," *Lesbian Connection*, February 1975, 8–9.

24. Nancy Williamson, "The Mean Mothers," *Lesbian Tide*, December 1973, 10.

25. *The Real Live Lesbian Show*, WBAI Radio, New York, 1978, WBAI Collection, Spoken Word Audio Files, LHA.

26. Jeanne Jullion, interview with author, Oakland, CA, May 21, 2002.

27. *Lesbian Connection*, May 1978, 15.

28. "Laura," *Amazon Quarterly: Special Double Issue* (Fall 1973): 53.

29. Helen Lane, "Washington Womenspace Report," *Lesbian Connection*, September 1975, 5. One year after this was written, Sappha Survival School was planning the construction of a "children's space." *Lesbian Connection*, September 1976, 13.

30. *Mom's Apple Pie*, January 1976, 5.

31. "Lesbian Mother's Day," Everywoman's Space, WBAI Collection, Spoken Word Audio Files, LHA.

32. Ibid.

33. I discuss the emergence of activism by the children of lesbian and gay parents in detail in chapter 7.

34. Becky Logan, interview with author, Seattle, WA, May 13, 2005.

35. Kate Alfaro, interview with author, Ithaca, NY, July 29, 2005.

36. Cynthia McCabe, interview with author, Albany, CA, December 21, 2002. McCabe also remembered hearing about Marxism and other anticapitalist ideas as a child.

37. "Collectives Collectively," *Lesbian Tide*, June 1972, 7.

38. Laurel Galana and Gina Covina, *The New Lesbians: Interviews with Women across the U.S. and Canada* (Berkeley, CA: Moon Books, 1977), 38.

39. Cynthia McCabe, interview with author, Albany, CA, December 21, 2002.

40. Biren, *Eye to Eye*, 72.

41. *Mom's Apple Pie*, September 1976, 7.

42. The Journal Staff, "Lesbian Mothers Interview," *Women: A Journal of Liberation* 4, no. 3, 37.

43. "L.C. Interview: A Lesbian Mother," *Lesbian Connection*, October 1974, 11.

44. Jon Givner, interview with author, Brooklyn, NY, July 9, 2005.

45. Adrian Hood, interview with author, New York, NY, April 12, 2005.

46. Judie Ghidinelli, interview with author, Oakland, CA, April 15, 2003.

47. "Women Loving Women Loving Children" flyer, Dykes and Tykes (Org. and Legal Custody Ctr.) NYC folder, Organizations Files, LHA.

48. "Unclassifieds," *Mainely Gay* (formerly the Maine Gay Task Force Newsletter), January 1977, 58.

49. Womanstar, "Non-Sexist Education: Limited to Girls," *Lesbian Connection*, November 1979, 7.

50. Buckwheat Turner, "A Woman's Place—Women's Utopia: Roughing It in Reality," in Cheney, *Lesbian Land*, 19–23.

51. "Redbird Reflections: An Interview with Gail Gordon for the LHA," Spoken Word Audio Files, LHA. See also "Redbird," in Cheney, *Lesbian Land*, 121.

52. See Combahee River Collective, *The Combahee River Collective Statement*, in *Home Girls: A Black Feminist Anthology*, ed. Barbara Smith (New York: Kitchen Table—Women of Color Press, 1983), 272–82; and Cherríe Moraga and Gloria Anzaldua, eds., *This Bridge Called My Back: Writings by Radical Women of Color* (Watertown, MA: Persephone Press, 1981).

53. "Arco Iris," in Cheney, *Lesbian Land*, 30–40.

54. Juana Maria Paz, *The La Luz Journal* (Fayetteville, AR: The Paz Press, 1980), 2, 24, 62. Many Jewish lesbians did feel that lesbians of color did not understand the history of Sephardic Jewry as the struggles of an Arabic people of color. On issues faced by Jewish lesbians, see Evelyn Torton Beck, ed., *Nice Jewish Girls: A Lesbian Anthology* (Trumansburg, NY: The Crossing Press, 1982).

55. Adrian Hood and Alix Dobkin, interview with author, New York, NY, April 12, 2005. See also Majoie Canton and Rogi Rubyfruit, "Alix Dobkin and Liza Cowan on Money, Motherhood, and Mutes," *Lesbian Tide*, July/August 1977, 12.

56. *Lesbian Connection*, March 1977, 11.

57. "A Lesbian Tells Her Daughters to Forget Labels," *Poughkeepsie Journal*, March 27, 1983, 28.

58. Kate Alfaro, interview with author, Ithaca, NY, July 29, 2005.

59. Melanie was interviewed by Joan Biren in 1978. "Lynne and Susie Tape 1," Spoken Word Audio Files, LHA.

60. "Interview with a Lesbian Mother," *Desperate Living*, Spring 1975, 6.

61. Celeste Cole, interview with author, Seattle, WA, March 18, 2005; Kay, interview with author, New York, NY, April 19, 2005; Carolyn Selene, interview with author, Lynnwood, WA, March 13, 2005.

62. Letter, *Lesbian Connection*, May 1978, 22.

63. Paz, *The La Luz Journal*.

64. Bryant, "Lesbian Mothers," 137.

65. Kate Alfaro, interview with author, Ithaca, NY, July 29, 2005; Mary White, interview with author, Ithaca, NY, April 24, 2005.

66. Maxine Wolfe, interview with author, Brooklyn, NY, July 29, 2002; Judie Ghidinelli remembers her and her partner, Kate, telling their son Guthrie the same thing—not to mention lesbianism outside the household. Judie Ghidinelli, interview with author, Oakland, CA, April 15, 2003.

67. The Boston Women's Health Collective, *Ourselves and Our Children: A Book by and for Parents* (New York: Random House, 1978), 175. This quote appeared in a section on lesbian and gay parents. The book credits Wendy C. Sanford with writing the section and gives special thanks to the Lesbians with Children Group at the Cambridge Women's Center, which is probably the group mentioned.

68. Kay, interview with author, New York, NY, April 19, 2005; Ann, "Being a Dyke Means . . .," *Atalanta: The Newsletter of the Atlanta Lesbian Feminist Alliance*, March 1980, 5.

69. Nicole Joos, "Building Izbushka," *Womannews*, May 1981, 6.

70. *Mom's Apple Pie*, November 1977, 1.

71. Charlotte Bunch, "Learning from Lesbian Separatism," in *Lavender Culture*, ed. Karla Jay and Allen Young (New York: New York University Press, 1978), 433–57.

72. On the emergence of black political separatism in the Student Non-Violent Coordinating Committee, see Clayborne Carson, *In Struggle: SNCC and the Black Awakening of the 1960s* (Cambridge, MA: Harvard University Press), 144, 191–211. See Bette S. Tallen, "Lesbian Separatism: A Historical and Comparative Perspective," in *For Lesbians Only: A Separatist Anthology* (London: Onlywomen Press, 1988), 132–44 (originally prepared for delivery at the National Woman's Studies Association Conference in Columbus, Ohio, 1983).

73. Margaret Sloan-Hunter, "The Issue Is Woman-Identification," *Plexus: West Coast Women's Press*, June 1976. Cade explained to me her period of lesbian separatism in the early 1970s as a time of "breaking habits." As she realized that she had been conditioned to habitually defer to men and to limit her own power, she decided that she needed time away from male-dominated space to change those patterns. Cathy Cade, interview with author, Oakland, CA, June 23, 2004; Jill Lippett, interview with author, Jenner, CA, December 5, 2003.

74. As Alix Dobkin stated, "it depends on which separatist you ask, because separatism has many meanings." Alix Dobkin, interview with author, New York, NY, April 12, 2005.

75. *Lesbian Separatism: An Amazon Analysis* (Seattle: Lesbian Separatist Group, 1973).

76. Lois, "Me, the Boys and Our Struggle," *Moonstorm*, 1975 (issue on separatism), 11–12.

77. Gorgons, "Amazons Again," *Out and About: Seattle Lesbian/Feminist Newsletter*, May 1977, 21–22, Newsletter Collection, LHA.

78. Alix Dobkin, interview with author, New York, NY, April 12, 2005.

79. "Lesbian March Flyer," *Out and About: Seattle Lesbian/Feminist Newsletter*, July 1978, 8, Newsletter Collection, LHA.

80. "Forum to Discuss Male Children," *The Lesbian Tide*, July/August 1977, 35.

81. "Alix in Wimminland," *Out and About: Seattle Lesbian/Feminist Newsletter*, May 1977, 9, Newsletter Collection, LHA.

82. "Lesbian Center's Struggle for Support Ends," *Lesbian Connection*, May 1978, 3.

83. Discussion of ALFA policy on male children of lesbians and its history in "ALFA General Meeting Minutes," *Atalanta: The Newsletter of the Atlanta Lesbian Feminist Alliance*, November 1982, 5; letter from a woman protesting the presence of a teenage son of an ALFA member in the ALFA House in *Atalanta: The Newsletter of the Atlanta Lesbian Feminist Alliance*, October 1982, 8.

84. Janet Dey, four-page essay, July 19, 1978, Subject Files, Lesbian Mothers folder, Lesbian Mothers Narratives 08201 folder, LHA.

85. *The Real Live Lesbian Show*, WBAI Radio, New York, 1978, WBAI Collection, Spoken Word Audio Files, LHA.

86. "Mother of a Male Child," *Moonstorm*, December 1979, 3.

87. Judie Ghidinelli, interview with author, Oakland, CA, April 15, 2003.

88. *Atalanta: The Newsletter of the Atlanta Lesbian Feminist Alliance*, October 1982, 9.

89. This attendance estimate comes from a description of the first festival in the 10th Annual Michigan festival program, Subject Files, Music: Michigan Women's Festival (8–12th MWMF) folder, LHA.

90. Beth Greenfield, "Intense, Unique No-Man's Lands," *New York Times*, May 26, 2006. For a history and discussion of women's music festivals, see Bonnie J. Morris, *Eden Built by Eves* (Los Angeles: Alyson, 1999).

91. The program for the eighth annual festival in 1983 stated that "providing a completely female environment for womyn of all ages has continually been one of our priorities."

92. Adrian Hood, interview with author, New York, NY, April 12, 2005.

93. See programs for Michigan festivals, Subject Files, Music: Michigan Women's Festival (1–7th MWMF) folder, LHA. For details on childcare and male child policies, see the letter from a woman in Bloomington, Indiana, in *Lesbian Connection*, October 1978, 10.

94. *Lesbian Connection*, October 1978, 10.

95. Ibid.

96. Susan J. Wolfe, "Jewish Lesbian Mother," in Beck, *Nice Jewish Girls*, 173.

97. "ARF," in Cheney, *Lesbian Land*, 15; "Adobeland" in Cheney, *Lesbian Land*, 19–23, 27.

98. "Arco Iris," in Cheney, *Lesbian Land*, 30.

99. "D.W. Outpost," in Cheney, *Lesbian Land*, 47–49.

100. "Golden," in Cheney, *Lesbian Land*, 51.

101. *Lesbian Connection*, September 1976, 13.

102. "Lesbian Living Space," *Lesbian Connection*, March 1977, 23.

103. "Redbird," in Cheney, *Lesbian Land*, 116–24.

104. Cynthia McCabe, interview with author, Albany, CA, December 21, 2002; *Lesbian Feminist Flyer*, November 1978, 6. Susan Krieger writes about the tension and support one lesbian mother felt for her struggles raising her son in a lesbian feminist community in a midsized midwestern town. Krieger emphasizes the ways in which the community valued group process and decided to support the mother even though some women in the community had expressed dissatisfaction with the boy's presence. Krieger, *The Mirror Dance*, 114–15.

105. Jill Johnston, "Return of the Amazon Mother," in *Amazon Expedition: A Lesbian Feminist Anthology*, ed. Phyllis Birkby et al. (New York: Times Change Press, 1973), 66.

106. Sally Gearhart, *The Wanderground: Stories of the Hill-Women* (Watertown, MA: Persephone Press, 1979).

107. Charlotte Bunch, "Lesbians in Revolt," *The Furies: Lesbian/Feminist Monthly* 1 (January 1972): 9.

108. Laurel Galana, "Radical Reproduction: X without Y," *Amazon Quarterly* 2, no. 3, 4–19.

109. *Lesbian Connection*, March 1976, 3.

110. *Lesbian Connection*, April 1977, 24.

111. Suzi Kehler, "Why Separatism," *Lesbian Connection*, July 1977, 14.

112. "Matriarchy: Past and Present," *Lesbian Feminist Flyer*, August 1978, 5.

113. *Daughter Visions* 1, no. 1, 4.

114. Ibid., 3.

115. Ibid., 6.

116. For a historical discussion of parthenogenesis and lesbian separatism, see Greta Rensenbrink, "Parthenogenesis and Lesbian Separatism: Regenerating Women's Community through Virgin Birth in the United States in the 1970s and 1980s," *Journal of the History of Sexuality* 19, no. 2 (May 2010): 288–316.

117. Cathy Cade, interview with author, Oakland, CA, June 23, 2004; *Lesbian Front*, September 1975, 2, Newsletter Collection, LHA.

118. These underground networks of lesbians and gay men committed to reproductive freedom are a strong example of pre-AIDS political coalition between lesbian feminists and gay men. Cathy Cade, interview with author, Oakland, CA, June 23, 2004.

119. Looking back, Cade recalls that she was influenced in this decision by the activism of adopted lesbian feminists, just beginning at that point in time, for the right to know their birth parents. Cathy Cade, interview with author, Oakland, CA, June 23, 2004.

120. Cathy Cade, *A Lesbian Photo Album: The Lives of Seven Lesbian Feminists* (Oakland, CA: Waterwomen Books, 1987), 78.

121. Sioux Sawyer, "Conceiving Little Women," *The Lesbian Tide*, July/August 1977, 25.

122. *Moonstorm*, June 1979, 7.

123. "How to Get Pregnant without Getting Screwed," *Lesbian Connection*, November 1979, 14

124. Cathy Cade, interview with author, Oakland, CA, June 23, 2004.

Chapter 7

1. Roberta Achtenberg, "Donor Insemination," NGHEF Sixth Annual Lesbian and Gay Health Conference, June 16–19, 1984, Spoken Word Audio Files, LHA.

2. Gina Kolata, "Lesbian Partners Find the Means to be Parents," *New York Times*, January 30, 1989.

3. See letters to the Lesbian Mothers' National Defense Fund, LMNDF Files. A workshop on "lesbians considering motherhood" was held at Janus House, a lesbian counseling center in Cambridge, Massachusetts, in 1979. The workshop covered "adoption, artificial insemination, and having a male partner." Twenty-five women attended, and many others called in. Liz Hjetness and Alice Fisher, "Lesbians Consider Motherhood," *Gay Community News*, March 31, 1979. Anthropologist Kath Weston describes the explosion of interest in insemination among lesbians in the San Francisco Bay Area in her book *Families We Choose: Lesbians, Gays, Kinship* (New York: Columbia University Press, 1991), 165–93.

4. I follow Roberta Achtenberg and Donna Hitchens of the Lesbian Rights Project, after 1989 known as the National Center for Lesbian Rights (NCLR), in using the phrase "donor insemination." Both "artificial insemination" and "alternative insemination" suggest something exclusively original or authentic about heterosexual intercourse.

5. Donna Hitchens, *Lesbians Choosing Motherhood: Legal Implications in Donor Insemination* (San Francisco: Lesbian Rights Project, 1984), 5.

6. Letter dated October 6, 1987, LMNDF Files.

7. Nancy A. F. Langer, "Mothers By Choice," in *Lesbians Choosing Motherhood: Legal, Medical, and Social Issues* (New York: Lambda Legal Defense and Education Fund, n.d.), 3, LMNDF Files.

8. Jack and Jill (pseud.), *Artificial Insemination: An Alternative Conception* (San Francisco: Lesbian Health Information Project, 1979), 2, LMNDF Files.

9. Martha Heath, "Do It Yourself Artificial Insemination," *Lesbian Tide*, September/October 1978, 27.

10. "Proposal to Initiate Alternative Insemination at the Fenway Community Health Center," Subject Files, Artificial Insemination folder, LHA.

11. Barbara Kritchevsky, "The Unmarried Woman's Right to Artificial Insemination: A Call for an Expanded Definition of the Family," *Harvard Women's Law Journal* 4 (1981): 1–42.

12. Achtenberg, "Donor Insemination."

13. Georgia Dullea, "Artificial Insemination of Single Women Poses Difficult Questions," *New York Times*, March 9, 1979.

14. Marie Anoped, "Artificial Insemination for Lesbians," *Seattle Gay News*, March 2, 1979, 6.

15. Maidi Nickele, interview with author, Seattle, WA, July 17, 2006; Susan Stern, "Lesbian Insemination," *CoEvolution Quarterly* (Summer 1980): 108–17.

16. Mary O'Donnell et al., *Lesbian Health Matters* (Santa Cruz, CA: Santa Cruz Women's Health Center, 1979), copy in LHA library; Sarah and Mary Anonymous (pseud.), *Woman Controlled Conception* (San Francisco: Womanshare Books, 1979), copy in LHA library and LMNDF Files; Jack and Jill, *Artificial Insemination: An Alternative Conception*, 2, LMNDF Files. Although the booklet, *Woman Controlled Conception*, was originally published anonymously, one of the authors was Cathy Cade, who was instrumental in organizing early insemination networks in the San Francisco Bay Area. A third copy is in her collection at the Bancroft Library, University of California at Berkeley. Personal communication with Cathy Cade, June 12, 2012.

17. Maidi Nickele, interview with author, Seattle, WA, July 17, 2006. See also letters in LMNDF Files. On circulation of materials in the San Francisco Bay Area, see Anne Taylor Fleming, "New Frontiers in Conception," *New York Times Magazine*, July 20, 1980, 23.

18. Maidi Nickele, interview with author, Seattle, WA, July 17, 2006.

19. Stern, "Lesbian Insemination," 108.

20. Ibid., 112; Achtenberg, "Donor Insemination."

21. Stern, "Lesbian Insemination," 109. One woman from Madison, Wisconsin, got pregnant by arranging to have sex with a gay male friend. Langer, "Mothers by Choice," 5.

22. Mary Brennan, "Lesbian Moms and Kids," *Seattle Source*, May 9, 1986, 1; Sunny Rivera, interview with author, Seattle, WA, September 17, 2006.

23. Maidi Nickele, interview with author, Seattle, WA, July 17, 2006.

24. On the Los Angeles clinic, see Francie Hornstein, speech given at the 11th Annual Women and the Law Conference, San Francisco, March 1, 1980, LMNDF Files. On the Vermont Women's Health Center, see "Proposal to Initiate Alternative Insemination at the Fenway Community Health Center," Subject Files, Alternative Insemination folder, LHA. The Fenway proposal cites predecessors in Burlington, Vermont; Oakland, California; and Seattle, Washington.

25. Sandra Morgen, *Into Our Own Hands: The Women's Health Movement in the United States, 1969–1990* (New Brunswick, NJ: Rutgers University Press, 2002). The Vermont Women's Health Center specifically focused on providing lesbians with insemination services because of the discrimination they faced in dealing with other fertility clinics. Liz Clark and Bosha Gordon, interview with Barbara Kritchevsky, April 17, 1980, Burlington, VT, cited in Barbara Kritchevsky, "The Unmarried Woman's Choice of Artificial Insemination: A Call for an Expanded Definition of Family," May 1, 1980, 79, paper submitted in satisfaction of written work requirement, Harvard Law School, LMNDF Files.

26. "Proposal to Initiate Alternative Insemination at the Fenway Community Health Center," Subject Files, Alternative Insemination folder, LHA.

27. Jill Wolfson, "Toby's Mothers," *West Magazine San Jose Mercury News*, December 18, 1983, Sunday edition. See also Langer, "Mothers by Choice," 2.

28. Kolata, "Lesbian Partners Find the Means to be Parents."

29. In response to a 1988 letter from a woman in Madison, Wisconsin, requesting recommendations on sperm banks or clinics that would release sperm to a single woman in the "Wisconsin, Illinois, or Minnesota region," a member of the Lesbian Mothers' National Defense Fund suggested both the Blackwell clinic and the Oakland Feminist Women's Health Center. Letter dated February 19, 1988, LMNDF Files.

30. On Ident's relative size in 1987, see Elizabeth Noble, *Having Your Baby by Donor Insemination: A Complete Resource Guide* (Boston: Houghton & Mifflin, 1987), 109. One letter to the Lesbian Mothers' National Defense Fund from a woman in Knoxville, Tennessee, who donated one hundred dollars to the organization and said, "I'm trying, wish me luck!" recommended Ident as a source of sperm for insemination. Letter dated June 1, 1987, LMNDF Files. The proposal for the Fenway A.I. program identified Ident as one source for sperm used by the Vermont Women's Health Center since 1974. "Proposal to Initiate Alternative Insemination at the Fenway Community Health Center," Subject Files, Alternative Insemination folder, LHA. By 1990, the Fenway program was using the Oakland sperm bank. Jenifer Firestone, interview with author, Atlanta, GA, September 12, 2012.

31. Laurene Mascola, M.D., M.P.H., and Mary Guinan, M.D., Ph.D., "Semen Donors as the Source of Sexually Transmitted Diseases in Artificially Inseminated Women: The Saga Unfolds," *Journal of the American Medical Association* 257, no. 8, 1093–94. See also "Semen Banking, Organ and Tissue Transplantation, and HIV Antibody Testing," *Morbidity and Mortality Weekly Report* 37, no. 4 (February 5, 1988): 57.

32. The notes on a Lesbian Mothers' National Defense Fund telephone log entry that records a conversation with a woman in Iowa City, Iowa, say that sperm donations were being tested for AIDS so stringently at the Blackwell clinic that sperm had been dying as a result and success rates were in possible decline. LMNDF Telephone Log, LMNDF Files.

33. "Artificial Insemination and AIDS Link Tested," *New York Times*, August 21, 1985.

34. Donor Form, LMNDF Files.

35. "44% of Doctors Report Tests for AIDS on Donated Semen," *New York Times*, August 11, 1988.

36. "AIDS and Artificial Insemination," *Lesbian Connection*, March/April 1986, 4.

37. Maidi Nickele, interview with author, Seattle, WA, July 17, 2006.

38. It is important to note that this increasing availability of insemination for lesbians still varied greatly according to region. One woman in Oklahoma described what it was like for her and her partner to try and get pregnant in a state where they were "very much a minority." The two women had twin daughters in 1988 after "many years of searching for a physician that would cooperate." In 1993, they still did not know any other lesbian mothers of young children in their area. "Mom to Mom," *Momazons*, February/March 1994, 11, Newsletter Files, LHA.

39. Bill Jones, interview with author, Sausalito, CA, May 19, 2004.

40. In a 1985 article, Washington, D.C., attorney Sue Silber wrote that even though the D.C. family code prohibited taking into account sexual orientation in adoptive or foster parent evaluations, gay men and lesbians had better chances of being approved if they filed as single-parent adoptions rather than being open about their sexuality. Bonita Becker, "The Pursuit of Family: Part Three," *Washington Blade*, September 27, 1985, 13. The D.C. legislation protecting gay and lesbian parental rights, Bill 1–36, was passed into law in late 1976 and may have helped spur on the Anita Bryant campaign in Florida a year later. "D.C. Judiciary Committee Approves Custody Protection for Gay Parents," *Washington Blade*, June 1976, 1.

41. Bill Jones, interview with author, Sausalito, CA, May 19, 2004; Kevin Mckinney, "How to Become a Gay Father," *The Advocate*, December 8, 1987, 47.

42. Don Harrelson, interview with author, Seattle, WA, June 30, 2003.

43. Roberta Achtenberg and Wendell Ricketts, "The Adoptive and Foster Gay and Lesbian Parent," in *Gay and Lesbian Parents*, ed. Frederick W. Bozett (New York: Praeger, 1987), 92.

44. "Gay Male Couple Seeks Custody of Son," *Washington Blade*, January 7, 1983.

45. "Families by Adoption: A Gay Reality," *The Advocate*, August 28, 1974, 1.

46. On the Illinois program, see "Agency Reveals Kids Placed with Gay Couples," *Advocate*, August 15, 1973, 2. On the New Jersey program, see Brenda Maddox, *Married and Gay* (New York: Harcourt Brace Jovanovich, 1982), 151.

47. George Vecsey, "Approval Given for Homosexual to Adopt a Boy," *New York Times*, June 21, 1979. In a Harrisburg, Pennsylvania, case, a fifteen-year-old lesbian was placed with a lesbian foster parent. The placement was negotiated by the Committee on Criminal and Juvenile Justice of the Governor's Council on Sexual Minorities. "News Shorts," *Mainely Gay*, February 1977, 10.

48. Vecsey, "Approval Given for Homosexual to Adopt a Boy."

49. Essay by Will Dixon Gray, History Files, CKA.

50. "Joint Adoption: A Major Victory for LRP," *Lesbian Rights Project Newsletter* (Spring 1987), 1, box 1, file 35, Wendell Ricketts Papers, 1961–2004, HSC.

51. Essay by Will Dixon Gray, History Files, CKA.

52. In her rigorous and detailed history of adoption in the United States in the twentieth century, historian Ellen Herman argues that right-wing attempts to limit same-sex adoption have been a critical component of struggles over definitions of the family since the 1970s and as such are tied to the struggle for same-sex marriage. Ellen Herman, *Kinship by Design: A History of Adoption in the Modern United States* (Chicago: University of Chicago Press, 2008), 291–93. On Anita Bryant and the Dade County campaign, see Fred Fejes, *Gay Rights and Moral Panic: The Origins of America's Debate on Homosexuality* (New York: St. Martin's Press, 2008).

53. For a detailed discussion of the case, see Achtenberg and Ricketts, "The Adoptive and Foster Gay and Lesbian Parent," 99–105. See also "A Model Foster-care Policy" *Boston Globe*, May 28, 1985, and the Phil Donahue Show, May 31, 1985.

54. Georgia Dullea, "Gay Couples Becoming an Issue in Adoption," *Plain Dealer*, February 14, 1988.

55. "America's Waiting Children: A Report to the President from the Interagency Task Force on Adoption," March 31, 1988, box 2, file 3, Wendell Ricketts Papers, 1961–2004, HSC; Chris Bull, "Presidential Group Slams Les/Gay Adoption," *Gay Community News*, December 20–26, 1987, 1.

56. Rebecca Smith and Anne Affleck, interview with Wendell Ricketts, February 27, 1988, box 2, file 12, Wendell Ricketts Papers, 1961–2004, HSC.

57. *Matter of Appeal in Pima County Juvenile Action B-10489* (1986).

58. Steven Fritsch Rudser, interview with Wendell Ricketts, July 31, 1988, box 2, file 12, Wendell Ricketts Papers, 1961–2004, HSC.

59. *Sharon S. v. Superior Court*, 31 Cal. 4th 417 (2003). For the overruling of a denial recommendation by DSS, see Jacqueline Cutler, "Lesbian Couple Fought County to Jointly Adopt AIDS Boy," *Oakland Tribune*, November 16, 1989.

60. Achtenberg, "Donor Insemination"; Hitchens, *Lesbians Choosing Motherhood*, 1, LMNDF Files.

61. *Jhordan C. v. Mary K.*, 179 Cal. App. 3d 386 (1986).

62. Letter from Mary K. to the Lesbian Mothers' National Defense Fund, August 5, 1985, LMNDF Files.

63. Achtenberg, "Donor Insemination."

64. *Thomas S. v. Robin Y.*, 618 N.Y.S. 2d 356 (N.Y. App. Div. 1994).

65. *C.O. v. W.S.*, 639 N.E. 2d 523 (Ohio Ct. Com. Pls. 1994).

66. Jenifer Firestone, interview with author, Atlanta, GA, September 12, 2012. Sociologist Laura Mamo has also argued that as lesbians increasingly rely on high-tech technologies and sperm banks, there is a danger that lesbian childrearing will become commodified, controlled, and separated from lesbian feminist political commitments to women's autonomy and community formation. Laura Mamo, *Queering Reproduction: Achieving Pregnancy in the Age of Technoscience* (Durham, NC: Duke University Press, 2007), 224–50.

67. Jenifer Firestone, interview with author, Atlanta, GA, September 12, 2012. On Firestone's family, see Tinker Ready, "She Is Changing the Family Profile," *Boston Globe*, June 13, 1999. For gay men and lesbians creating nontraditional family structures together, see Bennett Drake, "Johnny Has Two Mommies—and Four Dads," *Boston Globe*, October 24, 2010; and David Tuller, "Gays and Lesbians Try Co-Parenting: Families with 2 Moms, 2 Dads," *San Francisco Chronicle*, February 4, 1993. In 2012 a law was introduced into the California state legislature that would address the needs of these non-nuclear families. Jim Sanders, "California Bill Would Allow a Child to Have More Than 2 Parents," *Pittsburgh Post-Gazette*, July 8, 2012.

68. Langer, "Mothers by Choice," 10–11. See also Ramon Coronado, "Lesbian 'Father' Gains Right to Visit Child She Had With Former Lover," *Oakland Tribune*, November 20, 1984; and "She Can Be 'Father' For Now, Says Court," *New York Daily News*, April 30, 1983.

69. Box 1, file 35, Paula L. Ettelbrick Papers, 1986–93, HSC.

70. On the New Mexico case, see box 2, file 2, Paula L. Ettelbrick Papers, 1986–93, HSC; box 2, file 13, Paula L. Ettelbrick Papers, 1986–93, HSC.

71. David Margolick, "Lesbian Child-Custody Cases Test Frontiers of Family Law," *New York Times*, July 4, 1990.

72. Box 2, file 14, Paula L. Ettelbrick Papers, 1986–93, HSC.

73. In re Matter of T.L., 1996 WL 393521 (Mo. Cir. Ct.).

74. Second-parent adoption is also referred to sometimes as "co-parent adoption" or "same-sex adoption." I use the term second-parent adoption to distinguish it from "co-parent custody cases" where one partner in a lesbian couple sues another for custodial or visitation rights. Carole S. Cullum, "Co-Parent Adoptions: Lesbian and Gay Parenting," *Trial* (June 1993): 28.

75. There is some dispute over where the very first second-parent adoption in the United States took place. Wendell Ricketts and Roberta Achtenberg have said that the first case was in Oregon, while Nancy Polikoff states that it was in Alaska. Both reports place it in 1985, and neither identifies the case or the participants. The local

and private nature of these early cases makes them hard to confirm, in contrast to the more public work of the Lesbian Rights Project on second-parent adoption a few years later. Ricketts and Achtenberg, "The Adoptive and Foster Gay and Lesbian Parent," 98; Nancy D. Polikoff, "Lesbian and Gay Couples Raising Children: The Law in the United States," in *Legal Recognition of Same-Sex Partnerships: A Study of National, European, and International Law*, ed. Robert Wintemute and Mads Andenaes (Oxford: Hart Publishing, 2001), 159.

76. Petitioner's Trial Brief, In the Matter of the Adoption Petition of Nancy L. Davis, Adopting Parent, No. 18086, 28, box 1, file 31, Paula L. Ettelbrick Papers, 1986–93, HSC; Anonymous Interview, July 4, 1988, box 2, file 12, Wendell Ricketts Papers, 1961–2004, HSC.

77. Copy of Petitioner's Trial Brief, In the Matter of the Adoption Petition of Nancy L. Davis, box 1, Hitchens/Davis Adoption Case [San Francisco] folder, Wendell Ricketts Papers, 1961–2004, HSC.

78. *Matter of Evan*, 153 Misc. 2d 844 (N.Y. Co. Surr. Ct. 1992); Elliot Pinsley, "N.J. Lesbian Adopts Mate's Child: Groundbreaking Ruling on Parent Rights," *The Record*, August 11, 1993, 1; Kimberly Griffin, "Judge Clears Way for Adoption by Lesbian Co-Parent," *Windy City Times*, March 17, 1994.

79. See letter from Paula Ettelbrick, November 29, 1993, box 1, file 31, Paula L. Ettelbrick Papers, 1986–93, HSC. See also National Center for Lesbian Rights, "Newsletter" (Spring 1992): 9, box 1, file 34, Wendell Ricketts Papers, 1961–2004, HSC.

80. Known as the National Gay Task Force before 1985.

81. "News Release—Ettelbrick to leave Lambda Legal Defense," November 10, 1992, Lambda Legal Defense Fund, New York, folder 6, Organizations Files, LHA.

82. Lambda and the Lesbian Rights Project submitted *amicus curiae* briefs together for co-parent cases such as *A.C. v. C.B.*, 829 P. 2d 660 (N.M. Ct. App. 1992); *Kulla v. McNulty*, 472 N.W. 2d 175 (Minn. Ct. App. 1991); *Nancy S. v. Michele G.*, 228 Cal. App. 3d 831 (1991); and second-parent adoption cases including, *Adoptions of B.L.V.B. and E.L.V.B.*, 628 A. 2d 1271 (Vt. 1993), and *In re Adoption of Katherine Mary*. In one 1991 Los Angeles second-parent adoption case involving the petition of a gay man, Michael D., to adopt his partner Gene's daughter, a supportive declaration written by a Lambda staff attorney described talking with Roberta Achtenberg at the Lesbian Rights Project. *In the Matter of the Adoption Petition of Michael D.* All *amicus curiae* briefs in the Paula L. Ettelbrick Papers, HSC.

83. Lambda Legal Defense Fund, New York, folder 1, Organizations Files, LHA.

84. "A Note from Legal Director Paula Ettelbrick about Lambda's Family Relationships Project," Lambda Legal Defense Fund, New York, folder 6, Organizations Files, LHA.

85. "NGLTF Hires New Staff Person, *Washington Blade*, April 7, 1989.

86. "NGLTF Hires Young as Director of New Project," *Seattle Gay News*, April 7, 1989.

87. Kelly Harmon, "Fighting for Our Families: Ivy Young Heads the Families Project," *Windy City Times*, August 23, 1990.

88. On the Families Project's goals and the state of domestic partner legislation at its founding, see "The Lesbian and Gay Families Project," draft pamphlet, box 85, folder 1, National Gay and Lesbian Task Force Records, HSC.

89. Records of the commission's hearing, box 86, folder 51, National Gay and Lesbian Task Force Records, HSC.

90. Paula L. Ettelbrick, "Since When Is Marriage a Path to Liberation?," *Out/look: National Lesbian and Gay Quarterly*, no. 6 (Fall 1989): 9, 14–17. For a brilliant discussion of these political shifts and their implications and an argument for a broad, inclusive domestic partner–based notion of personal rights, see Nancy D. Polikoff, *Beyond (Straight and Gay) Marriage: Valuing All Families under the Law* (Boston: Beacon Press, 2008), esp. 83–109.

91. Jenny Sayward, interview with author, Edmonds, WA, July 18, 2006.

92. Don Harrelson, interview with author, Seattle, WA, June 30, 2003; Suzanne Putman, Executive Vice-President, GLPCI, "Women's Leadership," *GLPCI Annual Report*, 1992–93, 3, CNOF.

93. Jim Pate, "Report from the President," and "History of GLPCI," *GLPCI Annual Report*, 1991–92, 1–2, 8, CNOF.

94. "Gay and Lesbian Family Week in Provincetown, Mass. August," *GLPCI Network* (Winter/Spring 1996): 13, CNOF.

95. Martha Sidell, " 'Center Kids': Completion of the Puzzle," *Sappho's Isle: The Tri-State Lesbian Newspaper*, April 1989, 1; Terry Boggis, "News from Center Kids," History Files, CKA.

96. "Task Force at Center," *Family Talk: A Publication of Center Kids*, May/June 1986, 3, Newsletter Files, CKA.

97. "Momazons," Newsletter Files, LHA.

98. Hope Berry, "*Just for Us* and Hope Berry: The History of an Organization and the Learning Experience of a Lifetime," CNOF. See also "History of GLPCI," *GLPCI Annual Report*, 1991–92, 8, CNOF. There is also evidence that smaller regional groups of kids of lesbians and gay men were operating at this time, suggesting that the emergence of these groups, including COLAGE, was a part of the growth of lesbian and gay families during this period. In Indianapolis, the local chapter of the GLPCI reported that it had a teenage support group called "Our Parents Aren't Straight." *GLPCI Annual Report*, 1991–92, 9, CNOF. By 1993, there was an Adolescent Children of Gay and Lesbian Parents Group organized out of the Fenway Community Health Center in Boston by COLAGE co-founders Anna and Molly Heller. Jenifer Firestone, interview with author, Atlanta, GA, September 12, 2012. See also Lisa Calvelli, Wendy Loveland, and Jennifer Polk, "The Brady Bunch? Not! Teenage Kids of Lesbian and Gay Parents," *Conceptions: Lesbian and Gay Family & Parenting Services* 10 (Fall 1993), LMNDF Files. On the Hellers and the founding of COLAGE, see "Strong Foundations: A Conversation with COLAGE Co-founder Molly Heller," *Just for Us* 16, no. 3 (2004): 1.

99. "COLAGE Groups," *Just for Us* (Spring 1996): back page, CNOF.

100. Letter dated March 2, 1996, Membership and Donors, 1996–98 folder, COLAGE (Children of Lesbians and Gays Everywhere) Records, 1982–2000, GLBTHS.

101. Membership slip and attached note dated June 16, 1997, Membership and Donors, 1996–98 folder, COLAGE (Children of Lesbians and Gays Everywhere) Records, 1982–2000, GLBTHS.

102. COLAGE Pen Pal Application, CNOF.

103. Resume and letter from Laura Bernard, Hiring and Internship Materials, 1994–95 folder, COLAGE (Children of Lesbians and Gays Everywhere) Records, 1982–2000, GLBTHS.

104. "Ian, Code Name 'Boo,' a Superhero—an interview with Ian Mobley," *Gay Parent* (March/April 1999): 4–5.

105. COLAGE Pen Pal Application, CNOF.

106. Ibid.

107. I have withheld the names of the town in these three instances; they are so small that this information could expose these individuals. COLAGE Pen Pal Applications, CNOF.

108. "Camp It Up!" brochure, box 1, file 30, Wendell Ricketts Papers, 1961–2004, HSC.

109. Camp Lavender Hill brochure, box 1, file 30, Wendell Ricketts Papers, 1961–2004, HSC. See also *Camp Lavender Hill*, documentary, 1997, directed by Michael Magnaye.

110. In 1995 Mountain Meadow was in Chadds Ford, Pennsylvania, and in 2001 and 2002 it was in northern New Jersey. Advertisements for Mountain Meadow Summer Camp, *Gay Parent* (May/June 2001): 15, and *Gay Parent* (May/June 2002): 3. See also Rachel Milenbach, "Mountain Meadow Summer Camp—I Miss Getting 100 Hugs A Day—First Person Account," *GLPCI Network* (Winter/Spring 1996): 11, CNOF.

111. "Keshet Camp at Camp Towanga," *Gay Parent* (January/February 2000): 4.

112. "Camp Ten Trees Prepares for Growth in Second Year," *Gay Parent* (March/April 2002): 14.

113. Lesléa Newman *Heather Has Two Mommies*, illustrated by Diane Souza (Boston: Alyson Publications, 1989); Michael Willhoite, *Daddy's Roommate* (Boston: Alyson Publications, 1990); Lesléa Newman, *Gloria Goes to Gay Pride*, illustrated by Russell Crocker (Boston: Alyson Publications, 1991); Anne Heron and Meredith Maran, *How Would You Feel If Your Dad Was Gay?*, illustrated by Kris Kovick (Boston: Alyson Publications, 1991). See also William A. Davis, "New Books for Gay Couples' Kids," *Boston Globe*, November 17, 1990.

114. Lance Morrow, "Family Values," *Time Magazine*, August 31, 1992, 26; Donna Seese, "Kids' Book about Gay Father Sets Town Abuzz," *Raleigh News and Observer*, July 24, 1992.

115. "More Controversy for *Daddy* and *Heather*," *GLPCI Network* (Fall 1993): 9, LMNDF Files.

116. The measure failed but the alliance succeeded in getting several local initiatives passed in the early 1990s. Vernon Bates, "Rhetorical Pluralism and Secularization in the New Christian Right: The Oregon Citizen's Alliance," *Review of Religious Research* 37 (September 1, 1995): 46–64; Timothy Egan, "Oregon Measure Asks State to Repress Homosexuality," *New York Times*, August 16, 1992.

117. "How a 'Rainbow Curriculum' Turned into Fighting Words," *New York Times*, December 13, 1992.

118. Katherine Q. Seelye, "Senate Backs Cuts for Schools That Endorse Homosexuality," *New York Times*, August 2, 1984.

119. On Gluckman's experience, see Anne Wallace Allen, "Out of the Closet about Gay Mom," *South Coast Today*, September 8, 1996. On the outcome of the hearing, see "Vt. Library Won't Restrict Book," *Boston Globe*, June 16, 1995, 42.

Epilogue

1. Elisabeth Bumiller, "The Egg Roll (Again!) Becomes a Stage for Controversy," *New York Times*, April 10, 2006; Joseph Curl, "Gay Parents' Children Find Easter Eggs, But Not Bush," *Washington Times*, April 18, 2006, A4. On the controversy over the PBS show, see Julie Salamon, "Culture Wars Pull Buster into the Fray," *New York Times*, January 27, 2005, E1.

2. One article called it "the largest instance of media visibility for queer parents and their children in history." "National" column, *Just Out*, October 19, 2007, 18. The head of Family Pride Coalition claimed that the presence of lesbian and gay families at the egg roll "received coverage on CNN, Good Morning America, Fox News, ABC, and over 600 local affiliate TV stations." Angeline Acain, "At the Forefront of Family Pride and Social Justice: An Interview with Jennifer Chrisler," *Gay Parent* (January–February 2007): 14.

3. In 2005, Family Pride Coalition had a budget of $800,000. In 2006, that budget had increased to $2 million. Both of these numbers give an indication of the power of the group, as well as the growing significance of the struggle for domestic/parental rights in the mainstream LGBT freedom struggle. Although these budget amounts clearly separate FPC from earlier grassroots lesbian mother organizations, they are still very small compared to the conservative groups that are opposed to LGBT domestic and familial rights. In 2010, for example, Focus on the Family had an annual revenue of $95 million. On the FPC budgets, see Greg Hernandez, "It's All about Our Children," *The Advocate*, April 25, 2006; for the Focus on the Family revenue figures, see "Focus on the Family 2010 Federal 501(c) Form 990." Copy in author's possession. In 2009, the Family Equality Council (FEC) defined itself as "dedicated specifically to advocating at a national level for equality for families headed by queer parents." On the 1998 name change, see *The Family Tree: A Publication of the Family Pride Coalition* (Autumn 1998): 1. Copy in Family Tree, Family Pride Coalition folder, Periodicals Collection, GLBTHS. On the 2009 name change and the stated mission of the group, see "National" column, *Just Out*, October 19, 2007, 18.

4. "Rainbow Families Moves Forward with Merger," *Lavender*, March 28, 2008.

5. While the scope of this book, for both practical and historical reasons, has limited its focus to lesbian and gay parents, leaving the important work of uncovering the history of bisexual and transgender parents to future research, in this epilogue I use the acronym LGBT to reflect the realities of the more recent political organizing. Parental rights have been part of the focus on domestic rights in the mainstream LGBT movement, and that movement has come to define itself as including bisexual and transgender people, in spite of the continuing marginalization experienced by these groups within the mainstream movement.

6. R.S. *v.* A.S., Court of Appeals of Virginia. Copy of appellate decision in author's possession.

7. *McGriff v. McGriff*, 140 Idaho 642; 99 P. 3d 111; 2004. See also Jen Christensen, "Custody: Parent vs. Parent," *The Advocate*, December 21, 2004, 27–28.

8. "Pennsylvania Superior Court Overrules Quarter-Century Homophobic Precedent in Child Custody Dispute," *Lesbian/Gay Law Notes* (March 2010): 31–32.

9. "Gay Dad Can Be Out," *Echo Magazine*, April 8, 2004, 29–30.

10. "Louisiana Appeals Court Rules for Gay Dad in Custody Dispute," *Lesbian/Gay Law Notes* (Summer 2009): 128.

11. *Mongerson v. Mongerson*, 678 S. E. 2d 891 (2009).

12. Changes in adoption and foster care policies for LGBT parents have also been significant, though not necessarily linear. They have varied significantly, with some states moving solidly in the direction of lesbian and gay adoptive rights in the period from 2003 to 2011 while others have passed legislation banning gay and lesbian adoption and foster parenting. By 2011, gay and lesbian adoption was expressly illegal in Utah and Mississippi, while bans had been overturned in Florida and Arkansas, and a ban on gay and lesbian foster care had been repealed in New Hampshire. Other states, such as Arizona, required state workers to give preference to heterosexual homes. The adoption story requires more space than I have in this epilogue to tell—by 2004, studies showed that somewhere around 65,000 children were living with a gay or lesbian adoptive parent. For recent developments dealing with gay and lesbian adoption in the past ten years, see Patrick Roland, "An Unexpected Family," *Echo*, June 12, 2008, 36; Ellen Wright, "American Bar Passes Resolution in Support of Gay Adoptions," *Lesbian News* (September 2003): 15; Sabrina Tavernise, "Adoptions Rise by Same-sex Couples, Despite Legal Barriers," *New York Times*, June 14, 2011: A11; Michelle Norris, "Anti-Gay Adoption, Foster Measures Fail," *Lesbian News* (June 2005): 11.

13. "Pennsylvania Appeals Court Affirms Custody for Co-Parent Over Biological Mom on Best Interests Grounds," *Lesbian/Gay Law Notes*, October 2005, 193.

14. "Oregon Court Finds Same-Sex Lesbian Partner to be a Parent," *Lesbian/Gay Law Notes* (May 2011): 84–85.

15. "New York Court of Appeals Rules in Lesbian Custody and Child Support Disputes," *Lesbian/Gay Law Notes* (June 2010): 79–80.

16. "Another New Jersey Court Recognizes Expanded Partner Rights: Co-Parent Status," *Lesbian/Gay Law Notes* (June 2005): 113.

17. On the outcome, see Elizabeth Weill-Greenberg, "Md. Court Overturns Custody Ruling against Gay Father," *Washington Blade*, March 31, 2006, 10. On the use of *Lawrence* as a legal precedence in the case, see Lou Chibbaro Jr., "Gay Father Invokes Lawrence in Custody Appeal," *Washington Blade*, April 15, 2005, 7, 21.

18. Susan Moss, "Casenote: McGriff v McGriff: Consideration of a Parent's Sexual Orientation in Child Custody Disputes," 41 Idaho L. Rev. 593 (2005): 1.

19. "Alabama Appeals Court Rules against Lesbian Mom in Custody Appeal," *Lesbian/Gay Law Notes* (January 2005): 9–10.

20. James Vaznis, "Lawsuit Invokes Religious Freedom; Parents Say Beliefs Ignored By School," *Boston Globe*, May 4, 2006, Globe Northwest Section, 1; "National Briefing New England: Massachusetts: Gay Topics and Schools," *New York Times*, February 24, 2007, 13; Lisa Keen, "U.S. Supreme Court Refuses Lexington Case," *Boston Globe*, October 9, 2008, B2; Robert Skutch, *Who's in a Family?*, illustrations by Laura Nienhaus

(New York: Random House Children's Books, 1997); Stern Nijland and Linda De Haan, *King and King* (New York: Random House Children's Books, 2003); Nancy Garden, *Molly's Family*, illustrated by Sharon Woodling (New York: Farrar, Straus and Giroux, 2004).

21. A similar controversy erupted in Alameda County, California, when the school district approved a new curriculum, Lesson 9, designed to alleviate antigay bullying and attitudes among school children. The curriculum included a strong focus on family diversity, including the book *And Tango Makes Three*, about two male penguins raising a small penguin. A group of parents sued the district for not being allowed to opt-out of the new lessons. In 2009, the parent's lawsuit was denied. Amy Lai, "Tango or More? From California's Lesson 9 to the Constitutionality of a Gay-Friendly Curriculum in Public Elementary Schools," *Michigan Journal of Gender & Law* (2011): 17.

22. *Parker v. Hurley*, 474 F. Supp. 2d 261 (D. Mass. 2007).

23. Ibid.

24. Ibid.

25. Testimony by Thomas Minnery, Senior Vice President for Public Policy, Focus on the Family, Senate Judiciary Committee Hearing, July 20, 2011.

26. Dan Aiello, "Mass. Couple Pushes Prop 8," *Bay Area Reporter*, October 23, 2008.

27. Lisa Leff (Associated Press), "Prop 8 Backer Questioned about Child Sex Comment," *Newsday*, January 13, 2010.

28. "Kids Fight for LGBT Parents' Rights with Valentine's Project," *Vanguard: The Monthly Newsletter of the L.A. Gay and Lesbian Center* (February 2008): 4.

29. Leslie Robinson, "General Gayety" Column, *Outlook Weekly*, November 27–December 3, 2008, 6.

30. On the participation of COLAGE members in the San Francisco protest, see *Just for Us* 21, no. 1 (2009): 8; on Samuel Berston's speech, see "COLAGE Reports Back from the Prop 8 Oral Arguments in California," March 5, 2009, http://www.colage.org/uncategorized/colage-reports-back-from-the-prop-8-oral-arguments-in-ca; "Proposition 8 Ruled Unconstitutional: On to the Supreme Court?" Washingtonpost.com, published February 7, 2012.

31. Chuck Colbert, "Gay, Catholic, and Parents of Three," *National Catholic Reporter*, March 23, 2007, 12.

32. "Testimony of 12-Year-Old with Two Moms Moves Some Vermont Legislators to Support Gay Marriage Bill," *Democracy Now*, April 8, 2009. For the full text of Evann Orleck-Jetter's speech, see Evann Orleck-Jetter, "Daughter: 'Time to Honor—Families Like Mine,'" *Valley News*, March 21, 2009.

33. Sarah Wildman, "Children Speak for Same-Sex Marriage" *New York Times*, January 21, 2010. On the internet distribution of the video of Zach Wahls's speech, see Allen McAlister, "Letting Love Speak for Itself: Zach Wahls Goes from College Student to Internet Sensation With His Stirring Speech in the Iowa House of Representatives," *Out & About*, April 2011: 15, 25; and Stacey Cosens, "Plea for Marriage Equality Tops You Tube Most Watched," *Pink Paper*, December 23, 2011, 14.

Bibliography

Primary Sources

Archival Collections

Gay, Lesbian, Bisexual, and Transgender Historical Society, San Francisco, CA
    COLAGE (Children of Lesbians and Gays Everywhere), 1982–2000
    Donald Stewart Lucas Papers, 1941–98
    Phyllis Lyon and Del Martin Papers, 1924–2000
    Newsletter Files
    Oral History Files
    Periodicals Files
    Protests, etc.—Marches on Washington Ephemera
Human Sexuality Collection, Carl A. Kroch Library, Cornell University, Ithaca, NY
    Paula L. Ettelbrick Papers, 1986–93
    National Gay and Lesbian Task Force Records
    Wendell Ricketts Papers, 1961–2004
John J. Wilcox Jr. Archives, William Way LGBT Community Center, Philadelphia, PA
    Subject Files
Lesbian Herstory Archives, Brooklyn, NY
    Before Stonewall Special Collection
    Boots of Leather/Slippers of Gold Special Collection
    Daughters of Bilitis LHA Video Project Special Collection
    Renee Hanover Special Collection
    Jezebel Productions Interview Transcripts Special Collection
    Lesbian Defense Fund Special Collection
    Blue (Doris) Lunden Special Collection
    Newsletter Files
    Organizations Files
    Periodicals Files
    Mary Jo Risher Special Collection
    Spoken Word Audio Files
    Subject Files
    Maxine Wolfe Special Collection
    Deborah Goleman Wolf Interviews
M. E. Grenander Department of Special Collections and Archives, State University of
    New York–Albany, NY
    Steven F. Dansky Papers, 1968–2006
New York Public Library, Manuscripts and Archives Division, New York, NY
    International Gay Information Center Archives Collection
ONE Institute and Archives, University of Southern California, Los Angeles, CA
    Subject Files
Sophia Smith Archives, Smith College, Northampton, MA

Joan E. Biren Papers
Old Lesbian Oral Herstory Project
Old Lesbians Organizing for Change Records

Personal Collections
(Copies of all material cited in author's possession)

Geraldine Cole
Bill Jones
Jeanne Jullion
Carole Morton
Jenny Sayward (Lesbian Mothers' National Defense Fund Files)

Institutional Records
(Copies of all material cited in author's possession)

Center Kids Files, Center Kids Archives, Lesbian, Gay, Bisexual and Transgender
Community Center, New York, NY
COLAGE (Children of Lesbians and Gays Everywhere) National Office Files, San
Francisco, CA

Interviews Conducted by Author

Alfaro, Kate. Ithaca, NY. July 29, 2005.
Anger, Zia. Ithaca, NY. August 1, 2005.
Bereano, Nancy. Ithaca, NY. April 26, 2005.
Boggis, Terri. New York, NY. August 9, 2005.
Bogut, Linda. Minneapolis, MN. September 25, 2006.
Bolles, Hilary. Seattle, WA. May 18, 2005.
Bradford, Fred. Los Angeles, CA. June 31, 2003.
Cade, Cathy. Oakland, CA. June 23, 2004.
Callahan, John. Los Angeles, CA. June 20, 2003.
Camille (pseud.). Palm Springs, CA. October 29, 2006.
Carr, Jesse. San Francisco, CA. March 20, 2005.
Cerasaro, Sam, and Richard Mason. Rancho Mirage, CA. January 28, 2006.
Cole, Celeste. Seattle, WA. March 18, 2005.
Cole, Geraldine. Seattle, WA. March 14, 2005.
Conway, Phil. San Francisco, CA. March 6, 2005.
Cooperberg, Dave. San Francisco, CA. March 31, 2005.
Couvillon, Jan. San Francisco, CA. October 5, 2006.
Davies, Rosalie. Haverford, PA. September 12, 2002.
Dobkin, Alix. New York, NY. April 12, 2005.
Earth, Ellen. Seattle, WA. May 13, 2005.
Firestone, Jenifer. Atlanta, GA. September 12, 2012.
Ghidinelli, Judie. Oakland, CA. April 15, 2003.

Givner, Jon. Brooklyn, NY. July 9, 2005.

Graham, Kurt. Palm Springs, CA. October 28, 2006.

Green, Richard, M.D. San Francisco, CA. April 22, 2006.

Haddad, Emily. Brooklyn, NY. July 16, 2004.

Hallum, Andrew. Lynden, WA. June 27, 2003.

Hank (pseud.). San Francisco, CA. October 6, 2007.

Harrelson, Don. Seattle, WA. June 30, 2003.

Harris, Wendy. Seattle, WA. July 19, 2006.

Hart, Melissa. Eugene, OR. March 10, 2005.

Hiner, Jo. Minneapolis, MN. October 21, 2006.

Holland, Dan. Sebastopol, CA. February 22, 2005.

Hood, Adrian. New York, NY. April 12, 2005.

Iguina, Zulma. Newfield, NY. July 28, 2005.

Isis (pseud.). Jersey City, NJ. June 28, 2005.

Johnson, Robert. Pasadena, CA. June 18, 2003.

Jones, Bill. Sausalito, CA. May 19, 2004.

Jones-Hennin, ABilly S., and Christopher Hennin. Washington, D.C. June 29, 2012.

Jullion, Jeanne. Oakland, CA. May 21, 2002.

Karls, Marty. San Francisco, CA. August 9, 2004.

Kaufman, Kate. Santa Cruz, CA. June 9, 2012.

Kay (pseud.). New York, NY. April 19, 2005.

Keeley, Pam. Seattle, WA. March 17, 2005.

Ken (pseud.). Santa Barbara, CA. May 21, 2004.

Klein, Allen. Telephone interview. March 23, 2005.

Kolb, Gina. Freeville, NY. April 22, 2005.

Krause, Patricia. Minneapolis, MN. October 23, 2006.

Laine, Jody. Seattle, WA. September 18, 2006.

Lee, Patricia. Seattle, WA. May 13, 2005.

Leicty, Derek. Los Angeles, CA. June 19, 2004.

Lippett, Jill. Jenner, CA. December 5, 2003.

Logan, Becky. Seattle, WA. May 13, 2005.

Lunden, Linda. Key Biscayne, FL. March 17, 2012.

Mackenna, Greg. Oakland, CA. June 16, 2004.

Mager, Don. Charlotte, NC. March 28, 2008.

Mahaney, Ruth. San Francisco, CA. May 15, 2003.

Malkin, Michelle "Mo." Seattle, WA. March 16, 2005.

Martin, Del, and Phyllis Lyon. San Francisco, CA. February 17, 2006.

Martin, Vera. Apache Junction, AZ. September 22, 2006.

Mastrostefano, Cara. Minneapolis, MN. October 22, 2006.

McCabe, Cynthia. Albany, CA. December 21, 2002.

McCarthy, Jilda. Minneapolis, MN. October 21, 2006.

McCarthy, Sarah. Minneapolis, MN. October 21, 2006.

McKenna, Clancy. New York, NY. August 2, 2002.

McClung, John. Apple Valley, CA. May 22, 2003.

Melroe, Kieran. Seattle, WA. May 13, 2005.

Melroe, Kris. Seattle, WA. May 15, 2005.
Merrill, Mimi. Ridgecrest, CA. September 26, 2006.
Miller, Stacy. Brooklyn, NY. June 25, 2005.
Mon, Kendra. Petaluma, CA. November 29, 2006.
Moon, Jannelle. Berkeley, CA. March 16, 2007.
Morton, Carole. San Francisco, CA. March 10, 2007.
Natalie (pseud.). Ithaca, NY. April 23, 2005.
Nicholas (pseud.). Los Angeles, CA. February 10, 2003.
Nickele, Maidi. Seattle, WA. July 17, 2006.
Pearce, Tricia. Seattle, WA. May 12, 2005.
Perry, Troy. Los Angeles, CA. April 10, 2008.
Pitchford, Kenneth. New York, NY. September 19, 2009.
Pittell, Joan. Seattle, WA. May 14, 2005.
Pollack, Sandy. Ithaca, NY. April 21, 2005.
Pullen, Peggy. Seattle, WA. May 17, 2005.
Quartarola, Bob. Oakland, CA. June 16, 2004.
Reinstein, Shad. Seattle, WA. September 17, 2006.
Rhodes, Anne. Freeville, NY. April 22, 2005.
Richard (pseud.). Berkeley, CA. June 1, 2004.
Rivera, Sunny. Seattle, WA. September 17, 2006.
Robinson, Susan. Ithaca, NY. July 24, 2005.
Ron (pseud.). Santa Barbara, CA. May 7, 2003.
Rubaii, Munna. Ithaca, NY. July 27, 2005.
Rubaii-Barrett, Nadia. Ithaca, NY. July 27, 2005.
Sangenilo, D. Palm Springs, CA. October 29, 2006.
Sangenilo, Joe. Palm Springs, CA. October 29, 2006.
Saul, Judith, and Regi Teasley. Ithaca, NY. July 30, 2005.
Sayward, Jenny. Edmonds, WA. July 18, 2006.
Selene, Carolyn. Lynnwood, WA. March 13, 2005.
Selene, Michele. Lynnwood, WA. March 11, 2005.
Sklute, John. San Francisco, CA. March 31, 2005.
Sonenberg, Fred. Guerneville, CA. June 6, 2004.
Stewart, Annalee. Minneapolis, MN. October 19, 2006.
Stokes, Rick. San Francisco, CA. January 15, 2007.
Stone, Arion. Mountain View, CA. February 4, 2006.
Swift, Mike. Stanford, CA. April 25, 2005.
Tarsky, Alan. Los Angeles, CA. February 25, 2003.
Ted (pseud.). Los Angeles, CA. February 22, 2003.
Thetford, Lois. Seattle, WA. March 15, 2005.
Visser, Hal. Santa Barbara, CA. May 2, 2003.
Warner, Jack. San Francisco, CA. October 6, 2006.
White, Mary. Ithaca, NY. April 24, 2005.
Widmer, Candace. Ithaca, NY. July 24, 2005.
Wilson, Clay. San Jose, CA. October 7, 2007
Wolfe, Maxine. Brooklyn, NY. July 29, 2002.

Newspapers, Magazines, and Newsletters

Amazon Spirit, 1978–80 (Helena, MT)

Atlanta Lesbian Feminist Alliance Newsletter (later *Atalanta: The Newsletter of the Atlanta Lesbian Feminist Alliance*), 1973–94 (Atlanta, GA)

Azalea, 1977–83 (New York, NY)

Big Mama Rag, 1973–84 (Denver, CO)

Country Women, 1974–77 (Albion, CA)

Daughters of Bilitis San Francisco Chapter Newsletter, 1959–70 (San Francisco, CA)

Desperate Living, 1973–77 (Baltimore, MD)

Dinah, 1979–81 (Cincinnati, OH)

The Furies, 1972–73 (Washington, D.C.)

Gay Liberator, 1971–76 (Detroit, MI)

Gay Parent, 1998–2003 (Forest Hills, NY)

The Ladder, 1956–72 (San Francisco, CA/New York, NY)

Lavender Woman, 1974–76 (Chicago, IL)

Lesbian Connection, 1975–97 (East Lansing, MI)

Lesbian Feminist Flyer, 1976–94 (Richmond, VA)

Lesbian Feminist Union News, 1975–78 (Louisville, KY)

Lesbian Front, 1975–77 (Jackson, MS)

Lesbian Tide, 1972–78 (Los Angeles, CA)

Mainely Gay, 1976–79 (Portland, ME)

Mattachine Review, 1955–66 (San Francisco, CA)

Momazons, 1993–2000 (Columbus, OH)

Mom's Apple Pie: The Newsletter of the Lesbian Mothers' National Defense Fund, 1974–93 (Seattle, WA)

Moonstorm, 1973–83 (St. Louis, MO)

The Newsletter (Triangle Area Lesbian Feminists), 1981–95 (Durham, NC)

ONE Magazine, 1953–67 (Los Angeles, CA)

Out and About: Seattle Lesbian/Feminist Newsletter, 1976–80 (Seattle, WA)

Published Sources

Abbott, Sidney, and Barbara Love. *Sappho Was a Right-on Woman*. New York: Stein & Day, 1972.

Achtenberg, Roberta, and Wendell Ricketts. "The Adoptive and Foster Gay and Lesbian Parent." In *Gay and Lesbian Parents*, edited by Frederick W. Bozett, 89–111. New York: Praeger, 1987.

Armanno, Benna F. "The Lesbian Mother: Her Right to Child Custody." *Golden Gate Law Review* 4, no. 1 (1973/1974): 1–18.

Barnhart, Elizabeth. "Friends and Lovers in a Counterculture Community." In *Old Family/New Family: Interpersonal Relationships*, edited by Nona Glazer-Malbin, 90–115. New York: D. Van Nostrand Company, 1975.

Barret, Robert, and Bryan Robinson. *Gay Fathers*. Lexington, MA: Lexington Books, 1990.

Basile, R. A. "Lesbian Mothers I." *Women's Law Reporter* 2, no. 2 (December 1974): 3–25.

Bates, Vernon. "Rhetorical Pluralism and Secularization in the New Christian Right: The Oregon Citizen's Alliance." *Review of Religious Research* 37 (1 September 1995): 46–64.

Bayer, Ronald. *Homosexuality and American Psychiatry: The Politics of Diagnosis.* New York: Basic Books, 1981.

Beck, Evelyn Torton, ed. *Nice Jewish Girls: A Lesbian Anthology.* Trumansburg, NY: Crossing Press, 1982.

Benkov, Laura. *Reinventing the Family: Lesbian and Gay Parents.* New York: Crown Trade Paperbacks, 1994.

Bernstein, Mary. "Abominable and Detestable: Understanding Homophobia and the Criminalization of Sodomy." In *The Blackwell Companion to Criminology,* edited by Colin Sumner, 309–24. Oxford: Blackwell Publishing, 2004.

———. "Liberalism and Social Movement Success: The Case of the United States Sodomy Statutes." In *Regulating Sex: The Politics of Intimacy and Identity,* edited by Elizabeth Bernstein and Laurie Schaffner, 3–18. New York: Routledge, 2005.

Berube, Allan. *Coming Out Under Fire: The History of Gay Men and Women in World War Two.* New York: Free Press, 1990.

Biren, Joan (JEB). *Eye to Eye: Portraits of Lesbians—Photographs by JEB.* Washington, D.C.: Glad Hag Books, 1979.

Black, David. *The Plague Years: A Chronicle of AIDS, the Epidemic of Our Times.* New York: Simon and Schuster, 1985.

Blount, Jackie. *Fit to Teach: Same-Sex Desire, Gender, and School Work in the Twentieth Century.* Albany: State University of New York Press, 2005.

The Boston Women's Health Collective. *Ourselves and Our Children: A Book by and for Parents.* New York: Random House, 1978.

Boyd, Nan Alamilla. *Wide Open Town: A History of Queer San Francisco to 1965.* Berkeley: University of California Press, 2003.

Bozett, Frederick, R.N., D.N.S. "Gay Fathers: Evolution of the Gay-Father Identity." *American Journal of Orthopsychiatry* 51, no. 3 (July 1981): 552–59.

Breines, Wini. *Young, White, and Miserable: Growing Up Female in the Fifties.* Boston: Beacon Press, 1992.

Bryant, Barbara S. "Lesbian Mothers." Master's thesis, California State University at Sacramento, 1975.

Bunch, Charlotte. "Learning from Lesbian Separatism." In *Lavender Culture,* edited by Karla Jay and Allen Young, 433–57. New York: New York University Press, 1978.

Buring, Daneel. *Lesbian and Gay Memphis: Building Communities Behind the Magnolia Curtain.* New York: Garland Publishing, 1997.

Cade, Cathy. *A Lesbian Photo Album: The Lives of Seven Lesbian Feminists.* Oakland, CA: Waterwomen Books, 1987.

———. *My Family, the Movement, and Me: How My Being in the Civil Rights Movement Affected My White Family.* Self-published, 2002.

Cain, Patricia. *Rainbow Rights.* Boulder, CO: Westview Press, 2000.

Campbell, Ross. "Child Custody: When One Parent Is a Homosexual." *Judge's Journal* 17, no. 2 (Spring 1978): 38–41, 51–52.

Canaday, Margot. *The Straight State: Sexuality and Citizenship in Twentieth-Century America.* Princeton, N.J.: Princeton University Press, 2009.

Carrington, E. et al., eds., *The Rights of Gay People: The Basic ACLU Guide to a Gay Person's Rights.* New York: Sunrise Books, 1975.

Carson, Clayborne. "Civil Rights Reform and the Black Freedom Struggle." In *The Civil Rights Movement in America: Essays,* edited by Charles W. Eagles, 19–32. Jackson: University Press of Mississippi, 1986.

———. *In Struggle: SNCC and the Black Awakening of the 1960s.* Cambridge, MA: Harvard University Press, 1981.

Carter, David. *Stonewall: The Riots That Sparked the Gay Revolution.* New York: St. Martin's Press, 2004.

Castells, Manuel. *The City and the Grassroots: A Cross-Cultural Theory of Urban Social Movements.* Berkeley: University of California Press, 1983.

Cheney, Joyce, ed. *Lesbian Land.* Minneapolis, MN: Word Weavers, 1985.

Chesnut, Saralyn, and Amanda C. Gable. "Women Ran It": Charis Books and More and Atlanta's Lesbian-Feminist Community, 1971–1981." In *Carryin' On in the Lesbian and Gay South,* edited by John Howard, 241–84. New York: New York University Press, 1997.

Clark, Richard. "City of Desire: A History of Same-Sex Desire in New Orleans, 1917–1977." Ph.D. diss., Tulane University, 2009.

Clendinen, Dudley, and Adam Nagourney. *Out for Good: The Struggle to Build a Gay Rights Movement in America.* New York: Touchstone Press, 1999.

Combahee River Collective. "The Combahee River Collective Statement." In *Home Girls: A Black Feminist Anthology,* edited by Barbara Smith, 272–82. New York: Kitchen Table–Women of Color Press, 1983.

Coontz, Stephanie. *The Way We Never Were: American Families and the Nostalgia Trap.* New York: Basic Books, 1992.

Cott, Nancy. *Public Vows: A History of Marriage and the Nation.* Cambridge, MA: Harvard University Press, 2000.

Crawford, Vicki. "Beyond the Human Self: Grassroots Activists in the Mississippi Civil Rights Movement." In *Women in the Civil Rights Movement: Trailblazers and Torchbearers, 1941–1965,* edited by Vicki L. Crawford, Jacqueline Anne Rouse, and Barbara Woods, 13–26. Bloomington: Indiana University Press, 1990.

Davies, Rosalie. "Representing the Lesbian Mother." *Family Advocate* 1, no. 3 (Winter 1978): 21–23, 36.

Davies, Rosalie, and Minna Weinstein. "Confronting the Courts." In *Politics of the Heart: A Lesbian Parenting Anthology,* edited by Sandra Pollack and Jeanne Vaughn, 43–45. Ithaca, NY: Firebrand Books, 1987.

Davis, Angela Y. "The Legacy of Slavery: Standards for a New Womanhood." In *Women, Race, and Class,* 3–29. New York: Random House, 1981.

D'Emilio, John. "The Homosexual Menace: The Politics of Sexuality in Cold War America." In *Making Trouble: Essays on Gay History, Politics, and the University,* 57–73. New York: Routledge, 1992.

———. *Sexual Politics, Sexual Communities: The Making of a Homosexual Minority in the United States, 1940–1970.* Chicago: University of Chicago Press, 1983.

Duberman, Martin. *Stonewall*. New York: Dutton, 1993.

Edwards, Laura. *Gendered Strife and Confusion*. Urbana: University of Illinois Press, 1997.

Eisenbach, David. *Gay Power: An American Revolution*. New York: Carroll & Graf, 2006.

Eskridge, William. *Dishonorable Passions: Sodomy Laws in America, 1861–2003*. New York: Viking Press, 2008.

Ettelbrick, Paula L. "Since When Is Marriage a Path to Liberation?" *Out/look: National Lesbian and Gay Quarterly*, no. 6 (Fall 1989): 9, 14–17.

Evans, Sara. *Personal Politics: The Roots of Women's Liberation in the Civil Rights Movement and the New Left*. New York: Vintage Books, 1980.

Faderman, Lillian. *Odd Girls and Twilight Lovers: A History of Lesbian Life in Twentieth-Century America*. New York: Columbia University Press, 1991.

Faderman, Lillian, and Stuart Timmons. *Gay L.A.: A History of Sexual Outlaws, Power Politics, and Lipstick Lesbians*. New York: Perseus Books, 2006.

Fineman, Martha. *The Illusion of Equality: The Rhetoric and Reality of Divorce Reform*. Chicago: University of Chicago Press, 1991.

Frank, Gillian. " 'The Civil Rights of Parents': Race and Conservative Politics in Anita Bryant's Campaign against Gay Rights in 1970s Florida." *Journal of the History of Sexuality* 22, no. 1 (January 2013): forthcoming.

Freedman, Estelle B. *Feminism, Sexuality, and Politics: Essays by Estelle B. Freedman*. Chapel Hill: University of North Carolina Press, 2006.

———. *No Turning Back: The History of Feminism and the Future of Women*. New York: Ballantine Books, 2002.

———. " 'Uncontrolled Desires': The Response to the Sexual Psychopath, 1920–1960." *Journal of American History* 74, no. 1 (June 1987): 83–106.

Freedman, Estelle B., and John D'Emilio. *Intimate Matters: A History of Sexuality in America*. New York: Harper & Row, 1988.

Freeman, Susan K. "From the Lesbian Nation to the Cincinnati Lesbian Community: Moving toward a Politics of Location." *Journal of the History of Sexuality* 9, no. 1/2 (January–April 2000): 137–74.

Galana, Laurel, and Gina Covina. *The New Lesbians: Interviews with Women across the U.S. and Canada*. Berkeley, CA: Moon Books, 1977.

Gallagher, John, and Chris Bull. *Perfect Enemies: The Religious Right, the Gay Movement, and the Politics of the 1990s*. New York: Crown Publishers, 1996.

Gallo, Marcia. *Different Daughters: A History of the Daughters of Bilitis and the Rise of the Lesbian Rights Movement*. New York: Carroll & Graf Publishers, 2006.

Garnett, Blynn. "Memoirs of a Lesbian's Lesbian Daughter." In *Lavender Culture*, edited by Karla Jay and Allen Young, 315–24. New York: New York University Press, 1978.

Garrison, Dee. "Our Skirts Gave Them Courage: The Civil Defense Protest Movement in New York City, 1955–1961." In *Not June Cleaver: Women and Gender in Postwar America, 1945–1960*, edited by Joanne Meyerowitz, 201–26. Philadelphia: Temple University Press, 1994.

Gates, Gary J., and Jason Ost. *The Gay and Lesbian Atlas*. Los Angeles: Urban Institute Press, 2004.

Gearhart, Sally. *The Wanderground: Stories of the Hill-Women*. Watertown, MA: Persephone Press, 1979.

Giddings, Paula. *When and Where I Enter: The Impact of Black Women on Race and Sex in America*. New York: William Morrow, 1984.

Gifford, Guy, with Mary Jo Risher. *By Her Own Admission: A Lesbian Mother's Fight to Keep Her Son*. Garden City, NY: Doubleday, 1977.

Goodman, Bernice. *The Lesbian: A Celebration of Difference*. Out and Out Books: New York, 1977.

———. "The Lesbian Mother." *American Journal of Orthopsychiatry* 43 (1973): 283–84.

Gordon, Linda. *Heroes of Their Own Lives: The Politics and History of Family Violence*. New York: Viking, 1988.

———. *Woman's Body, Woman's Right: Birth Control in America*. New York: Grossman, 1976.

Green, Richard. "Sexual Identity of 37 Children Raised by Homosexual or Transsexual Parents." *American Journal of Psychiatry* 135, no. 6 (June 1978): 692–97.

———. *Sexual Science and the Law*. Cambridge, MA: Harvard University Press, 1992.

Gutman, Herbert. *The Black Family in Slavery and Freedom, 1750–1925*. New York: Vintage Books, 1976.

Halberstam, Judith. *In a Queer Time and Place*. New York: New York University Press, 2005.

Harris, Barbara. "Lesbian Mother Child Custody: Legal and Psychiatric Aspects." *Bulletin of the American Academy of Psychiatry and the Law* 5 (1977): 75–89.

Herman, Ellen. *Kinship by Design: A History of Adoption in the Modern United States*. Chicago: University of Chicago Press, 2008.

Hitchens, Donna. "Social Attitudes, Legal Standards, And Personal Trauma in Child Custody Cases." *Journal of Homosexuality* 5, no. 1 (Fall 1979): 89–96.

Hitchens, Donna, and Barbara Price. "Trial Strategy in Lesbian Mother Custody Cases: The Use of Expert Testimony." *Golden Gate University Law Review* 9, no. 2 (1978): 451–80.

Hoagland, Sarah, and Julia Penelope, eds. *For Lesbians Only: A Separatist Anthology*. London, UK: Onlywomen Press, 1988.

Howard, John. *Men Like That: A Southern Queer History*. Chicago: University of Chicago Press, 1999.

Hunter, Nan, and Nancy Polikoff. "Custody Rights of Lesbian Mothers: Legal Theory and Litigation Strategy." *Buffalo Law Review* 25, no. 3 (Spring 1976): 691–733.

Hurtado, Albert. *Indian Survival on the California Frontier*. New Haven: Yale University Press, 1988.

Jay, Karla. *Tales of the Lavender Menace: A Memoir of Liberation*. New York: Basic Books, 1999.

Jensen, Joan. "Native American Women and Agriculture: A Seneca Case Study." In *Unequal Sisters: A Multicultural Reader in U.S. Women's History*, edited by Ellen DuBois and Vicki Ruiz, 51–65. New York: Routledge, 1990.

Johnson, David K. *The Lavender Scare: The Cold War Persecution of Gays and Lesbians in the Federal Government*. Chicago: University of Chicago Press, 2004.

Jullion, Jeannie. *Long Way Home: The Odyssey of a Lesbian Mother and Her Children*. San Francisco, CA: Cleis Press, 1985.

Kaplan, Laura. *The Story of Jane: The Legendary Underground Abortion Service*. New York: Pantheon, 1995.

Kaplan, Morris. *Sexual Justice: Democratic Citizenship and the Politics of Desire*. New York: Routledge, 1997.

Keller, Yvonne. " 'Was It Right to Love Her Brother's Wife So Passionately?' Lesbian Pulp Novels And U.S. Lesbian Identity, 1950–1965." *American Quarterly* 57, no. 2 (June 2005): 385–410.

Kennedy, Elizabeth Lapovsky, and Madeline D. Davis. *Boots of Leather, Slippers of Gold: The History of a Lesbian Community*. New York: Routledge, 1993.

Kenney, Moira Rachel. *Mapping Gay L.A.: The Intersection of Place and Politics*. Philadelphia: Temple University Press, 2001.

Kirkpatrick, Martha, M.D., et al. "Lesbian Mothers and Their Children: A Comparative Survey." *American Journal of Orthopsychiatry* 51, no. 3 (July 1981): 545–51.

Krieger, Susan. *The Mirror Dance: Identity in a Women's Community*. Philadelphia: Temple University Press, 1983.

Kritchevsky, Barbara. "The Unmarried Woman's Right to Artificial Insemination: A Call for an Expanded Definition of the Family." *Harvard Women's Law Journal* 4 (1981): 1–42.

Kunzel, Regina. *Fallen Women and Problem Girls: Unmarried Mothers and the Professionalization of Social Work, 1890–1945*. New Haven: Yale University Press, 1993.

Lai, Amy. "Tango or More? From California's Lesson 9 to the Constitutionality of a Gay-Friendly Curriculum in Public Elementary Schools." *Michigan Journal of Gender & Law* (2011): 315–48.

Latham, Jack. "Faggot Father Speaks Out." *Gay Sunshine Journal* 24 (Spring 1975): 10–11.

Leitch, Patricia. "Custody: Lesbian Mothers in the Courts." *Gonzaga Law Review* 16, no. 1 (1980): 147–70.

Lewin, Ellen. "Lesbianism and Motherhood: Implications for Child Custody." *Human Organization* 40, no. 1 (Spring 1981): 6–14.

———. *Lesbian Mothers: Accounts of Gender in American Culture*. Ithaca, NY: Cornell University Press, 1993.

Loftin, Craig. *Masked Voices: Gay Men and Lesbians in Cold War America*. Albany: State University of New York Press, 2012.

Lomawaima, K. Tsianina. *They Called It Prairie Light: The Story of Chilocco Indian School*. Lincoln: University of Nebraska Press, 1994.

Maddox, Brenda. *Married and Gay*. New York: Harcourt Brace Jovanovich, 1982.

Mamo, Laura. *Queering Reproduction: Achieving Pregnancy in the Age of Technoscience*. Durham, NC: Duke University Press, 2007.

Marcus, Eric. *Making Gay History*. New York: Harper Collins, 1992.

Mascola, Laurene, M.D., M.P.H., and Mary Guinan, M.D., Ph.D. "Semen Donors as the Source of Sexually Transmitted Diseases in Artificially Inseminated Women:

The Saga Unfolds." *Journal of the American Medical Association* 257, no. 8 (1987): 1093–94.

Mason, Mary Ann. *The Custody Wars: Why Children Are Losing the Legal Battle, and What We Can Do about It.* New York: Basic Books, 1999.

———. *From Father's Property to Children's Rights.* New York: Columbia University Press, 1994.

May, Elaine Tyler. *Barren in the Promised Land: Childless Americans and the Pursuit of Happiness.* New York: Basic Books, 1995.

———. *Homeward Bound: American Families in the Cold War Era.* New York: Basic Books, 1988.

McGuire, Danielle. *At the Dark End of the Street: Black Women, Rape, and Resistance—A New History of the Civil Rights Movement from Rosa Parks to the Rise of Black Power.* New York: Random House, 2010.

Meeker, Martin. *Contacts Desired: Gay and Lesbian Communications and Community, 1940s–1970s.* Chicago: University of Chicago Press, 2006.

Meyerowitz, Joanne. "Beyond the Feminine Mystique: A Reassessment of Postwar Mass Culture, 1946–1958." In *Not June Cleaver: Women and Gender in Postwar America, 1945–1960*, edited by Joanne Meyerowitz. Philadelphia: Temple University Press, 1994: 229–62.

Miller, John C. " 'My Daddy Loves Your Daddy': A Gay Father Encounters a Social Movement." In *Queer Families, Queer Politics: Challenging Culture and the State*, edited by Mary Bernstein and Renate Reimann, 221–30. New York: Columbia University Press, 2001.

Miller, Neil. *Sex-Crime Panic: A Journey to the Paranoid Heart of the 1950s.* New York: Alyson Books, 2002.

Moraga, Cherrie, and Gloria Anzuldua, eds. *This Bridge Called My Back: Writings by Radical Women of Color.* Watertown, MA: Persephone Press, 1981.

Morgen, Sandra. *Into Our Own Hands: The Women's Health Movement in the United States, 1969–1990.* New Brunswick, NJ: Rutgers University Press, 2002.

Morris, Bonnie J. *Eden Built by Eves: The Culture of Women's Music Festivals.* Los Angeles: Alyson, 1999.

Murdoch, Joyce, and Deb Price. *Courting Justice: Gay Men and Lesbians v. the Supreme Court.* New York: Basic Books, 2001.

Murray, Heather. *Not in This Family: Gays and the Meaning of Kinship.* Philadelphia: University of Pennsylvania Press, 2010.

Mushroom, Merril. "At Yalla's Place—1960." *Common Lives/Lesbian Lives: A Lesbian Quarterly*, no. 11 (Spring 1984).

———. "Bar Dyke Sketches—1959." *Common Lives/Lesbian Lives: A Lesbian Quarterly*, no. 5 (Fall 1982).

Nestle, Joan. *A Fragile Union: New and Selected Writings.* San Francisco: Cleis Press, 1998.

Nestor, Bryon L. "Attitudes of Child Psychiatrists toward Homosexual Parenting and Child Custody." *Conciliation Courts Review* 17, no. 2 (September 1979): 21–23.

Noble, Elizabeth. *Having Your Baby by Donor Insemination: A Complete Resource Guide.* Boston: Houghton Mifflin, 1987.

Payne, Charles. *I've Got the Light of Freedom: The Organizing Tradition and the Mississippi Freedom Struggle.* Berkeley: University of California Press, 1995.

Paz, Juana María. *The La Luz Journal.* Fayetteville, AR: Paz Press, 1980.

Pleck, Elizabeth. *Not Just Roommates: Cohabitation after the Sexual Revolution.* Chicago: University of Chicago Press, 2012.

Polikoff, Nancy D. *Beyond (Straight and Gay) Marriage: Valuing All Families under the Law.* Boston: Beacon Press, 2008.

———. "Lesbian and Gay Couples Raising Children: The Law in the United States." In *Legal Recognition of Same-Sex Partnerships: A Study of National, European, and International Law,* edited by Robert Wintemute and Mads Andenaes, 153–67. Oxford: Hart Publishing, 2001.

———. "This Child Does Have Two Mothers: Redefining Parenthood to Meet the Needs of Children in Lesbian-Mother and Other Nontraditional Families." *Georgetown Law Journal* 78 (1990): 459–575.

Reilly, Philip. *The Surgical Solution: A History of Involuntary Sterilization in the United States.* Baltimore: Johns Hopkins University Press, 1991.

Rensenbrink, Greta. "Parthenogenesis and Lesbian Separatism: Regenerating Women's Community through Virgin Birth in the United States in the 1970s and 1980s." *Journal of the History of Sexuality* 19, no. 2 (May 2010): 288–316.

Rich, Adrienne. "Compulsory Heterosexuality and Lesbian Existence." In *Blood, Bread, and Poetry: Selected Prose, 1979–1985,* 23–75. New York: W. W. Norton & Co., 1986.

Richman, Kimberly. *Courting Change: Queer Parents, Judges, and the Transformation of American Family Law.* New York: New York University Press, 2009.

Riley, Marilyn. "The Avowed Lesbian Mother and Her Right to Child Custody: A Constitutional Right That Can No Longer Be Denied." *San Diego Law Review* 12, no. 4 (1975): 799–864.

Roberts, Dorothy. *Killing the Black Body: Race, Reproduction, and the Meaning of Liberty.* New York: Random House, 1997.

Rosario, Vernon A. "An Interview with Martha J. Kirkpatrick, M.D." *Journal of Gay & Lesbian Psychotherapy* 6, no. 2 (2002): 85–98.

Rosen, Ruth. *The World Split Open: How the Modern Women's Movement Changed America.* New York: Viking, 2000.

Ross, Susan Deller, and Ann Barcher. *The Rights of Women: The Basic ACLU Guide to a Woman's Rights,* rev ed. New York: Bantam Books, 1983.

Shilts, Randy. *The Mayor of Castro Street: The Life and Time of Harvey Milk.* New York: St. Martin's Press, 1982.

Solinger, Rickie. *Wake Up Little Susie: Single Pregnancy and Race before Roe v. Wade.* New York: Routledge, 1992.

Stein, Marc. *The City of Brotherly and Sisterly Loves: Lesbian and Gay Philadelphia, 1945–1972.* Chicago: University of Chicago Press, 2000.

Stevenson, Brenda. *Life in Black and White: Family and Community in the Slave South.* Oxford: Oxford University Press, 1996.

Stryker, Susan. *Transgender History.* Berkeley, CA: Seal Press, 2008.

Stryker, Susan, and Jim Van Buskirk. *Gay by the Bay: A History of Queer Culture in the San Francisco Bay Area.* San Francisco: Chronicle Books, 1996.

Tallen, Bette S. "Lesbian Separatism: A Historical and Comparative Perspective." In *For Lesbians Only: A Separatist Anthology,* edited by Sarah Hoagland and Julia Penelope, 132–44. London: Onlywomen Press, 1988.

Teal, Don. *The Gay Militants.* New York: Stein & Day, 1971.

Trennert, Robert. "Educating Indian Girls at Nonreservation Boarding Schools, 1870–1920." In *Unequal Sisters: A Multicultural Reader in U.S. Women's History,* edited by Ellen DuBois and Vicki Ruiz, 224–49. New York: Routledge, 1990.

Van Deburg, William. *New Day in Babylon: The Black Power Movement and American Culture, 1965–1975.* Chicago: University of Chicago Press, 1992.

Weiss, Jessica. *To Have and to Hold: Marriage, the Baby Boom, and Social Change.* Chicago: University of Chicago Press, 2000.

Werth, Barry. *The Scarlet Professor—Newton Arvin: A Literary Life Shattered by Scandal.* New York: Nan A. Talese, 2001.

Weston, Kath. *Families We Choose: Lesbians, Gays, Kinship.* New York: Columbia University Press, 1991.

Williams, Kathie D. "Louisville's Lesbian Feminist Union: A Study in Community Building." In *Carryin' On in the Lesbian and Gay South,* edited by John Howard, 224–40. New York: New York University Press, 1997.

Wolf, Deborah Goleman. *The Lesbian Community.* Berkeley: University of California Press, 1979.

Wolfe, Susan J. "Jewish Lesbian Mother." In *Nice Jewish Girls: A Lesbian Anthology,* edited by Evelyn Torton Beck, 164–73. Trumansburg, NY: Crossing Press, 1982.

Young, Perry Deane. *God's Bullies: Power Politics and Religious Tyranny.* New York: Holt, Rinehart, and Winston, 1982.

Index

Note: Page numbers in italics refer to photographs.

Doidge, William, 68

Domestic partnerships, 174, 183, 186, 195, 196, 197, 199, 210. *See also* Same-sex marriage

Domestic violence, 40, 82, 87, 101, 102, 103, 141, 151, 236–37 (n. 5)

Donor insemination, 10, 49, 83, 105, 169–70, 173, 174–81, 189–90, 192, 195, 198, 200, 203, 217 (n. 4), 229–30 (n. 8), 255 (nn. 3, 4), 256 (n. 24), 257 (n. 30); and concerns about AIDS/HIV, 179–80, 257 (n. 32); in medical clinics, and discrimination against lesbians and single women, 169, 173, 175–76, 178–81, 183, 186, 188, 256 (nn. 24, 25), 257 (n. 38); self-insemination networks, 165–71, 173, 175, 176–78, 186–88, 256 (n. 16). *See also* AIDS/HIV crisis; Custody cases; Lesbian nationalism; Parthenogenesis; Reproductive rights; Women's health movement

Downer, Carol, 179

Drag, 37, 40, 120, 123

Driver, Nancy, 98

Dubin, Ali and Carrie, 200

Dukakis, Michael, 184

Dykes and Tykes, 4, 51, 55, 86–88, 95, 96, 98–101, 100, 104, 105–6, 107–8, 146, 150, 160–61, 193, 234 (n. 75), 238 (n. 20); Dykes and Tykes Legal Custody Center, 87

East Coast Lesbian Mothers Defense Fund, 86–88

East Village (New York), 35, 45. *See also* Greenwich Village

Effeminism, 114–17, 120

Elizabeth Blackwell Health Center for Women (Philadelphia), 179, 256 (n. 29), 257 (nn. 30, 32). *See also* Donor insemination; Women's health movement

Elliott, Carl, 14

Elwell, Anne, 234–35 (n. 79)

Employment discrimination: against gays and lesbians, 3, 18, 21–24, 37, 48, 55, 56–57, 72, 77, 84, 109, 121, 122, 154, 196, 211–12, 218 (n. 8), 221 (n. 22), 228 (n. 3), 229 (n. 7), 231 (n. 26); against women, 17, 156, 221 (n. 22). *See also* Antigay legislation/attitudes; Teachers

English, Katherine, 67

Equal Rights Advocates, 109

Equal Rights Amendment, 218 (n. 8)

Erickson, Erik, 67. *See also* Psychiatrists/psychologists

Ettelbrick, Paula, 195, 197, 199

Evans, Sara, 82

Fagelson, James, 197

Family Equality Council, 207–8, 263 (n. 3)

Family Pride Coalition, 207–8, 263 (nn. 2, 3)

Family values rhetoric, 6, 122, 123, 143. *See also* Religious conservatives

FBI (Federal Bureau of Investigation), 24

Feminist Karate Union, 86

Feminist Women's Health Center (Los Angeles and Oakland), 179–80, 256 (n. 29). *See also* Donor insemination; Women's health movement

Femme identity. *See* Butch-femme identity/communities

Fenway Community Health Center (Boston), 169, 175–76, 179, 188–89, 256 (n. 24), 257 (n. 30), 261 (n. 98). *See also* Donor insemination; Women's health movement

Fertility clinics. *See* Donor insemination

Fineman, Martha, 230 (n. 12)

Fire Island (New York), 30

Firestone, Jenifer, 188–89

Fleming, Jennifer, 236–37 (n. 5)

Florez, Kathy, 74, 108

Flournoy, Mary, 189–90

Focus on the Family, 213, 263 (n. 3). *See also* Religious conservatives

Quest, 101

Race/racism, 7–8, 16, 17, 24, 58, 61–62,
    77, 81, 82, 96, 97, 98, 99, 101, 102,
    110, 151–53, 181–82, 218 (n. 8). See also
    Women of color
Radicalesbians, 81, 94, 141
Rainbow Curriculum, 205
Rainbow Families, 208
Rape, 7, 82, 97, 159; rape crisis centers,
    171; rape crisis hotlines, 141
Rat, 116
Reagan, Ronald, 123, 184
Redbird, 89, 151, 165. See also Communal
    living experiments
Religious conservatives, 6, 8, 56, 79,
    100, 121, 122, 123, 126, 184, 205,
    207, 213, 218 (n. 8), 228–29 (n. 5),
    230 (n. 9), 263 (n. 3). See also Antigay
    legislation/attitudes
Reproductive rights, 5, 9, 80, 82, 83,
    96–97, 99, 100, 101, 102–3, 110,
    133, 171, 176–77, 178–79, 254
    (n. 118), 259 (n. 66). See also Abortion;
    Donor insemination; Sterilization,
    involuntary; Women's health
    movement
Revolutionary Male Homosexual (RMH),
    116
Reynolds, Darlene, 63
Rich, Adrienne ("Compulsory
    Heterosexuality and Lesbian
    Existence"), 2, 146
Richman, Kimberly (Courting Change),
    69–70
Ricketts, Wendell, 259–60 (n. 75)
The Rights of Gay People (Carrington),
    231 (n. 27). See also American Civil
    Liberties Union
The Rights of Women (Ross and Barcher),
    229–30 (n. 8). See also American Civil
    Liberties Union
Risher, Mary Jo, 59, 60, 68, 92, 93. See
    also Custody cases; Friends of Mary Jo
    Risher

Rivera, Rhonda, 67
Rivera, Sunny, 178
Roberts, Dorothy, 7
Roe v. Wade, 82, 97. See also Abortion
Rosen, Ruth, 82
Ross, Alan, 125, 126, 135–36
Ross, Susan Deller (The Rights of Women),
    229–30 (n. 8)
Rothman, Lorraine, 179
Roy, Ronald, 70, 71
R.S. v. A.S., 209
Rudser, Steven, 185
Rural communes. See Communal living
    experiments
Rustin, Bayard, 33

Sabol, Terri, 191
Same-sex marriage, 7, 111, 113, 122,
    123, 174, 186, 192, 197, 207, 208,
    209, 210, 212–14, 217 (n. 5), 218
    (n. 10), 258 (n. 52). See also Domestic
    partnerships; LGBT freedom struggle
Sanders, Betty, 16
Sanders, Helen, 28
Sanford, Wendy (Ourselves and Our
    Children), 252 (n. 67)
San Francisco Bay Area Gay Fathers
    (SFBAGF), 118, 120, 121, 122–26, 124,
    127, 129, 130–31, 132–33, 134, 181,
    243–44 (n. 14), 244 (n. 22)
San Francisco Freedom Day, 124, 142
Santamasso, Gene, 245 (n. 34)
Sappha Survival School, 146–47, 250
    (n. 29). See also Communal living
    experiments; Lesbian separatism
Sappho Was a Right-On Woman (Abbott
    and Love), 234 (n. 67)
Save Our Children campaign, 3, 55,
    121–22, 184, 237 (n. 7). See also
    Antigay legislation/attitudes; Bryant,
    Anita; Schools
Sawyer, Sioux, 170–71
Sayward, Jenny, 198
Schindelman, Ellie, 203
Schools: alternative education for

children of gays and lesbians, 140,
141, 150–52, 171–72; discrimination
against gay and lesbian teachers, 3,
55, 109, 122, 154, 211–12, 218 (n. 8),
228 (n. 3), 229 (n. 7), 231 (n. 26);
experience of children of gays and
lesbians in, 25, 150, 154, 199, 204–5,
206, 211; LGBT advocacy in, 202,
203–5, 207, 209, 211–13, 241–42
(n. 84), 265 (n. 21). See also Communal
living experiments; Save Our Children
campaign
Schuster v. Schuster, 64, 75
Seattle Lesbian Resource Center, 86, 176
Selene, Carolyn, 108, 155
Serria, Jose, 84
Sexual Freedom League, 94
Sexual Privacy Project, 55, 74, 234–35
(n. 79)
Sexual revolution, 5, 82, 102
Sikorski, Gino, 125, 134
Silber, Sue, 257 (n. 40)
Single parents, 40, 50, 71, 80, 99, 101,
110, 131, 155–56, 160, 173, 175–76,
178–79, 181, 183, 185, 186, 192, 211,
230, 256 (n. 29), 257 (n. 40). See also
Adoption; Custody cases; Divorce;
Donor insemination; Poor families/
communities; Welfare programs/
activism
Sister, 152
Sisterhood of Black Single Mothers, 99
Sisterspace, 145–46
Sloan-Hunter, Margaret, 158
Smith, Catherine, 70, 71
Smith, Rebecca, 184
Smith, Robert, 205. See also Helms-
Smith Bill
Smith v. Smith, 68
Socarides, Charles, 68, 69
Social workers, 9, 17, 59, 61, 92, 185,
241–42 (n. 84)
Society for Individual Rights, 48
Sodomy/sodomy laws, 24, 56–57,
62–63, 78, 109, 185, 208, 211, 225

(n. 5), 229 (n. 6), 231 (nn. 26, 27).
See also Bowers v. Hardwick; Lawrence
v. Texas
Solinger, Rickie, 7
Sommer, Susan, 211
Sonenberg, Fred, 129
South Bay Gay Fathers, 126. See also San
Francisco Bay Area Gay Fathers
Spellings, Margaret, 207
Spence, Susan, 64, 232 (n. 37)
Spence v. Durham, 64, 232 (n. 37)
Sperm banks. See Donor insemination
Sperm Bank of Northern California
(Oakland), 175. See also Donor
insemination
Spock, Benjamin, 70
Stearn, Jess (The Grapevine), 221 (n. 16)
Steinhorn, Audrey, 70
Steinman, Wayne, 183
Stephens, Mark, 130
Sterilization, involuntary, 5, 9, 23, 79,
80, 82, 96, 98, 99, 100, 101, 102, 110,
230 (n. 9). See also Abortion; Poor
families/communities; Reproductive
rights; Women of color
Steuart, James, 48–49
Stokes, Rick, 23–24
Stonewall riots, 114, 242 (n. 2). See also
Bars, gay and lesbian; Greenwich
Village; Police
The Straight State (Canaday), 6
Student Non-Violent Coordinating
Committee (SNCC), 97, 98, 158. See
also Civil rights movement; New Left
Surrogacy, 10, 173, 198, 200, 217 (n. 4)
Swislow, Lee, 100–101

Tam, William, 213
Tapia, Rebecca, 131–32
Teachers: discrimination against gay
and lesbian, 3, 55, 109, 122, 154,
211–12, 218 (n. 8), 228 (n. 3), 229
(n. 7), 231 (n. 26). See also Acanfora
v. Board of Education of Montgomery
County; Briggs Initiative; Employment

discrimination; Save Our Children campaign; Schools

Tearoom Trade (Humphreys), 18–19

Terkel, Judith, 199

Thetford, Lois, 84, 94, 98, 101, 103, 108, 239 (n. 32)

Tillery, Linda, 86

Today Show, 246 (n. 42)

Tooker, Richard, 22, 43

Townend, Lorraine, 85

Townend v. Townend, 69

Traditional Family Coalition, 213. *See also* Religious conservatives

Transgender issues, 2, 9, 37, 54, 109, 111, 147, 174, 199, 218 (n. 6), 263 (n. 5). *See also* LGBT freedom struggle

Transsexuals, 71

Trull, Teresa, 86

Truman, Harry, 15

Urban communities of gays and lesbians. *See* Bars, gay and lesbian; Bohemians; Butch-femme identity/communities; Greenwich Village; Police

Van Deburg, William (*New Day in Babylon*), 140

Van Dyke, J. J., 84

Vanguard, 242 (n. 2)

Vermont Women's Health Center, 179, 256 (n. 25), 257 (n. 30)

Vice raids. *See* Bars, gay and lesbian; Police

Vilas, Hank, 14, 30

Village Voice, 127, 141

Violence against women and homosexuals. *See* Domestic violence; Hate crimes

Visitation rights of gay and lesbian parents, 9, 18, 25, 29, 30, 54, 56, 62, 63, 64, 69, 73, 76, 78, 112, 121, 130–33, 135, 186–88, 189, 191, 195, 198, 209–10, 228 (n. 2), 232 (n. 41), 259 (n. 74). *See also* Antigay legislation/

attitudes; Custody cases; Divorce; Psychiatrists/psychologists

Voeller, Bruce, 70, 136, 182, 248 (n. 89). *See also* Gay Activists Alliance; National Gay Task Force

Wahls, Zach, 214

Wales, Margaret, 75, 76

The Wanderground (Gearhart), 166

Wanrow, Yvonne, 101

Watkins, Mary, 86

Weather, Stormy, 41

Weinstein, Mikki, 67, 236–37 (n. 5). *See also* Custody Action for Lesbian Mothers

Welfare programs/activism, 6, 79, 80, 87, 96, 98, 102, 110, 120, 152, 156, 157. *See also* Poor families/communities

West Coast Women's Music Festival, 170. *See also* Women's music festivals

We Want the Music Collective, 161. *See also* Women's music festivals

Wharton, Dave, 134

White, Byron, 78

White, Mary, 156

White House, 24, 207–8

Who's in a Family? (Skutch), 211–12

Willhoite, Michael (*Daddy's Roommate*), 204, 205

Wirthlin, Joseph and Robin, 211, 213

Wolf, Deborah Goleman, 143, 237 (n. 11)

Wolfe, Maxine, 156

Wolfe, Susan, 164

Woman Controlled Conception, 176, 256 (n. 16). *See also* Donor insemination

Womanstar, 151

Women in Transition, 236–37 (n. 5)

Women of color, 5, 7, 9, 10, 26, 33, 61–62, 79, 80, 82, 97, 98, 99, 100, 110, 151–53, 158–59, 164, 171, 251 (n. 54). *See also* African American families/communities; Poor families/communities; Race/racism; Sterilization, involuntary; Welfare programs/activism

Women's Coffee Coven (Seattle), 159–60. *See also* Women's music festivals

Women's health movement, 82, 83, 102, 110, 169, 179, 180, 189. *See also* Abortion; Donor insemination; Parthenogenesis; Reproductive rights

Women's music festivals, 82, 86, 88, 89, 92, 107, 158, 159–60, 161–64, 168, 170; Michigan Womyn's Music Festival, 89, 161–64, 162, 163, 168, 253 (n. 89)

Working-class families/communities, 8, 11, 19, 34, 35–37, 39, 40, 156, 225 (n. 10). *See also* Bars, gay and lesbian; Bohemians; Butch-femme identity/communities

Working People's Health Clinic (Chicago), 101

Yarrow, Irene, 147

Young, Ivy, 196, 197

Young, White, and Miserable (Breines), 32–33

Zellner, Dottie, 98

Ziem, Frederick, 235 (n. 80)

Zinn, Howard, 97